Fictions of Sappho

1546–1937

D1526078

Women in Culture and Society

A Series edited by Catharine R. Stimpson

Fictions of Sappho

1546–1937

Joan DeJean

The University of Chicago Press   *Chicago & London*

The University of Chicago Press, Chicago 60637
The University of Chicago Press, Ltd., London
© 1989 by The University of Chicago
All rights reserved. Published 1989
Printed in the United States of America
98 97 96 95 94 93 92 91 90 89   5 4 3 2 1

Portions of Joan DeJean's article "Fictions of Sappho," *Critical Inquiry* 13, no. 4 (Summer 1987):787–805 (© 1987 by the University of Chicago), are incorporated in this volume.

Portions of Joan DeJean's article "Sappho, c'est moi, selon Racine: Coming of Age in NeoClassical Theater," *Yale French Studies* 76(1989):3–19, appear in Chapter 3 of this volume in modified form.

♾ The paper used in this publication meets the minimum requirements of the American National Standard for Information Sciences—Permanence of Paper for Printed Library Materials, ANSI Z39.48-1984.

Library of Congress Cataloging-in-Publication Data
DeJean, Joan E.
    Fictions of Sappho, 1546–1937 / Joan DeJean.
        p. cm.—(Women in culture and society)
    Includes index.
    ISBN 0-226-14135-7 (alk. paper).—ISBN 0-226-14136-5 (pbk. : alk. paper)
    1. French literature—History and criticism. 2. Sappho in fiction, drama, poetry, etc. 3. French literature—Greek influences. 4. Women poets, Greek, in literature. 5. Lesbianism in literature. 6. Lesbians in literature. I. Title. II. Series.
PQ143.A3D45 1989   89-31843
840.9'351—dc20   CIP

For Froma Zeitlin

In all the centuries since history began we know of no woman who in any sense can be said to rival [Sappho] as a poet.

Strabon

As far as Sappho's body went, she was exceedingly disgusting to behold, being short and of dark complexion—resembling a nightingale whose tiny form was enshrouded in shapeless wings.

An Ancient Commentator on Lucian

[Sappho and Socrates] both appear to me to have practiced the same sort of friendship, he of males, she of females, both declaring that their beloved were many in number and that they were captivated by all beautiful persons.

Maximus of Tyre

Even Plato calls [Sappho] wise. I understand that there was another Sappho in Lesbos, a courtesan, not a poetess.

Aelian

A clever woman named Damophyla was said to have had girl companions just like Sappho, and to have composed love poems just as she did.

Philostratus

[Sappho] was accused by some of being undisciplined and having sexual involvements with other women.

A Second Century B.C. Hellenistic Biography

Some say nine Muses—but count again.
Behold the tenth: Sappho of Lesbos.

Plato

Contents

Contents

Illustrations

Series Editor's Foreword

"If you are squeamish," a Sapphic fragment warns, "Don't prod the beach rubble."[1] Fortunately, *Fictions of Sappho* is fearless. It probes a famous strand: literary history, especially that of France, since the sixteenth century. It is far more than the uncovering of the bones of a writer, the starfish arm of a text, or the bottle of a reading. *Fictions of Sappho* changes the picture of the beach itself. Apparently staunch stones of "historical fact" become the shells of an epoch's interpretations.

Since antiquity, Sappho's reputation has been battered more often than it has been burnished. She has been vulnerable for many reasons. We know almost nothing about her or about Greek female homosexuality. We cannot estimate how many of her poems we might have lost. Prejudice adores a vacuum. It rushes in and names the void away. Moreover, what we have is difficult. Standing at the beginning of Western literary history is a woman. She sees, speaks, and writes. She desires other women. Her fragments, however, are brutally cunning. Joan DeJean writes of "the polyphony of voices of sexual desire in her poetry." Her discourse is "self-conscious," self-aware of its own turns, indeterminate. To tame her, some commentators read the fragments as if they were Sappho's true story, others as if the poems were the commentator's own story. The critical error of reducing a narrative voice to an author's presence has alternated with the psychological and cultural error of projection.

Brilliantly, with zest and wit, DeJean traces the ways in which scholars and writers have read the Sappho they had and produced the Sappho they wanted. So doing, DeJean shows how scholarship and fictions, study and speculations, "contaminate" and influence each other within a given system of discourse. The French began to organize their modern Sappho in the sixteenth century. Although the figure they first made of her was capable of sexual diversity, the seventeenth century erased homoeroticism. Ironically, a man, Tanneguy LeFèvre, in a forgotten 1660 edition, had been straightforward about Sappho's desire for women. A woman, his own daughter, Anne LeFèvre Dacier, helped transform Sappho into "Sapho," an unhappy heterosexual who killed herself for love of a Phaon, a younger man. Textually, Anne LeFèvre Dacier substituted Ovid for her biological father. Translated into French, Ovid's fiction about Sappho, the fifteenth Epistle of his *Heroides,* was a complex female impersonation by a male poet that took over as a sign of "the female."

The creation of Sappho was neither sideshow nor pastime. Deciding what her literary identity was to be amounted also to a struggle over the part gender would play in the establishment of any cultural order, the power of woman writers, and the definition of female sexuality and desire. Woman writers, such as Madeleine de Scudéry, had claimed Sappho for themselves. By the late seventeenth century, however, the French had articulated authoritative theories of the canon that erased woman writers. The triumph of an Ovidian fiction about Sappho was a defeat for a Madeleine de Scudéry.

In the eighteenth century, in a prophecy of the Freudian drama of the family romance, the French linked Sappho to motherhood. Either happily maternal or a depraved violation of bourgeois maternal norms, she was heterosexual. As popular legends integrated and spawned fictions of Sappho ever more exuberantly, the focus of scholarship about her shifted to Germany. In the nineteenth century, French speculative fictions ran riot. Sappho was chaste, but redemptively so. No, she was wildly heterosexual, a sometime whore. No, she was a lesbian, but her homosexuality was less erotic delight than the mark of modernist alienation. No, there were actually two Sapphos: one a kindly poet/ teacher, the other a courtesan whom that irrepressible Phaon abandoned.

At the same time, German scholarship opposed French "sexual sensationalism." It rehabilitated Sappho through purging her of sexuality. Chaste and fair, she radiates purity, enthroned next to a gorgeous hunk of a Phaon, now idealized male body and compelling erotic object. Astutely, DeJean suggests that such translations were to influence English classical studies in the twentieth century. Their claims to objectivity about Greek and Latin are less tributes to science than masks of their ability to write out the female body.

At the beginning of the twentieth century, papyrus manuscripts of some of Sappho's poems were discovered and published. The recovery of "the real" stimulated its elaboration. For many woman writers, Sappho was to become the great, empowering figure—as a woman writer. For many lesbians, she was to become the great, empowering figure—as a lesbian. For lesbian writers, she was to become the myth that authorizes both sexual and literary desire. In 1985, the poet Judy Grahn tells of a Lesbos with "a long female-centered history":

> Sappho wrote to us from (this) island, a lavender-
> flowered island . . . to those of us holding Sappho in our
> mind's eye as *the* historic example both of Lesbianism and of
> Lesbian poetry, everything she represents lives on an
> island.[2]

Such lesbian writers in their passion have reinvigorated the struggle to represent female sexuality and authority through reclaiming the right to represent Sappho. Yet, even as Renée Vivien was translating Sappho into French, the second woman to do so, other French writers were lacerating lesbianism. The contests about Sappho were not limited to the control of a single nation's discourse. After they renewed their interest in her, French scholars argued with German academic interpretations, their double rhetoric echoing the fatal discourse of modern European nationalism.

DeJean's last fictioneer is Marguerite Yourcenar, whose grammar of the erotic may be as sly, as unstable, as that of Sappho herself. DeJean's vivid narrative is a warning, however, against such phrases as "Sappho herself." "Sappho" is a magnificent text in fragments. Writing, rewriting, rehearsing, replaying, and denying each other, later literatures have given these fragments their illusory wholeness and meaning. Or, to extend my first metaphor, "Sappho" is a treasure ship that broke apart millennia ago. Over time, bits have floated in. When and if we find them, we display them in maritime museums near the shore that compete against and succeed each other. Built of manuscripts, images, and self-reflecting mirrors, these museums interpret the past and set terms for the present. One of Sappho's fragments might serve as a preface to catalogs about her:

> I have no complaints.
>
> Prosperity that
> the golden Muses
> gave me was no
> delusion: dead, I
> won't be forgotten.[3]

Fictions of Sappho admires the audacity of this voice. It also takes an exacting measure of many of the museum architects and curators who have remembered Sappho but never learned that historical memory and cultural laws too often compound forgetfulness, fantasy, special pleadings, and fear.

Catharine R. Stimpson

Series Editor's Foreword

1. Mary Barnard, "84," *Sappho: A New Translation,* Foreword by Dudley Fitts (Berkeley: University of California Press, 1958), n.p.
2. *The Highest Apple: Sappho and the Lesbian Poetic Tradition* (San Francisco: Spinsters, Ink, 1985), p. 5.
3. Barnard, "100," n.p.

Acknowledgments

Several years ago, after I had published a book in which I thanked a number of people with sincere but apparently, to some at least, overly zealous enthusiasm, I received an anonymous letter (with a Yale University Library letterhead) mocking what the author considered my "treacly" expressions of gratitude. Since I didn't figure out at that time what rule of critical *bienséance* I had broken, my infraction now will probably be greater still: never have more friends and colleagues come to my aid than on this project, and never have colleagues been of greater help. I would not have explored many fascinating nooks and crannies of literary history, and certainly not have had as much fun doing so, without the participation of the following cast of characters.

Peter Allen dropped off on a number of occasions articles he thought might be of interest. Jean Alter xeroxed material from the University of Pennsylvania Library. Charlie Bernheimer gave the kind of critical reading of the manuscript's first draft for which I was only grateful in the long run. He frequently suggested useful references and provided translations of German texts. From the vast resources of his erudition, Frank Bowman produced a number of properly obscure (and very helpful) references; he also commented on part of the manuscript. Anne Carson provided a productive critique of an early version of chapter one. Joe Consoli never tired of trying to make the computer turn up leads on texts I had given up hope of finding. (Some we never did find, but Joe did manage to locate several obscure works.) Stanley Corngold made very elegant sense of Welcker's immensely contorted German. Natalie Davis was always there with support, interest, references (and usually the books as well). Maria Di Battista pushed the Wharton translation—which eventually proved to be the missing link in several lines of investigation—on me when I didn't want anything more to do with the late nineteenth century. Lance Donaldson-Evans sent references and even gave door-to-door service on what must have felt like a ton of essential books. Steve Ferguson ordered microfilms and did everything in his power to convince librarians to loan rare volumes. With great patience, Tony Grafton introduced me to the mysteries of reading seventeenth- and eighteenth-century Latin. Daniel Javitch gave a helpful critique of several sections of my manuscript. Karla Jay provided references and help in tracking down obscure works. Barbara Johnson saved her nickels for the Widener xerox machine and even provided delivery of materials to my hospital room. Elaine Marks supplied information and put me in touch with colleagues working in areas where I needed guidance. On several occasions, François Rigolot referred me to useful texts. Jamie Rohrer's word-processing genius saved me countless hours. Charlie Segal provided important references. Judy Stein generously shared information and photographs. Sally Tubach sent me her work on Sappho's fate in the German tradition. Jack Undank generously supplied references, loaned books, and was tireless in his support. Lucette Valensi and Avram Udovitch did the impossible and wrangled microfilms out of "incompetent bureaucrats" (at an institution that will remain nameless). Jack Winkler graciously allowed me to reprint his excellent translations of Sappho. And finally, Froma Zeitlin, alphabetically last as if to realize the proverb. Without Froma's indefatigable help, I would, quite simply, not have been able to write this study. She translated, and retranslated (and retranslated—sometimes probably wondering if she was dealing with stubbornness or simple stupidity), provided references and an invaluable critique of the first version of chapter one. She helped me track down citations. More important still, she always made me feel as if the work I was doing was of interest to someone besides myself. Everyone struggling with difficult material should have a friend like Froma to make the going easier and more fun.

Critical Inquiry allowed me to incorporate throughout the text, in substantially revised form, material from the article "Fictions of Sappho" (Summer 1987), vol. 13, no. 4 (© 1987 by the University of Chicago; all rights reserved). Revised material previously published in *Yale French Studies* now appears in chapter 3. A fellowship from the John Simon Guggenheim Memorial Foundation made it possible for me to complete a final version of this project. The Princeton University Committee on Research provided funds for initial research and for typing.

Introduction

Saphon, Sappho, Sapho, Sappho, Sapphô, Psappha

Sappho is a figment of the modern imagination. During her recovery by early modern scholars, she was completely a French fantasy. And throughout the entire span of her modern existence, she has remained largely a projection of the French imagination. The list of spellings that I use as my title here recapitulates her phantasmatic presence in France, from the mid-sixteenth to the early twentieth century. Behind each spelling there is a story, the fiction of what Sappho was for the period during which she bore a given name. This book is a particular kind of literary history. In a sense, it is literary history à la Flaubert: a history of received ideas. The following pages record a tradition of images and perceptions. This is a chronicle largely of fictions and seldom of facts.

The greatness of a number of writers from antiquity is so thoroughly unquestioned that they are always granted a place in the annals of literature. Yet none but Sappho has become a truly *legendary* figure: the few clichéd poses of classical literary figures—Socrates the teacher, for example—that inhabit the popular imagination can in no way be compared with either the variety or the narrative complexity of the fictions that have circulated about Sappho from antiquity to the present day. The tradition of Sapphic fiction-making began within centuries of the poet's death. (Scholars seem to agree that, while it is impossible to pinpoint the tradition's origin with absolute precision, it probably can be traced to old comedy.) All we know of the perception of Sappho shared by her contemporaries and near contemporaries before the inception of Sapphic fictions is the simple fact that she was known as "*the* poetess," the female counterpart, and presumably the equal, of "*the* poet," Homer. The

I would suggest that readers unfamiliar with Sappho's poetry begin with appendix 1 in which I provide a selection of recent translations of the two major odes and a brief survey of issues that have dominated the interpretation of these poems.

1

absence of information concerning the primal perception of Sappho the woman may indicate (and it has often been interpreted this way) a greater tolerance on the part of the early Greeks toward diversity of sexual preferences, or a relative lack of concern for the private person behind a writer's public persona. But in the absence of evidence it is impossible to draw conclusions.

If I learned one thing while working on this study, something for which I was totally unprepared, it is quite simply that Sappho makes a great many people nervous. A limited number of (unfortunately not very sophisticated) jokes rapidly became all too familiar because they were so often repeated when I mentioned my project. These were jokes that often seemed out of character for the individuals making them, as though Sappho had touched a particularly raw nerve. My lecture on Sappho's presence in the seventeenth century was once even pronounced "unsuitable for *un collège de jeunes filles*" by colleagues of the person who had invited me. A similar nervousness has affected Sappho's commentators and translators over the centuries. One phenomenon I explain in this way is their recurrent, stubborn refusal to mention female homosexuality under any name. (Commentators thus find themselves in the delicate position of attempting to disprove Sappho's homosexuality without actually naming that which they claim she was not.)

I foreground this nervousness for two reasons: first, in order to repeat that silences are not easily read, and second, in order to stress that a major cause of the unparalleled density of speculation centered around Sappho is the association between the poet and sapphism that creates an apparently inevitable stumbling block, a sort of critical repressed that, however emphatically it is denied or however ingeniously it is written off, is always sure to return. Sappho is, quite simply, a problem, certainly among the most sensitive issues in the history of literature. To retrace the development of fictions of Sappho is both to measure the standards imposed on female sexuality at any given period and to provide an index, across the centuries, not only of the received ideas about female same-sex love but also of what it was possible to write about that subject at any given period. (Thus, for example, we will witness several occasions on which scholars clearly have an intuition that would have led logically to controversial readings of certain poems but do not feel able to carry it through openly.[1])

This study retraces translations of Sappho. On the most obvious level, this means that I review nearly all the versions of Sappho's poetry available in France, from the first text (given only in Greek) of one of her two most famous odes, made public in 1546, to what is still the standard critical edition of Sappho in France, published in 1937.² Many, if not most, French translations of Sappho are of remarkably poor quality. Surely the proverbial expression about translators' betrayals has rarely been so apropos: during the four-century-long tradition we will examine, Sappho's French interpreters have most often deformed her poetry, sometimes almost beyond recognition. In these cases, rather than merely review a translator's errors, I will try to show how they influenced the image of a major writer. Therefore when I speak of the translation of Sappho in this sense, I have in mind a use of the word related to its origin in *translatio,* which means something close to our current term reception. Sappho thus translated is Sappho transformed, adapted to new purposes. This is, therefore, a study not of Sappho's timelessness but rather of the poet as she is anchored in every successive moment of what is always referred to as her "recovery," as though it were possible to strip away successive semantic transformations and reveal once and for all the original Sappho. This process could, however, more accurately be characterized as her continual recreation in the image, on the one hand, of each creator and, on the other, of the mentality of his or her day. In the following pages, I try to give a sense of the *timeliness* of Sappho's reception, of the factors that are responsible for each period's image of Sappho, both the woman and her poetry. These factors may be common to the period on the level of what our age terms the history of *mentalités,* or they may be largely personal to an individual writer. A final meaning of translation is close to transference in the psychoanalytic sense. Fictions of Sappho are, at least in part, a projection of the critic's/writer's desires onto the corpus, the fictive body, of the original woman writer.

I will be attempting primarily both to substantiate and to account for the existence of a special bond between the French literary tradition and the problem of Sappho—that is, Sappho in all the power of her poetic seductiveness and the full threat of her possibly deviant sexuality. In the canon of French literature as it has been drawn up virtually from the beginning of the existence of literary history in France, the earliest age to be recuperated as a period and packaged for educational consumption is the sixteenth century. However, the real beginning of modern French literature as a patriotic, nationalistic, and therefore eminently pedagogical enterprise is always traced to the so-called golden age of French literature, the period beginning in the 1660s and coinciding with Louis XIV's mature reign, during which the doctrine of French neoclassicism was shaped, practiced, and promoted. In a simultaneous development which, I came to be convinced, could not have been completely accidental, the modern creation of Sappho was rigorously simultaneous with the formulation of French literature as a canonical entity, with the birth of the French literary tradition. In the sixteenth century, the first period that pedagogues perceive as having a clear sense of identity, Sappho's poetry is recovered—and immediately becomes a source of inspiration, an object of desire, for virtually every major poet of the day. Yet, for the first century during which her poetry is known (1550–1650), Sappho is almost exclusively a disembodied voice, and biographical speculation does not yet generate fictions about the woman identified with the powerful cry of passion in the poems. However, by the time the French tradition was being constituted and its first canon drawn up, this speculation—centered, as always, on Sappho's sexual orientation—had begun. For the period now known as the generation of the great French classics (1660–80), Sappho is a figure of female homoerotic desire. Her poetic voice is woven throughout the fabric of that founding discourse of French nationalism, neoclassicism. This language threatening to the patriarchal order exerts an influence at the heart of the very discourse chosen by the self-proclaimed greatest of French monarchs as the fitting representation of his glory. This fact is one that the original canon shaper, Boileau, and his self-appointed heirs like Sappho's first eighteenth-century translator, François Gacon, struggle for decades to suppress.

Sappho's presence at the foundation of the French literary order once established, both her poetry and her person are, as it were, indissolubly bound up with the articulation of that tradition: while I was working on this project, it seemed that, virtually everywhere I looked, Sappho was there. The longevity and the intensity of the Sapphic presence within the French literary tradition explain the focus of my study. However, my concentration on the French Sapphic construct does not signify the exclusion of her presence in other national traditions. At first (until the early eighteenth century, when the English and the Germans really began to play a role), Sappho is almost exclusively a French preserve. Once other traditions become active, I refer to all the major contributions to the composite portrait of Sappho that originate outside France. I dwell especially on these foreign traditions when they create original fictions that subsequently serve as models for French authors. On occasion, when these innovations have a major long-term effect, I allow foreign influences to upstage French production. This occurs most prominently in chapter 3, when the politics of nineteenth-century German philology is featured, at times to the virtual exclusion of French scholarly activity. I do not, on the other hand, give detailed attention to foreign Sapphic configurations when these are neither original nor destined to wield a formative influence on subsequent fictions of the muse of Mytilene. Thus, for example, I mention only briefly the flowering of English Sapphic fictions in the early eighteenth century, even though this moment of English speculation, the most intense of any time, generated productions by important authors, from Addison's commentaries in *The Spectator,* to Pope's imitation of Ovid's Sapphic epistle, to Ambrose Philips's first English translation of Sappho's most famous odes. The English discovery of Sappho reproduces so closely the structure of her entry into the French tradition a half-century earlier that an analysis of its unfolding would have been repetitive, without being essential to an understanding of the future of Sapphic fictions.

When the entire span of Sappho's presence in the modern literary imagination is considered, it becomes obvious that the French tradition has played throughout its development a privileged role as the nexus of her fictionalization. French dominance over the scene of Sappho scholarship, virtually uncontested in the sixteenth and the seventeenth centuries, comes to an end at the dawn of the Enlightenment: the nineteenth and very early twentieth centuries belong to the Germans; the English have dominated since about 1920. The French claim to Sapphic glory comes from an unbroken chain of fictions, from the early seventeenth century to the 1940s (when I take leave of it). French Sapphic fictions begin a half-century before similar speculation in England, nearly a century before such activity in Germany, a century and a half before Italy. In addition, other national schools simply cannot approach either the longevity or the sheer magnitude of the French tradition of speculation. No other national literature has anything like this uninterrupted dialogue with Sappho, in which, across three centuries, texts build on precursor texts and in turn feed their successor texts, continuing strands of speculation and opening up new ones that correspond to the obsessions of each period. (Thus, for example, the legend of Sappho's political involvement is initiated in France in the 1790s.) Over time, authors of French Sapphic fictions create a series of Sapphos, each of which represents the poet of Mytilene to at least a generation of readers. Certain elements are carried over from fiction to fiction; some manage to infiltrate scholarly commentaries, where a few are still firmly ensconced, even today.

This continuous obsessive involvement with Sappho has been fueled by men and women of letters. Over the centuries, the poetess has served time and again—more frequently than any other writer—as the precursor against whom subsequent writers measure themselves. These individual associations with the original poet of female desire have taken three radically different forms. A significant number are classic examples of the phenomenon Hélène Cixous terms "coming to writing" (*la venue à l'écriture*). Cixous coined the phrase to characterize the process by which a woman is empowered as a writer and becomes able to assume her literary gift. Since the time of Sappho's recovery for modern literature, with which the "coming to writing" of the original French female erotic poet, Louise Labé, is rigorously simultaneous, major women writers have come into their literary powers, as Labé did, in Sappho's name, assuming the title "the Sappho" of the age.[3] Many such involvements are true rites of passage in which these women take on authorial authority by means of their identification with Sappho. They fuse poetic voices with her; they propose alternative Sapphic fictions to the dominant plot inevitably dictated by their male contemporaries—this is the essence of the process by which they become able to assume the literarily deviant role of woman writer.

However, the history of writers' involvement with the poetess will lead us to foreground far more often two male variants of Cixous's coming to writing. By far the more visible phenomenon, historically the most frequently encountered involvement with Sappho, is a male rite of authorial passage that is a complex, and disquieting, version of the phenomenon Harold Bloom calls "the anxiety of influence." In these cases, which I term "coming of age" to distinguish them from Cixous's paradigm, young male writers strive for literary manhood by enacting their simultaneous double attraction to a male and to a female literary origin. Unlike Bloom's model, in which the fledgling writer demonstrates his hostile attraction to the precursor poet whose authority he hopes to inherit, in cases of coming of age literary novices display only admiration for the male predecessor while displacing their hostility onto Sappho in her role as the original woman writer. Coming of age is always a collective phenomenon: a cluster of closely connected, aspiring men of letters collectively makes its claim to literary maturity by updating either the vision of Sappho's poetry (I think in particular of a group of the major lyric poets of the sixteenth century) or the story of Sappho's life (a notable example is the circle of poets centered around Baudelaire in the late 1840s). In all instances of coming of age, according to a pattern analyzed recently by Eve Sedgwick (following paradigms articulated by Luce Irigaray and Gayle Rubin), Sappho is reduced to the status of mere accessory to a double act of male poetic bonding, with other members of the literary collective and with the male precursor (Catullus and Racine in the examples mentioned above). Hence the absence in these texts of direct access to Sappho: the original woman writer is cited second-hand, through the mediation of the precursor poet who is always himself the inventor of a powerful, original vision of Sappho. Hence also the ease with which the attraction to a female literary origin, the founding expression of female desire by a woman writer, is camouflaged behind admiration for the male precursor and ultimately expressed only as often violent hostility. The fictions of Sappho that are the product of a coming of age are always the most unsettling: the fledgling writers are empowered by Sappho but then, as though rejecting their authorial proximity to a figure of female sexual deviance, revel in fictions in which Sappho is transformed into the archetypal abandoned woman, is physically humiliated, and in which her sexuality is normalized.[4] These Sapphic fictions reveal the central role played in male initiatory rites by received ideas of the female experience, by a drama of literary transvestism in which writers, using Sappho's words, perform an imitation of female desire designed to be accepted as real by their male contemporaries.

However, the obsessive recurrence of this hostile, oblique relation to Sappho should not blind us to the existence of the small number of exceptional cases in which a male writer forges a bond with Sappho so powerful and so personal that it is possible to speak of a case of poetic doubling, of impersonation or ventriloquism rather than mere transvestism. These instances are closer to Cixous's coming to writing (even though the man of letters is not necessarily a novice), an individual empowerment through a blending of a personal fiction of female desire and Sappho's expression of that desire. In these cases—I think most notably of Ovid, Catullus, Racine, and Baudelaire—the male writer's motivations are far more complex than that behind the simple act of appropriation that empowers the young writers who are coming of age. In fact, in the history of representations of Sappho, it is almost always writers of lesser talent who forge the kind of predictable relation to Sappho that is founded on an attempt to contain her voice of female desire.

Historically, the most influential fictions of Sappho and her poetry have been conceived by those male authors somehow able to identify with the original woman writer, to succeed in a special variant of what Froma

Zeitlin calls "playing the other," in this case, re-voicing a most problematic other, a woman who wrote of woman's desire for women. These writers strive for more than mere recognition by their male contemporaries: they seek somehow to become "authentically" Sapphic. For them, any corruption of the Sapphic image is less easily interpreted than the violence against Sappho's person enacted in fictions founded on what Irigaray terms a hom(m)osexual bond. For example, Racine's blackening of his Sapphic heroine (the portrayal of her lascivious, murderous maternity) might be said to express a denial of his attraction to Sappho. I use denial in the psychoanalytic sense of the term, to refer to the process by which the individual disavows a perception even as he or she retains it. Racine's denial of his proximity to Sappho would translate both a desired union with the female literary origin and the fear that he might identify too uncannily well with the woman's voice. The male poet who is able to speak with an "authentic" Sapphic voice, to continue an argument developed by Anne Freadman, finds himself in the disquieting position of having elected a muse with an independent existence in her own poetry, a muse who has no need of his voice in order to speak (see 152–55).

In France, fictions of Sappho have always loomed larger than her life and her poetry. Throughout the following pages, I try to keep the distinction clear between what was known about Sappho and what was imagined at a given period. I also try, whenever possible, to indicate through orthography the successive phantasms of the muse of Mytilene. I had originally intended to use "Sappho" whenever referring to fictive characters, like the heroine of Ovid's fifteenth heroical epistle, but decided this was too cumbersome. However, I have maintained all the different spellings imagined by French authors and commentators throughout Sappho's history in France. For example, when describing the fictions of the late seventeenth century (when what has been through the centuries the most common French spelling is first adopted), I refer to their heroine as Sapho, whereas for fictions of the late nineteenth century I write Sapphô. Likewise, I have maintained all spellings adopted for persons and places from antiquity: my reader will thus encounter Alcée, Athis, Mytilène. We do not Anglicize the names of characters in foreign literary traditions: my use of contemporary spellings is intended as a reminder of the fabulation that consistently surrounds Sappho, even in what appear to be the most serious scholarly commentaries.

I adopt two additional peculiarities of orthography. First, I often write "Sapphic" when normal usage might seem to require "Sappho's," as in the phrase "Sapphic sexuality" characterizing the erotic configuration of one of her poems. I do so in order to stress that I am referring to the sexual orientation not of the poem's author but of the poem itself. Second, I maintain throughout a distinction between "Sapphic" and "sapphic" and between "Sapphism" and "sapphism." In lower case, adjective and noun correspond to standard usage and refer to female same-sex eroticism: they do not necessarily (indeed, at most periods, do not) imply a vision of Sappho's sexuality. In upper case, adjective and noun convey the plot decreed for Sappho at a given period. By Sapphism, in other words, I mean the changing vision of what was believed to be Sappho's story. The Sapphic plot need not—and at many, if not most, periods (the entire eighteenth century, for example), did not—include female homosexuality.

A number of fictions of Sapphism that I will describe are so unlikely that readers might well feel they could be dismissed as the ravings of critical crackpots. It is important to remember that no vision, however strange, is simply a personal invention: each commentator constructs a composite of elements culled from a variety of sources, to which he or she may add only a pinch of fantasy—but it is that unexpected veering off course that, time and again, alters the future of Sapphism. By retracing the history of both the predictable elements and the swerves of fantasy, we will come to understand the creation of a legend. It is also important to remember that, with few exceptions (to which I call attention), the fictions explored here in most detail are not only those with the greatest influence on the history of Sapphism, but those created by scholars whose knowledge of antiquity and classical languages gave them the intellectual authority that guaranteed respect for their opinions. Again and again, in fact, the least expected theories of Sapphism are those imagined by the most prominent Hellenists, scholars without whose erudition Sappho's corpus as we know it today would not have been restored to us.[5]

This phenomenon serves as further confirmation of the unsettling effect Sappho seems inevitably to produce. I came to wonder if it might not also be possible to attribute, at least in part, to this critical discomfort the fact that in the four centuries of Sappho commentary that I analyzed for this project, I encountered only three instances in which Hellenists call for the application to the study of Sapphism of what literary critics today consider the most elementary principles: a distinction between the speaking subject or narrator of a literary work and the biographical individual known or presumed to have authored that work, and the concomitant distinction between literary word and actual deed. Since examples of critical modernity have been so rare, I would like to foreground them briefly here.

Not before the mid-nineteenth century does it occur to a scholar to question the absolute identity between the narrator and the author of the poems attributed to Sappho: in 1847, Emile Deschanel (socialist, soon to be exiled for his political activity in the aftermath of 1848) writes with regard to the fragment in which the narrator advises a suitor to find a younger woman, "Here Sappho is only speaking relatively, if in fact in this fragment (and we are saying this once and for all), she is speaking about herself" (342).[6] But Deschanel's resounding "once and for all" remains without echo for some fifty years, until 1898, when Alfred Croiset delivers the most virulent and sustained attack to date on the interpretive stance dominant through the centuries.[7] Here are but scattered fragments from Croiset's rejection of the most common critical coin in readings of Sappho: "It is impossible to see a declaration of love in all the verse in which [Sappho] made a woman in love speak. . . . In such matters, one must avoid drawing conclusions . . . about behavioral habits from stylistic habits" (2:232, 235). Nearly another half-century passes before Aimé Puech, in the preface to the still standard French edition of Sappho (Reinach-Puech, 1937), again takes a stand against the reduction of the poetry to a reflection of Sapphism: "We know with certainty that Sappho did not exclusively limit herself to the expression of her own feelings" (179).

Three Hellenists in four centuries do not an interpretive tradition make; it is impossible, therefore, to speak of organized opposition to the reduction of Sappho to the sexual fictions promoted for her. And whether the chosen plot turns on a suppression or a promotion of sapphism seems to do little to alter the validity of the axiom K.J. Dover formulates from his study of commentary on male same-sex eroticism: "I know of no topic in classical studies on which a scholar's normal ability to perceive differences and draw inferences is so easily impaired" (vii). Anyone who still believes that scholarship can be ideologically neutral has only to turn to virtually any monument in the history of Sappho interpretation to learn just how innocent this view is.

Many explanations help account for the attempted suppression of sapphism: the fear of depopulation and the threat to the patriarchal order posed by communities of women are historically the most frequently recurrent. On the other hand, the promotion of sapphism could be seen as the result of a conscious or an unconscious autobiographical projection.

Following this line of reasoning, one could argue, for example, that the fact that Christina of Sweden saw Sappho's poetry as unequivocally homoerotic whereas her contemporary Madeleine de Scudéry gave a far more ambiguous reading of the same corpus tells us something about the sexual orientation of these two women. However, such autobiographical deductions about Sappho's commentators seem to me highly suspect, constructions as fragile as the rebuildings of the poet's biography on the basis of her poems—if for no other reason than the impossibility of weighing the influence of variables as important as personal and official censorship. Therefore, whereas I try to remain sensitive to the ambiguities in fictions of Sapphism that suggest that an author was aware of possibilities not officially admitted in his or her day, it is not clear to me that the effects of a commentator's sexual orientation on his or her commentary can be measured.

As I worked on this project, classicists whom I approached with requests for information would often respond with something like "We know this now; why would we want to know when it was discovered?", a response that implies that knowledge, once acquired, is permanently acquired, something the history of Sappho scholarship resoundingly disproves. This book is an unbroken narrative of Sappho's history from the mid-sixteenth to the mid-twentieth century. An important raison d'être for this story's existence is to pinpoint those moments (most strikingly, the dawn of the Enlightenment) at which knowledge of Sappho is lost or suppressed. These moments will probably seem the driest parts of this study, perhaps even to specialists of the period in question. However, by reading the introductions to each section, readers should be able to follow the story's unfolding without reading each section in its entirety. Had I left out elements of lesser general interest, the narrative chain would have been broken, and it would have been impossible to give a sense of the daring and the creativity that eventually led to break-throughs. Especially during periods when Sapphic knowledge is being or has been repressed, the imagination of fiction-makers tends to become more limited, and their productions may consequently appear to be mere variations on a theme. But even rote repetition is, in and of itself, of some importance: I came to believe that the most insistent refusal of change might well be indicative of the degree to which the opposing, suppressed scenario constituted a threat. It is clear that Sappho's numerous interpreters did not feel that they were merely repeating already tired material— only very rarely, and then only as confirmation of the widespread acceptance won by the most outlandish scenarios, do I include dictionary entries or other compilations that could be classified as hack work. Often tiny innovations were sufficient to win attention, even authority, for a commentator.

My three chapters correspond to the three moments in the French obsession with Sappho. Each chapter covers a phase in the constitution of Sappho's corpus as well as a phase in Sapphic fiction-making. Both my critical strategies and the context in which I attempt to situate Sapphic speculation vary from chapter to chapter, both because Sappho's corpus is so different in each of the three periods, and because the types of fictions inspired by Sappho are generically so varied. I begin with a preliminary section on the first steps, in the sixteenth century, toward the organization of a Sappho for modern times. By the end of that century, the then remaining texts have all been published in Greek, although only in a haphazard manner, scattered throughout editions devoted principally to other poets. My initial chapter is devoted to the construction of a French Sapho. This means first of all the constitution and the dissemination of a corpus in French. During the last quarter of the seventeenth century, certain of Sappho's poems are made available to a broader public when they are translated into French and packaged as an independent, unified corpus (1670, 1681, 1684).[8] However, the creation of a French Sapho actually begins nearly fifty years earlier in 1612, when the wide dissemination in French and broad success of Ovid's *Heroides* is inaugurated. The epistle that Ovid imagines from Sappho to her legendary lover Phaon is quite simply the most influential Sapphic fiction ever: fictions of Sappho begin when Ovid and Sappho intersect in the early modern imagination. The first phase of Sappho's French history is centered around the struggle to claim her authority for each of the discourses that were then rivals for dominance of the literary scene: Sappho's voice is heard, therefore, both in neoclassicism and in the most prominent anticlassical strain, the various forms of prose fiction that collectively are recognized as the earliest manifestations of what we today know as the novel. The first phase of Sappho's French presence is over when, during the decades 1690–1710, the French dominance over Sappho scholarship (and Hellenic studies more generally) comes to an end. At this time, both the scope of Sapphic fictions and the corpus attributed to Sappho become radically restricted.

The second phase of the French Sapphic romance is in every respect the most limited and the most limiting. From 1710 to 1816, Sappho's heterosexuality is uncontested. This reduction of narrative possibilities never means, however, that her presence in French letters abates. In the course of the eighteenth century, the center of Sapphic activity is gradually transferred from the novel to the theater, but the pace of that fiction making never slackens. During the same period, Sappho's corpus is both reduced—so that, for example, the general reader in 1715 was led to believe that fewer fragments of her poetry had survived than his or her counterpart in 1685 would have thought—and deformed, virtually beyond recognition. Nothing less than the severing of the bond between Ovid and Sappho is required to set fictions of Sapphism on a new course.

Only at the end of the Napoleonic period do woman and work break out of the restraints that the Enlightenment seems to have felt obliged to impose on the poetess. In the second and third decades of the nineteenth century, both Sappho scholarship and Sapphic speculation take a radically new turn. As far as Sappho's corpus is concerned, the energy then released culminates, for the first time since the sixteenth century, in Greek editions of all available fragments (most prominently, Bergk, 1854; Lobel and Page, 1955) and the first complete translations (in particular, Wharton, 1885; Lebey, 1895; Vivien, 1903; Reinach-Puech, 1937). Each of these editions in translation presents the reader with a radically different vision of Sappho and her poetry, an inevitable consequence of the explosion in Sapphic fictions whose beginning is simultaneous with the movement to recover her work from the state of regression to which the Enlightenment had consigned it. In the course of the nineteenth century in France, Sappho leaves behind the often modest and always timid heterosexuality in which she had been disguised for nearly a century to reemerge as a figure of highly charged sexuality, first a courtesan, later a (sometimes depraved, sometimes oversexed) lesbian.

It is during the nineteenth century that national scholarly traditions part ways most violently on the subject of Sappho. German Hellenists decree Sappho's "chastity" at the same time that their French colleagues are beginning to explore possibilities for Sapphism that have been suppressed for nearly a century and a half. This interpretive divergence along national lines indicates what I take to be the heart of the most recent phase of Sappho's history. Throughout the nineteenth century and at least until after World War II, Sappho is almost always implicated in a nationalistic struggle: by this, I mean that Franco-Prussian politics will color her interpretation, and also that nationalistic interests will often determine the shape of Sapphic fictions. The most striking illustration of this phenomenon is one that I analyze at length, the bond between the study of Sappho and that of *pederastia* that German philologists forge to replace the tie they sever between Sappho and Ovid. The question of the role Sapphism and sapphism will be allowed to play in the modern polis underlies the most influential discussions of the poetess from the advent of a new nationalism in the early nineteenth century to the most recent redefinition of national boundaries and nationalism after the Second World War.

I reconstruct both the separate development and the interconnections among three strands of Sapphic texts. The first is *scholarship*—editions, translations (including some translations in which even minimal scholarly standards are not respected), and scholarly commentary published outside of editions, such as the entries on Sappho in Bayle's 1697 *Dictionnaire*. Second is *scholarly speculation,* a somewhat slippery intermediary category that includes, on the one hand, commentary like Allier de Hauteroche's 1822 *Notice sur la courtisane Sapho,* which succeeded in passing for scholarship even though it is only a tissue of flagrantly invented elements; and, on the other, works like Barthélemy's 1788 *Voyage du jeune Anacharsis,* a novel whose erudition is for the most part on a level higher than that found in many learned commentaries. Finally, there are *fictions,* a category in which I include both serious literary texts like Baudelaire's "femmes damnées" cycle and popular Sapphic fantasies such as D'Auvigny's 1724 novel, *L'Histoire et les amours de Sapho de Mytilène.* I reserve the term commentator almost exclusively for writers whose contributions belong in my first category, although I do on occasion use it in reference to the more reliable authors in the second category. I set commentator in opposition to fictionist or fiction-maker, to convey the difference between those who presumably believe that they are presenting facts, like Sappho's most influential seventeenth-century commentator, Anne Le Fèvre Dacier, and those who are deliberately trying to depart from the received ideas of their day, like Le Fèvre Dacier's contemporary, Madeleine de Scudéry, whose Sapphic scenario must be termed a fiction, despite its irreproachable erudition, because of her occasional, major departures from both contemporary scholarly tradition and what could then or ever be recovered about Sappho (most strikingly, her claim that Sapho never married).

Throughout this reconstruction of Sappho's presence in modern thought, I shift back and forth between scholarship and fictions to show how the different levels of commentary constantly contaminate each other. Indeed, the relation between scholarship and speculation is often so intense, even as recently as the early twentieth century, that on a number of occasions I expose the roots of scholarly theories in popular fiction. My principal concern throughout is to convey a sense of how a tradition was kept alive and shaped. Therefore, I privilege fictions, such as Baudelaire's, that bring together the elements most crucial to an understanding of each period's Sapphic vision, and fictions, Scudéry's for example, whose revisions provoke the kind of controversy that results in opposing fictions of Sapphism (in this case, Boileau's and Racine's). My focus thus obliges me almost to efface the distinction between high and popular culture: pulp fiction like D'Auvigny's novel was often far more influential in determining the future of the received ideas about Sapphism than texts with literary merit.

On the other hand, I do not discuss a number of works of recognized quality by well-known authors which feature a character named Sappho when the plot imagined for that heroine bears no resemblance to any scenario imagined for the actual Sappho of Mytilene: by fictions of Sappho, I mean only texts in which received ideas of Sapphism are evident and not works that simply traffic in the poetess's name, much as does a current French pop singer who has adopted the sobriquet "Sapho." In Brantôme's *Les Dames galantes,* for example, Sappho figures solely as a personification of the threat of female same-sex love. Even though in the second half of the sixteenth century the basic elements of the Sapphic plot (whose survival contemporary humanism was in the process of guaranteeing) were only beginning to circulate in the public domain, the contemporary biographical sketch by André Thevet (1584) proves that Brantôme had access to a fairly complex Sapphic plot. However, Sappho enters Brantôme's annals of female "gallantry" only because she serves to confirm his theory that husbands should not make the mistake of tolerating sapphism on the grounds that it is less dangerous than adultery: just as "the lesbians' mistress" gave up women for "her friend Faon," so women always become dissatisfied with other women and turn to male lovers because "they must bathe in running water, which is so much more refreshing than still water" (192–93).[9] Fontenelle's dialogue "Sapho et Laure" (*Nouveaux Dialogues des morts,* 1683), in a chaster vein, uses Sappho's name to figure no longer female homosexuality but female erotic drive. (This shift may be an early signal of the heterosexualization of Sappho.) In the dialogue, Sapho defends the opinion that women should be more aggressive in lovemaking, while Laure contends that they should let men make the first move. Fontenelle—despite the fact that he is writing near the end of the most intense early period of Sapphic dissemination in French—demonstrates no knowledge of Sappho herself and only borrows her name in an attempt to profit from its notoriety to commercialize his own work.

There are, finally, a few scattered examples of authors who exploit the name "Sappho" without reference to the sexual sensationalism generally associated with it. The most interesting of these is Lawrence Durrell's 1950 verse play *Sappho*. Durrell uses several characters related either intimately (Phaon) or intermittently (Pittakos, the tyrant of Sappho's Lesbos) to Sapphic fictions; he also occasionally employs proper names found in Sappho's poetry, although in dramatically altered contexts ("Dika," for example, the name of one of Sappho's "beloved girls," becomes here the name of a pet monkey). These echoes prove that Durrell is conversant with the tradition of Sapphic speculation but chooses not to belong to it: his Sappho is a poet without being a fiction of Sappho.

To the French belongs the credit for having made the fictionalization of Sappho into a national obsession, but they did not invent the genre. As for all the genres rooted in French neoclassicism, this tradition is based on classical precedent. Nearly every element used through the centuries of Sapphic fiction-making can be found in embryonic form in commentaries in antiquity. The legends about Sappho's life that were then formulated time and again take a recurrent form: biographers imagine that a series of dubiously historical figures can be seen as doubles for Sappho. The least troubling of these doubling fictions are those in which the Sappho character is something like a line-by-line copy of a commonly held view of the original. Thus Philostratus cites the example of a "clever woman" Damophyla who "was said to have had girl companions like Sappho, and to have composed love poems just as she did" (*Life of Apollonius of Tyana* 1.30). More intriguing are the fictions in which Sappho is replaced with a pair of Sapphos and the poet's attributes are divided between them. The doubles in this category are either courtesans or women humiliated by their *male* lovers. Aelian, for example, alleges the presence in Lesbos in Sappho's day of another woman named Sappho, a courtesan (*Historical Miscellanies*). Those who do not make the other Sappho a lover of many men rather than of many women describe this double as wild with love for one man, a male lover whose betrayal drives her to commit suicide by leaping from a cliff. Witness the account in the ancient lexicon, the Suda, of this other Sappho: "a Lesbian of Mytilene, a lyre player. She threw herself from the Leucadian Cliff for love of Phaon the Mytilenaean. Some authorities say that she, too, was a lyric poetess." These doublings make it possible to distinguish between a female sexuality judged unorthodox, even disreputable, and a respectable female sexuality, or even between female sexuality and poetic genius. This splitting, which is traditionally explained as the desire to separate a sexually disreputable Sappho from the poet and thereby protect the poet from criticism, provided nevertheless the basis for subsequent fictions of Sappho in which is evident the desire to humiliate the woman in order to assume control over her literary legacy.

Dover describes the "*horror vacui* which led ancient biographers to treat mere possibilities as established facts" (173). In Sappho's case, even the "mere possibilities" are far from numerous. The biographical details on which there is something like a consensus in the earliest sources are few indeed and, in addition, narratively uninspiring (possible names of her parents, names of from one to three brothers). There are two exceptions, both of which have important futures in fiction: the report of a quarrel with a brother, Charaxus, over his dissolute behavior (a foundation of nineteenth-century German philology's Sapphic vision), and the mention, recorded on an ancient historical stele known as the Parian marble, of a voyage to Sicily (a foundation of the rival nineteenth-century French Sapphic scenario). Indeed, as Mary Lefkowitz argues, almost all components of what has been presented through the ages as Sappho's biography are fabrications based on a literal reading of some part of her corpus as if it were an exact transcription of her life. What this means most crucially is that every bit of Sappho's impressively varied and constantly varying sexual biography is a projection of the biographer's sense of the erotic vision of her poems—which are, in turn, variously distorted and simplified until they provide a clear illustration of the orientation the commentator wishes to promote for Sappho. This vision of bio-poetic harmony is founded on an absolute identification between speaking subject and author, an identification that of necessity blinds commentators to the most complex aspects of the major Sappho odes, the evasively undefinable internal signature and the calculated avoidance of stable erotic orientation.[10]

Now I am trying to suggest here the importance and the complexity of a double problem: on the one hand, the basis for the definition of Sappho's own sexuality and, on the other, the basis for the interpretation of Sapphic eroticism, that is, the sexual orientation of Sappho's poetry. The first part of this issue, the definition of Sappho's personal eroticism, is irresolvable, if it is to be decided independently of the "evidence" of her poetry. As Dover stresses (174), no surviving text indicates the existence of commentary on Sappho's erotic relationships before old comedy (some two centuries after Sappho's time). Moreover, what information has survived about these first fictions of Sappho in literary works indicates only general portraits of Sappho as a center of erotic interest, or references to her sexual involvements with *men,* from Phaon to Anacreon (see Dover's descriptions of what is known about these plays, 174). Dover points out in addition that "no one who speaks of Sappho's eros for her own sex can be dated with complete certainty before the Augustan period" (174). He has in mind the references and fictions made by Horace and, more importantly, Ovid, the founding texts—despite their enormous distance from Sappho's time—for the discussion of Sappho's sapphism. Horace's stance has often been seen as "blame" (see, for example, Bonnet, 27), but there is no consensus about the meaning of his famous "mascula Sappho"; Ovid's ambiguity is more complete still. It would appear, therefore, that Sappho is initially portrayed as a lover of women only by those writing in response to a tradition that had enshrined her (satirically) as a lover of men, and only by writers unwilling or unable to take a clear stance on the issue of female homosexuality.

This lack of contextualization in the Augustan age is related to, and may well result from, a final insurmountable obstacle to knowledge of Sappho, the fact that the original silence surrounding *her* sexual person is part of a larger silence with regard to female homosexuality in antiquity in general. Commentators from John Addington Symonds to John Boswell remark what Boswell terms "the overwhelming disproportion of data regarding male and female sexuality" (*Christianity,* xvii). Indeed, it would appear that Boswell's conclusion is an understatement, to say the least, if Dover's claim is even nearly correct: "Classical Attic literature refers once, and once only, to female homosexuality" (172).[11] And this unique mention must be contrasted with the abundant tradition of commentary on male homo-erotic relations, at least in their official, public incarnation as the pedagogic-military union between older man and youth known as *pederastia.* No one in antiquity, in other words, seems to have had, or at least was willing to express, an opinion on female same-sex love, much less on Sappho's potential relation to this phenomenon. Small wonder that subsequent commentators, from the founding Augustans to Sappho's most recent editors, have enormous difficulty in defining a position with regard to what has every appearance of a taboo subject. For all of them, sapphism in antiquity is no more and no less than the woman who gave it her name, even though strictly no evidence remains about that woman's sexual biography. Small wonder, too, under these circumstances, that commentators have contested for centuries every word of Sappho's poetry that could be seen in any way as related to the phenomenon otherwise without a past and virtually without a name. For the burden of proof lies there, and only there.

As to the mystery surrounding Sappho's person and the larger question of female homosexuality in antiquity, it seems fruitless to speculate about the origin of the absence of information. But Sappho's poetry is a different matter, for in this domain it is difficult to believe that at least some of the perplexing ambiguity is not an intentional creation of its author. If antiquity were the invention of modern writers, Sappho would be Borges's creation: an author who cries out for interpretation because of the controversial nature of her subject matter, but an author whose works time and again deny the reader an absolute response to questions of sexual orientation that the poems themselves elaborately stage and oblige the reader to pose. As Dover concludes, "the evidence for [Sappho's] homosexuality is fragmentary." By this, he means that since only two of her poems have come down to us in something like an integral version, in most cases editors and readers alike are faced with only fragments of poems, often only fragments of lines. Dover further concludes that "the evidence is also fragile and ambiguous" (174). Here, he refers to two interrelated issues, the problems in transmission caused by Sappho's Lesbian dialect, and what I would describe as "breaks" in manuscripts, passages in which a key word or phrase is either missing or has never been interpreted in a manner that satisfies all authorities.

Dover never suggests that the obscurities in Sappho's texts are the result of editorial dishonesty, and I have come to believe that this implicit view is probably correct. For a long time, however, I was convinced that, as Edith Mora claims on several occasions, editors must simply have decided to alter manuscripts. This view often infiltrates critical presentation of Sappho's sexual textual history—see, for example, Louis Crompton's attribution of translators' use of a male object of desire in the "Ode to Aphrodite" to a conscious attempt to obscure Sappho's homosexual message (93). We will never be able to determine the role played by homophobia in the destruction of the part of Sappho's work apparently forever lost to us.[12] The modern transmission of Sappho's text, on the other hand, has been a complicated process, but one that we can reconstruct. It is, furthermore, a process certainly not accounted for by any one explanation alone. We will witness, for example, numerous emendations proposed through the centuries for Sappho fr. 31 (the ode cited by "Longinus," familiarly known in French as "A l'aimée" and in English as "Peer of the Gods"), all of which aim to normalize the Sapphic erotic configuration: in every case will be evident, to varying degrees, dishonesty, homophobia, and/or fear of the forceful expression of female desire.[13] But there are at the same time very real textual problems in Sappho's corpus of the type Dover is trying to account for, as we will see in particular in the example of Sappho fr. 1 (the "Ode to Aphrodite"). To his multifaceted description of the origin of the difficulties Sappho presents, I would add one final factor, what I had in mind when I referred to Sappho's Borgesian stance: the undeniable role Sappho herself plays in the creation of sexual confusion, most notably in her two most celebrated odes (fr. 31 and fr. 1), both of which make their threatening sexuality evident only belatedly, and in a manner so devious that it appears teasing. It is as if Sappho had been fully conscious of the controversial nature of her subject matter—and had sought actively to enhance it.

For centuries, students of Sappho have shared the dream of recovering her for modern times: by this, they mean establishing, once and for all, the truth about her sexuality. After studying the textual history of Sapphism over more than four centuries, I would offer this conclusion, which the following pages will attempt to justify: the sexual orientation of Sappho's poetry is not unidirectional, as it would have to be to allow us to draw conclusions about its author's person. When Dover announces that the evidence for Sappho's homosexuality is "fragile and ambiguous," he is cautioning that the currently prevalent view—Sappho's poetry is homosexual and she was herself a lesbian—cannot be incontrovertibly established.

It seems to me that the most interesting definition of the problem of Sappho lies elsewhere, in the polyphony of voices of sexual desire heard in her poetry. The example of the ultimate sexual undecidability of the "Ode to Aphrodite," for which the gender of the object of desire cannot be determined, is only part of what I have in mind here. The most powerful expressions of Sapphic desire must be termed homosexual.[14] But this voice can also be characterized with the Bakhtinian term "polyphonic," not in its sense of "containing opposing meanings in suspension of judgment" in which I just used it, but rather in the sense of self-conscious discourse, a discourse that includes a commentary on its own functioning as well as its primary message. Just as Sappho measures the distance separating her poetic standards from those of epic, notably in the fragment (LP 16) referring to the Trojan war, so she on occasion can be said to make her reader aware of the distinction between her erotic vocabulary and that of other erotic situations, for example male homosexuality. A number of the most influential nineteenth-century philologists (see, for example, Müller and Welcker in chapter 3) already note Sappho's use of the vocabulary of male homoeroticism. Dover discusses the proximity between Sapphic expression of desire and that of the older lover in pederastic relations (174); he also compares her use of "hetaira" ("companion") to heterosexual usage ("mistress") (20). At times, this terminological proximity or contamination contributes to the erotic undecidability of Sapphism, for example in LP 102, when the female narrator expresses her love for a "pais," a word that can mean "boy," "girl," or the neuter "child," but is also the term used by the dominant pederastic lover for his passive partner (Dover, 16). This is but one striking example of Sappho's creation of sexual ambiguity; rather than use the alternate, truly neuter word for "child," she elects the term that invites a determination of its gender, something her poem then denies the reader. But Sappho's self-consciousness with regard to the very discourse of homoerotic desire (the discourse that, in the feminine, may well be her contribution to the Greek language) also implies a commentary on homoerotic relations, male and female. Dover, like others, astutely points to the existence of what he terms a "marked degree of mutual eros" as the distinguishing characteristic of Sapphic relations (177). Indeed, the absence in Sappho of the configuration basic to male homosexuality in antiquity, the absolute distinction in *pederastia* between a dominant or active partner and a subordinate or passive partner, is constitutive of Sapphism: Sapphism, antiquity's only exemplar of sapphism, defines itself in opposition to a dominant male tradition.[15]

Such an unambiguous choice of erotic ambiguity would seem to position Sappho as the ultimate post-structuralist author, a poet who proclaims the death of the subject, the prophet of today's widely prevalent critical desire for a subject that celebrates (in terms both literary and sexual) a mode beyond difference, beyond categories such as male/female, masculine/feminine. Sappho could also be seen as the archetypal lesbian writer, according to Teresa de Lauretis's recent definition of her as a writer who seeks "variously to escape gender, to deny it, transcend it, or perform it in excess" (159). A major lesson to be learned from the tradition of Sapphic speculation is that received ideas about gender have always dominated what has passed for Sappho commentary. However, commentators have been led down that garden path by Sappho herself. Her consistent refusal to be confined within stable definitions of gender and sexual identity invites, as it were, her readers to project their prejudices onto what has been denied them. Thus, Sappho, in a manner not unrelated to the post-structuralist inquiry, forces the reader to pose basic questions about literary sexuality: Can we determine the sex of an author from internal textual evidence alone? What is the relation between the sex of an author and the gender of the speaking subject in his or her work?

The history of Sappho's fictionalization has much to teach us about the evolving discourse of gender, the construction of sexual difference through notions of the feminine and the masculine. All fictions of Sappho are fictions of the feminine: they transmit received ideas about female desire, its expression, its plot, and its fate. The tradition I reconstruct here can help historicize our understanding of the cultural function of fantasies of Woman. In particular, the material I uncover could serve as the basis for studies of two interrelated aspects of the history of gender: a history of the function of the feminine in the transmission of what Irigaray terms hom(m)osexual culture, and a history of writers' attempts to undermine that culture by recreating the Sapphic position beyond gender. This book, however, is neither of those histories. I stress the role of fantasies of the female in the production of male culture, in particular whenever I analyze instances of literary coming of age. However, my goals are too diverse to concentrate only on the history of the functioning of gender. I hope that others will find these materials useful for their contributions to that history.

I began this project under the illusion that the history of Sappho must be one of progress, in stages, toward the reclaiming of the poetess from the obscurity that surrounded her for her first modern editors. While I still believe that the stages that inspired the book's division into chapters existed, I no longer see her history as a progression toward greater knowledge. It now seems to me that the first erudites who worked to recover Sappho—notably Henri Estienne and one of the last to guarantee the survival of humanism's ideals in the seventeenth century, Tanneguy Le Fèvre—knew more about Sappho than any other pre-nineteenth-century scholars. This seems more comprehensible if we accept that, in Sappho's case, "knowledge" seems ultimately to be synonymous with undecidability, with the realization that we do not know most of what has for centuries been accepted as fact. In the sixteenth century, "knowledge" is also synonymous with willingness to admit the possibility of her sapphism, an openness to sexual diversity that has rarely been part of Sappho's modern history. Without the daring necessary to violate sexual taboo and express the existence of female homoeroticism, an intellectually valid view of Sapphism has never been possible.

But personal daring alone was not enough to create scholarly open-mindedness. Retracing Sappho's history allows us to pinpoint those few moments when French code(s) of sexual propriety, those unwritten laws that made female homosexuality the unpronounceable, were relaxed enough to allow scholars to accept for themselves this reading of Sapphism and to make it public. If Sappho is an index, as she must be, sapphism was conceivable in a public literary-scholarly forum at four moments: (1) off and on from the mid-sixteenth century to about 1660—at the end of this period, we encounter perhaps the most forthright commentator in the entire French tradition, Le Fèvre, who simply states his position (Sappho loved women) without either condemning or defending female homosexuality. After this, female homosexuality is unthinkable, or at least unpronounceable, until, (2) faintly and very briefly in the 1820s, a glimmer of recognition appears. (3) Briefly again, but far more brazenly, in the decade from 1847 to 1857, most spectacularly around *Les Fleurs du mal,* sapphism gains public recognition. (4) Finally, at no time in the French tradition has female homosexuality been so openly displayed as during the period from 1895 to 1910, when first Pierre Louÿs and then the members of the "Sapho 1900" circle for the first time made sapphism the most frequently encountered reading of Sapphism.

Throughout the four centuries of her French presence, therefore, Sappho has rarely been openly sapphic. Instead, I believe, a more socially admissible translation of Sapphism has often replaced the suppressed erotic configuration: Sappho as the primal voice of female (literary) desire. This reading originates with the early modern view of Ovid's Sappho, when she was seen simultaneously as the archetypal woman in love and the archetypal woman writer. From the late seventeenth century until at least the early nineteenth century, Sappho presides over a scenario in which woman's amorous passion and women's writing are synonymous: uncontrolled, spontaneous, excessive outpourings.

The credit for rewriting the terms in which the critique of Sapphism was formulated goes to proponents of this interpretation of Sappho as the origin of absolute spontaneity and raw physicalness in the expression of woman's desire. The new theory receives its first careful articulation in prominent *arts poétiques* of the eighteenth century. At the period during which the possibility of sapphism was most effectively suppressed, the Sapphic style was shown to be instinctive as a prelude to a subtle depreciation of all women's writing. Witness the abbé Batteux, who in his 1747 *Cours de Belles-Lettres* explains that, in literature, the real (*le vrai*) is less valuable than the real-seeming (*le vraisemblable*), because only the real-seeming can inspire true pleasure and admiration in the reader (1:322). Ultimately, the theory of Sapphic spontaneity is the basis for a devaluation of Sappho's poetry — and of all work (whether or not written by women) seen as conforming to her model — as *merely* authentic desire rather than the more highly prized artificially passionate.[16] Sappho (and therefore sapphism) is no longer threatening, and moral condemnation no longer necessary, when she can be dismissed on grounds of literary inadequacy.

Starting in the Romantic period, however, the theory of the Sapphic voice as speaking directly from the poet's heart becomes the basis for what is presented as a eulogy of her sublimity. Two near-simultaneous texts, the critic Sainte-Beuve's 1845 *Portraits de femmes* and the Hellenist Emile Deschanel's 1857 study of Sappho, enshrine Sappho as the patron saint of what Sainte-Beuve characterizes as a quite literal type of life writing, writing to stay alive. The principal literary chronicler of his age situates "the original genius" of women's writing on the limit between life and death: on the one hand, Sapphism is "the passionate suffering" of "unrequited love" and, on the other, "[women] *should* die . . . when they are no longer loved" (381, my emphasis). Deschanel defines Sappho's poetry as "born of her passion" and therefore "true" and "always natural." He describes the original woman poet quite literally *writing the body:* Sappho turned to poetry to "distract" herself from her "unfulfilled" passion; "her nerves would quiver . . . and broken song would flow from her trembling lips" (355–56). Finally, in a move that prefigures the dominant fin-de-siècle reading of all expressions of physical desire by women, Deschanel defines Sapphism as "hystérisme," the written out-pouring of "unfulfilled" desire (354). Ultimately, therefore, these panegy-rics are merely the flip side of the neoclassical dismissal of female spontaneity: they maintain the critical configuration used for decades to guarantee that "the female literary style" would remain only a literary curiosity.

Readings of Sappho's poetry as a primal throbbing of desire at least keep alive a sense, however undefined, of the erotic power of Sappho's poetry in the face of attempts, mainly by German scholars, to sublimate away that energy. It was left to an Austrian, writing in Paris at the exact time of the explosion of literature both Sapphic and sapphic known today as the "Sapho 1900" movement (1903–10), to give this originally Ovidian reading its most extreme expression and, above all, to integrate sapphism explicitly into the vision of women's writing as primal passion. Key passages of Rainer Maria Rilke's *Notebooks of Malte Laurids Brigge* portray Sappho as a "saint" of love, as the model for all the outpourings of female passion (some of which we would classify as clearly literary, some of which we would call, like him, "real") from Heloïse, to the Portuguese nun, to Julie de Lespinasse (207, 236). For Rilke, this Sapphic tradition (whose beginnings, in seventeenth-century France, we will retrace) is more than merely natural; it is nature itself: "the whole of nature joins in with the voice [of women in love]" (235). Rilke's Sappho is at the same time the original woman in love and the culmination of the very notion of female amorous passion: the force of her desire has incorrectly been qualified as "excess," whereas Rilke proclaims it instead "the new unit of measure for love and heart-grief" (241). Like Ovid's, Rilke's Sappho has loved one man and many women but, unlike Ovid's, she does not abandon sapphism for "true" heterosexual passion. The object of her desire is less important than the very nature and the continued existence of that desire. Rilke portrays Sappho as a model for lovers and for writers because he sees her poetry as a continuous longing "not for fulfillment but for greater longing," as an account of her unattainable quest for "the no longer possible one who had grown vast enough for her love" (242). Because she made desire into a search for the infinite, because she was in love with necessarily unrequited love, "her heart became a force of nature" (242).

I will not, for the moment at least, explore the uncanniness of the male writer's identification with the woman broken by the force of her desire and freely electing this martyrdom. For now, I merely want to stress the persistence of this image, as well as the fact that, through the centuries, this at times unsettling interpretive stance has guaranteed that Sappho be discussed as a *woman* writer, a consideration otherwise extremely rare.[17] Indeed, on occasion this long tradition of patronizingly gender-specific Sappho commentary is (uncomfortably) reminiscent of recent feminist theories of women's writing, in particular Cixous's canonical formulation of *écriture féminine,* "Le Rire de la Méduse." I will not, for the moment, dwell on this either, except to cite at some length for those who do not remember them key points of Cixous's definition of *écriture féminine* that parallel the definition of Sapphism elaborated by writers from Ovid to Sainte-Beuve to Rilke:

> A woman . . . throws her trembling body forward. . . . All of her passes into her voice, and it's with her body that she supports the "logic" of her speech. Her flesh speaks true. . . . In fact, she physically materializes what she's thinking; she signifies it with her body. . . . There is not that scission, that division made by the common man between the logic of oral speech and the logic of the text. . . . In women's speech, as in their writing, that element which never stops resonating . . . is the song: first music from the first voice of love which is alive in every woman. (251)

Cixous even repeats the ultimate move in Rilke's argument, the sort of metaphorization of female homoeroticism that situates an ill-defined vision of sapphism at the origin of woman's writing the body, and therefore at the origin of the poetry of desire: "We will rethink womankind beginning with every form and every period of her body. The Americans remind us, 'We are all Lesbians' " (252).[18]

I would never claim allegiance to this originally romantic myth of Sapphism as primal life-writing or body-writing, of Sappho as Ur-woman at one with nature and with her feminine nature spontaneously sobbing out, sibyl-like, her desire for infinite desire. However, I remain even less convinced by the tradition that, at least since the beginning of Sappho's translation into the modern imagination in the seventeenth century, has been defined in opposition to the theory of the Sapphic "heart" as "a force of nature": the theory of Sapphism as the ultimate in the controlled, *never* spontaneous, depiction of desire, as the artificially passionate that eighteenth-century theorists preferred to merely authentic passion. We will trace the origin of this counterdefinition to the Ovidian vision in seventeenth-century French neoclassicism. However, its most influential formulations date from the nineteenth and twentieth centuries and originate with the Germans who, at the turn of the nineteenth century, begin to proclaim Sappho's "chastity." All those who center their vision of Sappho on her artistic control are, wittingly or unwittingly, heirs to the original modern philologists, for whom her artistic control was implicitly synonymous with the absence of erotic drive, Sappho's heterosexuality, and even her asexuality. Commentators who proclaim that Sappho wrote from the head rather than the heart consistently downplay the power of the passion expressed in her poems and either are blind to or deny the importance of gender-specific readings. At the foundation of this tradition is the never explicitly formulated assumption that a great writer does not write as a woman.

Perhaps the purest representative of this august tradition (august because it has won the allegiance of virtually all those considered the finest Hellenists of the last two centuries) is among the most recent, Denys Page, coeditor of the currently definitive Greek text of Sappho. To understand the consequences of this interpretation, we need look no further than Page's reading of Sappho's two most celebrated odes in the companion volume to his edition, *Sappho and Alcaeus*. Here fr. 31 becomes the story above all of the man evoked in the poem's initial pronoun and the saga of a struggle for writerly mastery. For the "Ode to Aphrodite," Page emphasizes the presence of repetition, a presence, he contends, that proves Sappho's detachment: "This everlasting sequence of pursuit, triumph and ennui is not to be taken so very seriously" (16). Page stresses Sappho's "wit," her "good-humoured raillery" (15) (in the *Oxford Classical Dictionary,* Bowra speaks of her "badinage"), to show Sappho as involved not in her passion but in portraying "the vanity and impermanence of her passion" (16).

This vision of Sapphic "control" and "dispassionate[ness]" (18) is ultimately an attempt to deny the bodily presence that the opposing interpretive camp sees everywhere in Sappho's verse. In fact, representatives of the English school of sangfroid commentary are so little concerned with the question that is the foundation of all attempts to read Sappho's poetry as an extension of her person, her creation of a voice and a structure of desire that are inherently female, that they often (willfully?) fail to point out the sexual implications of the formal points they emphasize. Thus, for example, in his commentary on the "Ode to Aphrodite," Page does not indicate that the reading he prefers would change the female object of desire given in his Greek text (reproduced from Lobel and Page) to an object of desire of undeterminable sex (11, n. to line 24). Such all-encompassing formalism may mean that, for the control school, all questions of eroticism are, like the pursuit sequence in fr. 1, "not to be taken so very seriously." However, as I will be able to suggest more convincingly after we have examined the history of philology's relation to Sapphic chastity, it may also signify the most oblique attempt to date at establishing if not the heterosexuality, at least the asexuality of Sapphism.

From the turn of the nineteenth century on, the real fear for the philologist seems always to be that to speak of the body and eroticism in Sappho is to summon forth the specter of female homosexuality. Thus, at least according to today's reigning philologist, the future of Sappho studies is asexual.

For centuries, Sappho commentary has been torn between two radically opposed visions: on the one hand, Sappho as the abandoned woman, the essence of unmediated female suffering and pain; and, on the other, Sappho as detached and wry commentator on "the vanity and impermanence" of *human—not* essentially female—passion. The almost total absence of efforts to mediate between these positions is striking but, upon reflection, hardly surprising. For any attempt to break out of this critical deadlock would require first of all a major sidestepping or setting aside: commentators would have to cease writing with or against previous commentators, stop searching for the woman, and concentrate instead solely on what is left of her *oeuvre*. Finally, they would have to look at her poems in a way in which they have all too rarely been seen during the past four centuries: stripped bare of all the interpretive encrustations adhering to them that have originated in the tradition of Sapphic fictions whose slow but steady development we will now begin to retrace.

Preliminaries: The Sapphic Renaissance (1546–1573)

Sappho has known a fate unique in literary tradition: for centuries, her reputation has been grounded in her exceptional value as literary property, that is, her ability to function repeatedly in an age-old tradition of male poetic exchanges. Sappho continues to accumulate exchange value (a value that translates into Sapphic fictions) for reasons that vary from period to period. But the basic scenario remains the same. A part of her corpus gains wide currency when poets and commentators circulate new versions of it. This is the prelude to an instance of coming of age as a group of young writers reaches literary manhood by means of a struggle for Sappho. A woman writer is the natural conduit for male poetic bonding: she performs a traditional female role, according to the terms of the now classic discussion initiated by Lévi-Strauss of the exchange of women at the foundation of the social order. However, the central function performed by Sappho at the origin of the male cultural order could not have been fulfilled by just any woman writer. The force of the attraction exercised by Sapphic homoeroticism is particularly evident in the complex poetic configuration enacted around her in the sixteenth century: male poets strive to take over the powerful desire for woman she had originated, to put their poet figures in the place of Sappho's speaking subject. The scenario I trace here will establish the basic lines of a pattern we will see recreated, in greater complexity, throughout the Sapphic tradition. I will consider the poetic bonding generated by Catullus's Sapphic revision only briefly, as a backdrop to the more elaborate design inspired several decades later by Ovid's Sappho.

In modern times, interest in Sappho has almost always been a group effort: clusters of translators, commentators, and fictionalizers appropriate her work not only at the same time but also collectively. As we explore the history of Sappho's fictionalization, we will unravel a number of what could be called knots of influence, moments during which the poetic object, Sappho's founding text of amorous passion, is passed back and forth among writerly hands with such frenetic intensity that we are forced to wonder how much was at stake in her circulation. The first such knots of influence take shape immediately at the time of her recovery for modern readers. The perimeters of this brief foray into Renaissance humanism were in fact set by two such moments of collective desire for Sappho. I will not comment extensively on the first French Sapphic presence because the sixteenth century does not yet create true fictions of Sappho (Louise Labé comes closest). But these are the foundations on which, at the beginning of the seventeenth century, the French tradition of fictionalization will be constructed.

As I will repeatedly observe in this presentation of Sappho's history, she does not necessarily begin to circulate as soon as she is made known. At times, her text seems to fail to produce echoes because readers are unable or unwilling to confront her controversial expression of desire. At others, the lack of interest seems to have been just that: knots of influence take shape only when the right poem (or version of a poem) is made available at the right time. A case in point: for some twenty years, sixteenth-century French poets indulged in a collective obsession with fr. 31 while at the same time fr. 1 sparked little visible interest.[1] Indeed, whereas the "Ode to Aphrodite" was the first of Sappho's poems revealed to modern readers, initially it generated, with one important exception, remarkably little attention, and the attention it did get was slow in coming. The poem is published as early as 1546, in Robert Estienne's Greek edition of the rhetorician Dionysius of Halicarnassus, who cites Sappho as a model of stylistic and euphonic harmony (thereby inaugurating what we will find to be a recurrent practice among moderns, whereby Sappho's erotic vision is treated as a mere subset of metrics). In addition, fr. 1 is the first poem to receive independent publication: in his original (Greek-Latin) edition of Anacreon in 1554, Robert Estienne's son Henri tacks on, as though as an afterthought, with neither fanfare nor even a Latin translation, the Aphrodite ode and a poem whose attribution is questioned today, "La Lune a fui" ("The Moon Has Set").

The text the Estiennes provide is not the one I will discuss early in chapter 2, the controversial declaration of homosexual passion that readers today generally associate with Sappho's most celebrated ode. On the contrary, the Estiennes make sense of the manuscripts as all Sappho's editors for nearly three hundred years do. They make Sappho go public with her passion (this is the only poem with an internal signature identifying the speaker with the author) for the first time in her modern history with a declaration of unrequited love for an object of desire of undetermined gender (always assumed by Renaissance translators to be male). It is important to remember that this is the initial modern vision of Sappho, as the poet of woman's unhappy heterosexual passion. It is equally important to remember that this vision had none of the attraction for the poets of the mid-sixteenth century that it would have for their successors at the turn of the following century. Renaissance men of letters would shortly be drawn to a very different image of Sapphism: the obsession with Sappho that leads to the first instance of coming of age begins only when the Renaissance public is introduced to a Sapphic text celebrating a female object of desire. However, for Louise Labé, the lone woman poet of the Renaissance to be pulled into the Sapphic magnetic field, the situation is reversed. We will consider Labé's immediate identification with the heterosexual poet of the "Ode to Aphrodite." But before the exception, let us posit the rule, Sappho's fate in the hands of male poets.

In 1556, 1560, and 1566, Henri Estienne includes Latin translations of fr. 1 (by Hélias Andréas) in his editions of Sappho. Nevertheless, fr. 1 passes almost unnoticed through the Renaissance. Critics point out occasional reminiscences, few of which convince me that the poets had Sappho in mind.[2] The most interesting uses of the poem indicate that Renaissance male poets, following the example of Estienne's chosen translator, were unwilling or unable to understand the deviousness of the economy of desire that Aphrodite explains to the suppliant Sappho. In chapter 2, we will discuss in some detail the interpretive options presented by the alternate Greek texts of this ode. For the moment, I will simply mention that while Sappho's sixteenth-century editors elected a version not very different from the one dominant until the late nineteenth century, her contemporary translators added an element to that Greek text. Early French translations of lines 23–24 of the Greek text that Estienne gives usually read something like "If one/he (depending on whether the translator is faithful to the then accepted Greek text, or decides to normalize the undetermined sexual scenario) doesn't love you, one/he will conform to your law," a reading that at least suggests something of what commentators now consider the profound ambiguity of Sappho's text: it does not make clear just what that Sapphic law would be and thereby leaves open the possibility that it would not be simply a story of reciprocal passion. Andréas, however, inaugurates a practice that is generalized only in the sixteenth century, that of adding to line 24 "amabit" (one/he will love you), a verb that vastly simplifies the sense of the exchange between Sappho and Aphrodite. Jean de La Gessée's 1583 translation of the "Hymne à Vénus," like Antoine de Baïf's free translation (1573) before it, is even more resolute in its effacement of undecidability from the Sapphic erotic economy. The ode is made known in French under cover of a misreading of Aphrodite's promise to Sappho:

> *S'il te fuit ore, il te suivra pour vivre,*
> ....
> *S'il ne t'aime ore, un jour il t'aimera,*
> *Et tout enfin, pour te plaire, fera.* (1:490–91)[3]

Rather than Sappho's vision of the (eternal) nonreciprocity of desire, her initial French readers were presented with a boringly conventional erotic scenario: just be patient and the wayward lover will come round.[4]

Baïf's 1573 imitation of the ode is a determined rejection of Sappho's erotic suspense, a masculinization of Sapphism that makes it perfectly in tune with stereotypes of contemporary amorous poetry. Baïf even puts his own poet-double in Sappho's place as unhappy poet-lover: "What's the matter with you, poor Baïf?" Venus wonders (2:181). And so we learn that "pauvre Baïf" is asking for help with not one, but two wayward mistresses. Venus is quick to promise a solution to such an easy dilemma: "One we will give you to mercy more inclined. / . . . / This one will conform her desires to yours" (Baïf's novel reading of the troublesome line 24). Unrequited love has lost all its threat in this almost comic rendition of the lover's complaint: Baïf can be certain of a happy end, if either mistress will do. And the most intriguing suggestion of the end of Sappho's original, a cycle of passion founded on continuous dissatisfaction, is put to rest as soon as woman becomes an infinitely substitutable object of desire. This accomplished, the ode ceases to interest French poets for nearly a century.

The fate of fr. 1 at the hands of male poets of the sixteenth century suggests most strikingly the lack of attraction for this public of any possibility for heterosexuality that departed from contemporary stereotypes: the alternate scenario Sappho was thought to offer was quickly dismissed—not obsessively stamped out, as will happen when a period enjoys a more ambivalent relation to a Sapphic model. It also indicates what is overall the dominant feature of the Renaissance treatment of Sappho: unlike the seventeenth century, whose obsession with her can be traced to its desire to found a fiction of the woman in love, the sixteenth century is concerned almost exclusively with adapting all the erotic scenarios proposed by the primal poet of female desire to a male protagonist.

A parallel masculinization progressively translated fr. 31 into an even more stereotypical saga of male amorous passion, one readers today would identify with René Girard's mediated desire. Fragment 31 was not included in the first volume in which Sappho was published independently (that is, not as a citation in a classical treatise), Estienne's 1554 edition of Anacreon. However, the ode does appear twice in the course of that same year, albeit not in France, and as a citation included in the classical texts being edited (in Robortello's edition, published in Basel, of "Longinus" 's treatise on the sublime; and as part of Muret's commentary on Catullus, published in Venice). And this poem evidently struck a collective poetic nerve in a way fr. 1 had not, for this time Sappho took off. Whereas eight years pass between the "Ode to Aphrodite" 's appearance as citation and its independent publication, only two are necessary in this case: in the second edition of his Anacreon, Estienne—perhaps realizing the error of his initial decision to promote only fr. 1—adds fr. 31. In addition, rather than the simple Latin translations provided for all the poems in this edition, Catullus's revision (his ode 51) of Sappho's original follows fr. 31, either a fortunate or a clever decision. This linking of Sappho to a more familiar male poet from antiquity, which prefigures the association between Sappho and Ovid so important to the literary imagination of the following century, is the move that guaranteed her presence on the sixteenth-century French poetic scene. In modern times, it is only when the coming-of-age scenario can be fulfilled—a relation to Sappho mediated by a relation to a male precursor who had already been under her influence—that the original woman writer has become the object of male literary desire. Estienne followed this original masculinization of Sapphism with a Latin translation of the stanza most deformed by Catullus, the fourth stanza which contains the signature of the narrator's femininity. This decision both indicates his awareness that the Catullus poem could not provide a proper replacement for Sappho's for readers without Greek and suggests that he may also have sensed that it was the union of Sappho and Catullus (initially displayed by Muret) that would launch the poetess's modern career. Indeed, from this point on, there was no stopping the spread of her fame—but that fame was based almost exclusively on the success of a single ode, the poem that would become known in French as "A l'aimée."

Later the same year (1556), Sappho receives her first translation into French, when Rémi Belleau includes a version of fr. 31, based on Estienne's Greek text, as an appendix to his *Odes d'Anacréon*. (The influence of precedent is apparently so great in these matters that, once Sappho had been published twice as an appendix to Anacreon, the subordination of her poetic fate to his became a convention in the French tradition, destined to continue uncontested until the twentieth century.) However, it is unlikely that Belleau's translation would convince anyone of Sappho's sublimity. Sappho's inaugural appearance in French is, sad to say, a fitting beginning to her generally lamentable fate in French hands: Belleau prettifies, softens, and generally weakens the impact of Sappho's account of love's power. (One example: lines that in a recent translation read "sous ma peau / un feu subtil soudain se glisse" become "Un petit feu qui furette / Dessous ma peau tendrelette.")[5] Really the only positive aspect of Belleau's effort is his decision to follow Sappho rather than her Latin successor for this scene of unrequited love. Unlike the vast majority of the sixteenth-century poems allegedly inspired by fr. 31, this one owes nothing to Catullus. Most important, Belleau maintains the poem's erotic geometry, a triangle constituted from the angle of a female narrator when she observes a man as he observes the woman who is the object of their collective desire.[6]

No matter how inadequate, therefore, the translation at least proposes a vision directly onto the Sapphic original, whereas almost all of what is introduced as Sapphic imitation in Renaissance poetry explicitly deals at least primarily with Sappho only as already radically recast by Catullus. I have in mind here not only what are repeatedly mentioned as possible echoes of Sappho (for example, passages in the twenty-fifth sonnet of Joachim Du Bellay's *Olive*, and his "Sonnet dédié à la reine de Navarre") but also even the majority of what are presented as, and at first glance could be taken for, the major sixteenth-century adaptations of fr. 31. Let us consider briefly a pair of related poems, Baïf's "Qui t'ouït et voit vis à vis" and Ronsard's "Je suis un demi-dieu quand assis vis à vis" (Aulotte, 112–14). Although Baïf's is published only in 1573, at the end of Sappho's Renaissance history, its composition—in 1552–54, according to Robert Aulotte (112)—like that of Ronsard's 1556 poem, plays a generative role in the first moment of modern Sapphic speculation. Critics from the sixteenth century to today explain the close resemblances between the poems by suggesting that Ronsard must have had access to Baïf's text in manuscript (Aulotte, 113). This theory provides the earliest indication of a phenomenon repeatedly associated with Sappho's dissemination in modern times, a competition among male writers for a sort of unofficial copyright on Sappho's production, to see whose Sapphic text will win the greatest acclaim. In its original formulation, this scenario provides a transparent illustration of Sappho's total dispensability in these exchanges among men. Baïf's poem was composed, it would seem, before he could have had direct access to Sappho: it is clear that he is readapting Catullus's original adaptation of her ode and therefore dealing with Sappho only incidentally, as a subset of his rivalry with his Latin precursor.

Catullus is the first example we encounter of the male writer who sees himself as Sappho's poetic double: his confrontation with Sappho is a founding gesture in his establishment of the Latin personal erotic elegy as a continuation of the Greek tradition. In "Ille mi par esse deo videtur," Catullus puts a man in the place of Sappho's female narrator and, with this substitution, sets up triangular desire degree zero: a man desires a woman when he sees her desired by another man.[7] The geometry of Sapphic eroticism thus reconfigured, Catullus counterbalances Sappho's focus on the birth and the physical effects of desire with a new center of interest, the explanation of the process by which the male narrator comes into greater control over the erotic scene. Sappho portrays her female narrator in a position of situational inferiority: either an actual man or a male phantasm, any man who would be "near" the woman who is the object of desire, "equals the gods," whereas the narrator is both at a distance from their shared intimacy and in a state of total physical disarray. In Catullus, the rival—transformed into the pronominally more precise "he," with all hint of the possibility of his existence solely as a figure of speech removed—is more than equal to the divinity; he is, "if that is possible," "superior to the gods." This ascension does not, however, cause the male narrator's abasement: in what becomes the poem's turning point, he bestows on the beloved woman a name with obvious Sapphic overtones, "Lesbia," thereby taking possession of her for the class of archetypal mistresses. Catullus then reclaims for male poet-lovers the control over the gaze that positions the scene of desire. Men in love are saved from humiliation at the hands of a rival when the poem's second verb of sight ("aspexi") attributes to the narrator concrete action, rather than Sappho's more doubtful subjunctive. The narrator's possessive gaze and naming allow him finally to dominate the scene of desire: in the end, "nihil est super me."[8] The rival exists only so that his desiring gaze can render the woman more desirable, not to cause the narrator jealousy. Lesbia turns away, as it were, from him, to figure instead as the possession of the man who names her: from then on, Sappho's portrait of the abandoned lover's torment can be seen as simply a description of a man's agitation in the presence of his beloved. Baïf continues Catullus's recuperation of an uncontested space for male desire, most notably in the lines, "Car sitôt que je te vois, / Ma maîtresse, devant moi, / Parler, oeillader ou rire,"[9] in which he completes the annihilation of the rival. The object of desire loses her (Sapphic) proper name to become simply "his." She performs the spectacle of her desirability ("talking, laughing") before the poet-lover rather than, as in Catullus's version, before the nameless rival, thereby continuing the distortion Catullus initiates in order to focus attention on a reempowered narrator. Through this process, the male lover is implicitly elevated through the love of a beautiful woman above his mere mortality.

Ronsard's version is the perfect realization of the veering away from Sappho initiated by his precursor poets. He opens with the boldest formulation yet of the most evident goal of the masculinization of Sappho's erotic geometry, the divinization of the male poet-lover: "Je suis un demi-dieu quand assis vis à vis / De toi, mon cher souci, j'écoute les devis, / Devis interrompus d'un gracieux sourire."[10] Triangulation can be suspended, and the mysterious rival on whom the reader's attention was first directed eliminated, when Ronsard replaces the more common form of mediated desire with another exchange among men. In his name for a poetic mistress, Catullus commemorates Sappho as a sign of his direct dialogue with his female precursor; Baïf and Ronsard bury her name, as they eliminate her triangulation, because, for them, she has taken over the role Catullus assigned Lesbia (in her name): woman desirable because she is the object of another's desire. Sappho is passed from man to man as an accessory in a detour of desire by which a series of male poets position themselves with respect to each other.

And that process is not ended with Ronsard's entry. It continues, most notably at the end of Sappho's Renaissance presence, when Baïf and Ronsard start their rivalry up again. This time, Baïf's 1573 salvo has remained in manuscript, while Ronsard's contributions, written between 1568 and 1574, become part of the 1578 *Sonnets pour Hélène* (Aulotte, 115–16). The final examples of the genre, while slightly more Sapphic than those that announce the muse of Mytilene's arrival in France, remain nevertheless the apparently straightforward account of a man faced with his mistress's beauty: the real Sapphic activity takes place behind the scenes.

This traffic in Sappho among rival male poets, each seeking to become the new Catullus, is the force that made Sappho an active presence in the sixteenth-century French literary imagination. And the only poem to achieve exchange value is fr. 31. Estienne continues to make new poems available, but he is never again able to repeat his success. In 1560, he publishes a Greek-Latin edition of nine Greek lyric poets with additional fragments of Sappho's poetry. The second edition of this volume (1566) enlarges her corpus further still. Indeed, the reader with the patience to piece together three different sections in a volume without consecutive pagination gained access to the two odes and nearly forty fragments, the most complete Sappho corpus available before 1733 (Wolff's edition).[11] French poets, however, are unmoved by this expanding Sapphic vista and continue their exclusive relationship with fr. 31, the poem that Catullus had already made his by masculinizing the founding text for the modern tradition of sapphic literature.

As a result of this single-minded obsession, male poetic bonding eradicated the sapphism in Sappho's eroticism. Of the poems available to her original modern audience (at least in the versions initially made public), only fr. 31 proposes an undeniably sapphic economy of desire. Behind all modern attempts to retriangulate, even to detriangulate, the poem's original erotic configuration stood the fact of which Renaissance poets may or may not have been conscious) that without the female narrator's declaration of her desire for another woman in fr. 31, there would remain no proof of Sappho's sapphism—and, therefore, no proof of sapphism's existence in antiquity.[12]

This enterprise of depriving female same-sex love of its founding moment would have acquired a certain urgency because Sappho's sapphic potential was openly proclaimed at the time of her modern recovery. In fact, Estienne's 1566 volume begins and ends on this note. The three-page "Sapphus Vita" with which he prefaces his edition contains all the (largely invented) biographical information we will come to recognize as the standard baggage of early Sappho commentators. According to this vision, Sappho lives a respectable life until her husband's death, whereupon she embarks on what Estienne terms her "shameless" or "indecent" (*impudens*) "promiscuity" with youths of either sex (34). He even names names and, in so doing, portrays Sappho as almost exclusively sapphic: the long list of female "disciples" and "beloved girls" (*puellas amatas*) is counterbalanced with a lone male name, Phaon, the lover traditionally made responsible for Sappho's tragic end—and Estienne even diminishes Phaon's importance by immediately hinting that he was merely legendary.[13] Finally, Estienne closes his edition with the fifteenth epistle, the letter Ovid imagines from Sappho to Phaon. This may be an early indication of the central role Ovid's text would play, only decades later, in the birth of the French tradition of Sapphic fictions. It is surely a first indication of the exceptional status accorded Ovid's portrait of Sappho, virtually as authoritative biography, by nearly all her pre–nineteenth-century commentators. (Most of Estienne's "Life of Sappho" represents, in fact, a strict Ovidian line.) This means in particular that Estienne reiterates at his volume's close his belief in the existence of sapphism in antiquity, thereby, perhaps, fueling the final antisapphic poetic exchanges in the early 1570s that bring to an end Sappho's Renaissance presence.[14]

The antisapphism that is the end product of sixteenth-century male Sapphic poetry is, unlike all subsequent antisapphic movements, apparently a purely literary phenomenon. It has nothing of the seventeenth-century fascination with Sappho the woman. The next generation of Sapphic texts repeatedly makes Sappho figures choose men over women. Sixteenth-century Sapphic poems display first and foremost a desire to replace the woman poet, to put a male in her place. This need to keep poetic authority under male control could have been inspired by the presence of a number of contemporary French women poets, of whom Labé is but the most visible. It also says that a female "I" will not have the power to dictate the form of erotic poetry.

In the sixteenth century, the only poetry that is directly inspired by Sappho without Catullus's mediation is also the only poetry that provides a proto-fiction of Sappho. Like the contemporary male erotic poetry, it defines Sapphism as heterosexual. Unlike the male exchanges of poetic authority we have just examined, however, this Sapphic vision is not premised on the rejection of sapphism—for the simple reason that, of all the Renaissance poets who sought inspiration in Sapphism, Louise Labé alone found hers, principally if not exclusively, outside the same-sex eroticism of fr. 31.

The 1555 collection of Labé's poetry is the only evidence of serious interest, during the intense Sapphic speculation surrounding that Sapphic year 1554, in the two other texts then revealed, notably in the "Ode to Aphrodite."[15] As she brings fr. 1 into the French poetic mainstream, Labé positions herself at the origin of two phenomena central to Sappho's French history. To begin with, she is the first of a number of French women writers, notably Scudéry and Staël, elaborately to stage her accession to authorship through an identification with the original woman writer, as the process by which she becomes a Sappho in her own right. In addition, for her authorial self-portrait as the Sappho of her age, Labé inaugurates what has been, in the four centuries of the poetess's French presence, the dominant definition of Sapphism: unrequited heterosexual passion.

Sappho is explicitly evoked twice by Labé; some authorities also see in her ninth sonnet an allusion to the "La Lune a fui." Nowhere in Renaissance literature is Sappho conjured up with greater complexity or originality than in Labé's first elegy. Here, in terms that recall Sappho's self-placement with respect to epic, Labé characterizes her coming to writing, her empowerment by Phoebus, who "m'a donné la lyre, qui les vers / Soulait chanter de l'Amour Lesbienne" (107).[16] Initially, Labé defines this "Lesbian Love" only as painful, unhappy. She then opens an extended apostrophe to the women who will read the tale of her "past misfortunes." The lines are uncannily reminiscent of parts of Sappho's corpus that would have been inaccessible to Labé, in which her precursor poet traces the origin of women's poetry to shared female experience. Labé stresses the reciprocity of the process by which woman assumes an authorial voice: she asks her female readers to "sigh out with her her regrets"; in return, she may "one day" return the favor "and help your compassionate voice / To recount your travails and sorrows" (108).

To the reciprocity that she hopes will prevail in women's accounting for their amorous suffering, Labé contrasts the absolute nonreciprocity that she presents as the universal truth learned by women in love. In her demonstration of how "the noblest spirits" are brought low by love's power she moves ever closer to a definition of the "Amour Lesbienne" whose plot her poetic lyre knows so well. Labé considers one example in detail, that of Semiramis, queen of Babylon, who, after having led her people to impressive military victories, late in life found her "virile heart corrupted"—by love for her own son—until she became unrecognizable: "Ainsi Amour de toi t'a étrangée, / Qu'on te dirait en une autre changée" (109).[17] I will not yet consider the implications for the Sapphic plot of this scenario of incestuous mother love; I will return to this question only for our discussion of the seventeenth century's best known incestuous (step)mother, Racine's Phèdre, by which time Ovid's widespread influence on the French literary imaginary should make the inevitability of Sappho's relation to this paradigm more convincing. For the moment, I will simply point out that, even if Ovid's "Letter from Sappho to Phaon" is first linked explicitly to Sappho's poetry only in Estienne's 1566 edition, the *Heroides* were already well known at the time of Sappho's modern recovery, having been made accessible in French as early as 1505 in Octavien de Saint-Gelais's frequently reprinted translation. And thus it seems likely that the first of the two morals that Labé delivers to conclude her elegy—"Telle j'ai vu qui avait en jeunesse / Blâmé Amour: après en sa vieillesse / Brûler d'ardeur"[18]—also contributes to the definition of "Lesbian Love." Sapphism is implicitly portrayed, already in the true Ovidian vein, as the "burning" love of the older woman for a mere youth.

In the Sappho corpus of Labé's day, only one poem could be viewed as confirmation of this definition, the only available version of the "Ode to Aphrodite," whose undefined object of desire was always masculinized. In the seventeenth century, Ovid's portrait of the aging Sappho grieving for the youthful Phaon who had abandoned her would be married to that ode; from their union would be born a theory that was held up for one hundred and fifty years as proof both of this reading of the poem and of Ovid's biographical reliability: Sappho composed the "Ode to Aphrodite" after she had been abandoned by Phaon, in a desperate last attempt to win him back and turn thereby away from her suicidal drive. (In this theory, we can glimpse the origin of Sainte-Beuve's theory of women's writing as writing for one's life.)

The final lines of Labé's elegy found a relation between women's writing as a demonstration of female solidarity and female amorous passion as the sudden desire for a younger man that causes the aging woman to walk out on all her accomplishments. They provide a second, more universal, moral and at the same time the only truly accurate Renaissance commentary on Sappho's vision of the dynamics of eroticism:

> *Ainsi Amour prend son plaisir, à faire*
> *Que le veuil d'un soit à l'autre contraire.*
> *Tel n'aime point, qu'une Dame aimera:*
> *Tel aime aussi, qui aimé ne sera.* (110)[19]

The lyre Labé inherited is truly Sapphic, "so accustomed to singing the poetry of Lesbian Love" that the structure of her poem's ending is an unmistakable reference to fr. 1. In addition, her elegy ends up just where the "Ode to Aphrodite" leaves off, in a vision of desire as ongoing process, founded in eternal nonreciprocity. Labé's reading of Sappho is all the more remarkable because it is based only on intuition: as it was known in the sixteenth century, the message of fr. 1 might seem closer to what male poets of the Renaissance took it to be, a pledge of the eventual satisfaction of desire. Labé's vision of "Lesbian Love" could, therefore, be seen almost as a fiction of Sapphism that, on one major point at least, is also an uncanny prediction of the most recent theories of the functioning of Sapphic desire.

To be a true fiction of Sappho, Labé's elegy requires only the narrative fiber to bind the various elements into a vision of the poetess's life. By the end of the seventeenth century, it will be possible to see how her proto-Ovidian vision can be used to reinforce the erasure of sapphism that is the foundation of the Sapphic presence in the work of Labé's male contemporaries. Ironically, despite the fact that they are drawn up during the only period before the late nineteenth century when the existence of sapphism is openly expressed, the views of Labé and of her male contemporaries, when combined, add up to the fiction of Sappho that will be promoted throughout the eighteenth century, the period of the most stringent repression of sapphism.

In fact, we can trace the original formulation of that most conservative Sapphic scenario to the decade following the final expressions of Renaissance poets' involvement with the muse of Mytilene. André Thevet makes a place for Sappho in his 1584 compilation, *Les Vrais portraits et vies des hommes illustres,* but only the better to contain a figure he portrays as threatening.[20] Although Thevet opens his portrait with a eulogy of the poet's role as "interpreter of the Gods," a role which, he claims, women can play, he concentrates not on Sappho as poet, but on Sappho as woman with as normalized a biographical scenario as possible: married to a rich man, she had a good marriage and a daughter (2:57). Thevet suggests that crimes of what he, like Estienne, calls "indecency," at least in the case of the alleged passion for Phaon, should be attributed to another woman named Sappho, a suggestion whose potential will be realized in the nineteenth century. He is so violent in his denial of the possibility of sapphism that he clears even this other Sappho of having "perpetrated this crime, the horror of which is so great that it is more seemly for me to suppress it than to speak of it here" (2:56). Thus begins the tradition of Sapphic speculation in which Sappho is evoked chiefly in order to deny the unutterable abomination inseparable from her name.

＊

It may be that just the sanitized plot Thevet advocates was a necessary prelude to Sapphic fiction-making. Certainly fictions of Sappho tend to proliferate during periods when her sexual potential is stifled, as though fiction were generated by the tension between the heterosexual plot and the sapphic eroticism that no amount of repression can dissociate from her person. However, it is not clear that the particular French obsession with Sappho would ever have been initiated if the *Heroides* had not suddenly succeeded in capturing the collective literary imagination of the age that prepared the way for French neoclassicism. Once Ovid had provided an Ur-biography for Sappho, her status as a center of narrative interest was recognized and a process initiated that may only have abated in the decades since World War II.

1 Female Desire and the Foundation of the Novelistic Order (1612–1694)

Sappho Lost and Found

All individuals history takes hold of eventually become mythic.
The taste for *vies romancées* is not as new as one might think.
— François Jean-Desthieux,
Femmes damnées

Key figures in our theoretical modernity—most prominently Freud, Lévi-Strauss, and Irigaray—have given us essentially the same vision of the foundation of the sociocultural order: a band of young men shapes itself into an ordered assembly through the formulation of rules to govern the exchange of women. Patriarchal society is based on interdictions designed to guarantee that transfers of power will take place exclusively between men, with women only conduits for the bonding that results from such transfers. All founding rules, such as the prohibition against incest, provide for the orderly distribution of women: they help, therefore, to guarantee that young males will find a place in the cultural community and that the commerce on which that community depends will continue undisturbed.

Certain founding precepts are immutable. But the sociocultural order also depends on less stable entities, fantasies of possible conduct (both desirable and undesirable) rather than codes of correct behavior. The history of Sappho's fictionalization is a constantly evolving projection of fantasies of Woman, each of which enables contemporary male culture to ensure its continuity. According to Irigaray's account of woman's place in the system of exchange, Sappho's behavior, *in the vision that sixteenth-century poets wanted to have of her,* is doubly "male": "As soon as she speaks . . . , a woman is a man. As soon as she has any relationship with another woman, she is homosexual, therefore masculine" (*This Sex,* 194). Renaissance men of letters repeatedly staged a single Sapphic image (woman as speaking subject, declaring her desire for woman) in order to

43

prove that it can be reversed, that a male poet can displace the female subject from the position of control. For their seventeenth-century heirs, this scenario was apparently no longer complex enough to deal with the problem of Sappho that had been vastly complicated at the dawn of the century by the rapid and wide dissemination of Ovid's version of her life story. The fantasy of Sappho required for seventeenth-century male poetic bonding was Sappho no longer as writer but as sexually pitiable woman.

The creation of this new fiction of Sappho is inextricably bound up with that of the literary form, the novel, that its contemporaries would come to view as the essential manifestation of the female literary style and woman's expression of desire. In the modern novel's initial formulation in seventeenth-century France, for the first time in the history of literature heroines were allowed to speak openly, even to speak their desire, *without* this action being considered a usurpation of a male prerogative. The price of this new authority would be a redefinition of gender roles: new images of possible female behavior were being actively generated throughout the period of Sappho's modern recovery. Not only did the biography then promoted for Sappho enrich the expanded fantasy of the female: Sappho's increased presence on the literary horizon seems to have been the key factor behind the apparently widespread need to promote new images of female behavior.

*

The foundation of at least one domain in the literary order bears a striking resemblance to the scenarios that have been devised to account for the foundation of the cultural order. Whereas in general literary origins seem irretrievably lost, one form, the novel, has tantalized critics as dissimilar as Marthe Robert and Ian Watt with the possibility that its creation might be reconstructed. I will make no such comprehensive claim about the beginning of the novel but in the following pages will retrace instead the rise in seventeenth-century France of two subgenres, the historical and the epistolary novel. I will focus on the foundation of this particular literary order as the nexus where Sappho's presence first makes itself felt in modern literature: a multitude of aspiring literary figures came of age when they devised rules to govern not the exchange of women but the sharing of a fiction of female desire. In sixteenth-century France, the first step is made toward a recovery of Sappho after centuries of nearly total oblivion. In the following century, four literary phenomena—the rediscovery of Ovid's *Heroides,* the creation of a French Sappho, the birth of epistolary fiction, and the formulation of a new type of historical romance—are intertwined in complex ways, one of which I will unravel in this chapter. The thread I will follow through this literary maze, the fiber that binds together writers like the foremost poet of the age, Jean Racine, and translators of Ovid, some of whom were virtually unknown even in their day, is their relation to what they all perceived to be a primal voice of desire, an origin for the literary expression of passion, the discourse and the plot for eroticism Sappho devises in fr. 31.

At its inception, the novel enjoyed exceptional generic status because of its relation to generation. A literary foundling, it stood alone, without the backing of the unbroken procession of classical fathers that authorized the continuation of other genres. And this was a voluntary stance: despite the claims of the first theoreticians of prose fiction, those most influential in carving out the novel's initial territory in France apparently felt that epic had run its course. They seldom turned back to the primal literary father, Homer, and they thereby rejected what could have served as a legitimating tradition for their efforts, epic. Those first novelists elected instead more subversive classical precursors. The modern French novel was born when writers chose to sing no longer "of arms and the man" in prose fiction but of what Ovid termed "private battles" and amorous "campaigns" (*Amores* 2.18.12), when writers chose desire to be the language of their new masterpieces. Those writers looked, as Ovid had, to Sappho for their model.

Ellen Moers defines "heroinism" as "the challenge to tell the woman's side of the love story in her own words" (160). She identifies Ovid's *Heroides* as the founding text for all literary narratives of passion told from the woman's point of view and suggests that these feminocentric accounts were influential in the development of the modern novel.[1] Yet Moers leaves out one crucial distinction, that between the efforts of male and female writers in defining the boundaries of "heroinism" and of the woman's point of view on her (love) story. Moers recreates the literary status of the woman's point of view at the time of the modern French novel's creation, when the literary style commonly accepted as authentically female was just as likely to have been created by a man as by a woman. In this tradition which challenges any easy assumptions about stylistic sexuality, Ovid was designated spokesman for the woman's voice in literature, and his *Heroides* were seen as having set the standards for the female literary plot. On the basis of the *Heroides,* heroinism was defined as a state of physical paralysis produced by a longing for love both lost and treacherous, limiting therefore its territory to tales of betrayal and abandonment. Because of Ovid's founding influence, a novelistic heroine, unlike her male counterpart, traditionally was almost always unhappy and unlucky in love. When literary critics trace the novel back only as far as the *Heroides,* they reinforce both male literary authority at the expense of its female counterpart and the plot for heroinism prescribed by a male writer.[2]

The story of Ovid's generic influence over the developing French novel becomes more dramatic when we examine the sexual politics that accompanied the rising prominence of the fiction of the feminine that was considered his invention. The *Heroides* was a crucial pretext for the developing French novel, because Ovid's text was seen as having set the standard for the language of female "autobiographical" passion. In seventeenth-century France, however, Ovid's authority to speak for the woman in love was not always accepted as legitimate. Certain writers challenged Ovid's influence on the development of prose fiction. They responded in particular to what they proclaimed the signature piece of the *Heroides,* the letter from Sappho to Phaon. In Ovid's fifteenth epistle, the archetypal woman writer is portrayed as having been deserted by both the man she loves and her poetic inspiration. To counter Ovid's authority, seventeenth-century novelists proposed an alternate vision of female desire in relation to literary authority: they thereby invented what were destined to become the two most influential novelistic forms of the seventeenth and eighteenth centuries, the epistolary and the historical novels. Contemporary writers responded to their generic innovations with a defense of what was seen as the Ovidian scenario for the woman, and in particular the woman writer, in love. Their defense took many forms, from repeated translations of the *Heroides,* to new fictional incarnations of Ovid's plot, to elaborate attacks on the fledgling novel's rising prominence.

The history of the novel's invention is the repeated reenactment of this struggle for the right to speak with the voice of female desire and to dictate the plot of female passion. Each confrontation highlights issues also important to the recent debate on women's writing. In particular, the ongoing struggle to control the language of woman in love forces those who analyze it to come to terms with the opposing views now advanced to explain gender's role on the literary scene. On the one hand, seventeenth-century Sapphic discourse is often beyond gender: it does not matter whether its author is male or female, only whether, and why, a creation succeeds in passing as authentically female. On the other, seventeenth-century Sapphic fictions often foreground situations in which the author's sex is the determining factor. Their authors, most often women, use Sappho as an illustration of the difficulty for the woman (writer) of escaping received ideas of female conduct. In the seventeenth century, each confrontation over Sapphic discourse and Sapphic plot produces a new articulation of the literary form that we now recognize as the novel.

The widespread acceptance of Sappho as a literary origin by writers of the French classical age creates a prototype for poetic inheritance not accounted for by existing theories of literary influence. Neither Moers's study of women writers' reception of their female precursors, nor Harold Bloom's model for the "anxious" influence male authors exercise on their followers, nor Gilbert and Gubar's revision of Bloom's theory to include the woman writer's position with regard to her male precursors imagines the male writer's relation to the priority of a female voice. The history of Sappho's fictionalization provides numerous examples of male writers' confrontation with a female literary origin: with an actual female precursor whose proximity they recognize, with a literary structure given its original expression by women writers, or with a literary medium accepted as authentically female. Situations of female priority seem to provoke three radically different responses. When writers such as Boileau realize that a certain literary form—the novel, in Boileau's case—had a female origin, they attempt simply to eradicate that female literary primacy. Writers who use a fiction of the female as an initiatory coming-of-age rite transvest themselves in order to use the appeal of female stereotypes for self-promotion. Finally, writers such as Ovid and Racine function as literary ventriloquists because they recognize not only female priority but also their own close affinity with the prior female voice.

In modern times, Sappho's poetry has consistently been a *succès de scandale*. Until recently, what passed for critical commentary was in large part a response to the scandal of Sappho's poetry that was at the same time a response to the scandal of Sappho's person.[3] Sappho's commentators through the ages have responded in particular to two characteristics of her work, her presentation of the context of poetic creation and her configuration of the plot of female passion. Sappho portrays both the composition and the performance of her verse as an exchange among women, as the product of a female community whose members are united by bonds both personal and professional. Her *oeuvre* is most famous and most notorious because of its celebration of a type of female friendship that commentators try to understand through reference to the biographical scenario they promote for Sappho. Commentators thus most often consider Sapphic friendship solely in terms of that they believe to be its sexual content and react to the subject with moral condemnation or sympathetic defense, or even with attempts to deny the sexual content of her poetry. Yet this female bond can be considered in purely literary terms as an attempt to bypass male literary authority and to deny men any primary role in the process of poetic creation. Sappho presents poetic creation as a gift handed down from woman to woman, as literature written by women for other women and about other women. In this poetic universe, males are relegated to a peripheral, if not an intrusive, role. Most strikingly, the Sapphic narrator, a woman, repeatedly assumes a classically male prerogative. She is the desiring subject. Because the object of her desire is also a woman, she is in control of the gaze that objectifies the beloved woman, thereby giving the poem its visual focus and creating its geometry of desire.

Both the Sappho odes widely known by the early seventeenth century share this scandalous erotic geometry.[4] Probably because seventeenth-century editors respect the reading of fr. 1 proposed by Sappho's humanist commentators, at no time in the century does this ode generate even a zero-degree fiction like Louise Labé's. The enormous attraction to Sappho then played out has a unique source in her poetry, fr. 31. Yet the new involvement with this poem is far more complex than the reconfiguration to which it had previously been repeatedly subjected. Commentators enrich their interpretations through reference to the biography Sappho was then acquiring. Sappho's influence on writers is no longer limited to simple adaptations; in addition, writers no longer traffic in fr. 31 only as already reconfigured by Catullus. For the first time in Sappho's modern history, poets turn directly to an authentic text of her poetry of desire. Once the detour via Catullus has been eliminated, Sappho is no longer placed in an extreme position, as woman who speaks her desire and is therefore a cultural man. (Sappho will be positioned in the extremist margins again only in the nineteenth and twentieth centuries.) In the seventeenth and eighteenth centuries, Sapphic fictionalization is born from the desire to take Sappho out of the margin, to make her a sort of Everywoman, that is, a vision of the desiring woman designed to assure the continued functioning of the cultural order. This exceptional situation can, I believe, be explained by two factors: at no time in the French tradition were women writers more active than from the early seventeenth century to the early eighteenth century, and at no other period was the woman's first-person account of her passion a more viable literary commodity. Rather than take the risk that the literary scene would be overrun by literary women (including the transvested men of letters who passed off their creations as autobiographical tales), contemporary image makers constructed a Sapphic fiction that transformed the elements then most attractive until they were no longer transgressive.

As a backdrop to the history of Sappho's seventeenth-century presence, let us look briefly at the poem that represented the poetess to her first modern readers in order to locate those elements from which her initial French public constructed their fictions of the feminine. Here is a recent translation by Edith Mora. (The feminine forms essential to my argument are retained in French; English translations are found in the appendix.)

> *Il égale les dieux je crois*
> *l'homme qui devant toi vient s'asseoir*
> *et qui tout près de toi entend*
> *ta voix tendre*
>
> *et ton rire enchanteur qui a, je le jure,*
> *affolé mon coeur dans ma poitrine*
> *Car si je te vois un instant je ne peux*
> *plus rien dire*
>
> *ma langue est brisée, sous ma peau*
> *un feu subtil soudain se glisse*
> *mes yeux ne voient plus, mes oreilles sont*
> *bourdonnantes*
>
> *une sueur glacée me couvre et un*
> *tremblement*
> *me prend toute et je suis plus verte*
> *que l'herbe, tout près de mourir*
> *il me semble . . .*
>
> *Mais il faut tout oser car même*
> *abandonnée . . .*

The poem recounts what appears at first to be a rather banal story: the narrator is a voyeur, observing from a distance the woman who is the object of desire while this woman is demonstrating her love for a man. However, it quickly becomes apparent that the elements on which erotic poetry is generally founded have been replaced here with constructions either blatantly unstable or slightly unstable at best.[5] To begin with, the triangle of desire is unlike either of those formations that literary portrayals of love have schooled the reader to expect. Whereas the beloved's sex is determined in the initial stanza (in two feminine participles in lines 3–5), the narrator's femininity is not immediately stressed. The appearance of the narrator's signature as a woman ("je suis plus verte") (line 14 of the original) comes therefore as a shock, an invasion. The poem is meant to be initially mistaken for just what Catullus turns it into, the most common literary love triangle, in which a man desires a woman when he sees her in the arms of another man. This is the scenario termed triangular desire, which René Girard proposes as the origin of the novel. The functioning of triangular desire is familiar from theories of the founding of the cultural order: woman is confined to a passive role, as the object exchanged in a rite of male bonding. However, with the narrator's feminine signature in fr. 31, male bonding is suspended: Sappho's female "I" displaces the male from the dominant, active role as viewer. Nor can the triangle configured after this displacement be assimilated by the reader with what has become (because, as I will attempt to show, of Sappho's overturning of triangular desire) the stereotypical literary love triangle. This scenario, involving two women and one man, is designed to eradicate the possibility of female bonding, as one woman laments her abandonment for the woman traditionally known as the "other woman."

And this is not even Sappho's most subversive gesture against poetic erotic stability: she also casts doubt on the reality of the lone male figure present at the scene of desire. Fragment 31 has almost always been interpreted according to Catullus's revision, as though its opening line referred incontrovertibly to "the man who." Scrupulous commentators have on occasion pointed out that Sappho chooses an indefinite rather than a definite relative pronoun here, and that the line reads therefore "the man whosoever." But these commentators elect to reaffirm the stability of the male presence by explaining that the indefinite pronoun suggests only that the narrator does not know the man's identity.[6] However, the reading of the pronoun consistent with the poem's teasingly self-conscious presentation of sex roles would be "any man who sits opposite you." Rather than "*the* man," a concrete male presence, Sappho would be evoking "*any* man," the male as a mere figment of the female narrator's imagination (see Winkler, 76).

Sappho's erotic geometry, like the literary scenes that Girard presents as the key examples of triangular desire, concerns much more than the creation of a structure: fr. 31 is designed to provoke a reflection on the function of the model it sets up for both the lover and the poet. In particular, by leaving the male presence at the scene of desire in suspension between fact and fantasy, Sappho forces her reader to recognize the powerful attraction of constructions of gender, fictions of behavior, in the generation of desire. This is not to present fr. 31 as a female equivalent of triangular desire, with the narrator's attraction to the woman determined by her jealousy of the man.[7] On the contrary, Sappho makes the man indefinite to complete her undoing of the male model for (poetic) eroticism. The man is evoked in order to demonstrate his superfluousness: the erotic experience concerns the two women alone, united by bonds that are purely personal, with none of the sociocultural function associated with triangular desire.[8]

The three-hundred-and-fifty-year-old tradition of Sapphic speculation that we will now begin to retrace will show us that, consciously or unconsciously, readers have consistently been drawn to those elements in fr. 31 that force them to confront their expectations about the sexual construction of the scene of desire. The tradition of Sapphic fictionalization originates in just such a confrontation. Girard portrays the novel, the essential form of the modern literary order, as founded on triangular desire. However, when we examine the novel's initial articulation in seventeenth-century France alongside the contemporary commentary on Sappho, it becomes apparent that Girard's scenario accounts for only one of the novel's early variants. Sappho's influence spreads beyond her limited Renaissance presence only when writers no longer simply, in Mora's expression, "remodel the erotic face" (137) of her poetry by returning control over the gaze and the discourse of desire to a male poet figure. As soon as modern literary figures suggest, via Sappho, that a woman could become an active subject in the expression of desire, threatening thereby the foundation of the cultural order, they inspire a variety of neo-Sapphic discourses. They also make it necessary to recontain this discourse which undermines the continued orderly functioning of male poetic exchanges. Ovid's canonical fiction of Sappho (according to the seventeenth century's interpretation of his project) is employed to this end. Ovid's vision is the origin of the new fictional triangle that the French classical age offers in response to Sappho's reconfiguration of the scenario basic to male (poetic) bonding: the fiction of the abandoned (older) woman complaining to the man who has deserted her for another (younger) woman.

The element essential to this fiction is, of course, *the* man, a concrete identity for the male fantasy in the margins of fr. 31. That figure is conveniently supplied not only by Ovid but by other authors from antiquity. Scholars today believe that, in some poem now lost to us, Sappho must have evoked a certain Phaon. They believe that she was naming not an actual individual but perhaps a mythical figure, the ferryman Phaon who was said to have transported an old woman without remuneration. The old woman revealed herself to be Aphrodite and, to thank Phaon for his generosity, transformed him into a perfectly handsome young man. The goddess then proceeded to fall so madly in love with Phaon that she tried to hide him to keep him from other women. Other scholars argue persuasively that Sappho used the name Phaon simply as a symbol, to designate the name's root meaning, the light. Phaon, according to Gregory Nagy, is another name, a doublet, for Phaethon. Anxious to be recognized as a legitimate son of Phoebus, Phaethon begs his father to let him drive the chariot of the sun for a day. But he is unable to dominate the horses, and they veer wildly out of control. In order to protect the earth from conflagration, Zeus is obliged to hit Phaethon with a thunderbolt, and he plummets to his death.

We can only guess at the explanation for Sappho's invocation of Phaon-Phaethon. Howard Jacobson sums up the prudent stance on this issue: "It is generally believed that Sappho alluded to the mythical Phaon in some such way that later readers were able to misinterpret it (willfully?) as a personal relationship."[9] I will break with critical prudence and allow myself a moment of speculation in an attempt to account for the fascination with Phaon's desertion as the cause of Sappho's humiliation and suicide, a fascination prominently displayed in the first phase of Sapphic fictions. Given all surviving examples of Sappho's poetry, it seems unlikely that Phaon figured as part of the plot in which, as in the ferryman-Aphrodite legend, the young man deserts the older woman.[10] Sappho's biographers from antiquity could have transformed a reference to the luminosity at the root of "Phaon-Phaethon" into a personal reference. The history of Sapphic speculation provides countless examples of the tendency to literalize references in Sappho's poetry in order to make them into elements from which a biography can be constructed. This tendency is most often triggered by just those moments in which Sappho refuses to legitimate androcentric erotic scenarios, most prominently her reduction of the man to a female fantasy in fr. 31. A reference by Sappho to Phaon-Phaethon could have been understood as a similar attempt on her part to indicate the possible fragility of male control over the social order. The desire of the son to put himself in Phoebus's place and his failure to carry out his father's role could be used to figure both male sexual inadequacy (the unsuccessful completion of the young man's sexual rite of passage) and the breakdown of the system that guarantees the son a place in the sociocultural order.

The ancient lexicon, the Suda, mentions the existence of another Sappho who committed suicide when abandoned by someone named Phaon. The first male author who made the actual Sappho, rather than her double, the lyre player from Mytilene, commit suicide for love of a man named Phaon triply reassured his male audience: the desiring woman rejects her love for women; the woman writer loses her poetic gift; and Phaon-Phaethon is triumphant and completes his sexual rite of passage, while the older woman is hurled into the sea in his place. In modern times, Sappho, the poet who deprived the man of the right to dictate the plot of desire, becomes a major force on the literary scene only once she has been transformed into an exemplar of rejected female passion.

Let us turn now to the raw material on which the original French Sapphic fictions were based. We will begin by examining Sappho's first modern biographies and the earliest French editions of her work. We will then consider the other inspiration for early Sapphic speculation, Ovid's *Heroides,* as well as the tradition of Ovid's interpretation in seventeenth-century France. The limits to the period's knowledge of Sappho thus established, we will review the original French fictions of Sappho, first those imagined by members of the century's dominant literary tradition, classicism, and finally the counterfictions created in response both to the French classics and to Ovid.[11]

The Birth of "Sapho"

The ancients preserved for us a fiction of Sappho, whose thoroughly cheerful nature is imbued with the grace and the delicacy that characterize her writings.

Poinsinet de Sivry,
Anacréon, Sapho, Moschus, etc.

The modern reconstruction of Sappho was initiated in seventeenth-century France. She was simultaneously recreated as poet and as woman. Editors gathered together the available fragments to constitute a small body of work, but one presented as a corpus. In addition, this corpus was published in volumes whose title pages granted Sappho equal status with Anacreon. (In the previous century, she was published only in collective editions.) Her seventeenth-century editors also initiated the practice of prefacing the poems with a "life of Sappho," a review of what is always presented as historical evidence about her existence, even though this alleged evidence is largely a combination of the speculation of ancient authors and that of modern editors. Nevertheless, these sketches deserve our attention because they show us how, at the very period in which the vocabulary of biography was being codified, Sappho began to acquire a biography in the sense of a life story.[12] By the end of the seventeenth century, Sappho's name had been Gallicized as "Sapho." Even as they introduced Sappho to modern readers, her first French editors and biographers also laid the foundation for the French tradition of her fictionalization, the tradition that created a Gallic version of Sappho which has continued to follow the evolution of French literary taste and French norms for acceptable sexual conduct ever since.

The rapidly shifting face of Sappho scholarship in seventeenth-century France provides ample evidence to inspire or support virtually any fiction of the original woman writer. Throughout the second half of the century, debate about Sappho's biography was more intense and generated more divergent opinion than at any subsequent period. (The early twentieth century alone rivals it, but only if the entire spectrum of European opinion is considered, whereas in the late seventeenth century the conflicting scholarly energy was generated solely in France.) Perhaps because the debate was so open and so genuine, the scene of Sappho scholarship remained firmly centered in France until the end of the century, a phenomenon never since repeated. In the seventeenth century, as in the sixteenth, French Hellenists controlled, with virtually no competition from any other national school, the recovery of Sappho and her packaging for introduction to a broad audience.

Curiously, after half a century during which what was thought to constitute Sappho's *oeuvre* was reedited virtually without interruption, the end of the sixteenth century marks a temporary hiatus in her modern recovery. During the first half of the seventeenth century, Sappho yields to Ovid, and the text being restored to a general audience is the *Heroides*. During this period, Sappho and Ovid become completely intertwined: by the mid-seventeenth century and for virtually the next two hundred years, until German Hellenists decree the inauthenticity of Ovid's fifteenth epistle partly in order to disentangle the two literary voices, it is nearly impossible to disengage Sappho from the neo-Ovidian vision of her that had been widely promoted by Ovid's early French disciples. Indeed, only the very first of Sappho's French translators make public a figure more or less uncolored by speculation clearly traceable to Ovid's original fiction. Interestingly, and in the long run perhaps predictably, the work and the theories of the only two non-Ovidian spokesmen for Sappho have been completely eclipsed by those of their successors who aligned themselves most openly with a perspective on the poet and her poetry inspired by Ovid's fiction of heroinism.

The individual who produced the largest body of Sappho scholarship in the seventeenth century is also the last true heir of the sixteenth-century humanist tradition, Tanneguy Le Fèvre.[13] For his 1660 edition of Sappho's poetry, Le Fèvre follows the custom inaugurated by his precursors Estienne and Belleau and presents Sappho's *oeuvre* as a mere supplement to the vastly more extensive corpus of Anacreon's verse. He also adopts the sixteenth-century practice of providing only a Latin translation of the Greek text. In notes appended in Latin, he indicates his reading of the poems, the controversial nature of which can best be appreciated when it is examined in tandem with what is surely the most startling contribution to seventeenth-century Sappho scholarship, the biographical sketch found in Le Fèvre's 1664 *Abrégé des vies des poètes grecs.* The *Abrégé* is a pedagogical compilation destined for the twelve-year-old comte de Limoges. In this overview of the Greek canon in mid-seventeenth-century France, Sappho is given a prominent rank, ahead, for example, of the poet who would later replace Anacreon as her inevitable partner, Alceus.

The entry on Sappho is startling because of Le Fèvre's stand on Sappho's sexuality and its relation to her poetry. He provides the most forthright justification ever given in France for the reading of fr. 31 that would remain uncontested until the eighteenth century: "ode of sixteen lines addressed to a girl with whom she was in love" (22). He then goes on to explain what he terms "the word that slipped out when speaking about this ode" and, even though he never pronounces "the word" in question, Le Fèvre nevertheless makes his view quite plain: "I mean, Monsieur, that Sappho was of a very amorous complexion, and that not being satisfied with that which other women find in the company of men who are not disagreeable to them, she wanted to have mistresses" (24). Le Fèvre completes his lesson on Sappho's sexual biography by dismissing all legends linking her romantically with her illustrious male contemporaries. But perhaps the greatest mark of his originality is a silence. Le Fèvre, along with the early eighteenth-century German Hellenist Fabricius, alone among Sappho's pre—twentieth-century biographers, pays no attention whatsoever to any male role in Sappho's affective life: he does not even mention the two most frequently alleged presences, the husband Cercola and the unfaithful lover Phaon.

I use the adjective "startling" to characterize my reaction to Le Fèvre's text because I am never able to overcome my disbelief at the fact that a noted Hellenist dared to publish such views in 1664—several years after the inception of the personal reign of Louis XIV, at the dawn of the age of French neoclassicism, in a period, in other words, when the norms for political and literary behavior were becoming ever more confining. He made his opinion public, furthermore, in a pedagogical dialogue with the child of a prominent family. The ultimate sign of Le Fèvre's pivotal position is stamped on his contribution to the modern recovery of Sappho. He is the last French scholar to spell her name consistently with two *p*'s: after him, the preferred orthography will be "Sapho," and the second *p* will only be restored to "Sappho" in the twentieth century. The new spelling is adopted at the time when the French tradition, increasingly blinded by the inability to admit the existence of any but hetero-sexuality, made the first moves that would eventually cost it its dominance over European Sappho scholarship. I would be tempted to suggest a relation between orthography and tolerance of sexual diversity if Le Fèvre's use of "Sappho" had been imitated by any subsequent defender of Sappho's sexuality.[14]

In the balance he strikes between biography and commentary, Le Fèvre adheres to standards that subsequent editors would have done well to respect: he makes Sappho's life subservient to her poetry, mentions only those biographical elements he considers relevant to his description of her odes, and concentrates on providing a conclusive demonstration of Sappho's extraordinary literary status in antiquity. Indeed, Le Fèvre's sole regressive move is his decision to present only the two best-known odes as though they were all that remained of Sappho's *oeuvre,* whereas he had access, in the repertoire of texts edited by his sixteenth-century precursors, to approximately one hundred fragments cited by authors in antiquity. His decision to limit her canon was ratified by Sappho's French editors for the next hundred and fifty years. They thereby passed up the opportunity of reconstructing Sappho's *oeuvre,* a challenge taken up instead by eighteenth-century German Hellenists.

What should be known as the first edition of Sappho in French has simply been written out of the history of scholarship. Jacques Du Four de La Crespelière published his translation in 1670, eleven years before the edition generally referred to as the first, that of Le Fèvre's daughter.[15] The most evident explanation for the occultation of the individual who called himself the "Poète goguenard" is that he shows none of the prudery that has dominated Sappho studies. Like Le Fèvre, he does not avoid the controversy associated with Sappho: for example, he makes clear his placement of fr. 31 by entitling it "Ode de Sapho à son Amie." He opens his preface by declaring that the language of his translation is so "honnête" that "chaste ears will not be offended by it."[16] Indeed, he produces a version of the two odes that makes them into perfect examples of the frivolous love poetry in vogue in the salons of his day. In 1670, Sappho apparently could not scandalize if properly Gallicized.[17]

The translation that would be enshrined by posterity as the original French version of Sappho was first published only in 1681, by Le Fèvre's daughter Anne, the future Madame Dacier, a young woman who would prove to be the most influential seventeenth-century French Hellenist. Anne Le Fèvre Dacier's volume of *Les Poésies d'Anacréon et de Sapho* is the contrary of Du Four de La Crespelière's easy version for a frivolous public. She sets out to introduce Sappho to a general audience without sacrificing the standards of her erudition. She prefaces her prose translations with a twenty-page "life of Sapho" and also includes notes on the poems to document her readings. Le Fèvre Dacier's most important biographical strategy is her decision to oppose resolutely her father's belief in the poet's sapphism. The first editor to promote the soon to become standard French spelling "Sapho" presents the original woman writer as an active heterosexual, with a husband who dies when she is young, numerous suitors, and a passionate affair with Phaon. Le Fèvre Dacier brings up the theory of her sapphism only to dismiss it in a manner so discreet that a reader not already informed could not know what is at stake: "I believe . . . that envy inspired those who wrote the calumnies with which they attempted to blacken her" (393–94).[18] This position determines her reading of Sappho's poetry, and even the limits she sets for the Sappho corpus. For example, she characterizes fr. 31 as "an ode that she wrote for one of her friends [*amies*]," as though it were a platonic celebration of the joys of friendship (403). To attenuate its force, she retitles it "à son amie," removing thereby the "beloved" that signals female passion, and also excises the narrator's unique female signature, the phrase "plus verte que l'herbe" (403).

Le Fèvre Dacier's most original editorial decision is also the crowning gesture in her century's transformation of Sappho into a model of unhappy heterosexuality. She blends into her life of Sappho a number of the fragments cited by authors in antiquity but never before published in French under Sappho's name. The fragments thereby become part of Sappho's life rather than her *oeuvre,* and this transfer allows Le Fèvre Dacier to inaugurate the dominant tradition of modern Sappho commentary: the manipulation of her poems so that they seem to prove whatever biographical scenario the commentator wishes to establish. In this case, the dominant objective is to establish Sappho's heterosexuality. Thus the poem in which the speaker advises a suitor to choose a younger wife is introduced as "a fragment of a letter that Sappho wrote to a man who was seeking her hand in marriage," testimony therefore to both Sappho's heterosexuality and her attraction to younger men (394).[19] Second, Le Fèvre Dacier further tampers with the Sappho corpus by willfully limiting what she makes public to that which will prove her point. She integrates into her biography only those fragments, like the two epitaphs for Timas and Pelagon, that cannot be seen as sexually compromising, and she excludes any texts that challenge the vision at whose service she places her formidable erudition.[20]

Le Fèvre Dacier's ultimate goal is to prove the reality of *the* man — the triumphant male figure whose existence makes Sappho sexually pitiful and her ambiguous discourse of desire an unambiguous complaint of the woman scorned. She is determined to find evidence of an unrequited passion for Phaon: thus, for example, she presents the ode to Aphrodite as an effort to provoke the return of Sappho's inconstant lover (396). It follows logically that she also contends that Sappho, unable to win Phaon back, committed suicide by leaping from the White Rock of Leukas, even though she is unable to provide any evidence from Sappho's poetry to support this theory. The only citation regarding such a death that she does include is almost certainly, although as usual she does not identify her source, a reference to Strabo's account of this cliff: "As part of their annual festival [of Apollo], the Acanarians always chose a condemned criminal and had him thrown from this promontory" (399). Le Fèvre Dacier does not make clear the relation she sees between this "historical" curiosity and Sappho's life. The implications of her elliptical juxtaposition are only revealed, as we will see, by reading Ovid in the context of the seventeenth-century fictions he inspires.

We can accurately measure the bias of the most famous seventeenth-century edition by comparing it with an edition that, according to its translator, was already in progress when Le Fèvre Dacier's volume appeared. The baron de Longepierre's 1684 *Les Poésies d'Anacréon et de Sapho* challenges the authority of Le Fèvre Dacier's vision by presenting a Sapho who is in effect a compromise between the views of each Le Fèvre, père et fille. Thus in his "Life of Sapho" he affirms on the one hand her sapphism—nothing "can cleanse her of a stain that her works clearly admit" —and on the other her heterosexuality—after an early marriage, her "most violent" passion was reserved for Phaon (352). Longepierre's more active sexual biography is reflected in his view of the Sappho corpus: his 1684 edition is actually the most complete, and the most correct, text available before the French editions of the 1840s. That it never gained a measure of the authority that was its due—nineteenth-century French editors, for example, turn exclusively to German editions of the eighteenth century in their attempt to enlarge Sappho's French *oeuvre*—can surely be at least partially explained by the baron's unwillingness to promote a unified view of Sappho, his lack of concern with uncovering correspondences between life and work that would make each a reconfirmation of the other.

This editorial stance is most apparent in his presentation of the fragments with which he expands the classical French Sappho corpus, the two odes. Longepierre separates life and work and introduces the fragments as supplements to the *oeuvre* rather than as autobiographical remains. He includes all the fragments found in Le Fèvre Dacier as well as several she excludes, undoubtedly because they cause problems for her theory of unchallenged heterosexuality. Most notably, Longepierre accords full poetic status to a poem in which the speaker laments her abandonment by Athis for, in his translation, "the beautiful Andromède" (383; Mora, 12; LP 131). He leaves no doubt about the poem's triangle of desire for, in his "Life of Sapho," he lists Athis as "one of Sapho's beloved girls." At the same time, the baron also includes a fragment whose sexual orientation is today generally considered open to debate, but which until recently was always seen as proof of Sappho's heterosexuality, the poem in which the speaker admits to her mother that the love of a "beautiful child" (either male or female) had made her unable to attend to her weaving (384; see Mora, 78; LP 102).[21]

To conclude: the first editions in a modern language give us a profoundly ambiguous Sappho: homosexual, heterosexual, sometimes both. One cannot even detect a continuous evolution toward one dominant view. Before the end of the century, however, order would be imposed, and Le Fèvre Dacier's heterosexual Sappho would become the foundation for a staggeringly vast eighteenth-century tradition of fiction-alization. I chose to interrupt the development of my argument and to present the first translations in chronological order in order to stress several points. First, Hellenists and translators were in no hurry to bring Sappho to the French public — the Greek texts were available for a full century before they were packaged into editions — so her commercial value was not quickly perceived. Second, this judgment seems borne out by the fact that neither the earliest French editions nor Longepierre's most comprehensive volume were reprinted. The only Sappho able to arouse the interest of the seventeenth-century French public was the poet of unhappy heterosexuality proposed by Le Fèvre Dacier. The contemporary code of sexual propriety seems to have had little, if anything, to do with this choice: editors discuss sapphism more openly than at any time prior to the mid-nineteenth century. Sappho, in Le Fèvre Dacier's version, finally becomes a popular poet in French in the 1680s because native French versions of Ovid's heroinism as diverse as *Phèdre* and the *Lettres portugaises* had responded to and shaped the most ardently desired contemporary fiction of the feminine. To understand the origin of the first commercially successful modern Sappho, we must return to the beginning of the century and explore the recovery and the interpretation of the version of Sappho that replaced Sappho's own poetry for more than half a century, Ovid's canonic fiction of Sappho in the fifteenth of his *Heroides*. I will examine first Ovid's heroic epistle and then the key Ovidian fictions produced at the period of the *Heroides'* greatest influence in France.

"The Secretary of Ill-fated Heroines"

> Sappho's mad behavior would never have been made public, if she herself had not chosen to immortalize it. In order to impose silence on posterity, she should have loved Phaon passionately and remained silent. Or if Sappho could no more stop herself from writing than from loving, she should have loved, and written beautiful poetry in Athena's honor.
> — Madeleine d'Arsant de Puisieux,
> *Conseils à une amie*

Ovid's *Epistulae Heroidum* is a collection of fictive epistles addressed by women to men, for the most part to men who have betrayed their love and abandoned them for other women. With these letters, Ovid, like his heirs Richardson and Rousseau, established both a model for epistolarity and a model for women's writing. For centuries, interpretation of Ovid's goals in the volume commonly known as the *Heroides* has been overshadowed by two factual issues: the authenticity of some or all of the epistles, and the order in which Ovid intended the letters to appear, including whether or not the six "double letters" (three pairs of letters in which the heroines receive a response) should be considered part of the collection. For the present, I will defer consideration of these issues and, following current critical practice, consider the first fifteen epistles independently from the six "double letters" and assume the authenticity of all fifteen epistles.[22] In due time, I will trace the development of these challenges to the integrity of Ovid's enterprise in the *Heroides* in order to suggest that they were caused by his identifying, however ambivalently, his own poetic voice with that of the greatest female precursor poet, Sappho.

The following section will depart from the rules generally imposed on this study in several ways. For once, I will not present arguments only as they took shape in a historical development. Instead, I will use recent criticism to help analyze Ovid's place on the literary horizon at the time of Sappho's introduction into the French tradition in the seventeenth century. Crucial to an understanding of how Sappho's presence became inextricably intertwined with Ovid's female impersonation in the *Heroides* is a sense of what the *Heroides* stood for in the early seventeenth century, when the volume began to play its most important role in the development of the French tradition. At this time, when a major challenge to writers seeking to make a name for themselves on a rapidly evolving literary scene was the invention of a discourse of female desire, Ovid's relation to the voices of heroism he created was the central issue in the *Heroides'* interpretation.

A comparison of the two most recent studies of these verse epistles, Howard Jacobson's *Ovid's "Heroides"* (1974) and Florence Verducci's *Ovid's Toyshop of the Heart* (1985), permits a rapid assessment of the range of interpretations that have been advanced to account for Ovid's multivoiced, extended writing as a woman. I will not attempt to give a complete sense of Jacobson's and Verducci's arguments, only to contrast their visions of Ovid's relation to these fifteen outpourings of female desire.

Although Jacobson avoids an explicit ideological stance, according to his presentation, Ovid's intentions in these self-portraits could be characterized as feminist. I have in mind here a particular usage of that term, which has recently gained some currency in classical studies: it designates male writers from antiquity who are seen as reversing the narrative focus of traditional accounts, where attention is centered on the male as a nexus of continued adventures, to allow women previously condemned to silence to present their sides of well-known tales. Thus critics now speak of Euripidean and Ovidian feminism: Jacobson argues, for example, that both these authors "had a remarkable ability to see through the eyes of women" and that the monologues in which Euripides' heroines dare to give voice to their desire were the most evident precursor text for Ovid (7). Because of this feminized viewing angle, the *Heroides* becomes for Jacobson a "deheroization of the mythic material," a "rejection of the male viewpoint," and therefore "a denial of the Augustan (and Vergilian, at least as envisioned in the *Aeneid*) ideal" (7).

Jacobson's analyses of the individual epistles consistently present them as reversals of earlier perspectives on Ovid's heroines that Jacobson views as male-centered. Thus, he promotes Ovid's "new Dido" (*Heroides* 7) as the product of "a moral stance quite different from Vergil's, a Dido whose 'case' is promoted in the most advantageous ways and whose position is justified while Aeneas' is blackened" (93). Briseis (*Heroides* 3) "does not appear as the stolid, impassive, and resigned heroine" (her character in the *Iliad*), but shows a "sense of pride and desire for recognition as a person" (35). Jacobson does not, of course, maintain this perspective through-out—for example, he makes no claims for a whitewashing of Medea by Ovid—but his analyses of the voices given to heroines silenced in previous accounts is dominated by the conclusion that Ovid sought primarily to create an atmosphere of true pathos: "The sense of . . . seemingly inevitable doom . . . [is] the heart of [*Heroides* 10, Ariadne to Theseus]" (227). In this view, Ovid is portrayed as sympathetic to his heroines insofar as he seeks to generate pity for the plight of the abandoned woman.[23] The only factor that Jacobson allows on occasion to threaten his interpretive design is the presence that he almost grudgingly admits in the *Heroides* of a comic voice, a voice to which Ovid's early modern readers were almost totally insensitive, but the voice that has come to dominate more recent discussions of his intentions in these verse epistles. Thus Jacobson laments the presence of "the words of the great Homeric heroes in the mouth of a mere girl" as a source of "delight and amusement" that *Heroides* 3 "could well do without . . . since it invests the character of Briseis with an element of unconscious self-parody" (41). He explains these moments when pathos is shattered as the result of a sort of failure of pathetic will: "Unfortunately, even when Ovid fully sympathizes, he is incapable of fully empathizing, though this is perhaps more a function of his art than of his character" (41).

What Jacobson calculates as the occasional distance between "sympathy" and "empathy" is for Florence Verducci the omnipresent, dominant tension in the *Heroides,* the slippage from pathos to bathos. Even more insistently than Jacobson, Verducci calls attention to Ovid's conscious rewriting of the visions of his heroines already available to his original readers. Jacobson, however, views the comic or parodic displays as an artistic brake occasionally applied to the personal empathy for the heroines that inspired Ovid to revise these tales, whereas Verducci reverses Jacobson's hierarchy to present the display of witty artistry as the force motivating Ovid's revisionary fictions, and sympathy as at times restraining his displays of rhetorical virtuosity. Verducci's thesis is above all a response to the major tradition of nineteenth- and twentieth-century interpretation of the *Heroides* in which critics denounce the text as a failure because its "excessive" wit calls too much attention to Ovid's poetic persona, thereby undermining dramatic illusion in the poems.[24] For Verducci, Ovid's witty persona is created in reaction against what he felt to be outmoded literary visions and is intended to deflate the "romantic" pathos of his heroines' self-portraits. Verducci sees wit not as an occasional intervening voice unsympathetic to the heroines but as the *Heroides'* dominant mode, the almost constantly operative force whose presence positions the text in the domain of Bakhtin's polyphonic.

In Verducci's view, the *Heroides* is constructed as a double hostile dialogue, between the poet and his precursors and between the poet and his heroines. Like Jacobson, Verducci sees Ovid as an unruly son struggling against a series of powerful literary fathers: "Briseis the slave exhibits the poet's literary freedom, his sedulous independence vis-à-vis the tradition he inherits" (120). Unlike Jacobson, however, she does not view this independence as a result of Ovid's desire to present these tales "through the eyes of women": "Part of that independence is the freedom to be unkind to his characters in the name of a larger, more obscure sympathy" (120).

Let us analyze Verducci's vision of Ovid's "unkindness" first. She considers a central aim of the ever-present wit in these fictive epistles to be the reduction of what other critics perceive as female uniqueness to rhetorical clichés, set pieces of amorous discourse, "excessive but revealing conceits" (233). Ovid anchors his heroines firmly in their "banality" in order to "undercut the pathos granted at the outset, exposing his heroines' delusions, obsessions, . . . follies" (260). Instead of the newly "justified" heroines "seeking recognition as person[s]" that Jacobson gives us, Verducci uncovers a "diminish[ed]" Dido, a "blacken[ed]" Phaedra, a "debase[d]" Ariadne ("[*Heroides* 10] ruins Ariadne") (85, 246). The goal of this repeated female debasement, as Verducci sees it, is "to push [these heroines] beyond the limits [of pathos]—toppling [them] into selfish bathos" (285). And what is the "larger, more obscure sympathy" that Verducci promotes as a replacement for Jacobson's theory of Ovid's empathy for his heroines? Verducci never spells out an answer—she is no more explicit on the subject of her methodological investment than Jacobson—but it seems to be a sympathy rooted in literary polemic, in a broad sense of the term. According to Verducci, the tonality of the *Heroides* is a "react[ion] against" Vergil, Catullus, Euripides, and Homer and "a challenge to the Roman 'classical' heritage, a challenge which . . . adjusts the fictions of the past to the complicated, urbane, skeptical . . . integrity of a new and different world" (85).

By now it should be evident that the *Heroides* confronts the reader with an interpretive dilemma reminiscent of that generated by Sappho's corpus. Except in one instance, to which I will return shortly, Ovid's text avoids the question of the orientation of sexual desire. However, Ovid's reader is forced to choose between diametrically opposed options in two areas also fundamental to Sapphic interpretation, the author's personal investment in the desire to which the poem gives voice, and the authenticity of that desire. Most important, the reader is asked to decide whether Ovid was dealing in literary transvestism. Was he attempting to forge a discourse of female desire that would gain currency as a model of writing in the feminine, thereby appropriating for the male author the right to speak for women in love? Was he inspired by sympathy for Woman or did he hope to debase her?

The approach to Ovid's writing as a woman most congenial to recent critical modernity takes Verducci's insistence on the overriding literarity of Ovid's investment in his heroines to an extreme she stops well short of. I refer readers to Linda Kauffman's *Discourses of Desire: Gender, Genre, and Epistolary Fictions,* in which Ovid is presented as the originator of a tradition of epistolarity in which authors male and female speak desire as a woman, not from any "naive" belief that a writer can translate the essence of female, or male, experience, but in order to expose the artificiality of any attempt to construct gender in literature. Kauffman's analysis of the *Heroides* is reminiscent of Verducci's theory of an author intent on transmitting, rather than a straightforward vision of experience, a sense of contradictory perceptions of an experience. However, instead of stressing, as Verducci does, the distance that separates, say, Vergil's Dido and Ovid's, Kauffman makes the more radical suggestion that Ovid is unable to present an unproblematic identification with the female experience because "he is skeptical about the very idea of a center, a self, and about language's representation of such concepts" (19). In her view, Ovid's "obsession" with "the lack of interiority" led him to create in the *Heroides* a shifting surface of textuality designed to denounce as mere representations all attempts to write as a woman and to confound readers who might imagine that writing inevitably betrays the gender of its author.

Kauffman's new French feminist view of the *Heroides* is diametrically opposed to the vision of Ovidian epistolarity that we will see most commonly accepted in the seventeenth century, when Ovid was reduced to real-life precursor of Molière's Dom Juan, reveling sadistically in his ability to tap the wellspring of female passion and in his enjoyment of the humiliation of the woman who dares speak openly of her desire. My brief discussion of the *Heroides* in its current critical situation is designed to serve as a reminder of the kind of interpretive fact so obvious that it can seem forgotten during a complicated trajectory through diverse, and often opposing, interpretations of a text: the *Heroides* enjoyed such a durable and rich fantasy life on the early modern European literary scene because Ovid's text is at the same time so complex that it contains all the elements on which successive readings are founded, and so elusive as to baffle critics who seek to reduce to a monologic experiential truth the polyphonic dialogue in which Ovid presents female abandonment. In addition, I have foregrounded the interpretive controversy surrounding Ovid's relation to his heroines because it serves as an excellent introduction to the problem that concerns me most, the exceptional nature of the epistle with which Ovid closes the initial volume of the *Heroides,* the letter from Sappho to Phaon.

"It is primarily the critical failure to separate the voice of the poet from the voice of his creature which confounds the attempt to assess the tone of Ovid's fictive epistles" (81). Verducci's warning about the limitations of a monologic view of the *Heroides* also points to the limitations of her theory of the text's construction when that theory is applied to the volume's final poem. In the *Heroides,* Ovid brings together a collection of the best-known icons of female abandonment from classical literature and legend. Into this group of heroines of similar status, he introduces, in a fifteenth epistle that leaves his volume suspended in slight asymmetry, a single historical figure, Sappho, an individual whose prior literary existence is radically unlike that of Ovid's other women. The voice of this "creature" was available to Ovid, not for once in the works of his great male precursor poets, but in her own words, that is, her own poems, from which Ovid borrowed extensively for his verse epistle, as has been demonstrated most thoroughly by Jacobson (280–85) and Mora (83).

When we consider the related question of Ovid's sources for the version of Sappho's life story he presents, we find that the fifteenth epistle is often described by critics as though it shared the status of the other verse letters, a crucially misleading evaluation. For example, Verducci contends that Ovid's sources are Menander, Diphilus, and Plato Comicus, and this may have been partly so. However, as her notes reveal, none of these works is extant, so it is impossible to measure the extent to which Ovid's creation of Sappho is a (hostile) dialogue with these precursors, in the way in which, say, his Ariadne can be shown to overturn Catullus's. Other critics, Jacobson for example, mention that Ovid may have had access to "some kind of Hellenistic biography of the poetess" (280), a theory that is plausible since alleged biographies of major literary figures were often compiled in antiquity. Yet, once again, this theory cannot be established, since no trace of such a biography has survived. And, even had such a text existed, it would in all likelihood have been largely a reconstruction based on the literalization of the deliberate ambiguity of Sappho's poetry, as Jacobson admits and as Mary Lefkowitz's research on the lives of the ancient poets demonstrates. It seems probable that the Sappho Ovid created in the *Heroides* was a distillation of fragments of various visions of the archetypal woman writer: scenes from what appear to have been flagrantly caricatural comedies; a handful of undoubtedly contradictory references in diverse sources (the allusions in Aelian, the Suda, and Maximus of Tyre probably give a sense of the information thus transmitted); and any literal reductions of Sappho's poetry that Ovid himself elected to carry out. Ovid chose among contradictory interpretations of Sappho those that suited his overall intention and then threaded those fragments together with a story line to create the sort of biography of a famous writer that flourished in Hellenistic times.

And this is exactly how the fifteenth epistle was read throughout the time of the *Heroides*' greatest prominence and the creation of the modern novel, as the life story of Sappho, the authenticity of which was guaranteed by Ovid's rising poetic authority. When Ovid's epistle reaches a broad public in French translations, it first generates debate among those who, on the basis of their knowledge of the relatively extensive Sappho corpus available in the sixteenth century, contested the veracity of this version of her biography. Well before the end of the century, however, this dissent had been almost entirely silenced, and Ovid's fiction of Sappho had become what it remained, virtually without challenge, until the early nineteenth century: Sappho's "authorized" biography. Before I attempt to reconstruct the process by which Ovid's myth was grafted onto Sappho's corpus in order to efface its ambiguity, I would like to return to the question of his intention in creating the type of portrait we find in the fifteenth epistle. I do so not from a belief that it is possible to settle debate on this issue, but from a conviction that Ovid sets a model for the most intricate type of involvement with Sappho on the part of a male writer, a type of uneasy literary symbiosis that merits further exploration, if only to measure the considerable distance that separates this relation of fearful attraction from more banal instances of Sappho's appropriation by writers anxious to suppress the menace of her poetic voice.

Nowhere in the fifteenth epistle does Ovid indicate that in this instance he is imagining a historical rather than a legendary figure. Yet for his double portrait of Sappho as poet and Sappho as woman he makes no attempt to focus attention solely on the private persona, the abandoned woman. (This was a move almost universally adopted by Ovid's seventeenth- and eighteenth-century heirs, who conceived of the "new heroides" as a means of demonstrating that illustrious historical figures were less impressive because they were in their private lives *only* women in love, according to the fiction then being purveyed, that is, women seduced and betrayed.) On the contrary, in the fifteenth epistle the problem of stature—taken both literally and in the sense of the measure of a life, especially a poet's life—is a key concern for Ovid's Sappho. He has the poet, traditionally believed to have been short, pronounce poetic authority the true measure of a life. "My name is already sung abroad in all the earth. . . . I am slight in stature, yet I have a name that fills every land; the measure of my name is my real height."[25] However, when Sappho thus proclaims the rewards of genius, her canonization as writer is only granted in exchange for her humiliation first as woman and then as writer. For his allegedly "heroic" presentation of Sappho, Ovid portrays her no longer in full possession of her literary powers, but at a time when her genius and towering poetic stature have diminished: "My former power in song will not respond to the call; . . . mute for grief is my lyre" (197–98). Ovid poses Sappho on top of the White Rock of Leukas, poised for the suicidal leap that she hopes will bring her much desired oblivion, the ability to forget the beautiful young man, Phaon, for whom she has abandoned her sapphism, and whose subsequent betrayal has silenced her poetic gift. ("My genius had its powers from him; with him they were swept away." [206]) Her fictive epistle is the retrospective account of how she came to embody what Verducci sees as Ovid's vision of heroinism, the woman of "momentous stature" "diminished" and "debased."

In the fifteenth epistle Ovid portrays what could be seen as a solution to sapphism: deviant female sexuality has been tamed, and the female bond often presented as the inspiration for Sapphic poetic creation has been erased. Ovid has Sappho renounce sapphism as a youthful transgression — "my eyes joy not in Atthis as once they did, nor in the hundred other maids I have loved *to my reproach*" (*non sine crimine*, "not without blame or wrongdoing") (19, my emphasis). His heroine has realized that one man is preferable to a multitude of women, to the female community frequently celebrated by Sappho in her poetry: "The love that belonged to many maids you alone possess." Furthermore, her acceptance of the superiority of an *ars amatoria* much like Ovid's over that which she had formerly preached has brought about her public humiliation. Ovid's Sappho is a madwoman (139), consumed with a desire for a man who has betrayed her, a desire so strong that it "embarrasses" her, a desire that, like her lover, constantly betrays her: "Modesty and love are not at one. There was no one who did not see me; yet I rent my robe and laid bare my breast" (121–22). In the final image of what would become for the modern tradition of Sapphic speculation the inaugural fiction of the woman poet, Sappho declares that unless her letter provokes a quick response from her unfaithful lover, she will "seek [her] fate in the Leucadian wave" (220). In the *Amores,* Ovid alludes to the existence of a reply from Phaon in which the repentant lover reaffirms his love for Sappho (2.18.34). Such a "double" letter, however, is an impossible fiction, against the grain of the canonical plot for the heroic love story: as decreed by Ovid, it cannot have a happy end. Sappho can win no stay of execution.

Modern commentators on the fifteenth epistle are always made uncomfortable by the "unkindness" of Ovid's portrait of Sappho the woman. "The real Sappho . . . has degenerated into a grotesque pursuer of material luxury and corporeal lust" (Jacobson, 298). "Ovid cannot be said to be kind to Sappho in any simple sense. He omits nothing in her situation that would reduce her dignity or degrade her infatuation"

(Verducci, 137). However, the critics find explanations for this diminishment, even if, to do so, they must be unfaithful to the interpretive stance they otherwise maintain. Thus, Jacobson, unable to advance his usual reading of sympathetic defense, is forced to speculate without conviction: "We can be fairly sure that Ovid did not write this poem to denigrate the Greek poetess, for whom he probably had sincere admiration. It is, I submit, not the poet Sappho who is being mocked, but the *persona* of the lover-poet of which Sappho is virtually the paradigm" (297). Verducci sounds closest to Jacobson when she proposes a reading of the fifteenth epistle as a work whose "higher sympathy" lies not with the literary values necessary for a new age but with a far more autobiographical meditation on the incompatibility of sexual desire and the poetic calling. After stressing that the most sexually explicit passages in *Heroides* 15 (41–50 and 123–34) "are unique in the collection and perhaps even unique in the Ovidian corpus" (161), Verducci concludes that Ovid chose Sappho as a heroine in order to interpret the scandal surrounding her name in antiquity as a warning to poets that "such enslavement to the senses meant the end of poetry for her." In this light, the fifteenth epistle becomes a cautionary tale about the necessity of maintaining "artistic distance" (163).

Ovid's early modern readers, too, were sensitive to the victimization of Sappho in *Heroides* 15. However, none of them detected any trace of admiration on Ovid's part for the precursor whose humiliations he recounts in such lavish detail. On the contrary, those who introduced Sappho to a French public, most notably Le Fèvre Dacier, not only accepted Ovid's scenario as biographical fact but put forth additional evidence to suggest that his project had a goal parallel to their own: to contain the deviance of a poetry of female desire so powerful that it threatened to provide an alternate model to the Ovidian scenario of heterosexual abandonment. Thus, in her life of Sappho, Le Fèvre Dacier has the poet complete the leap for which she is positioned at the end of *Heroides* 15, and she justifies her conclusion with an unidentified citation from Ovid's contemporary Strabo, who mentions both Sappho's alleged suicide and an ancient cult practice associated with the cliff: "Every year, some criminal was cast down from the white rock into the sea below for the sake of averting evil" (399). This ritual sacrifice followed a model, as Girard has analyzed, frequently chosen in antiquity for scapegoats (216). With her reference to Strabo, Le Fèvre Dacier creates an implicit link between the means elected for Sappho's suicide and her ability to function as a scapegoat. She made Sappho's leap into water the crucial moment in Ovid's biography, the completed exorcism of inadmissible sexuality. For Le Fèvre Dacier and the generations of commentators who adopted her position, Ovid's Sappho functions as a scapegoat, for her suicidal leap guaranteed the continuing orderly functioning of life inside the literary city. For Sappho's seventeenth-century commentators, when Ovid lent his authority to the fiction of her suicide, he completed her reincarnation as "mascula Sappho," a phrase coined by his contemporary Horace in his first epistle (composed during the same period as one of the most influential canon-forming texts of antiquity, his *Ars poetica* [*Epistles* 19.1.28]). At other periods, in addition to obvious sexual connotations, the adjective has been seen as a commentary on Sappho's authoritative prosody (see Bonnet, 28). But under Ovid's influence in seventeenth-century France "mascula" was most frequently interpreted as a synonym for "heroic," designating the courage Sappho demonstrated when she made the fearful leap.[26] The early modern commentators who stress the male virtue of Sappho's leap all echo Le Fèvre Dacier's implicit conclusion: having recognized the "crime" of her original sapphism, the poet, by her leap, performs the action of her own scapegoating, thereby taking back in the end a measure of the control over her life she had abandoned to Phaon.

And what of the control over her poetry that Ovid has her surrender at the same time? For Sappho's early modern commentators, this was a question simply settled. They did not perform the systematic research of today's critics, but they were nonetheless sensitive to the presence of Sapphic echoes in Ovid's epistle. Most notable is the passage (lines 110–13), based on the celebrated images from fr. 31, that evokes the physical power of the narrator's desire for another woman: here they are used to convey the extent of the humiliation suffered by the woman when the man who had at last taught her the full force of desire abandons her. Taking this appropriation at face value, those I will present as Ovid's heirs made their master into a reincarnation of the sixteenth century's vision of Catullus: in their view, Ovid had simultaneously recovered for men the right to make women suffer in love and for the male writer the right to portray the force and the torments of female desire. And since the inheritors preferred Sappho's voice filtered through Ovid's and Sappho's geometry reconfigured by Ovid, they presented the epistle as an extended citation from Sappho and, as such, a work that could replace Sappho's actual poems.

Verducci's interpretation of the relation between the two poetic voices in *Heroides* 15 is actually not far removed from the early modern position: "The subject of *Heroides* 15 is . . . the failure of poetry; it must still be conceded that Ovid's poem is a victory of conscious craft over its subject" (156). The "artistic distance" Sappho has lost as a result of her "enslavement to the senses" becomes another victory for Ovid: this time, he proves his superiority to a previous writer in that writer's own words and in that writer's own (fictive) self-image. Jacobson comes closer to capturing the epistle's uncanny portrait of the artist as woman writer no longer sure of her artistry: he suggests that the Sappho epistle enjoys exceptional status within the collection because Ovid reveals himself so intimately in this poem. And what he reveals, according to Jacobson, is a proximity to literary maternity, a desire to be Sappho: "here alone in the *Heroides* Ovid means to transform a second-hand poem into an original, that is to say, to eliminate the poet (himself) who intrudes between the subject (the heroine) and the object (the poem). . . . Ovid, in brief, wanted this poem to ring . . . Greek, exotic, Sapphic" (286). Jacobson stresses the exceptional nature of this strategy: he argues, for example, that *Heroides* 7 reveals no such intimate identification with the precursor poet to counterbalance the hostile takeover of Vergil's portrait of Dido that both Jacobson and Verducci document. I would like to pursue Jacobson's intuition and allow myself a moment of speculation in the hope of better understanding the feasibility of Ovid's literary self-portrait as Sappho.

Ovid expressed on several occasions his sense of the proximity between his *oeuvre* and Sappho's. In his attempt in the *Ars amatoria* to teach women how to avoid the fate of the abandoned woman, he advises them to read the great erotic poets, including himself and Sappho, whom he characterizes as the most "lascivious" of all (3.331). When he writes Augustus begging to have his exile revoked, he tries to justify his *Ars amatoria* by evoking the authority of the poet he describes as his precursor in the art of amorous pedagogy: "What did Lesbian Sappho teach the girls if not love?" (*Tristia* 3.365). The *Heroides,* Ovid's first and best-known confrontation with Sappho, shows that his original vision of his female precursor is at odds with this later portrait of Sappho: she is neither in control of her "lascivious" art, as in the *Ars amatoria,* nor does she address her teaching to other women, as in the *Tristia.* Yet it is Ovid's original fiction of Sappho that indicates the crucial role she plays, first for Ovid and then time and again for modern writers, as the unique standard against which the fledgling writer felt obliged to measure his or her originality.

Jacobson presents the early development of Ovid's career as an extended confrontation with elegy, a genre that, in Jacobson's reconstruction of Ovid's view, "as it had been taken over from the Greeks with such brilliance by the Latin poets of the first century, had reached the end of its road" (5). So, first in the *Amores* and then in the *Heroides,* Ovid set about moving elegy onto a new course, an effort that leads in the *Heroides* to his decision to complicate the themes and the plots of the erotic by "incorporating elegy into the world of myth" (Jacobson, 6). In both these works, Ovid signals his deviation into new poetic territory by means of a Roman elegiac convention, *recusatio* (refusal). This is a rhetorical negation or denial of competence: the poet responds to an implicit demand that he devote himself to more serious poetry with a refusal to do so on the grounds that he is not worthy of the task. The *Amores* features a standard use of the figure when Ovid paints his literary self-portrait as author unable to create in the most noble genre, the epic; he is a poet not of war and public exploits but only of his "private battles" and his amorous "campaigns" (*resque domi gestas et mea bella cano*) (*Amores* 2.18.12). The refusal of competence, however, is immediately counterbalanced by an affirmation of originality, suggesting that *recusatio* may function as a denial in the psychoanalytic sense of a disavowal that acts simultaneously as an avowal. Ovid claims for himself mastery in a less public and therefore apparently less glorious double literary domain, "teaching the art of tender love" and writing "the tearful complaints of abandoned [women]" (*Amores* 2.18.19, 22).

The treatment of literary authority in *Heroides* 15 is far more oblique. To begin with, Ovid speaks his authorial denial of competence in the name of Sappho. The Sappho epistle is initially presented as a poem about the importance of an author's name, the signature that stamps a work with its creator's literary authority. Sappho distinguishes between two different signatures. Her love poems have won her great literary stature, and her name is associated with a type of poetry authenticated, as it were, with an implicit signature, the mark of Sappho's genius. She would have no need to sign this work, because it is so evidently hers. "And even now the whole world is alive with the sound of my name" (15.28).[27] When *Heroides* 15 opens, however, this relation has been dissolved; Sappho has lost her implicit signature. "Tell me, when you looked upon the characters from my eager right hand, did your eye instantly know whose they were—or, if you had not read their author's name, Sappho, would you have known the origin of this brief work?" (15.1–4). Sappho has recourse to an explicit signature because she knows that she is now unrecognizable not only as woman, but also as author. Her complaining epistle still relies on a Sapphic vocabulary, but the story it tells marks a complete break with the Sapphic model for female erotic passion. Ovid's heroine therefore opens this wayward production by stamping it with her authorial signature, "auctoris nomina Sapphus" (15.3), in an attempt to authenticate it.

These lines, and those that follow—"And perhaps you will ask why I write in elegy's rhythms / when I am better suited to the lyric mode" (15.5–6)—are, as Verducci has noted, a less predictable use of *recusatio* than Ovid's rejection of the epic mode in the *Amores*: "The opening to Sappho's epistle is mannered, precious, and amusing. It almost reads as a parody of the Callimachean literary apology, a parody become a convention of the Latin *recusatio* theme and one frequently employed elsewhere by Ovid" (150). What Verducci reads as parodic overworking of the expected rejection of expected literary standards, I see instead as a different mode of what Bakhtin terms the dialogic. The opening is a *recusatio* that explores the functioning of *recusatio* in order to make clear that the alleged denial of authorial importance acts simultaneously as an affirmation of a writer's originality. *Heroides* 15 confronts us not with authorial impotence but with a writer's struggle to invent a radically new voice.

Ovid abandons *recusatio* for open eulogy when in the *Ars amatoria* he relinquishes the pose of canonic inferiority, maintained completely in the *Amores* and partially in the *Heroides*, and asserts his originality by saying of himself, objectified in the third person, "He first invented this art unknown to others [*Ignotum hoc aliis ille novavit opus*]" (*Ars amatoria* 3.346). The "opus," "artistic form" or "structure," in question is the letter ("epistola") as articulated in the *Heroides*. Ovid claims that his invention of this form will save his works from being abandoned in the river Lethe and will inspire the addition of his name to the list of great writers—from Callimachus to Vergil, of whom Sappho is the only woman—with whom he compares himself (*Ars amatoria* 3.329–40).

The two sides of Ovid's literary self-portrait—the minor poet who sings of love rather than noble, manly deeds; the proud innovator who is confident of his literary immortality—together illustrate Gordon Williams's view of *recusatio*'s function in the Augustan era, to attribute a renewed seriousness to the poet and to the originality of his poetic message (134).

They also add up to an uncanny prediction of the evolution of genre, the foretelling of a canon to come, which was indeed being formulated at the time of the *Heroides'* rediscovery for modern literature. This new canon would valorize a genius very much like Ovid's own: private, amorous battles would take precedence over military exploits. Ovid would therefore be recognized as the origin of its dominant style and structure. *Heroides* 15 recounts Ovid's accession to literary primacy, his "invention," *through* Sappho, of a form that was to guarantee his immortality.

Among Ovid's heroines, Sappho alone is writing not simply as a woman but as a woman author. While commentators have often pointed this out, they fail to stress sufficiently Sappho's exceptional status within the collection. In the final epistle, Ovid forces his reader to confront the problematic essence of his authorial innovation in this work, this young writer's "coming to writing" with the invention of a model for writing the *female* body, what our critical modernity would term an *écriture féminine*. This explains Ovid's obligatory deviation from the pattern otherwise evident in the *Heroides,* creation of the woman's voice through a dialogue with a male precursor poet, which defined the articulation of female desire as a poetic exchange among men. Ovid could have retained this pattern for *Heroides* 15. Indeed, logically he should have presented Sappho's voice, too, as the product of an exchange with a male precursor—in this case, Catullus, a natural object for Ovid's rivalry, both because of his reconfiguration of Sapphic discourse (most notably in Catullus 51) and because of his pivotal role in claiming the Greek elegy for Latin poets. Yet Catullus, like all male precursor poets, is conspicuously absent from the *recusatio* in the *Heroides,* where Ovid simultaneously denies the importance of women's writing and affirms the originality of his vision of the discourse of female desire. Ovid brings the *Heroides* to a close by writing not only as a woman, and in the name of a woman writer, but as a woman writer. In what may be his most subversive gesture against traditional male values, he makes common cause with Sappho's opposition to the male poetic order. *Heroides* 15 is Ovid's signature piece, the epistle that closes his signature volume, the collection intended to add his name to the list of classic authors. "Auctoris nomina Sapphus" is Ovid's signature in the feminine, the author's name he devised to take possession of his prototype for the literature of a new age.

The opening lines of *Heroides* 15 make plain that Sappho is still conscious of her choice of mode and structure. Ovid portrays her as experimenting in a literary form unlike those previously associated with her name, as having invented this work, this "opus." This is the same term he later employs to characterize his own creation of the *Heroides*. Sappho's epistle is presented as an extension of her passion, as writing that strives for immediacy and intensity rather than formal control. Ovid thus places his secret sharer in what may be the most precarious authorial position, on the borderline between art and uncontrolled personal outpouring. When Ovid made this formal innovation the final evolution of Sappho's career, he guaranteed that his vision of the discourse of female desire would reactivate the original debate about women's writing: is it an uncontrolled outpouring or an artful recreation of literary impotence brought about by the intense experience of passion? This debate was undoubtedly inaugurated in the controversy generated by Sappho's poetry, in which these antithetical positions are recurrent. Those who try to undermine Sappho's importance as an origin dismiss her poetic intensity as a lack of control bordering on madness. And those who praise her artistry, most prominently "Longinus," see the mark of her control in her ability to convey the effects of passions so intense that they threaten the desiring subject's self-mastery. To the end Ovid suspends his volume in polyphony and does not take a stand in the debate on the nature of women's writing. He chooses rather to reactivate that debate and even to render it more problematic. By placing Sappho on the border between life and art, Ovid assured that the *Heroides* would make him Sappho's heir. Whenever the creation of a discourse of female desire would become a literary issue, Sappho's name and her literary authority would be bound up with Ovid's. In addition, to the undecided essence of writing as a woman would be added a new, equally undecidable issue: is it necessary to be a woman to speak an authentic language of female desire?

Ovid's poetic voice in *Heroides* 15 demonstrates a response to Sappho's *oeuvre* that is far more intricate than simple "admiration." Ovid filters his homage through a *recusatio*, Sappho's proclamation of her sense of creative inadequacy, in order to suggest the difficulty of identifying with the female inventor of the language of woman's desire. His use of elegiac convention here seems related more than functionally to denial in the psychoanalytic sense, the process by which the individual disavows a perception even as he or she reproduces it. Freud's theory of disavowal originated in his discussion of castration: faced with woman's lack of a penis, children "disavow the facts and believe they *do* see a penis, all the same" (19:143–44). Denial, like this *recusatio,* operates in the domain of the (child's) phantasmatic and translates a complex coming-to-terms with sexuality. Denial signals, on the one hand, the child's desire for union with the pre-oedipal mother, for an all-encompassing female origin, and, on the other, the fear of the loss of individual identity through engulfment in the maternal. In similar fashion, Ovid's denial of authorial competence in Sappho's name might be said to translate both a desired union with the female literary origin and the fear that he might identify so uncannily well with the woman's voice that in the end it would not be clear if his author's name, "auctoris nomina Sapphus," is male or female.[28] Ovid's ability to fuse with Sappho is at once the basis of his originality and the principal threat to his authorial status: the debate about the authenticity of *Heroides* 15 is perhaps the most appropriate response to Ovid's conflicted desire for Sappho.

Ovid requires a polyphonic texture for *Heroides* 15 so as to convey the complexities not only of the debate on the nature of women's writing but also of his claim to authorial originality. His canonic transgression consists in "inventing," in the name of the archetypal woman writer, the most subversive language a woman can adopt, the declaration of her desire. This is the literary force that, in Charles Segal's words, "refuses ultimately to be confined . . . as the secure possession of a univocal language" (*Language and Desire*, 211). Unlike Sappho, who creates a polyphonic erotic discourse as part of a self-conscious exploration of the nature of desire, Ovid equates the dialogic and a variant of *écriture féminine* in a way that invites the reader to evaluate the relation between the direct expression of female desire and the literary fate assigned the desiring woman. He confines an explosive, Sapphic language to a literary construction of femininity, an unequivocal plot reminiscent of those assigned the transgressive heroines of the first fourteen epistles. It seems likely that his decision is the result of his uncanny ability to predict the evolution of genre: the form Ovid chose for the "epistola" looks forward to the time when the love letter that generates the epistolary novel will be defined as the lament of the woman seduced and abandoned.[29]

Ovid revived Sappho's seemingly reckless spontaneity in a novel form ("novavit opus"), a form revived in turn as the novel. In the seventeenth and eighteenth centuries, after the canonic revision Ovid predicted had been accomplished, Ovidian revisions of Sapphic erotic spontaneity came into their full value in the literary economy. The tale of female masochism, the narrative of the sexually pitiable woman that Ovid was seen as having canonized in the *Heroides,* was a familiar fictional model to generations of readers, who found a seemingly endless source of indiscreet pleasure in the voyeuristic position they felt Ovid had taught them to assume. Those who proclaimed themselves Ovid's heirs repeatedly made his portrait of Sappho the abandoned woman the founding archetype for their fictions of women's writing as the narrative of female abandonment.

Ovid's heirs simplify the terms of his involvement with Sappho. They turn his intricate denegation of authority in the feminine into a brutal usurpation of female literary authority: in this vision, Ovid makes Sappho fall from the White Rock of Leukas and from the heights of literary glory so that he can rise and take her place. The expression of Sappho's loss of her original identity becomes Ovid's literary innovation, the signature of his originality. Ovid's heirs felt that the deranging of Sappho had empowered Ovid as writer, just as female suffering empowers many illustrious classical literary heroes, the Theseus figures whose amorous exploits Ovid persistently chronicles. They saw Ovid as a literary Theseus, and his involvement with Sappho in the *Heroides* as a paradigm for the assumption of male literary authority. We will encounter this paradigm repeatedly in the age of the creation of epistolary fiction. Whenever novelists came to their authority in and through the dissolution of an original voice of female passion, they felt themselves to be following Ovid's model. Hereafter, when I speak of the Ovidian model for Sappho, I will be referring to the seventeenth-century view of his project in the *Heroides*.

Ovid's inheritors also simplify the terms of his involvement with Sappho's primal discourse of female desire by consistently reducing the polyphonic texture of his *écriture féminine* to a monologic union in which the male writer transvests himself in order to portray the woman author as the agent of her own humiliation. These early masters of the epistolary form exploit the heroine's unrequited passion to drive the heroine out of herself and into her (re)creator. The female voice finally exists only in its male recreation, and the female signature stands for male literary authority. "Sappho, c'est moi."

I speak of these heroines as recreations because, even if the Julies and the Clarissas of the mastertexts of epistolary fiction are not revisions of actual women writers like Ovid's Sappho, they were nevertheless created in response to the female literary origins of their creators' day. Ovid's fiction of Sappho proved so attractive—so useful, I am tempted to say—that it successfully dominated public opinion of Sappho until the nineteenth century. From time to time, however, a renewal of interest in the archetypal woman writer prompted attempts to strip away the Ovidian overtones in order to recover an authentic Sapphic voice. Such efforts inevitably inspired a new campaign in the struggle Ovid initiated for control over Sappho's literary authority. Each campaign was associated with a new articulation of the novelistic "opus" which Ovid had given its original shape in the *Heroides*.

I will present in detail the interaction between a battle for the right to speak as Sappho and a redefinition of the novel that took place in seventeenth-century France. I stress from the outset, however, that the phenomenon I will be describing is not unique. Similar scenarios could be uncovered, for example, in England at the time the modern novel took shape there, and in France in the early nineteenth century during the first major realignment of the French novel.

"Ovid's Disciples"

In seventeenth-century France, writers rediscovered the alliance between allegedly spontaneous epistolarity and female abandonment that was arguably Ovid's most important long-term legacy. The *Heroides* thus played a generative role in genre formation when they became the central model for the epistolary fictions of women seduced and abandoned, such as the *Lettres portugaises,* that were among the century's most influential texts. The importance of the *Heroides* as an epistolary model in seven-teenth-century France has been acknowledged by a number of recent critics.[30] However, commentators have failed to recognize the intricacy of the Ovidian design in classical prose fiction.

The letter, fictional and nonfictional, came into its own in seventeenth-century France. Its stature was commensurate with the rise of epistolary compilation. As the best-known correspondences were collected into volumes, a variety of distinctive epistolary styles became available as models. A second type of compilation, the letter manual, displayed the broad range of possible epistolary modes. For all types of compilation, Ovid's creation of a literary work from a mosaic of individual letters remained a crucial, according to some critics *the* crucial, model (Bray, *L'Art de la lettre,* 14). Indeed, Octavien de Saint-Gelais's often reprinted 1505 translation initiated a series of translations and imitations of the *Heroides* whose number grew more impressive throughout the seventeenth century. Bernard Bray describes a three-stage process which he feels can account for the integration of the heroic epistle into the French literary sensibility in the course of the seventeenth century: (1) *translation* introduces the *Heroides* to a broad public; (2) *adaptation* brings about "an intimate blending of ancient and modern substances," resulting in (3) *acquisition*—"by the time of the great French classics the contact between Ovid's art and the style of the love letter is definitively realized" (*L'Art de la lettre*, 14–16). Bray's account promotes a simplified view of Ovid's influence as a process of smooth and steady assimilation by those he terms the "great French classics." Had he been aware of the sexual politics surrounding Ovid's reception, he might have concluded that those writers now seen as classic, as having set the standards against which all French literature must be measured, adopted without exception what was seen as the Ovidian position on the fate of Sappho—and even that such a stance was a prerequisite for acceptance as classic by their contemporaries. All those who questioned Sappho's Ovidian fate found themselves excluded from canonic status by the architects of classicism, notably Boileau.

French intellectuals of the seventeenth century routinely compared their era to the century of Augustus when they wished to suggest the standards against which their art was to be evaluated.[31] For epistolary fiction, the *Heroides* made it possible for them to posit a more precise connection with this precursor golden age. The volume's first seventeenth-century translator, Pierre de Déimier, is thus able to justify his undertaking: "This book is an image of the domination that Love exercised on souls in the first centuries, and today on the hearts of my friends and on mine" (ii). Writing in 1612, Déimier intuits that his century would share the fascination with the power of eros that he sees as the common bond between Ovid's day and the mythic original erotic age ("the first centuries") inhabited by Ovid's heroines. Like Ovid, the female secretaries of the seventeenth century portrayed their era as a reincarnation of the heroic age of amorous passion; like Ovid, they decided that writers should speak with the voice of Sappho. But erudites of the seventeenth century also created an original variant of the debate that still continues about the paternity of the Sappho epistle. This theory gives eloquent testimony to the uncanny effect of Ovid's Sapphic voice. Those who knew Sappho's *oeuvre* best consider the fifteenth *herois* the gem of the collection, but because it reveals Sappho's genius rather than Ovid's: "The Roman poet wrote nothing but what the tenth muse [Sappho] had dictated to him" (Le Fèvre, *Abrégé*, 24). Thus the scholars who first promoted Sappho as a locus of literary originality insisted that the voice of female literary origin was dominant: Sappho had replaced Ovid, had driven him out of himself.[32]

The same erudites who hear only Sappho's voice in the poem also give her credit for the generic innovation that Ovid saw as the origin of his future glory. They proclaim that Sappho's hand should be recognized in both the "tender," "touching" tone of the epistle and even in the choice of the letter form (Dacier, 403; Longepierre, 344).[33] The second seventeenth-century translator of the *Heroides,* Jean de Lingendes, formulates the most radical variant of this hypothesis. In effect, early commentators created a contest of authority: was Ovid or Sappho to be credited with the invention of the discourse whose attraction for the seventeenth-century public was becoming more and more evident?

By 1626, Ovid's third seventeenth-century translator, Bachet, resorts to flagrant redundancy to guarantee his proclamation of Ovid's originality: "Ovid's creation [of the epistle] was without example; he was the first inventor of this type of poem" (3). This disagreement on the origin of the epistolary form can be related to an early seventeenth-century debate on epistolary style that served as a springboard for one of the first articulations of the classical aesthetic. The early translators of the *Heroides,* including Déimier and abbé J.B. Crosilles (1619), in addition to believing in Sappho's originality, were also proponents of an epistolary model whose economy was not overt, of a discursive logic which later in the century would be considered anticlassical. Moreover, in the context of the parallel debate on women's writing, the model they promoted could also be seen as having affinities with the allegedly "natural," "spontaneous" epistolary style that was viewed as a female preserve. Déimier and Crosilles formulated their position in an attack on a widely influential early seventeenth-century epistolary stylist, Guez de Balzac, a staunch defender of male literary superiority who scornfully dismissed literary women as "intellectual transvestites" (237). Two vigorous opponents of their view, François Ogier and Michel de Marolles, helped in their defense of Balzac's model to articulate what has been seen as the first important formulation of classical standards for French prose.[34] When they subsequently joined forces to enter the contest for Sappho's authority, they contributed a monument to Ovid's renewed influence in the second half of the seventeenth century.

The frontispiece by François Chauveau to Marolles's 1660 translation of the *Epîtres héroïdes* plainly demonstrates that the attraction of Ovid's model for those who defended his literary originality was not his alleged invention of the love letter, but his equation of that form with the complaints of abandoned women (fig. 1). Chauveau's engraving shows about twenty women either alone or in groups of three or four, scattered about on the edges of a jagged sea coast. All look mournful: several have

Fig. 1. François Chauveau, frontispiece, Marolles translation, *Heroides* (1660).
Reprinted by permission of the Bibliothèque Nationale, Paris. Phot. Bibl. Nat.
Paris.

downcast eyes; a few sit with gaping mouths. One is rushing to the shore, arms outflung, racing in the direction of a ship leaving the port. Although she is farthest in the background, it is on her that the spectator's gaze is ultimately focused. Also in the background, another woman is placed in the center of a building in ruins, putting pen to paper, an activity in which one of the women in the foregrounded group also engages. The engraving is followed by a preface, in which Ovid is called "the secretary of the amorous heroines of antiquity." In the seventeenth century, those who elected the secretarial position did so in order to exploit a vision of female abandonment that contributed to their own literary glory even as it detracted from that of the literary women whom they portrayed amidst the ruins of their lives, no longer able to control the script of their passion.

The Marolles edition opens with a lengthy preface by Ogier, in which Balzac's supporter reveals that, at the time when he and Marolles began their careers, they coupled their defense of the nascent classical aesthetic with a conscious decision to follow in Ovid's footsteps and win literary authority from transvested fictive autobiography. To justify the by then traditional claim that his century was closely aligned with Ovid's, Ogier provides several examples of female abandonment. He recounts the unhappy adventures of wealthy young women from good families who had succumbed to "passion" for the "galants" who courted them with "ardor." Immediately thereafter, "*postquam avidae mentis satiata libido est*," their lovers "abandoned" them to the disgrace of public divorce or enforced imprisonment in a convent. The only people to come to their defense were "[Ovid's] disciples" who

> readily lent their pens to their complaints and had circu-
> lated, as though they were translated from that poet [Ovid],
> the letters they wrote their treacherous lovers. The first,
> written by the hand of a young man of twenty, provoked a
> great scandal in the midst of the [divorce] hearing. . . .
> The second made [the suffering woman] speak so touch-
> ingly, with such ingenious and delicate fictions [*inventions*],
> that [the author] received much esteem and honor. (n.p.)

The initial confusion in the paragraph about the letters' origin is revealing. Three possibilities are given: young women wrote the letters to their lovers and their secretaries made them public; Ovid's disciples circulated the letters as though they were a translation of the *Heroides;* aspiring male authors wrote fictive epistles and presented them as their inventions. The complicated scenario is, however, faithful to the contemporary understanding of the Ovidian compositional model, and the letters that result from it are in that sense translations of Ovid. To produce a true heroic epistle, the male writer must achieve a total identification with a female speaker which threatens the boundaries between reality and fiction. He becomes that speaker, takes over her identity to such an extent that he can proclaim that she wrote the letters that came from his pen: the female speaker loses all authorial status and all control over her own story.

Ogier has no doubts about the moral status of this undertaking, for he takes pride in revealing that this tale of the author as knight in shining armor is autobiographical: he was the first young man to take up his pen in defense of female virtue betrayed. He is blind to his own parallel betrayal of that virtue when he disrupted the divorce proceedings and made the young woman's shame more public in order to draw attention to his budding literary talents. He speaks of his imitation of Ovid as the "door by which I entered my reputation." Ovid's disciples have traditionally been dangerous secretaries. They allegedly take the woman's side, but their fictions, which Ogier describes as "ingenious lies" (*inventions*), are the literary equivalent of the mythic lovers' perfidy. The heroic secretary works to efface the origin of his production. Whenever this Ovidian scenario is reenacted, the unknown man becomes known, wins literary stature—"esteem" and "honor," in the case of Ogier's second example— and acquires an author's name by signing the name of the woman who thereby loses her independent identity and lives on only as a male fiction.[35]

Marolles eventually came to be accepted as Ovid's authoritative commentator in the seventeenth century; his was the translation most often reprinted during the decades that witnessed the recuperation of Sappho for a Francophone public. The frontispiece and preface to his translation reveal the origin of the *Heroides'* authority in his day. In 1660, what Dorothy Backer terms the "precious decade," the period during which literary women in the salons exerted dramatic influence in the republic of letters, was not yet over, and female literary power was at its highest level. It must have seemed to Ovid's disciples and proponents of the classical (epistolary) aesthetic that female literary originality was attaining ever more dangerous prominence. The rise of the novel, the rise of epistolarity, and the accession to prominence of a female voice of what was intended to be seen as spontaneous passion were all intertwined. Because of the *Heroides,* Sappho had come to represent the female voice of passion at the origin of the novel. In the mid-1660s, at the summit of female literary influence, the poet who established the guidelines according to which the canon of French literature was established, Boileau, composed the *Dialogue des héros de roman,* in which it becomes evident that fictions of Sappho by French male authors are at the same time attempts to check the spreading feminization of literature. I will return to this dialogue at the end of my discussion. First, I will make a chronological leap into the 1670s in order to consider Sappho's presence at the center of the classical aesthetic for whose advancement Ogier and Marolles became dangerous secretaries in the decades we have just considered.

Sapho and/in the "Great French Classics"

In 1674, when epistolary fictions of women seduced and abandoned knew their greatest popularity, a decade after Tanneguy Le Fèvre's biography of a homosexual Sappho and nearly a decade before the first French editions that sanitized and normalized Sapphism, Boileau published two works designed to make him the equal of the great theoreticians of antiquity, *L'Art poétique* and a translation of the *Traité du sublime.* The *Art poétique*—in which, significantly, Boileau scornfully dismissed all the novelistic forms rising to new prominence in his day—displayed his inheritance of Horace's canonic gift. His translation of "Longinus" 's[36] treatise on the sublime reinforced Boileau's self-portrait as master theoretician. It may also have been part of a bid by Boileau and his fellow royal historiographer Racine to align themselves with the Ovidian camp by discrediting Sappho's presentation of female desire and therefore her claim to poetic originality.

Because "Longinus" cited fr. 31 in its entirety in the *Traité du sublime,* he both guaranteed the survival of Sappho's poem and made it accessible to scholars through the centuries. Furthermore, "Longinus" was arguably the most "feminist" theoretician of antiquity. He presents the ode in a manner that is both favorable and equitable. He analyzes the poem's strengths without trying simultaneously to judge or to correct the poem's author. On the contrary, "Longinus" presents Sappho not as a woman whose craft has been sacrificed to her passion but as an author whose control is revealed in her ability to present the sundering effects of passion as though she were herself in the process of being torn apart. On these terms the ode is pronounced incomparable because of the graphic power of Sappho's imagery:

> When Sappho wants to paint the furor of love her skill is
> revealed above all in her choice among all its features of

those that put the greatest stress on love's excess and its violence. . . . Notice how many contradictory movements agitate her. She freezes, she burns, she is mad, she is sage. . . . In a word, one would say that she is not overcome by a single passion, but that her soul is the meeting place of all passions. (Boileau, 356–57)[37]

This critical objectivity may have forced "Longinus" to deny himself the possibility of commenting on a major component in the ode's forceful impact, the invasion of the narrator's femininity in its second half. The very equitableness of his analysis seems to have condemned him to neutralize the ode's sexual constructions.

That sexuality was portrayed differently by the same seventeenth-century French commentators who promoted the influence of the *Traité du sublime*, most notably Boileau. His translation is at the same time an interpretation, however discreet, of "Longinus" 's presentation of fr. 31.

> *Heureux qui près de toi pour toi seule soupire;*
> *Qui jouit du plaisir de t'entendre parler;*
> *Qui te voit quelquefois doucement lui sourire!*
> *Les dieux dans son bonheur peuvent-ils l'égaler?*
>
> *Je sens de veine en veine une subtile flamme*
> *Courir par tout mon corps sitôt que je te vois;*
> *Et, dans les doux transports où s'égare mon âme,*
> *Je ne saurois trouver de langue ni de voix.*
>
> *Un nuage confus se répand sur ma vue;*
> *Je n'entends plus; je tombe en de douces langueurs:*
> *Et pâle, sans haleine, interdite, éperdue,*
> *Un frisson me saisit; je tremble, je me meurs.*
>
> *Mais quand on n'a plus rien il faut tout hasarder,* etc.
>
> (356–57)[38]

Boileau's rendering of Sappho's ode was immediately attacked as bland and flat. (This did not prevent it from being accepted as the authoritative French version of the poem, virtually until the end of the eighteenth century.) This blandness, however, is a function of his attempt to weaken the poem's impact. In particular, faithful to his self-elected role as the new arbiter of literary taste, Boileau decided to suppress some of the poem's most powerful imagery. For example, as he explained in the remarks he appended to his translation, he changed Sappho's phrase "comme l'herbe" (actually "greener than grass") to "pâle" (see line 11, Boileau's translation) because "this is not said in French" (416). Boileau's attitude of grammatical infallibility (willfully?) obscures the fact that this substitution removes the only legitimate signature of the narrator's threatening femininity in the original. More pointedly, he eliminated her expression "a cold sweat" on the grounds that "the word 'sweat' can never be pleasing in French and leaves an unpleasant image in the mind" (416). This implicit attempt to contain the sublimity of Sappho's ode, according to the very terms in which "Longinus" used the ode to define the sublime, is coupled with an insistence on the Sapphic narrator's madness. "Longinus" stresses the narrator's simultaneous self-knowledge and insanity: "She is mad, she is sage." Boileau portrays the narrator as more completely given over to her delirium. He devotes the most extensive commentary to his rendering of the Greek "phobeitai" (a word generally translated as "terrified") as "entièrement hors d'elle-même" (completely beside herself).[39] Boileau's convoluted and learned excuse is intended to obscure his attempt, initiated with his removal of the "greener than grass" image, to translate the expression of the fear inspired by love's power into a portrait of woman abandoned to madness.[40]

This semiotic transfer was subsequently amplified by Boileau's most influential reader, Racine. Racine knew "Longinus"'s treatise in the original but, three years after the publication of Boileau's translation, he nevertheless borrowed from his colleague's rendering of fr. 31 to fabricate his own fiction of Sappho. Racine's contemporaries note almost immediately that what are perhaps the best-known lines of his masterpiece *Phèdre* (1677), its heroine's *aveu* of her forbidden love, are an adaptation of Sappho's ode. Thus, Longepierre points out that Racine "might well have remembered [Sappho's ode] when he made his Phèdre say pathetically

> *Je le vis, je rougis, je pâlis à sa vue;*
> *Un trouble s'éleva dans mon âme éperdue;*
> *Mes yeux ne voyaient plus, je ne pouvais parler;*
> *Je sentis tout mon corps et transir et brûler."*
>
> (Longepierre, 375)

The adverb "pathetically" indicates the perhaps unintentional key revelation of Longepierre's formulation: when he introduced Sappho's discourse into Phèdre's plot, Racine completed the translation, initiated by Boileau, of the figure "Longinus" proposed as an archetype—woman torn by passion but still in control of it—into woman betrayed and humiliated by her passion as much as by the lover who rejects her. Even though her creation precedes the publication of Le Fèvre Dacier's edition, the edition most influential in shaping Sappho's initial modern biography, Racine's Sapphic heroine testifies to the growing prominence of the fiction of the feminine that also permeates the vision of Sappho's life that Le Fèvre Dacier chooses to promote.

Phèdre's confession of her guilt (especially the above-cited lines 1.3.273–76 and 305–06) reproduces all the elements found in each successive exploitation of Sappho's famous ode: her body is simultaneously hot and cold; a fire is burning under her skin; she can no longer see; she can no longer speak; and finally, she is outside of or beside herself, unrecognizable, mad. The adjective Racine uses most prominently to display Phèdre's alienation is "éperdue" (1.3.274), "distracted" or "out of herself"—an adjective, as we have seen, also featured by Boileau.[41] His choice of a plot from antiquity allows Racine to echo the remodeling of Sappho's triangle of desire that Ovid had promoted: Phèdre is fragmented into physical contradiction by her love for a man who prefers another woman. The fourth of Ovid's *Heroides,* the letter from Phaedra to Hippolytus, has been cited as a pretext for Racine's interpretation of his heroine, but Ovid's Phaedra does not know physical humiliation, does not feel the effects of love in bodily extremes.[42] Ovid's Sappho, however, provided Racine with a graphic portrayal of the physical degeneration of the abandoned woman.

We encounter all three of these heroines, Ovid's Phaedra, his Sappho, and Racine's Phèdre, as they turn away from a past way of life. A comparison of their trajectories indicates that Racine set Phèdre on a Sapphic course, forging a similarity that is even more evident when one takes into account the vision of Sappho that Ovid's seventeenth-century translators created for Racine's first public. Phèdre's entrance scene is accented with a double rejection. She first throws off her "ornaments" and "veils" and complains that she is burdened by the intricate arrangement of her hair (1.3.158–61). She thus echoes Sappho's rejection of her adornments (73–76), a moment foregrounded in all seventeenth-century translations of the *Heroides*. Phaedra, however, mentions no such vestmental alteration, despite the fact that she has just embarked on a more active, masculine existence: in her desire to emulate Hippolytus's accomplishments, she has taken up riding and hunting (4.37–52). Both Sappho and Phèdre, on the other hand, have rejected their past activities to become more passive; they flee the light of day and seek shelter in the forest's darkness. In the first complete new translation of the *Heroides* after the publication of *Phèdre,* Marie-Jeanne L'Héritier makes their proximity evident. In her reading of Ovid's lines 135–38—"to flee the light, I seek out caves and woods: as if these somber places could console my love" (360)—Sappho invents the evasion scenario Racine has Phèdre repeat (1.3.176–78). Most revealing, however, is the comparison of the force of these heroines' desire. Sappho, not Phaedra, is Ovid's lascivious heroine. As Jacobson stresses in his commentary on lines 45–50, "this is the most explicit and graphic description of sex in the *Heroides,* set out with such relish that one senses a vicarious recreation of the moment in Sappho's imagination" (293). In fact, the most disquieting implications of the scenario Ovid established for female desire only become evident in the story of Racine's heroine.

In both these archetypal fictions of the desiring woman, abandonment leads to self-abandonment: unrequited love drives the abandoned woman mad. In the Ovidian vision, a suicidal leap into the sea is the toll of Sappho's self-alienation. Rather than a tale of woman left to die on a rock-bound sea coast, like Sappho or another woman forsaken by Thésée, Phèdre's sister Ariane,[43] Racine wanted a more complicated plot for his vision of female abandonment. Before Phèdre dies, she provokes the death of the man who had rejected her. If the fate of Racine's heroine is superimposed on that of Ovid's Sappho, both these male fictions of female desire can be seen as attempts to stage the threatening power of that desire.

According to the legend Ovid promoted, Sappho killed herself for love of a handsome young man, Phaon. You will remember that Phaon is a doublet for Phaethon, the son of Phoebus who died a victim of his premature ambition to take over his father's role. Racine's choice of the story of Phèdre allows him to examine Phaethon's ambition and to suggest another explanation for his death. In *Phèdre,* it is Hippolyte, the Phaon-Phaethon figure, who dies the precipitate, watery death Ovid had reserved for Sappho. He dies, like Phaethon, because he is unable to retain mastery over his horses. They are frightened by a sea monster breathing fire on them, and Hippolyte loses control of his chariot, which is smashed to pieces on the rocks. His death is caused by his own precocious attempt to take over his father's role—and by his stepmother's monstrous desire.[44]

As Racine stresses in his preface, the potential violation of Hippolyte's chastity that Aricie represents is one of his most striking alterations of this legendary plot. While he does not invent Aricie—he lists the classical sources linking Hippolyte to this figure—he grafts her onto the story of Phèdre and her stepson. Racine thereby remodels the plot for Phèdre to make it conform to the reconfiguration of Sappho's erotic triangle proposed by his contemporaries.[45] He may even have contributed to the most important innovation to result from the Sapphic speculation of the late seventeenth and eighteenth centuries: the invention of the other, younger woman for whom Phaon betrayed her. In a roughly simultaneous development, French men of letters conspire to make Phaedra and Sappho over in their preferred image of female abandonment. Racine's depiction of Hippolyte may offer an explanation for this widespread desire to reconfigure the plot of the woman in love.

In Racine's version, Hippolyte's story is above all his coming to sexuality, the rite of passage by which a boy becomes a man. Hippolyte's most telling autobiographical revelation is not his admission of love for a woman forbidden to him on political grounds, but his guilty attraction to his father's promiscuous sexual prowess. Hippolyte rehearses what he sees as his family romance, Thésée's story ("l'histoire de mon père"), as he learned it from his teacher, Théramène: it is the narrative of a monster killer and a lady-killer, a man who has seduced and abandoned numerous women. From the beginning, Hippolyte fears that his ambition for a rite of passage may be as yet unfounded:

> *Qu'aucuns monstres par moi domptés jusqu'aujourd'hui*
> *Ne m'ont acquis le droit de faillir comme lui!*
>
> (1.1.99–100)[46]

Nevertheless, upon Thésée's return, Hippolyte approaches him, as Phaethon did the Sun God, with a plaintive request to be allowed to step into his father's shoes, in the hope of winning thereby recognition as a legitimate son, a son worthy of "un si glorieux père" (3.5.945).

> *Souffrez, si quelque monstre a pu vous échapper,*
> *Que j'apporte à vos pieds sa dépouille honorable;*
> *Ou que d'un beau trépas la mémoire durable*
> *Eternisant des jours si noblement finis,*
> *Prouve à tout l'univers que j'étais votre fils.*
>
> (3.5.948–52)[47]

The monster against which Hippolyte struggles to win his manhood and his filial legitimacy fulfills the intuition of his account of "[his] father's story." As Francesco Orlando has suggested, the monster responsible for Hippolyte's death may be seen as the "aggressive revenge" of Phèdre's desire (30):

> *Indomptable taureau, dragon impétueux,*
> *Sa croupe se recourbe en replis tortueux.*
>
> (5.6.1519–20)[48]

Orlando argues that the monster is "both Minotaur and Labyrinth" because he sees the sinuous path of its tail as a figure for the maze from which Thésée escaped with the aid of Ariane's thread (75). I would add that the monster is labyrinth because it represents Phèdre's revenge, in the name of Ariane, on those who consign women to a tragic fate.

Phèdre's confession of forbidden love is most startling because she superimposes Thésée's past onto his son in the hope of rewriting that story to remove all trace of female abandonment:

> *Oui, Prince, je languis, je brûle pour Thésée:*
> *Je l'aime, non point . . .*
> *Volage adorateur de mille objets divers,*
> ....
> *Mais fidèle . . .*
>
> (2.5.634–38)[49]

In this fiction ("dans ce dessein"), Phèdre would replace Ariane (2.5.653) to accompany the newly feminized Thésée-Hippolyte into the Labyrinth, where together they would either "lose" or "find themselves" ("se serait avec vous retrouvée, ou perdue" [2.5.662]). But Thésée's son refuses to cooperate with Ariane's sister in her attempt to efface their families' past involvement in scenarios of female abandonment. He deserts her—that he never returned her love is irrelevant, because Phèdre has identified him with her fickle husband—for another, younger woman. Hippolyte thereby forces Racine's heroine to prove that, just as women can save the Thésée figure from the Labyrinth, so they can destroy the youth who refuses to enter the labyrinth of passion with them. Ovid's Phaedra, as the end of her letter to Hippolytus shows, is the direct descendant of the gods who were responsible for Phaethon's shattering, fatal fall: "from my ancestor's hand comes hurled the lightning-stroke. . . . The front of my grandsire, he who moves the tepid day with gleaming chariot, is crowned with palisade of pointed rays" (4.158–60). Like Phaethon, Hippolyte dies shattered on the rocks, fallen from the heights of his premature ambition.[50]

The superimposition of the plots decreed for Sappho and for Phèdre reveals that Ovid and Racine imply a causal relation between heroinism, "the woman writer's heroic resolve to write herself" (Moers, 147), and the death of the filial figure. The scenario they suggest, furthermore, absolves the representatives of the patriarchal order of any responsibility in the demise of the legitimate heir. Ovid's Sappho is an unfit mother on two counts. In her abandonment, her biological child, a daughter, is a source only of care and not of consolation: "A little daughter fills the measure of my cares," according to a recent translation of line 70. Ovid's self-proclaimed heir, Marolles, gives a translation that dispels any notion of maternal concern and leaves only an image of the woman writer as unfeeling mother: "I have a little girl who every day gives me much annoyance" (196). This unnatural mother has replaced her daughter with a most unnatural son: "You, Phaon, are my care" (15.123). Even in this elective maternal scenario, however, she proves herself unfit. Sappho compares herself in her grief over Phaon's abandonment to "the loving mother of a son whom death has taken [who] bears to the high-built funeral pile his empty frame" (15.115–16). In her abandonment, Sappho first desires Phaon's death, not her own.[51]

Ovid subsequently makes this portrait of literary woman as murderous mother more explicit in a passage whose full impact can only be assessed when Sappho's plot is linked to Phèdre's. "The Daulian bird, most mournful mother who wreaked holy vengeance on her lord, laments in song Ismarian Itys. The bird sings of Itys, Sappho sings of love abandoned" (15.153–55). Several of Ovid's seventeenth-century translators apparently sensed that this mythological reference would be incomprehensible when applied to Sappho's life. Lingendes amplifies his translation to identify the bird as "the swallow, that unmerciful mother who mourns her son Ithis whom she killed to take vengeance on her husband" (344). L'Héritier further clarifies Ovid's allusion by identifying the "unmerciful mother" as Procne (361). Despite their joint efforts, however, the comparison remains elusive, as Ovid must certainly have realized, for it was he who, in the *Metamorphoses* (6.437–674), set down what has become the standard version of the tale of Procne and Itys: after she was given in marriage to Tereus, Procne missed her sister Philomela so deeply that she sent her husband to bring her to live with them. Tereus, however, fell in love with Philomela and took her instead to a hut deep in the forest, where he raped her, cut out her tongue, and held her prisoner. Philomela told her story in a tapestry that she sent to Procne, who came to her rescue. For her revenge, Procne then killed her son Itys, who closely resembled his father, and she and her sister cut him up and served him to Tereus. When Tereus tried to pursue the two sisters to kill them, the gods changed them into a swallow and a nightingale.

While this tale of sisterly vengeance illuminates only a detail of the plot decreed for Sappho, it does cast direct light on Racine's vision of Phèdre.[52] Phèdre's position with respect to a sister betrayed by her husband parallels Procne's. And Ariane is Philomela's double in more ways than one. Both work with thread; they are practitioners of the only form of artistic creativity traditionally allowed women. Phèdre and Procne come to the defense of the sisters who, while they are not literary women, nevertheless figure female artistry. To avenge them, they kill the male heir who, in both cases, is his father's physical double. Their defense of a female creative origin thereby threatens to end the patriarchal order. The legend of Procne stands between the plots decreed for Phèdre and Sappho, making clear that, in these male fictions of the female desiring subject, Hippolyte's lascivious stepmother has a right to speak with the voice of the even more lascivious original woman writer. In addition, Racine turns to a second prominent borrowing from Sappho for one of Phèdre's most vengeful moments. Phèdre's monologue to Venus in act 3 rewrites the Aphrodite ode so that it figures the danger behind the expression of female desire. Phèdre ends her plea to Venus to help her win the youth who flees them both: "Goddess, avenge yourself: our causes are the same" (3.2.822), thereby highlighting the violent nature of this vision of Sappho's passionate voice.[53] The interwoven plots of Phèdre, Procne, Sappho, and Ovid's Sappho work together to demonstrate first that the literary woman is, in Lingendes's expression, a "mère impitoyable" and second that the literary woman who dares express her desire directly threatens the continuation of the patriarchal order.

Hippolyte's death makes clear another aspect of Ovid's use of Phaon as Sappho's unfaithful lover. Jacobson notes "the obvious allusions to Phaon's effeminateness and implications of his homosexuality," but adds "I do not see what Ovid's purpose is here" (296, n. 59). He does not admit the possibility of a causal relation between the two sexual portraits he uncovers in *Heroides* 15, the woman's "explicit and graphic" sexuality and the man's "effeminateness." Ovid's Sappho emasculates Phaon, thereby fulfilling the threat constituted by the female desiring subject, Phèdre or Sappho: by taking over the male prerogative, by assuming control over the gaze, she will unman the young male and thereby bring about his ruin. (I think, notably, of Phèdre's capture of Hippolyte's sword at the end of 2.5.)[54] Phèdre, like Sappho, must be punished for the raw physicalness of her desire. She is driven out of herself, and her humiliation is completed with her suicide under the viewer's gaze, a violation of seventeenth-century theatrical propriety justified by the purifying aspect of this expulsion of female desire.

Racine's involvement with Sappho repeats in key ways that of his precursor Ovid. Like Ovid, he is so successful at literary ventriloquism that the expression of female desire created as a result of his identification with "the poetess" is thoroughly dialogic, at the same time a valid re-voicing of Sappho *and* the most highly charged erotic poetry of Racine's invention. Racine's debasement of his Sapphic heroine might represent the denial of his proximity to Sappho, his simultaneous longing for a union with this female origin and reaction against his ability to speak with an "authentic" female voice. The saga of this involvement illustrates, as does Ovid's, the perhaps inevitable simplification of complex motivations by a strong writer's posterity: slowly throughout the eighteenth century and in particular in the early nineteenth century, writers seeking to become Racine's heirs reduce Racine's uneasily dialogic Sapphic discourse to a facile repression of the power of Sappho's voice. At the same time, they use Racine's Sapphic language, just as Ovid's was used by his early modern heirs, to infiltrate the authentic remains of Sappho's poetry, until they make Sappho resonate with ersatz Racine. Perhaps the most convincing illustration of this simplified reading of Racine's intentions occurs immediately. For with *Phèdre,* Racine repeated Ovid's rise to canonic status. Despite the fact that his tragedies were widely criticized by his contemporaries because the central place granted love allegedly made them a threat to civic virtue, Racine was immediately considered a "great French classic," even by Boileau, who normally saw no value in amorous literature.[55] But Boileau, as will become clear, was sensitive to the power of a contemporary female literary origin—and to what he saw as the need for male authors to assume the right to speak for the woman in love.

Boileau's and Racine's incursions into Sapphic territory were contemporaneous with the efforts of early French Hellenists to rescue what was for the seventeenth century the original voice of female passion. The decades 1660–80 were marked by an atmosphere of intense speculation about Sappho in which hostility to her poetic originality coexisted with the first modern *tradition* (in the sense of a series of commentators who consciously seek to build on each other's findings) of Sappho scholarship. That the efforts of the first French Sappho scholars are so generally forgotten today provides yet another example of the crystallization of seventeenth-century critical authority around Boileau's position.

One of those thus passed over, Tanneguy Le Fèvre, could be considered Boileau's rival in a domain on which Boileau's critical authority was founded. In 1663 he published a Latin translation, with commentary, of "Longinus" 's treatise on the sublime. When Boileau's own French translation appeared a decade later, Le Fèvre's stood as the principal introduction to this work destined to cast such a long shadow on classical French aesthetic thought. Le Fèvre's view of "Longinus" was taken seriously by the most distinguished scholars of the day. The Bibliothèque Nationale preserves the copy of his translation in which Pierre Daniel Huet—perhaps the most noted classical scholar of the century and the author of a treatise that defends the novel's seriousness against Boileau's attacks—made extensive marginal notes. Those who, like Huet, valued the seventeenth century's literary contributions did not always give Boileau's effort such flattering attention: Charles Perrault, for example, devotes much of his response to the commentary on "Longinus" to an attempt to challenge Boileau's linguistic capabilities and, therefore, his ability to serve as spokesperson for the ancients, an attempt for which Perrault claims Pierre Bayle's support (40). These three critics—Huet, Perrault, Bayle—who promoted the novel, women novelists in particular, and, in Perrault's case at least, women's rights, joined forces against Boileau's authority as a classicist in support of Le Fèvre's.[56]

In the preface to his edition of "Longinus," Boileau is careful not to reinforce rival authorities, even when he appears to commend the Le Fèvre family. He damns with faint praise the commentary by Le Fèvre's student and then future son-in-law, André Dacier, which Le Fèvre published as an appendix to his translation: "the very learned *little* notes he made on Longinus" (339, my emphasis). Of Le Fèvre's translation he says not a word; Le Fèvre himself is identified as though he were known only for his progeny: "father of that learned girl [*fille,* in this case an unmarried woman] to whom we owe the first translation of Anacréon in French" (339). The "learned girl" in question is Anne Le Fèvre (future Dacier), and the terms of her presentation—similar to those Boileau adopted to introduce Scudéry in the preface to the *Dialogue des héros de roman*—demonstrate that, for Boileau, silence is the surest indicator that he finds a female intellectual force threatening. The foremost early woman Hellenist is introduced through her relation to two male intellectuals, as though her merits were dependent on theirs; her name is never pronounced.[57] Boileau also omits the name of the literary woman in whose service Anne Le Fèvre, like her father, had placed her erudition: he credits her with having introduced Anacreon to a French public, but does not mention that her recent volume also contained what has come to be known as the first French translation of Sappho. Just as is true of the *Dialogue des héros de roman,* the chronology of Boileau's remarks indicates that his omissions are really occultations. The commentary on the Le Fèvre clan's erudition was added to the original preface for the volume's second edition in 1683. The family's principal contribution to scholarship relevant to "Longinus" 's treatise in the decade between the two editions of Boileau's translation is precisely what Boileau fails to mention, Anne Le Fèvre's French translation of Sappho.

Boileau's unspoken evaluation of Le Fèvre Dacier's potential menace to his authority was correct. Her translation would prove to be the most durable of the family's scholarly contributions, the most influential version of the writer whose name is, in more ways than one, synonymous with the genre Boileau repeatedly tried to destroy, the modern novel. Like her father, Le Fèvre Dacier marshals the weight of her impressive scholarship to resist the reduction of Sappho to her sexual notoriety. In the "Life of Sapho" that prefaced her edition, she theorizes that attempts to subjugate Sappho's poetry to her sexuality had originated in simple jealousy: "There is no doubt that her merit won her many enemies. . . . I believe that those whose poetry would have been found incomparable, had Sappho never composed any . . . were driven by envy to write the calumnies with which she has been blackened" (393–94). Anne Le Fèvre Dacier's most recent commentator, Fern Farnham, refuses to recognize an expression of female solidarity in this theory (81), but surely Sappho's first French translator was not blind to the parallels with the fate suffered by seventeenth-century women intellectuals, in particular to the similarity with her own situation. Farnham details the rumors about Le Fèvre Dacier's personal life that were circulated immediately after her death to "blacken" her reputation (24). A contemporary, Anne Bellinzani Ferrand—herself a novelist and the author of fictions that belong to the tradition of reactions against the Ovidian vision of the female heroic—

writes of the attacks on Le Fèvre Dacier's scholarship by "men [who] look with an envious eye upon erudition in women" (329).[58]

The wholesale promotion of Woman abandoned but still given over to the force of her desire is perhaps most prominent in the French tradition in the 1670s. The Portuguese Nun (*Lettres portugaises,* 1669) and Phèdre are but the most visible examples of a fiction of the feminine that held extraordinary appeal for contemporary literary figures and for their public as well. The Le Fèvre Dacier 1681 edition of Sappho is enshrined for posterity as the culmination of the French humanist tradition less as a tribute to its scholarship than because it promotes a fiction of Sappho that could be assimilated to the contemporary tradition of sexually pitiable females who strengthen rather than threaten the orders of male bonding. At the same time, Le Fèvre Dacier's recognition of the effects of male envy in shaping the reputation of a literary woman may signal her awareness of the existence in her day of a countertradition that attempted to resist the Ovidian model with a radically different fiction of Sappho. To understand this fiction's creation it will be necessary to return to the beginning of the century and the letter manuals that, in tandem with the *Heroides,* constituted the primary epistolary model of the period.

Recovering a Mother Tongue (1)
The Other Epistolary Heroinism

In the 1670s, the French literary tradition was in the process of establishing its standards. In this moment of canon formation, one of the voices making a bid for priority was explicitly identified with Sappho. That poetic voice had become prominent during the decades 1641–61, when the major novels of Madeleine de Scudéry, known to her contemporaries as Sapho, appeared. Today, *Ibrahim, Artamène ou le Grand Cyrus,* and *Clélie* are perhaps no longer taken for a powerful literary statement, but in the 1660s and 1670s, to judge from the violent response of the self-appointed arbiter of classical taste, Boileau, this was an *oeuvre* to be reckoned with. In these volumes, Scudéry drew out of the structures of romance fiction the forms that would be shaped by her successors into the modern French novel. Along the way, she won a huge audience for prose fiction. Most important, she realigned the narrative presentation, the point of view, of prose fiction, much as Sappho had realigned the viewing angle of erotic poetry. Scudéry's revision of the novel can be seen as a repeated attempt to rewrite Ovid's fiction. Her goal was nothing less than the overturning of his authority over Sappho's plot. Scudéry used Sappho as the heroine of a new fiction of the feminine. The vision she proposed was in reality far more than a fantasy: Scudéry compiled the first modern biography of Sappho. Scudéry initiated her assault on Ovid's authority by developing alternatives to the model for epistolary fiction presented in the *Heroides*. She began her career with an attempt to revise the plot for heroinism represented in her day by both Ovid's direct heirs and his less obvious successors, the editors of the first French letter manuals.

The letter manuals whose proliferation in seventeenth-century France was contemporaneous with the rise to prominence of the *Heroides* evolve for half a century ever closer to the epistolary novel. In the first stage of this evolution, the seed of the novel form is evident in compilations directly related to Ovid's epistles. Perhaps the earliest proto-epistolary work is François Des Rues's *Les Fleurs du bien dire* (1595), in which a translation of two of the *Heroides* (Helen and Phylis) is followed by a double series of love letters, the first from an unidentified man, the second from an unidentified woman. In each series, Des Rues exploits the letter form to introduce a narrative that presents one side of a love story, thereby suggesting that Ovid's influence on the early novel originated in the vision of the amorous experience projected by the entire collection of his epistles rather than in the status of the individual letters as examples of amorous rhetoric.

The second stage of the evolution from letter manual to novel is marked by attempts to use the epistolary collection to tell a story that deviated from Ovid's Ur-plot. In the preface to the first such attempt, *Nouveau recueil de lettres des dames tant anciennes que modernes* (1642), François de Grenaille proclaims himself "the secretary of ladies." Although his elected title is an unmistakable reference to the writers known as "Ovid's disciples," the two volumes of letters Grenaille collected—some appear to be actual historical documents, others are undoubtedly invented—turn the letter manual into a defense of a female heroic resolutely opposed to the Ovidian model. The majority of the letters are political documents, official directives from women in positions of power (his earliest examples are from Visigothic princesses) concerning the affairs of church and state. Even Grenaille's most recent examples, "complimentary" letters by his contemporaries, while concerned with more private matters, do not deviate from the collection's stance: Grenaille married the letter manual with a second pedagogical genre of the day, an offshoot of the end of the *querelle des femmes,* the treatise or the compendium illustrating female superiority, in order to create an epistolary model in which women avoid abandonment and exercise power rather than plead for the return of an unfaithful lover. His *Nouveau recueil* encapsulates the entire early history of women's political influence in France.

Grenaille's manual presents an alternative to the Ovidian vision so pervasive in his day, but he does not generate a narrative from his compilation. His collection fails therefore to indicate the evolution of epistolary form into the letter novel. However, the year before his compilation appeared, a volume was published that both offered a counterfiction to the sexually pitiable female and turned the letter manual into a proto-novel. With the *Lettres amoureuses de divers auteurs de ce temps,* Madeleine de Scudéry embarked on her literary career.[59] At the time of the volume's appearance, she had requested only the month before a *privilège* (the obligatory official permission to publish a work) for *Ibrahim,* her first historical novel—the genre known in French as the *roman héroïque,* the "heroic novel," of which she is the best-known representative. The *Lettres amoureuses* demonstrates that Scudéry initially considered epistolary rather than historical prose fiction the form of the future. It also demonstrates that the original literary instinct of "the French Sapho"—a title she deserved because more than anyone else she authorized a female literary tradition in France—was to undermine the authority of the Ovidian model for heroinism.

In tracing the origins of heroinism, Ellen Moers declares that "the letter form . . . is central." She pronounces Rousseau the earliest practitioner of "heroinical" epistolarity and notes no involvement by women authors in this development before the nineteenth century (147). Seventeenth-century French women writers would certainly have agreed that "the letter form is central," because it was the locus for a fiction that undermined female (literary) authority. Scudéry's example proves that as early as 1640 a woman writer saw the necessity of exploiting the letter form to provide an alternative perspective on female amorous conduct. Scudéry revises the pattern developed by "amorous secretaries" like Marolles and Ogier, who won a name for themselves by appropriating the voices of women seduced and abandoned. She maintains the definition of a "lettre amoureuse" standard in her day: her missives tell again and again a familiar story of cooling ardor, followed by avoidance, ending in abandonment. She severs, however, what other writers seem to accept as the indissoluble bond between femininity and the love letter defined as the litany of complaints of the lover left behind.[60] Scudéry turns the heroinical genre on end when she makes all the authors of her amorous epistles men.

Lettres amoureuses de divers auteurs de ce temps is composed of seven series of missives, each addressed by a male correspondent to a mistress, whose replies are not included. Initially, neither is identified, and in the course of each series, author and addressee acquire the kind of names most common in contemporary fiction—Daphnis, Angélique, Cléanthe, Caliste, and so on—suggesting the stereotyping essential to Scudéry's plan. She introduces a narrative progression into each set of missives, transforming the letter manual into a proto-novel. However, the stories thus told are virtually identical. Daphnis and his counterparts beg for the affections of Angélique and her counterparts, but she does not deign to answer his pleading missives—until, that is, he writes to say that he won't bother her anymore. At this point he acknowledges receipt of a letter that reactivates first his epistolary zeal and then his pleading for attention, for in no time at all Angélique gives him new cause for complaint. The only major variation on this theme is presented by the second and third series. In each case, our correspondent goes through the familiar progression, but, rather than disappearing from view at the end of his complaints, he reappears immediately to begin the same story from the beginning—this time, however, addressing his "lettres amoureuses" to a new, but equally unresponsive, mistress. Scudéry uses the letter manual to make it clear that men can fulfill just as readily as women the passive, complaining role assigned the heroines of Ovidian epistles, that women do not have to be called away to war and affairs of state to enjoy control over the unfolding of a relationship, and finally that the allegedly female psychology developed in traditional heroinical epistles can be transferred to a male speaker without the slightest modification.

The preface to her collection bears a title, "the publisher to the reader," familiar from many early novels. But for once this authorial mask is clearly justified, for the document reveals Scudéry's understanding of both the dangerous commercial attraction of fictions of female abandonment and the complicity between secretary and publisher when they conspire to violate epistolary privacy. The preface opens with a description of the letters' origin: "These letters were not written for publication . . . lovers rather than authors wrote them. . . . Love alone dictated them." Scudéry seems to hesitate over the authorship of the letters—authors, lovers, "love alone"—in order to make it clear that the status of the letters as real or fictional correspondence was ultimately unimportant. Once their letters have been collected by a secretary, the original authors must lose their status in order to supply readers with the voyeuristic pleasure that was the epistolary compilation's greatest charm. Scudéry then evokes the issue of authorial control over such spontaneous, natural (in the sense of nonliterary) expressions of passion: "Don't accuse these lovers of having made their passions public; they had no part in this publication, and I confess that I have no other permission to expose their letters to public scrutiny than that which the King gives me."

Scudéry's letter manual thus opens with a questioning of the right of self-appointed amorous secretaries to make private missives public. Those who consider themselves Ovid's disciples, as the preface to Marolles's translation reveals, claim to be working for the defense of abandoned women, even though, by their own admission, the "scandal" provoked when the women's seduction was advertised resulted in enforced seclusion for the ladies—and authorial status for their secretaries. Scudéry aspires to no such role of defender of helpless victims—the abandoned lovers she speaks for risked, after all, no fate worse than loss of face—but she wants her readers to reflect on a matter other amorous secretaries try to cover up. The last sentence of her preface begins "don't accuse," but what follows is an implicit laying of blame that traces the chain of responsibility from correspondent to secretary to publisher, all the way to the King whose *privilège* authorizes the indiscreet publication of personal outpourings.

With the *Lettres amoureuses,* Scudéry participated in the enterprise of epistolary vandalism that was one of the seventeenth century's great commercial success stories; she did so, however, in order to expose the motivations of those who worked together to assume the voice of female passion and thereby provide a vision of the desiring female subject that was reassuring to the patriarchal order. She may have chosen to end her preface by evoking the complex process through which purloined love letters came to increase the status of those who collected them and made individual stories part of a larger scenario of unrequited love because she sensed that the new model for fictions of abandonment she was proposing would never rival the success of the Ovidian plot. Her preface concludes with the type of contract that Scudéry, an enormously prolific writer, never failed to carry out: if this volume is successful, I'll publish a second one. That no second volume of heroical love letters appeared could only have meant that Scudéry was forced by her public to accept that the future of epistolary fiction was in female abandonment alone.[61]

Madeleine de Scudéry did not give up her challenge to Ovid's authority over the development of epistolary fiction when her *Lettres amoureuses* failed to become an influential countermodel. She renewed her challenge in *Les Femmes illustres ou Les Harangues héroïques* (1642), an even more explicit attack on Ovid's heroic model. Early commentators on women's writing note the work's affinity with the polemical texts that proclaimed women's superiority, especially with the Italian tradition initiated by Boccaccio (see Thomas, 4:71–72). Recent critics tend to stress its resemblance to the volume of Manzini's *Harangues or Academic Discourses* that Scudéry's brother Georges had translated in 1640 (see Mongrédien, "Bibliographie," 2:421). Only one eighteenth-century commentator has pointed out the work's proximity to a more influential model for prose fiction: "If the component parts had been written in verse, they could be seen as so many *Heroides,* in the manner of Ovid's" (La Porte, *Histoire,* 1:256). Even La Porte, however, misunderstands the nature of Scudéry's relation to her precursor in literary heroinism. He calls the *Femmes illustres* "a collection of developments on a theme [*amplifications*], such as professors of rhetoric assign their students." La Porte sees only the primary meaning of "harangue" and proposes the *Heroides* as Scudéry's model because he assumes that she considers Ovid's fictive epistles, as have numerous commentators through the centuries, as witty exercises in rhetorical flourish, harangues or academic discourses. For Scudéry, however, the stakes involved far more than oratorical brilliance.

The *Femmes illustres* makes it clear that she uses "harangue" in a different sense, a sense admitted almost as an afterthought in seventeenth-century dictionaries (Furetière, Académie Française): a complaint in the sense of a remonstrance or protest. The work is a collection of outpourings— "harangues" renders more successfully than any notion of epistolarity the spontaneity of these texts—of women silenced, women abandoned, in traditional historical accounts. For Scudéry and her contemporaries, the *Heroides* was influential not as an exercise in rhetorical control but as a model for the recreation of spontaneous passion. The year the *Femmes illustres* appeared, the verb "improviser" entered French. It provides, as Scudéry's opening outburst demonstrates, a more appropriate synonym than "academic discourse" for her use of harangue. The first harangue features Artémise, in mourning for her beloved husband Mausole. Her speech is presented as anything but the calculated flourishes of a practiced orator. On the contrary, Scudéry portrays Artémise's initiation into eloquence, the moment at which this heroine who describes herself as having remained in her husband's shadow is moved by "the excess of her love to forget that she is speaking" (2). Under the spell of this self-forgetting, Artémise finds a voice of spontaneous eloquence—and Scudéry becomes a precursor of Staël in her attempts to recreate improvisation and recover thereby what they imagined to be an original female verb. Scudéry's harangues give a series of illustrious women the opportunity to defend themselves against what she portrays as the slanders of history. As her title indicates, these harangues are more than protests. They are "heroic" protests, self-vindications that work collectively to suggest that many women might deserve such vindication. In the course of the volume, a positive valorization of the female heroic is presented that stands in resolute opposition to the Ovidian vision of the memorable heroine as one silenced and destroyed by her grief.

Just as in her epistolary compilation, in the *Femmes illustres* Scudéry refuses to display heroic women as authors of "lettres amoureuses." Her illustrious women, the women she proposes as heroines, write not to win pity for their suffering or to win back a delinquent lover, but to leave their mark on history. Like Ovid's, Scudéry's volume ends with a first-person outpouring imagined for Sappho, the first fiction in any language of Sappho as writer.[62] For this response to the Ovidian image of Sapphic poetic creation, Scudéry portrays her Sapho in full possession of her literary gift, addressing her younger disciple, Erinne, with an "exhortation," a plea to follow her literary example and become a poet.[63] This Sapho writes for her female friends and consciously seeks to found a female literary tradition. Sapho condemns the philosophy behind the rescripting of her poetry, a process initiated by Catullus and continued by poets such as Ronsard. Ronsard uses Sapphic poetry to script a *carpe diem* contract: the beautiful woman who is the object of the poet's desire has only to respond to his affections, and he will immortalize her ephemeral charms in his poetry. According to Scudéry's Sapho, the reader of such poetry "admires more the poets' imagination than the beauty [of the women]; their copies are taken for the originals" (438). Rather than passively accepting this imperfect immortality that preserves them only through the transforming filter of the male poet's desire, women should "find their own glory in themselves"; they should win immortality for themselves by proving their literary ability.[64] The harangue is an "exhortation" to all women to follow Sappho's literary example and to surpass her by reaching new heights of literary greatness (436).[65] The harangue was only the initial step toward the creation of the first original French fiction of Sappho.

Recovering a Mother Tongue (2)
The New Heroic Novel

The *Femmes illustres* was published early in Scudéry's career as a novelist, immediately after the shortest and the least typical of her novels, *Ibrahim ou l'illustre Bassa* (1641). It was her second, and final, attempt to develop the epistolary form that her contemporaries associated with Sappho's voice. When the *Femmes illustres,* like the *Lettres amoureuses* before it, failed to generate a new prose tradition, Scudéry embarked, this time definitively, on the generic avenue she first explored in *Ibrahim.* Despite her ultimate turning away from the epistolary form, Scudéry's discovery of Sappho, and in particular her decision to make Sappho an advocate for women's writing and to cast her in a generative role with respect to a female tradition, had a decisive impact on the evolution of both Scudéry's fiction and French prose fiction in general. In particular, Scudéry uses Sappho to realign historical fiction, to turn it away from the epic tradition over which Homer served as the presiding deity. When in the *Femmes illustres* Scudéry recuperates Sappho's voice for women writers, this is the first indication of the feminization of prose fiction for which she would eventually be responsible, a telling shift in the early development of the French novel away from tales "of arms and the man" that won for her an enormous readership and that may well have been the key factor in the articulation of what we now recognize as the modern novel.

In the *Femmes illustres,* Scudéry leaves Sappho's life a virtual blank; the reference to Erinna is the only indication that she had access to any information not found in Ovid's epistle. In the final volume of *Artamène,* published some ten years later, Scudéry introduces Sappho as a character for a second time and gives over the conclusion of her most extensive fiction to her, at the expense of the characters who had dominated its action for nine volumes. This time, she paints a fiction of Sappho remarkable both for its complexity and for the rigor of its documentation. Even though recently critics have begun to stress the thoroughness of Scudéry's historical documentation, it is never pointed out that her portrait of Sappho revises prior fictions of her life and that every detail of it is based on ancient commentaries on Sappho. The most remarkable aspect of Scudéry's erudition is the fact that it was accumulated in the absence of a French-language tradition of Sappho scholarship. Working over a decade before Le Fèvre's *Abrégé,* nearly thirty years before his daughter's "Life of Sapho," she was obliged to compile on her own biographical information not included by Ovid and, since she knew no classical language, to have these texts translated by her friends. Scudéry deserves therefore the title of Sappho's original French biographer. Significantly, the only acknowledgment of the quality of her contribution came from outside the French tradition. In the early eighteenth century, the foremost early Sappho scholar, Christian Wolff, treats her fiction as scholarship and reserves his highest praise not for any previous editor but for Madeleine de Scudéry for having described in *Le Grand Cyrus* "the accomplishments and the loves of Sappho with great elegance" (v).

The extent of Scudéry's knowledge of previous attempts to reconstruct Sappho's life is generally ignored because her portrait of Sappho has traditionally been read solely as a self-portrait. While only self-recognition in the facts and the legends of Sappho's life could explain the thoroughness of her documentation, Scudéry's portrait is most remarkable because of her painstaking effort to tell her own story only as it can be told through Sappho's, and thereby to suggest that her Sapho could serve as an example for future literary women. To this end, she stresses those elements that her life and Sappho's, as it was presented in the sources available to her, have in common—both were orphaned at an early age; both had only one brother; both were dark, and neither was known for her beauty, although both were redeemed by their vivacity and by certain charms, such as "brilliant" eyes and graceful hands, shown to their best advantage in a conversational situation (*Artamène,* 10:332).[66] This resemblance established, Scudéry proceeds to translate her Greek precursor into the ideal image of the French literary woman of the mid-seventeenth century.

Scudéry's fiction attempts to reverse previous reconfigurations of Sappho's poetry of desire. She defines Sapphic writing as an exchange among women, and she rescripts Sappho's life by proposing an alternative ending to the suicide of an abandoned woman. Nevertheless, I am unable to make the claim that would be most telling for the history of fictions of sexual propriety in France, that Scudéry plainly inscribes her Sapho's rejection of heterosexual relationships. It is possible that such a position would have been irreconcilable with the widespread acceptance Scudéry consistently tried to win for women's writing, a theory supported by the occultation of the seventeenth-century testimonies to sapphism that we have already discussed.[67] In this context, it is important to remember that

104

Scudéry seems to have succeeded in promoting both her view of Sappho's artistic centrality and her own identification with Sappho without appearing, in her own person, in the least threatening to contemporary structures of propriety. Early commentators point out time and again that Scudéry was known as Sapho because, in La Forge's words, in seventeenth-century France her intellectual position "equaled Sappho's in Lesbos." They then never fail to note, as La Forge did, that Scudéry "eclipsed [Sappho] with her virtue" (13).[68] It may be that this immediate disclaimer of Scudéry's sexual attraction to the Sapphic model covers up the commentator's confusion, or even embarrassment, over the evocation of a notorious woman writer as literary patron. In any event, this recourse to denegation has foreclosed recognition of the, for her time, enormously equivocal sexual scenario Scudéry proposes as the context for Sapphic literary creation.[69]

When Scudéry is read closely, it becomes clear that the French Sappho's position on sexuality and in particular on her precursor's sexuality is hardly so straightforward as it is generally considered. Even while she refuses to risk scandalizing her contemporary public, Scudéry consistently tries to reaffirm both the primacy of female relationships and the concomitant subordination of heterosexual bonds in Sappho's literary universe, and even to foster a certain ambiguity with regard to the sexual significance of this hierarchy. Thus, for example, she alters the name of Sappho's father, manipulating the historically verifiable "Scamandronymus," "named for the river Scamander" (the chief river of the Trojan plane), with a deformation so slight that commentators have failed to notice it, into "Scamandrogine" (10:330), an appellation that casts suspicion on paternal legitimacy at the same time that it creates doubt about the sexual placement of the androgyne's offspring.[70] This ambiguity is reinforced by Scudéry's presentation of Sapho's genealogy. The narrator of her story, Democède, announces that he will tell us "something of [Sapho's] *condition*" (330, my emphasis). The word simply refers to her social status, but it takes on new implications when followed by a clause that defines her "condition" as being the daughter of an androgyne. The end of the sentence repeats this pattern of genealogical stability undermined with a hint of deviance, a pattern equivalent to denegation: Scamandrogine's family has the "longest line of ancestors, the most illustrious and least *doubtful* genealogy" (330, my emphasis). Even while it establishes the paternal androgyne's blood lines, the passage nevertheless serves to undermine the stability of the familial description. Although it is denied, the specter of genealogical doubtfulness has been raised, providing the kind of hint of sexual instability that Scudéry weaves into her novelistic fabric so subtly that the overall design remains unthreatening.

Scudéry's portrayal of the sexual orientation of Sappho's poetry is more complex still. In Scudéry's revision, Sapho is constantly surrounded by four female friends—Amithone, Erinne, Cydnon, Athys—so close that they are described as the "inseparables" (340).[71] Indeed, when we meet her, Sapho's entire affective world is feminocentric. In any reference to her friends—and I do not have in mind allusions to the "inseparables," but simple collective expressions like "[Sapho] always had time for her friends" (336)—the object of Sapho's affection is never the grammatically dominant and therefore expected "amis," but always the feminine plural "amies." All of her poetry is addressed to these "inseparable" friends, and Scudéry seems to make no attempt to hide the nature of that verse. Phaon, who finds a place in her account as one of Sapho's suitors, discovers some of these poems, and we learn of their content through his reactions. In one poem, "he found things so moving, so tender, and so passionate that his heart was touched by his reading" (455). His reaction to "a poem that Sapho had written about a jealousy of friendship [*une jalousie d'amitié*] between Athys and Amithone" appears further to clarify the situation: "their jealousy had the true stamp of love" (456). Phaon is subsequently driven to his own excess of jealousy because he recognizes the authenticity of the strong passion he notes in these poems. However, it never occurs to him that the poems could really be, as we, and he, are repeatedly told that they are, addressed to other women: the only explanation he ever considers for the presence of such "ardor" is the existence of a *male* rival who has already taught Sapho the meaning of love. Scudéry eventually seems to resolve any confusion that may exist in the reader's mind by having Sapho address to Phaon a loose translation of fr. 31 into the idiom devised by literary women of her day, *préciosité* (472–73). Even this apparent victory of heterosexual object choice is counterbalanced, however, by the new ending she decrees for the legendary relationship between woman writer and man of the world.[72]

Scudéry makes it plain that the Phaon character has his roots in legend by recounting what she terms the "fable" of Phaon as Aphrodite's boatman (372–73). More important, even though she ultimately pays lip service to the code governing novelistic propriety in her day by allowing Phaon to supplant the "inseparable" women at the center of Sapho's affective life, Scudéry grants this substitution only on the condition that

Phaon be consigned to a permanently subordinate status in a feminocentric economy and, furthermore, that he agree to his displacement. Sapho sets up the terms on which she accepts Phaon's suit. Most crucially, she agrees to live with him only if he promises never even to mention marriage to her. Sapho thereby guarantees that she will never be submitted to the "long slavery" (343) that is woman's legal status in marriage and, moreover, that their love will survive: "in order to love each other forever with no loss of ardor, it is necessary never to marry" (607). Since their society would not accept such a situation, Sapho obliges Phaon to "retire" with her to the land of the Sauromates—according to Herodotus, the home of the Amazons. Scudéry portrays their country as what feminist thought of her day would have defined as a utopia, a domain governed by a queen, in which courts of love both regulate the economy of desire and give legal status to unions outside of marriage.[73]

The journey to the realm of the Amazons, like all voyages into utopia, is long and arduous. Scudéry has Sapho and Phaon stop along the way to admire a temple of Apollo built at the top of the White Rock of Leukas. Their tourism allows her to explain the origin of the story of Sappho's suicidal leap from this cliff. After her departure from Mytilène, her relatives discover that Sapho has left a will disposing of her possessions. She had done so, Scudéry explains, because she knew that they would be of no use to her in the land of the Sauromates, but her relatives invent another explanation for her gesture. When they learn that she has been sighted on the White Rock of Leukas, they decide that she had gone there, like other lovers in antiquity, to throw herself into the sea "to cure herself of her passion" for Phaon (603). Scudéry explains that, given all that was known about Sappho's character, such a belief was totally "implausible" (*invraisemblable*) (604, 605), but that "the masses" (*le peuple*) are so fond of "extraordinary" stories that they choose them over more "credible" explanations. Unlike Ovid's abandoned woman, Scudéry's Sapho suffers no physical humiliation because of her love for a man. On the contrary, Phaon is faithful to her because she retains control over the plot of her passion. In the Amazons' desert state, Sapho realizes the classic dream of numerous heroines of early women's novels, when she is obliged to give up neither Phaon nor her "peace of mind" (*repos*) (608). Nor does this Sappho pay for her love with any loss of authorial status: safe within the confines of utopia, Sapho continues "to write every day" (608).

This rescripting of the Sappho legend seems explicitly intended to discredit the fiction of the sexually pitiable woman. Scudéry's Sapphic vision is in fact permeated with fictions of the feminine, in particular with fictions of the woman writer. Scudéry continues the tradition of the doubling fictions consistently invented for Sappho in antiquity. For her other Sappho, Scudéry even builds on a legend initiated in antiquity and recorded by Philostratus: "A clever woman named Damophyla was said to have had girl companions just like Sappho, and to have composed love poems just as she did" (*Life of Apollonius of Tyana,* 1.30). On the basis of this legend fragment, Scudéry creates a double for her Sapho who allows her to exorcise both the image of the "ridiculous *précieuse*" as promoted, most prominently, by her contemporary Molière and the Ovidian vision of the woman writer in abandonment. The legends of the two Sapphos circulated in antiquity created in various ways a distinction between disreputable or destructive sexuality and poetic genius. Scudéry's doubling fiction distinguishes between serious and parodic presentations of the literary woman.

Her Damophile should not be confused with the madwomen that, as Gilbert and Gubar have shown, nineteenth-century English women novelists shut up in attics in an attempt to displace their "own anxiety and rage" and to distance their heroines from the threat of female excess (78). Unlike the figures in the doubling fictions they analyze, Damophile is not Scudéry's specular image, her denied self-portrait. She is instead her recreation of the male intellectual's projection of his female counterpart. Damophile tries so hard to make herself an exact replica of Sapho that she comes to be known as "the Sapho of her neighborhood" (350), or "the copy of Sapho" (376). Damophile has decided to "act the part of the learned woman" (*faire la savante*) (350). Rather than a perfect imitation of Sapho, Damophile is "foolishly learned," "a ridiculous learned [woman]" (352). She shapes herself according to male expectations of intellectual women, until she is identical to the parodic fictions of seventeenth-century literary women circulated by Molière and Boileau, among others.[74]

Damophile should not be taken for Scudéry's attempt to save a group of women considered superior intellectuals from ridicule at the expense of other, less talented literary women. She is a projection of the fears of men like Phaon. Scudéry accomplishes the ultimate exposure of Sapho's double as a male fiction by means of a vestmental exchange. When she learns that Sapho has agreed to sit for her portrait, Damophile immediately commissions a large portrait of herself for which she chooses to be "dressed as the muses are painted." The false Sapho, in other words, dresses for posterity in garments stolen from Sappho, known from antiquity as the tenth muse. Confronted with this portrait of the woman artist as male phantasm, Sapho decides to have her portrait painted "dressed as the shepherdess Oenone"—to appear, that is, in clothing taken from another of the forsaken women who cries out in the *Heroides* (the fifth epistle), and to assume the attributes of abandonment in which the desiring woman was presented to the mid–seventeenth-century public (447). Sapho is "laughing" when she decides on her costume, and no sooner is the portrait completed than Phaon makes it plain that clothes do not an abandoned woman make: "Rest assured that you will never know [Oenone's] fate, just because you wear her attire: for it is impossible, if you ever loved someone, that the one you loved would abandon you" (449). With this scene of parodic transvestism, Scudéry exposes as a fiction what was to become her century's dominant image of Sappho. She also causes her reader to suspect an awareness that her own Sapphic portrait, despite a documentation unequaled by even the most respected early modern Hellenists, also used Sappho to promote a fiction of the feminine.

Scudéry's Sapho is a poet, but she also writes in prose (333). With her characterization of Sapho's proto-novelistic art, Scudéry foreshadows Tanneguy Le Fèvre's definition of the original Sappho's genius as "that secret and admirable art of getting into hearts, . . . of touching the tenderest passions" (22). Sapho "knows so well how to recreate the anatomy of an amorous heart that she knows how to describe exactly all the jealousies, all the anxieties, . . . all the joys, . . . all the hopes . . . that are only accurately understood by those who have felt them [themselves]" (334). When Scudéry endows Sapho with the ability to understand "l'anatomie d'un coeur amoureux," she realizes in fiction the vision promoted by the Le Fèvres of Sappho as the origin of the modern novel; she has Sappho prefigure the genius of seventeenth-century French women novelists. In particular, Sapho defines as her artistic territory the field that Scudéry herself marked off as her novelistic property. The first historians of French women's writing recognize as the essence of Scudéry's talent her "extensive knowledge of the human heart" (Alletz, 1:323); recent historians of the novel point to her "minute analysis of the human heart" as the origin of the immense influence she exercised over subsequent French novelists (Showalter, 28–29).[75] Scudéry develops Sapho's story in such detail because she uses it as a *mise en abyme* of the model she imagined for the novel. She uses Sapho to authorize a prototype for prose fiction that takes its plot beyond marriage, beyond traditionally defined novelistic space, even beyond the novel as novelists, including Scudéry herself, had previously defined it.

Scudéry rejects marriage as a possibility for Sapho, even the story widely accepted in antiquity and repeated by Ovid of an early union, from which a daughter Cleis was born. Her decision to have Sapho and Phaon live together outside marriage, while it marks the end of Sapho's presence in *Artamène,* was ultimately the decisive use of the original woman writer for the future of the French novel. Scudéry uses Sappho to initiate a new female plot for the novel: the process by which woman rejects marriage, and the story of the life she creates for herself outside marriage. A seventeenth-century opponent of French women novelists, Valincour, condemns Scudéry's model as "conspiratorial" (339): in the new novelistic economy she initiates and later novelists, most notably Staël, develop, heroines lead the way and take heroes away from their paternal estates, beyond the novelistic spaces charted by men for male adventures designed to reinforce and prolong the patriarchal order, and into lands under female control, domains dedicated to the continuing exploration of Sapho's "amorous anatomy."[76]

Ritual Murder

> This is a conscientious study in which I have tried to make live—and die—she who was Sapphô; my study could even be entitled "The Punishment of Sapphô."
>
> —G.-A. Faure,
> *La Dernière journée de Sapphô*

Sainte-Beuve, characterizing what he terms a "pastoral nuance" of the early French tradition exemplified by Scudéry's novels, concludes that "the good sense of Louis XIV, aided by Boileau, tidied up . . . this moment in French literature" (13). Boileau certainly did his best to curtail what he saw as Scudéry's threat to the heroic model: "Is it love that has now become the measure of heroic virtue?" he has Diogenes inquire in his *Dialogue des héros de roman* (476). That Boileau understood the importance of the challenge posed by his century's revival of Sappho and by her presentation as model for women writers can be deduced from his creation of a fiction of Scudéry that disposes of the French Sappho, and even Scudéry's fiction of Sappho, as neatly as the Ovidian model had eliminated her classical precursor. His first canonic gesture, a decade before his edition of "Longinus" and his *Art poétique,* originated in his desire to efface from French literary history the novel and the threat of female literary primacy then synonymous with this form. Boileau's awareness that such an impulse lay behind his ambition to set himself up as judge and arbiter of literary taste, as well as his desire to keep this knowledge secret, are revealed by the compositional fiction with which he persistently surrounded the text that was the foundation of his critical authority.

Allusions to contemporary events make it clear that Boileau's parodic *Dialogue des héros de roman* was composed in 1664–66, at a time when Scudéry still enjoyed great renown and when the model she had invented for prose fiction still dominated the novelistic horizon. However, in a preface composed when he prepared the dialogue for publication shortly before his death in 1711, Boileau points out that until that time, he had not even committed it to paper but had preserved it "in [his] memory" where, although in poor health and at nearly seventy-four years of age, he had been able simply to "recover" it (446). As he explains it, this unusual authorial strategy was employed to avoid "distressing a girl [*une fille*, an unmarried woman] who, after all, had a great deal of merit" (445). The "girl" in question is identified—just as, in the preface to his edition of "Longinus," Boileau would later identify Sappho's other major female sponsor in seventeenth-century France, Anne Le Fèvre Dacier— as "Mlle de Scudéry, sister of the author with the same name" (444), as though her literary merits derived exclusively from her family ties. Boileau does not justify Scudéry's alleged worth: her novels "teach bad morals"; she herself had "more honesty than intelligence" (445). "Nevertheless," he waited to make his dialogue public until "*at last* death had struck her off the list of humans" (445, my emphasis). Boileau also points out that his charity has cost him authorial status: his dialogue's best parodic moments will never again be appreciated, for the literary production of this worthy woman, the two novels (*Artamène* and *Clélie*) that are the primary targets of his parody, has already "fallen into oblivion" (*tombé dans l'oubli*) (446).

The man who by 1711 was already accepted as "the arbiter of literary taste" would have us believe that he had finally consented to the dialogue's publication only after Scudéry's death. Significantly, however, his dialogue can be seen as driven toward the symbolic recreation of Scudéry's death or, on the model of the "leap" Ovid devised for Sappho, of her ritual murder. In the dialogue, Boileau's counterparts in the afterlife, the judges of the underworld Pluto and Phèdre's father Minos, condemn Scudéry's most successful characters on a charge that her pale imitations of the great heroes of antiquity have taken on the names and the trappings of illustrious dead men no longer able to defend themselves against her defamations. In their judgment, Scudéry has emasculated the proudest classical heroes, making them so "pretty" that they have become "the most foppish [*dameret*] and gallant sight imaginable" (452; see also 462, 467). Her deformation of the classic male heroic is condemned as a form of madness: Minos declares that all journeys across Scudéry's amorous thoroughfares destine the reader for the *Petites maisons* (madhouse) (464). These arbiters of literary taste warn that this mad effeminacy is a threat to the patriarchal order. In her novels, Scudéry's heroes forget war and the affairs of state to concentrate, like Ovid, on "private battles" and "amorous campaigns" (456). Boileau's judges condemn as "morally dangerous" the view of history that focuses attention on the crucial roles played by women.

Boileau's title refers only to "the heroes of novels," even though most of the dialogue is devoted to a parody of Scudéry's heroines.[77] Boileau uses its longest section for his scornful dismissal of Scudéry's female heroic. As the editors of the Pléiade edition of Boileau's works point out (1094–95, n. 14), the hideously grotesque portrait of the "illustre fille" Tisiphone that Boileau has his Sapho read in his dialogue (473–74) is a line-by-line parody of the portrait of Sapho in *Artamène* (10:332–33). Since this portrait of Sapho is simultaneously Scudéry's self-portrait and a portrait of the original woman writer, Boileau's disfigured Tisiphone attempts to eliminate the fiction of the feminine created in an attempt to encourage the development of women's writing.

Boileau's parody culminates in an elaborately staged ritual killing, Scudéry's punishment for her crimes against the (literary) state. The shades of Scudéry's ersatz literary creations are first "stripped" (*dépouillés,* a word Boileau repeats four times) of their deceptive clothing, "whipped" (*abondamment fustigués*) and then plunged "head first" into "the deepest part of the river Lethe" (218). "The mountains of ridiculous paper on which their stories are written" are tossed in after them. Lest their function as stand-ins be missed, moreover, the heroes cry out "in chorus" as they are led to their second death "Ah! Scudéry!" Boileau could have avoided inscribing the name of his adversary into his text—as he did in his imitation of Horace, the *Art poétique,* when he ridiculed *Clélie* without naming its author (171)—for he had already made the status of the heroes clear by calling them "phantoms" (485). Like the straw effigies (known as "fantômes") used in the seventeenth century to carry out symbolic executions when the criminal could not be found, Boileau chose for the shades the fate he hoped thereby to decree, if not for their author, for her literary production.[78] With the leap into water to which he condemned her Sapho, Boileau hoped to consign Scudéry to abandonment, to a literary fate parallel to the physical abandonment chosen for Sappho in the Ovidian model.

As Georges May points out, Boileau's claim that the novels he parodied in the dialogue were already "forgotten" by the time of its publication was blatantly erroneous: "Everything indicates on the contrary that these novels still held on for long years to an enthusiastic readership" (*Dilemme*, 21), a counterclaim supported by the memoirs of many major eighteenth-century novelists. The decree prematurely consigning Scudéry's works to the river of oblivion that closes Boileau's preface and is repeated at the end of his dialogue betrays his goal in finally authorizing its publication. Scudéry had been dead since 1701; had Boileau simply been waiting until she was no longer able to defend herself, the parody could have appeared much sooner. The editors of the Pléiade edition point out, for example, that he had refused to consent to its publication in 1707 (1090). Boileau's scornful attack in *L'Art poétique* in 1674 had eliminated neither Scudéry's name nor her feminocentric novel from the annals of French literature. A premonition of his own impending death may have prompted an eleventh-hour renewed attempt to revise the official presentation of the novel's early history.

The authorized version of the *Dialogue des héros de roman* which finally appeared in 1713 was prepared from a manuscript Boileau confided just before his death to Billiot, the publisher who served as his literary executor. The dialogue can be seen as Boileau's literary last will and testament, and also as proof that the career of the principal architect of the shape of French literature that the French educational system continues to pass on even today was unified by the desire to eradicate female literary primacy. The leap into water, as we have seen, was a form of death frequently chosen in antiquity for the scapegoat. Boileau's deathbed wish was to "strike [Scudéry's name] from the list of [French writers]" (445). The fall into Lethe of Scudéry's phantom figures the elimination of the original women novelists from the canon dictated by the heroes of classicism.

Boileau's attempt to cover up his lifelong preoccupation with the threat of female literary authority was exposed even before the dialogue's official publication by one of Scudéry's heirs, Marie-Jeanne L'Héritier, niece of Boileau's enemy Perrault. The elaborate chronological fiction laid out in the preface to the *Dialogue des héros de roman* seems even more devious when one considers that the work had been published twice while Scudéry was still alive (in 1688 and 1693—even if, as the editors of the Pléiade edition contend, those editions appeared "without Boileau's consent" [1090]). The dialogue's initial publication prompted a quick response in the form of a combined attack on Boileau and defense of women writers by L'Héritier, whose translation of the *Heroides* (1732) would subsequently reveal her to be a student of both Le Fèvre Dacier's and Scudéry's visions of Sappho.[79] Her *Le Triomphe de madame Deshoulières, reçue dixième muse au Parnasse* (1694) is a celebration of the only seventeenth-century literary woman besides Scudéry whose talent was recognized by an award from the Académie Française. Deshoulières's "triumph" is her literary apotheosis, the coronation ceremony in which the inhabitants of Parnassus welcome her into their ranks. It is a ritual crowning echoing scenes in Scudéry's novels in which an entire city turns out to pay homage to one of her heroines—scenes that Staël recreates for her heroine's entrance in *Corinne*. L'Héritier passes the history of women's writing in review when she lists the literary women from various epochs, notably Sappho, gathered along Deshoulières's path to receive her into their assembly.

In L'Héritier's vision of the literary afterworld, just as in Boileau's, ritual ceremony is preceded by an act of judgment. Minos is called in for the trial of "a new type of misanthrope, who during his life was the irreconcilable enemy of women" (7). He decrees that the misanthrope's punishment will be "to receive from Cerberus as many bites as his slanderous tongue had hurled abusive gibes against women" (8). In the course of the coronation ceremony that follows the trial, it becomes clear that the nameless misanthrope is none other than Boileau. During the procession, the nymph of satire refuses to give her hand to Boileau because of his attacks on women (15). Indeed, at the ceremony's conclusion it is evident that this apotheosis of literary women functions above all as a warning to Boileau that his murderous fictions will not stem the rising tide of female literary influence. L'Héritier proclaims that Boileau "pours his ugly venom on this dear sex in vain"; "he storms out and thunders against [women] in vain" (22–23). In the vision of the literary day of judgment that L'Héritier sets in opposition to Boileau's, the female literary origin will not be struck off the face of French literary history as long as women writers join together to oppose the decree consigning their works to oblivion.

*

By the seventeenth century, as a result of nearly a century of struggle for control over the discourse of passion with which her name was synonymous, Sappho's *oeuvre* had passed as it were into the public domain. There it represented either the pitiful cries of woman seduced and abandoned or the forceful expression of women's right to literary authority. In reality, a choice between these two opposing fictions had already been made by the dawn of the Enlightenment. For nearly a century, Sappho was, for the only time in her modern history, no longer a subject of controversy. She was instead an ever more sexually pitiable woman, a conduit for the male poetic bonding that protected Boileau's standards and eventually erased every trace of rival literary models.[80]

2 Sappho's Family Romances (1697–1818)

The Promiscuous Mother

I've always been suspicious of the hearts and minds of women.
— François Gacon
(Le Poète Sans Fard)

Freud entitles "family romance" his fiction of the fictions that the (male) child invents in order to free himself from the authority of his parents and take his place in the patriarchal order.[1] He distinguishes between two phases in this primal fabulation: an initial, asexual phase during which the child in his fantasies replaces his parents with others of a higher social station, followed by a sexual phase during which the child imagines only his father replaced by one of superior birth, with whom his mother had engaged in an adulterous love affair. In *Roman des origines et origines du roman,* Marthe Robert uses Freud's model as the basis for her typology of the early novel. To Freud's asexual romances, she juxtaposes the utopian novel (*Don Quixote* is her paradigm) in which the orphaned hero tries to remake the world. To Freud's sexual fantasies, Robert compares the novel's realistic strain (in this case, *Robinson Crusoe* is her Ur-text), in which the hero, a bastard, strives to conquer the world. Had Robert taken the eighteenth-century French novel as the basis for her typology, she might have come to different conclusions. As has often been remarked, French prose fiction of the Enlightenment is more often feminocentric than its English counterpart. An important strain of its feminocentrism involves fantasies of the mother and motherhood.

In *Sexe et liberté au siècle des Lumières,* Théodore Tarczylo links the promotion of myths of the family and motherhood in the French eighteenth century to the fear of depopulation that he sees as an increasingly important phenomenon throughout the second half of the century. Others would situate the origin of this panic about depopulation somewhat earlier: the end of Louis XIV's reign at the dawn of the

116

eighteenth century, a period characterized by the proliferation of progressively more ambitious wars, is often cited as an origin. At this time, a new fiction of Sappho begins to be promoted, the first centered on her family roles as wife, mother, young widow. This fiction, like all major Sapphic fictions and like all influential fictions of the feminine, is reversible: Sappho is alternately a figure of happy, bourgeois maternity and an exemplar of depraved motherhood. Collectively, these visions of Sappho's family life correspond to the sexual phase of Freud's family romances: they simultaneously reinforce paternal superiority and promote an image of maternal promiscuity. Just as was the case for the seventeenth century, the negative face of this coin is ultimately dominant: the eighteenth century replaces the image of Sappho as sexually pitiable woman with the figure of Sappho as woman of easy virtue.

Throughout the century and without exception, that dissolute virtue is heterosexual. *The* man clung to in the seventeenth century to replace Sappho's own fiction of *any*man is replaced by a series of men to whom Sappho is bound by a variety of affective ties. The eighteenth century's capital Sapphic fictions are perhaps most striking because of the total silence with regard to the issue of sapphism. This avoidance of the traditionally most troublesome image of Sapphism would seem to support the position developed by Michel Foucault in *The History of Sexuality* that sexuality began to be morally problematic in the early eighteenth century. Certainly, at no time in their history have fictions of Sappho been less controversial. Witness the preface to Anne de La Roche-Guilhen's turn-of-the-century *Sapho ou l'heureuse inconstance* (1695, 1706): "The only recommendation a work needs is its title. . . . The name of Sappho is celebrated among scholars and even among women [*le beau sexe*]." La Roche-Guilhen uses "the name of Sappho" to "recommend" a true "lady's novel," according to George Eliot's expression: an early brush with Phaon's "inconstancy" is a "happy" experience because Sapho goes on to marry and become the mother of a daughter. At the dawn of the Enlightenment, thanks undoubtedly to the success of the fiction of her sexual pitifulness, Sappho's name had become so pure that it could be used to publicize the kind of tale of bourgeois maternal bliss that would later win the approval of Rousseau and Diderot the moralist.

How can we reconcile this turn-of-the-century vision of her morally correct maternity with the decree, some seventy years later, consigning Sappho's poetry to destruction by fire in Louis Sébastien Mercier's 1770 utopian vision, *L'An 2440*? In the chapter "The Royal Library," the librarian explains to Mercier's narrator that, "with unanimous approval," "we" had burned all books deemed "dangerous" to human "understanding." Among ancient authors, only four are chosen for this reenactment of the destruction of the library of Alexandria: Anacreon, Aristophanes, Herodotus—and Sappho (158). Faced with this condemnation, one might imagine that Sappho's poetry had, in the course of the eighteenth century, remained distinct from her person, still dangerous when her image had been neutralized, but we will see that this is not the case. The contradiction between these two Sapphos could also suggest a hypothesis far more difficult to demonstrate: the eighteenth century may have continuously reaffirmed Sappho's heterosexuality because the fear of her sapphism had not been eradicated.

It would be tempting to measure this hypothesis against evidence of an actual contemporary tradition of female homosexuality. However, the only surviving documents are difficult, perhaps impossible, to interpret. Jacob Stockinger contends that the proclamations of the philosophes brought about a greater tolerance for homosexuality in the course of the eighteenth century: "France had gone from the last public burning of a homosexual in 1784 to placing homosexuality on a more or less equal basis with heterosexuality in the constitution of 1791" (175). It is perhaps the moment to point out that, as Jeffrey Weeks stresses, the histories of male and female homosexuality are often divergent (281, n. 83). In this instance, when one examines the only evidence that Stockinger offers for the existence of a female tradition in the age of Enlightenment, it is tempting to conclude that in eighteenth-century France, homosexuality was not only an aristocratic privilege, as Stockinger admits, but a *male* privilege as well.

Stockinger's only source of information on a putative female homosexual tradition is a 1909 volume, *La Raucourt et ses amies,* by Jean de Reuilly (published under the pseudonym Vial). Despite its subtitle, *Etude historique des moeurs saphiques au 18ᵉ siècle,* designed to advertise its seriousness, Reuilly's study immediately reveals itself to be not history but what the French call *petite histoire,* a tale of gossip and rumors intended for titillation rather than information. By the end of my third chapter, readers will recognize Reuilly's volume as a perfect example of the lavishly antisapphic productions inspired by the late nineteenth-century tradition of "medical" commentary on female homosexuality. The fin-de-siècle works I have in mind make an ornate display of sapphism in order to profit commercially from the scandal surrounding its contemporary visibility.

Thus Reuilly concludes his initial chapter by linking the eighteenth century to his own day: "Famous lesbians are legion, but it is above all in the eighteenth century that they demonstrated publicly the scandal of their depravation" (11).

The principal sources on which Reuilly bases this allegation are eighteenth-century texts, to be discussed in this chapter, that I would not hesitate to classify as fictional. They are, in addition, the first precursors of the tradition to which Reuilly belongs, purveyors of lightly pornographic, titillating scandal. In addition, to prove the existence of a network of lesbian secret societies, "more mysterious than those of the Freemasons" (13), Reuilly cites Friedrich Melchior Grimm's *Correspondance littéraire*, a more respectable source, but one not entirely unrelated to the nineteenth-century texts of ever wider circulation that testify to that age's enormous fascination with an increasingly complex fiction of the lesbian. And, no more than I would take the scandal sheets that promoted, for example, wild tales of George Sand's sexual exploits for reality, would I draw conclusions about an actual female homosexual tradition during the French Enlightenment from Grimm's remarks. At most, I would cite Grimm's decision to circulate these tales to the elite pan-European public for which his *Correspondance littéraire* was destined as the first indication of the broad commercial appeal that fictions of sapphism were destined to enjoy from the 1840s to the 1930s.

In France, the eighteenth century may well be the period during which the rhetoric of prejudice—anti-Semitic, homophobic, and so on—is least evident. We could take this absence for a confirmation of the century's traditional image as the age of free thought. However, after having explored the period's Sapphic speculation, I am left with a nagging sense that this may be a hasty conclusion. In the case of Sappho, if the eighteenth century is relatively untouched by antisapphic prejudice, why is so much creative energy devoted to making certain that she will not regain a homosexual identity?

*

After the seventeenth century's complicated Sapphic chronology, the building of the eighteenth century's image is remarkably straightforward and untroubled. In the history of Sappho's involvement with French literature, no other period presents such a unified face: throughout the century, a single vision reigns unchallenged. Because of the uncontested hegemony of the tradition developing a heterosexual plot for the original woman writer, it is possible to retrace virtually every step in the creation of the Enlightenment's Sappho, to evaluate both the sources and the contribution of each writer. This unbroken, rational development was the most unexpected discovery of all my research on Sappho. In the history of the French Sapphic involvement, the eighteenth century—the age of Laclos, Restif de la Bretonne, Sade, not to mention numerous authors of erotic texts far less concerned with literary effects—appears without question the period of the most limited, and the most conventional, sexual imagination.

Writers of the age refuse to grant the most controversial Sapphic plot—Sappho as lover of women rather than men—textual status even as a subject for prurient speculation. Numerous pornographic novels feature a lesbian plot. Some, like the two works that are the basis for Reuilly's study, *La Nouvelle Sapho, ou Histoire de la secte anandryne* included in *L'Espion anglais* (1778) and the short story "Sapho ou les Lesbiennes," included in V.J.E. de Jouy's *La Galerie des Femmes* (1799), even feature a namesake of the original woman writer. However, these fictions are sapphic without being Sapphic: they use Sappho's name but pay no attention to the tradition of Sapphic speculation. It is as if the writers of the age of Enlightenment were collectively unwilling to admit the possibility of even the slightest hint of the sexual and therefore of the narrative deviance many of their seventeenth-century precursors had still connected with the original woman writer. Throughout the eighteenth century, "Sapho" referred either to a heterosexual poet authorized by an ever more complex tradition of biographical speculation, or to a lesbian heroine whose adventures were either completely fictional or an *à clef* fiction based, as Grimm and others would have us believe, on the lives of contemporary women. Before the late nineteenth century, the two traditions—fictions of Sappho and fictions of the lesbian—were never to intersect.

The sexual conservatism of the Enlightenment's Sapphic speculation is reinforced by its political conservatism. Eighteenth-century French Hellenists invent a political Sappho, exiled because of her role in an attempted revolution on Lesbos. This fiction predates the French political activity of the end of the century but, significantly, is never made to foreshadow it. The poets of the Revolution refuse to recognize in as controversial a figure as Sappho a precursor of their politically subversive activities. Their consignment of the hapless, heterosexual Sappho to the right wing of the political arena seems initially a superfluous gesture. The potential of this political placement is first exploited during the Napoleonic period and is only truly realized in the early twentieth century in fictions such as *La Dernière Journée de Sapphô* (1901) in which the Barrès protégé G.-A. Faure initially displays his heroine's sapphism with fin-de-siècle lushness and then brutalizes her to make her atone for the sin of sexual deviance. Nowhere is the ideological importance of this decadent Sappho more explicit than in Larnac and Salmon's 1934 "biography," in which the original woman writer, from the enemy of tyranny invented by the eighteenth century, has come full political circle to be presented as a royalist aristocrat, enemy of the people's class struggle.

Contemporary French Hellenists played an essential role in the development of a vision of Sappho that is the modern counterpart to Ovid's "heroic" fiction. It won for an entire century the kind of virtually uncontested allegiance that has been achieved at no other time and by no other plot decreed for the original woman writer. The work of Anne Le Fèvre Dacier—whose biography of Sappho was, significantly, the only unhesitatingly heterosexual scenario proposed by a seventeenth-century scholar—was enormously influential throughout the eighteenth century and was, for example, the central inspiration for the English rediscovery of Sappho that began at the turn of the century. Le Fèvre Dacier's edition was at the same time the final contribution to the recovery of Sappho initiated by sixteenth-century French humanists like Henri Estienne and Rémi Belleau; it marked the point at which the French tradition ceased to be the dominant influence in Sappho erudition and became instead the fountainhead of Sappho vulgarization. In the early eighteenth century, the scene of Sappho scholarship shifted to Germany, where the first of a long line of early German philologists began the painstaking work of reconstructing and ordering the fragments of Sappho's poetry, a reconstruction that culminated in the mid-nineteenth century with the Bergk edition, the most complete possible before the early twentieth-century papyri discoveries.

Thus, at the dawn of the Enlightenment, the French Sappho tradition veered off course. French Hellenists and translators continued to offer editions of her poetry throughout the century, but they were never to regain the position of philological dominance they had enjoyed in the sixteenth and seventeenth centuries. Furthermore, French Hellenists continued to aggravate their isolation by refusing to acknowledge the German breakthroughs, which were consistently made known in France only years, often decades, after their publication in Germany. (These editions were not even published in German, for German Hellenists continued the tradition which had been abandoned in France after Tanneguy Le Fèvre of publishing bilingual Greek-Latin editions.[2]) As it became increasingly provincial, the French tradition became at the same time increasingly popularized. French eighteenth-century translations of Sappho were exclusively in French; the editions seldom even included a Greek text. In addition, the editors took increasing textual liberties; Sappho's poetry was made over more extensively than at any time in the French tradition, until she came to sound like a typical popular poet of the day. This eighteenth-century Sappho reached a broad audience, as the range of fictions inspired by these translations demonstrates. More surprisingly, the French eighteenth-century Sappho, though a provincial and popular creation, had long-range effects on the "official" Sappho, the creation of serious philologists: the eighteenth century provides us with a unique example of the process by which even absolutely unfounded elements could be added to the Sappho legend. Some of the most pervasive and enduring myths of Sappho's life enter the scholarly tradition from the popular tradition, and some of the more tenacious misreadings of Sappho's poetry may, in addition, have been reinforced by it, indicating that Hellenists were, in the eighteenth and nineteenth centuries at least, more eclectic readers than might be imagined.[3]

In the following pages, I will recreate the construction of this heterosexual Sappho, whose plot made her a typical heroine of popular novels and romances. The inquiry into Sappho's life will of necessity be far broader than the field delimited for the seventeenth century. Sappho's unrequited love for Phaon and her suicidal leap remain the endpoint from which her life is measured. However, the eighteenth-century fictions are devoted to the many earlier episodes seen as an elucidation of this ultimate episode. At the same time, the focus on Sappho's work shifts radically. Whereas in the sixteenth and seventeenth centuries fr. 31 had been foregrounded, to the virtual exclusion of the other known poems, in the eighteenth century this same exclusionary focus shifts to fr. 1 which, after two centuries of critical neglect, takes over as Sappho's premier production (see Bayle's *Dictionnaire,* article "Sapho"). This shift of interest can be explained quite simply by the fact that the Aphrodite ode can more successfully be rewritten to promote a heterosexual biography for its author. In order to understand the process by which Sappho was transformed into a heterosexual figure, let us return briefly to the seventeenth-century editions of her work, to see the foundation on which eighteenth-century fictions were built.

Seventeenth-century editors provide a range of positions from which subsequent scholars could choose. Tanneguy Le Fèvre is the only seventeenth-century editor — and indeed, perhaps the only pre–twentieth-century editor — to reject every possible heterosexual scenario for his Sappho. He makes no mention whatsoever of her marriage or of her involvement with any man, and he dismisses the liaisons alleged by early commentators with Alcée and Anacréon as a product of "scandalous chronicles" (27) and "very apochryphal." (Le Fèvre, unlike many Hellenists before and after him, realized that Sappho and Anacreon could not have been contemporaries [49].) In a moderate stance, Longepierre grants sapphism the primary role but acknowledges the existence of both a husband, Cercola, and Phaon. Le Fèvre Dacier advocates a third position, an almost completely normalized affective plot. And, in a second founding gesture for the eighteenth-century tradition, she introduces a number of basic permutations for that plot, beginning the process by which Sappho's alleged biography was transformed into a popular novel. For example, Sapho's husband becomes "a wealthy man," acquiring the first touch of novelistic interest. Sapho herself becomes a widow when she is "very young": "nevertheless she never wanted to remarry, even though she was offered very advantageous prospects" (238). Le Fèvre Dacier thus suggests a first chronology for the heterosexual Sapho she is promoting. She even invents a scenario for one of the young widow's marriage prospects, introducing one of Sappho's poetry fragments as though it were an autobiographical document: "A fragment of a letter has come down to us in which she wrote to a man who was seeking her in marriage: 'if you are my friend, you won't think of marrying me; but you will choose a younger woman, for being older than you, I could never make up my mind to take you for a husband', " (238). With this fiction, Le Fèvre Dacier lays the groundwork for the eighteenth-century French Sappho tradition, during which the original woman writer gradually becomes no longer just an older woman humiliated by her love for one younger man, but a woman with a complicated heterosexual past in which a number of involvements prefigure the culminating episode with Phaon.

In the course of the eighteenth century in France, every fiction linking Sappho to any male is removed somehow from the realm of speculation: the attempt by seventeenth-century Hellenists to restore Sappho to her place in literary tradition is replaced by an effort to install the original woman writer in the world of men, first erotically and then literarily. All the texts from antiquity connecting Sappho to male literary figures — for example, the Suda's entry portraying her as a contemporary of Alceus and also of Stesichorus; Hermesianax's poem representing Alceus and Anacreon as rivals for her hand—are resurrected to authorize this speculation. At the dawn of the Enlightenment, only German scholars try to advance Sappho's literary stature. Christian Wolff's 1733 *Fragmenta et elogia* was the first edition devoted solely to Sappho, a practice continued in the century by, among others, Stählin and A.G. Raabe. In France, however, no such edition appeared before Louis Planchon's 1846 *Sapho retrouvée.* Initially, eighteenth-century French editors follow the seventeenth-century practice of appending Sappho's *oeuvre,* almost as an afterword, to that of a male poet—at first only Anacreon, but later Bion, Moschus, and others. And as a result of the fiction-making simultaneously developing, in the course of the century such couplings came to appear biographically justified. As an example of the disparity between the French and the German positions at the turn of the century, I would like to contrast briefly the article on Sappho in Bayle's *Dictionnaire* (1697) and the entry on her in Fabricius's *Bibliotheca Graeca* (1704). I will then review the elements in the "Ode to Aphrodite" that made possible its transformation into the founding text of Sappho's heterosexuality.

The opening sentence of Bayle's article sets the tone for his presentation of the original woman writer: "Sapho was one of the most famous women of all antiquity because of her verse and because of her loves." By setting her "loves" on an equal footing with her "verse," Bayle opens the door to the delectation in Sappho's alleged sexual excesses, which soon begin to receive as much attention as her poetry. This emphasis increasingly leads to the replacement of her poetry with verse that corresponds to the plot of the new biographical fantasies. Furthermore, throughout his article Bayle only aggravates this tendency by blending amorous and critical commentary and, in fact, by speaking relatively little about the verse and far more about the loves. In addition, he follows Le Fèvre Dacier's practice of treating the poem fragments as fragments of letters, thereby writing them out of the Sappho canon and into her biography. Bayle thereby effectively reduces the canon to the two best-known odes, of which he consistently privileges the Aphrodite ode. Fabricius's method could not be more different. Writing in Latin and therefore for a more limited, erudite audience, he adopts a miniature version of the organization of a critical edition: a biography in chronological order (as opposed to Bayle's *biographie romancée,* in which the only remaining facts, such as the names of her immediate family members, are tossed off only in the middle of the article), followed by a listing of the works of Sappho cited by classical authors. Fabricius makes every effort to distinguish between life and work and devotes the major part of his entry to information vital to the reconstruction of Sappho's *oeuvre*. His presentation initiated the building of the Sappho corpus that soon became the preserve of German Hellenists, led by his student Wolff.

Bayle consistently reveals a strong personal bias in presenting his material. Like so many of his French precursors, he does not question the authority of Ovid's epistle which, like them, he takes to be an "authentic" document: "Consider well what she herself writes with Ovid's pen." Because he accepts Ovid's text to the letter, he is obliged to take issue with the heterosexual scenario promoted by Le Fèvre Dacier, whose philological authority he nevertheless defends. Bayle—along with Sappho's first eighteenth-century translator, François Gacon—is thus alone in his day in advocating Longepierre's position: in Bayle's words, Sappho was initially "a notorious tribade," who forgot her sapphism once she knew true passion with Phaon.[4] Fabricius, on the other hand, presents an overview of the positions on Sappho's sexuality and the classical sources that support each viewpoint. For example, he mentions her love for Phaon only in passing, referring the reader to two sources for additional information, and makes no mention of her suicide.[5] He even grants prominence to one version of Sappho's life that no one will develop before the twentieth century, that she did not die young, but lived to old age. Not for another hundred and fifty years will Sapphism again be treated with such equanimity, or will a scholar so consistently play down Sappho's potential for scandal.

The differences between the presentations of Bayle and Fabricius cannot simply be explained away by the type of work each was composing, for these presentations are representative of the ways in which Sappho would be treated in their respective countries throughout the following century. Since so much of the eighteenth-century speculation is centered on fr. 1, as a backdrop to my discussions of the second wave of Sappho translations I would like to suggest some of the ways in which this celebrated poem lent itself to these distortions. Here is the poem known throughout the eighteenth century as the "Hymn to Venus" in a recent translation by Edith Mora:

> *Au trône d'arc-en-ciel immortelle Aphrodite*
> *fille de Zeus, tissant l'intrigue, je t'en supplie*
> *n'accable pas sous l'angoisse et sous la douleur*
> *ô vénérée, mon coeur*

mais viens, si jamais si une autre fois
entendant tout au loin ma voix tu l'as écoutée,
quittant le palais doré de ton père
    alors tu es venue

sur ton char attelé. Qu'ils étaient beaux te conduisant
les passereaux rapides autour de la terre assombrie
en un dense tournoiement d'ailes du haut du ciel
    à travers l'éther

Très vite ils furent là et toi, ô Bienheureuse,
souriant de ton visage immortel tu me demandais
ce qui me rendait alors malheureuse et la raison
    alors de mon appel

et ce que je voulais plus que tout dans mon coeur
fou. Qui encore supplies-tu Peithô
d'amener jusqu'à ton amour? de qui, ô
    Sappho, te plains-tu?

car si elle te fuit aussitôt elle te poursuivra
si elle refuse tes présents c'est elle qui t'en offrira
et si elle ne t'aime pas aussitôt elle t'aimera
    même contre son gré!

Viens donc à moi cette fois encore! Délivre-moi
de ce tourment trop lourd et réalise tout
ce que mon coeur désire. Ah viens toi-même
    m'aider à lutter!

$$(372)^6$$

Like the poem on which the seventeenth century's obsession was centered, fr. 1 reveals its sexual threat only deviously. When Aphrodite turns their conversation to the object of Sappho's desire, for a number of lines the sex of the beloved is camouflaged behind the neutral "who." It is in the next stanza (lines 20–24), when the reader's curiosity to know the identity of this "who" has been heightened by its repetition, that the poem's "problem" is located. Like Mora, translators generally are obliged to show their hand as early as the twentieth line, although they are in fact adding gender to neutral pronouns, renegotiating the poem's sexual configuration, as the other ode forces us to do, on the basis of an element near the end of the poem—in this case, the last word in the twenty-fourth line. The "elle" recurrent in lines 20–23 in Mora's translation is in the original the equivalent of the neutral "on." Mora is able retroactively to fill in this pronominal gap and avoid the less appealing but more correct "on" because she reads the word that closes the stanza as a feminine participle, "even if she [the love object] is unwilling."

And far more rests on the stanza than the interpretation of this single ode, especially in the period with which we are here concerned, when the Sappho corpus was so limited. When Aphrodite speaks to her in direct address—"about whom, Sappho, are you complaining?"—the poem's internal erotic subject is identified with its author. This same identification is always assumed by commentators on Sappho's poetry: it has almost always been taken for granted, for example, that the narrator addressing the "beloved girl" in fr. 31 is also the poem's author. Yet it is surprising that this critical assumption has so seldom been questioned, for in the absence of an internal signature it is not obligatory. It may be argued, therefore, that in the eighteenth century the burden of proof of Sapphic sexuality rests on her ode to Aphrodite—hence the poem's centrality in the age of Enlightenment.

The crucial identification of the beloved's sexual identity finally depends on the addition or subtraction of a single letter, the last letter in the eternally controversial line 24. If the last letter in the reading Mora proposes (following the majority of Sappho's editors since Bergk in 1854) is removed, the feminine participle modifying the erotic object is transformed into another form of the same verb, but in the second-person singular ("ethelois"). In this stanza, the second-person singular is the form Aphrodite adopts to address Sappho. The verb remains therefore feminine, but its femininity is shifted onto the poem's erotic subject, whose sex is already known and is acceptable—as long as that of the object remains unidentified. With this substitution, the line can be translated as "even if you [Sappho] are no longer willing," that is, are no longer interested in the beloved (sexually undetermined).

The crucial line is most remarkable because of the absolute integrity of its undecidability. After centuries of often heated debate, in which leading Hellenists throw their weight behind one reading or another, it is clear by now that the line cannot be deciphered with certainty—due perhaps to difficulties posed by Sappho's dialect and certainly to corruptions in existing manuscripts. We will consider a number of the quarrels launched when nineteenth-century scholars put forward emendations that they claim resolve the difficulty of the line by proposing at last a metrically flawless version. Ultimately, however, all these readings are grounded most firmly not in science but in sexual prejudice, in the view of Sapphism each scholar wishes to promote. The Enlightenment is innocent of this debate. Throughout the eighteenth century, the line remains unproblematic: it is always translated as if the last verb form in line 24 could only refer to Sappho. This allows translators, in something like good conscience, to define the undetermined object of Sappho's desire as a man. The absence of debate must not be taken to mean that Enlightenment scholars did not yet have access to science that the first generation of philologists would develop in the early nineteenth century, that they heterosexualized Sappho purely out of ignorance. The nineteenth-century scholars who reopen the debate on Sappho's homosexuality are armed not with new knowledge but with the personal (as opposed to scholarly) instincts that allow them to see that to which the eighteenth century is obstinately blind: the possibility that, given the overall vision of eroticism in Sappho's corpus, the object of desire in fr. 1 could well be female. At no time in the French eighteenth-century tradition of Sappho speculation is this possibility for dealing with the troublesome line evoked. At a time when all were striving to develop Sappho's promiscuity, the individual discussed by Aphrodite and Sappho in their dialogue could only be male.

I will now alternate between translations and fictions to illustrate the way in which editors and novelists conspire to create a heterosexual Sappho.

Sappho *au naturel*

> It's really only the plot of a novel:
> there's nothing solid, nothing historical;
> we must allow clever men such liberties.
>
> —Tanneguy Le Fèvre,
> dismissing the story of the
> loves of Sappho and Anacreon

In the initial phase of the eighteenth century's Sapphic reformation, the original woman writer acquired a biography notable for the centrality of what Bayle terms "les amours de Sapho." The textual price at which Sappho's sexual normalization was purchased can easily be calculated: first Ovid's Sapphic voice was sacrificed, then Sappho's corpus was confined within ever more deforming limits, and finally Sappho's poetic sublimity was eliminated. In the seventeenth century, Sappho's sublimity was recognized by those who decreed the rules of their century's *ars poetica* on the condition that she be made to love one man instead of many women. In the eighteenth century, the poet was made biographically promiscuous, but no longer as a prelude to her literary elevation. In a gesture initiated by Boileau's heirs, Sappho's threatening poetic power was contained when her poetry was also made promiscuous, indistinguishable from the eighteenth-century standard for mildly erotic verse. The second wave of Sappho's French translators thereby succeeded in eliminating her threat to the canonic standards of the age.

In *Heroides* 15, Ovid binds his poetic authority to Sappho's. Both his first French translators and Sappho's are sensitive to this intimate relation, and they propose various theories granting Sappho a share in the authorship of the epistle published under Ovid's name, the most common of which characterized Ovid as a mere translator of the great precursor poet. Such theories are undoubtedly at the origin of the first of two moments we will discuss during which Sappho's rising prominence eclipsed that of Ovid. At the dawn of the Enlightenment, the vogue of the *Heroides,* so enormous in the previous century, is markedly on the wane—and this is true despite the fact that the epistolary novel, in whose creation Ovid's innovative opus had played such a generative role, is finally becoming one of the dominant novelistic forms of the nascent century. This phenomenon, too, can be related to the changing vision of Sappho's sexuality: Ovid's importance diminished in direct proportion to the promotion of an exclusively heterosexual Sappho. Indeed, since Ovid portrays Sappho as originally homosexual, it was essential that the *Heroides* be eliminated so that the eighteenth-century's vision of Sapphism could reign supreme. Eventually, the fifteenth epistle is replaced by ersatz Ovid, a text rewritten to remove all trace of sapphism, a text therefore no longer in conflict with the Enlightenment's vision of Sappho.

By the end of the seventeenth century, the extraordinary multiplication of translations of the heroic epistles that had continued without interruption for nearly a hundred years is almost played out. During the first third of the eighteenth century, there are only two new translations of the *Heroides*—Richer (1723) and L'Héritier (1732)—plus one new translation of the Sappho epistle alone (1713). In addition, early in the century Barrin's 1676 translation and Bachet's 1626 edition are reprinted.[7] Subsequently, there are no new translations and after the 1730s no more reprints, and in the middle of the century the *Heroides* is replaced by the so-called *Héroïdes nouvelles,* Ovid *revu et corrigé* in the spirit of the age. However, the way had been prepared for this rescripting of Ovid both by the reprints of earlier translations and by the new early eighteenth-century translations. Significantly, the two seventeenth-century editions of the *Heroides* that are reissued early in the eighteenth century are those closest to the salon tradition of light, occasional verse. Thus Bachet recommends Ovid's volume because it is the richest source of "beautiful conceits" and "politeness" (3). Jean Barrin goes even further and portrays Ovid himself as a *galant homme,* a duc de Nemours *avant la lettre,* an historical precursor of the heroes whose inconstancy is the subject of his heroines' complaints (ii).

The new translations of the *Heroides* continue to promote this vision of Ovid as master of the codes of *politesse* and *galanterie.* The 1713 version of *Heroides* 15 appears in the *Mercure galant,* the public paper most closely aligned with aristocratic life and most acutely attuned to every refinement of the beautiful people's quickly shifting taste. The translation is a faithful one, but the anonymous translator makes Ovid's Sappho speak in perfect *Mercure galant-*ese, that is in the *galant* style of the day. Marie-Jeanne L'Héritier's 1732 translation of the *Heroides* is the culmination of this tradition that remodeled Ovid into an eighteenth-century society poet. L'Héritier, a disciple of Scudéry and other pillars of seventeenth-century salon society, provides a translation that is a tribute to the code of propriety those assemblies sought to impose: "I toned down Ovid a bit in the places where good taste would have been offended" (ix). To this end, for Ovid's references to his heroine's initial sapphism, L'Héritier substitutes her own version of Scudéry's *précieuse* Sapho, Sappho rendered unhesitatingly heterosexual, according to Le Fèvre Dacier's scenario. Thus Ovid's lines 18–20, the basis for subsequent "charges" of sapphism—"my eyes joy not in Atthis as once they did, nor in the hundred other maids I have loved to my reproach [*non sine crimine*]"—become the gentle lament of a woman who has been neglecting the companions of her salon days: "I no longer amuse myself, as I used to, with Athis, nor with the many other witty [*spirituelles*] individuals whom I cared for tenderly."[8] And, lest there remain any doubt as to the nature of the affection formerly shared and now Phaon's exclusive property, witness her watered-down version of the highly erotic remembrance of frenzied past lovemaking with Phaon (in Ovid, lines 139–50) that Ovid's Sappho "blushes to tell": "I remember that one day . . . I was singing: You took great pleasure in praising me. . . . I admit it, the tenderness of my glances responded to that of yours, and in these sweet moments we pledged an eternal love" (354).[9]

Against the backdrop of the declining influence of the *Heroides* and the waning authority of their increasingly tenderized author, appeared the first of the series of eighteenth-century "translations" of Sappho that betray her poetic voice more scandalously than those of any other period. The translator, François Gacon, signed it with his pseudonym, "Le Poète Sans Fard." His edition first appeared in 1712, but it was often reprinted throughout the eighteenth century, when it was, initially along with Le Fèvre Dacier's and later with Louis-Edmé Billardon de Sauvigny's, the dominant French version of Sappho's *oeuvre*.[10] The Poète Sans Fard is a self-proclaimed "disciple of Boileau" (clix). This self-definition helps explain the oblique gesture with which Gacon opens his edition of Anacreon and Sappho: a two-hundred-page preface which, while it contains occasional references to Greek poetry and even to the poets to whose *oeuvre* it allegedly stands as a pre-text, is really a contribution to the *querelle des anciens et des modernes* promoting a vision of the canon in perfect conformity with Boileau's views. Predictably, this is an "ancient" canon, one that privileges genres founded in antiquity and modern writers who position themselves in the wake of classical masters (cxxiii). Gacon even takes the time to combat the moderns on their own ground: "the moderns base their case on [the genres] dealing with what is known as *galanterie*, in which they claim to have gone well beyond the ancients" (cxxvi). He contests this position on the grounds that the ancients were well versed in "the natural expression of love," while the moderns speak only a language of passion so "contrived and verbose" that it is "ridiculous." When one considers that the authorized version of Boileau's *Dialogue des héros de roman* was published within months of Gacon's edition, this argument, Gacon's total exclusion of women writers from his modern canon, and the fact that the only examples of "artificial" modern literary passion that he proposes are Scudéry's *Artamène* and *Clélie*— all these appear the absolutely predictable gestures of a faithful "disciple of Boileau."[11]

However, at the end of the brief preface to his translation of Sappho, the Poète Sans Fard offers a more personal explanation for his exclusion of modern women writers: "Since I have always been suspicious of the hearts and minds of women, I've indulged myself as little as possible in that passion which keeps us under their control" (346). Gacon's independence from the modern female empire, he explains, means that he is not deceived by the artificial tongue that his contemporaries take for love's true language and can respond to Sappho's voice of primal passion. His translation, he assures us, will therefore not be restricted by the "coldness" that characterizes those of his predecessors Le Fèvre Dacier and Longepierre (346). However, despite his alleged admiration for this one woman writer, Gacon publishes only the two odes and excludes all the fragments included in the previous two editions. The poet-translator removes his makeup and reveals his true critical colors when he links this reduced canon to Sappho's sexuality: "But no matter how beautiful her verse, we should not worship it to the point of pardoning her shameful debauchery." The last move of his introduction and the reading he then offers for the two odes reveal the terms on which Boileau's disciple felt he could win canonic pardon for Sappho.

Gacon dismisses, on moral grounds, the work of his precursors. Tanneguy Le Fèvre is condemned as a bad Christian who "deserved to be publicly chastised by the Calvinists for having tried to excuse [Sappho] in spite of St. Paul's condemnation of her shameful passion." Le Fèvre's daughter has the merit of having tried to prove that Sappho had been a victim of "calumny," a position Gacon would defend if only "one of her odes did not offer visible proof that she had not been wrongfully accused" (344). Longepierre is attacked on two occasions and even more vehemently than Le Fèvre *père et fille,* both because he acknowledged her sapphism without condemning it, and because he committed the additional sin of going against Boileau's law of propriety by including in his translation of fr. 31 the image of the "cold sweat" ("a very disgusting image, as M. Boileau very correctly noted)" (346). For his edition, the Poète Sans Fard takes a novel, and far more devious, stance. For the first time in the French tradition, he explicitly links the by then familiar description of Sappho's poetry as the *natural* voice of passion to her sexuality. This connection in the long run allows him to justify readings of Sappho's odes that make them canonically acceptable, despite Gacon's loudly proclaimed view that her sexuality was scandalous.

His innovations in fr. 1 are centered on the problematic lines 20–24 and affect the portrayal of both erotic subject and object. Gacon takes full advantage of readings put forth more timidly by his French precursors. Since the ode had always been read as heterosexual, they had, with few exceptions, made the same choices as he. By exceptions, I refer to those translating into Latin, like Tanneguy Le Fèvre and all Sappho's eighteenth-century German editors, who are able to eliminate the pronoun designating the gender of the love object. Those translating into French, however, are obliged to be more specific. In the early translations, we witness the construction of a more and more concrete heterosexuality. To translate line 20, Longepierre elects the minimalist "il." Le Fèvre Dacier is more precise with her "young man," and Du Four de La Crespelière chooses the more *galant* "serviteur." The Poète Sans Fard further embroiders Sappho's text, first by filling in the gender blank of the neutral Greek pronoun with the totally unjustified "young and handsome boy," a supplement that reactivates the older woman abandoned by younger boy scenario. Gacon soon reveals that he has just this tradition in mind, when he further characterizes the younger man as "fier, farouche" ("proud, wild"), precisely the adjectives Phèdre uses to describe the object of her passion (2:5:638). Racine pillaged Sappho for his heroine's cry from the heart. The Poète Sans Fard puts adjectives from Racine into the mouth of Sappho's Aphrodite, thereby completing the founding transference in the French Sapphic tradition.[12]

Gacon introduces a similar amplification of previous readings of Sappho's line 24. Following Estienne's lead, Du Four de La Crespelière's original formulation had established a structure, maintained for decades, that skirts what are from the nineteenth century on seen as the two possibilities for the line ("even if [the beloved] is not willing"; "even if you [Sappho] would no longer be willing"): "in the future he will do whatever you order." Gacon gets this message across twice by having Venus[13] first tell Sappho "I'll bring him under your law," and then "he will constantly follow your lead" (349). Gacon's doubling technique could be seen as an attempt to win authority for a reading of a crucial line that even its own proponents felt somehow to be unsatisfactory. This reading is more correct than those proposed by early translators in other traditions, but its accuracy is merely accidental.[14] Gacon includes a Greek text with his translation, and it confirms that he follows the dominant manuscript tradition of his day in which the verb is a second-person singular form referring to Sappho's possible future lack of desire. The reading offered by Gacon and his precursors shifts the eventual unwillingness onto the beloved, where it rightfully belongs, while still asserting the beloved's masculinity.

Gacon's version of the second ode demonstrates his conscious subordination of accuracy to his desire to reform Sappho. After his translation of the Venus ode, he remarks that "one can't help feeling pity when hearing the author grieve amorously" (350). He contrasts this reaction with his response to Sappho's other ode "which contains a passion so infamous and debauchery so horrible that it is difficult not to condemn its shameful and criminal madness [*extravagance*]." He then justifies the measure he has adopted to spare others this painful sensation: "I believe that the precaution I've taken so that readers won't be shocked will not displease reasonable people. It was very easy to make the poem *natural* and therefore more beautiful" (350, my emphasis). He then unveils his innovation, entitled simply "Ode." The necessity for the altered title is immediately clear: "Happy, dear Phaon, is the young and tender beauty / On whom you cast the brilliance of your beautiful eyes." The Poète Sans Fard makes this poem heterosexual by shifting the angle of Sappho's love triangle. In his reconfiguration, as in Racine's Sapphic tragedy, Sapho is abandoned by a man for the other woman. Gacon displaces her jealousy so that she is no longer envious of the man she imagines with the beloved girl, but of the younger woman she visualizes in the arms of the younger man who never returns her affections.[15]

You will remember that the preface to Gacon's edition attempts to prescribe a canon and to set down canonic standards. His canonic posturing is a pre-text to justify his distortion of Sappho's *oeuvre:* if that *oeuvre* is restricted to two odes and if those odes are sexually homogenized, then their author's "indecency" can be erased. Sappho is "pardoned" by the canon on the condition that she be contained within the limits of weeping, pitiful heterosexuality. At the turn of the eighteenth century, a writer paid a high price for such confinement, as Gacon must have known. By making over Sappho, he guarantees that she will be deprived of her original canonic status. In Gacon's wake, Sappho will no longer stand for the sublimity for which "Longinus" singled her out, and which Boileau allegedly reaffirmed at the point of her entry into the French literary mainstream. "Reasonable people," Gacon claims, will not be displeased with his efforts to naturalize Sappho's poetry. However, in the age of reason a tearful (*larmoyant*) poetic voice would be kept far from the literary mainstream, restricted to the domain of melodrama, insignificant poetry, and third-rate novels. By removing Sappho's sexual makeup, the Poète Sans Fard consigns the original woman writer no longer to the waters of oblivion but to the company of the Enlightenment's lower-class literary voices.

Within that domain, her exploitation began immediately and accelerated throughout the century. The multiplication of fictions of Sappho is indeed so rapid that, from this point on, I will no longer try to present a complete picture of the French reconstruction of Sappho but will focus instead on the texts I consider representative of each major development.[16] Little more than a decade after Gacon's translation appeared the exemplary continuation of his methods in the popular domain, an extended (over four hundred pages) *biographie* flagrantly *romancée, L'Histoire et les amours de Sapho de Mytilène* (1724). This is the work that definitively seals the new fiction of Sapphic promiscuity, Sappho as an object exchanged among many men, even, perhaps especially, men of letters. Its author, Jean Du Castre d'Auvigny, does not invent the romance he adds to the biography; on the contrary, he documents his fiction as thoroughly as eighteenth-century translators do their editions, and he concludes his novel with a twenty-page "Lettre à Mme de S***," a lengthy discussion of his sources. However, this does not mean that D'Auvigny, any more than Gacon and his followers, is striving for accuracy in his reconstruction. Rather, the ostentatious display of sources is characteristic of the marriage between erudition and wild fantasy that is the hallmark of eighteenth-century popular fictions of the original woman writer. For hack novelists like D'Auvigny, it is as if erudition had become absolutely necessary to authorize their fantasies.[17]

In his epistolary postface, D'Auvigny enumerates a variety of sources, from Aristotle to Le Fèvre Dacier, from whom he has culled a list of men believed to have been contemporaries of Sappho. He pays no attention to discrepancies among his disparate sources or to authorities who question the reliability of any of his sources, for what he seeks are candidates to provide a heterosexual plot for Sappho—and it is essential that none of these candidates be of his invention. That heterosexual plot is what he terms "the economy of this work" (430). To support that novelistic economy, D'Auvigny dismisses the "little story" of sapphism with his own "little story," pure Rostand *avant la lettre*: "Couldn't we say that one of her friends incapable of describing to his mistress the ardor of his flame employed Sapho's pen? During his lifetime he harvested the glory of having composed this poem. . . . After the death of this friend, it was discovered that Sapho was its author, and someone who wanted to slander her accused her of having written so passionately to a woman, when it is really a lover writing to his mistress" (433–34). This obstacle out of the way, D'Auvigny is free to develop the economy of his choice.

In all doubling fictions of Sappho—whether explicit ones which claim the existence of two Sapphos, or implicit ones which distinguish a homo-from a heterosexual Sappho—Sappho is portrayed as a creative artist, even if an artist whose creativity is a thing of the past. The eighteenth century is the only period in Sappho's history in France during which there are no doubling fantasies. Sappho acquires her uncontested heterosexuality in eighteenth-century fiction at the cost of even a past memory of her poetic genius. D'Auvigny so denatures her creative life that it is no longer threatening. For example, he makes Sapho a *salonnière* only to bring this traditionally female-dominated sphere of influence under masculine control. At age fourteen, his Sapho is already the belle of Mytilène, and "the court of her suitors was getting bigger every day" (11). She deals very efficiently with the problem of having a house full of young men by setting up "a kind of Academy . . . which soon becomes the meeting place of the town's most polite and *galant* society" (12–13). The members soon decide that they need rules to govern their assemblies, and they ask Sapho to draw them up. The finished product is rather like the codes established by eighteenth-century neo-*précieuse* academies, with the exception of one rule that no French classical salon would have accepted: "The Academy will be composed of persons of both sexes. . . . To preserve the primacy accorded men by nature, they will always preside over assemblies and speak first: women, for whom modesty is the finest adornment, will only speak if asked to do so" (14–15).

Once the female threat to the literary economy has been contained, D'Auvigny inaugurates his century's tradition of biographical speculation in grand style, crafting an elaborately traditional amorous plot for his heroine. Sapho encounters her future husband at a meeting of her Academy, when he wins her heart by reciting passionate verse to her (25–26). While Cercala (D'Auvigny's variant on the then standard French spelling "Cercola") is still only a favorite suitor, he is called away by his father on a business trip, and the first of a series of unwelcome suitors, Alcée, tries to supplant him and is rejected by Sapho. Sapho and Cercala marry and have a daughter, Cleis, but Cercala is killed shortly after her birth. Sapho is a model widow until Cleis's sudden death at age twelve. At this juncture, D'Auvigny extends Sappho's plot beyond the limit previously prescribed for it and reveals the nature of his version of Sapho's family romance, Sapho portrayed as promiscuous mother.

Numerous suitors pursue the "young widow" (347), most notably a pair central to D'Auvigny's conception, the ever-present Phaon and the second in the series of poet-lovers to be decreed for Sappho on the basis of rumors from antiquity, Stésichore. In his postface, the novelist explains that he introduced Stésichore because the rival "provides a contrast" with Phaon and "gives more forcefulness to Phaon's love" (428). On the surface, it would seem that D'Auvigny's novelistic "economy" is simply one more confirmation of the centrality of René Girard's triangle of desire. When the two rivals are superimposed, however, we learn that the shared trait that makes the doubling fantasy possible is the fact that both men are considerably younger than Sapho. For her rejection of Stésichore,

D'Auvigny has his heroine employ a rough paraphrase of the Sappho fragment, cited in the seventeenth century as evidence of her refusal of Alcée, in which the poet tells a younger man that she cannot marry him and advises him to find a woman of his own age (348; see Mora, 47; LP 121).

By making the similarity between Sapho's major suitors their relative youthfulness, D'Auvigny is simply exerting gentle pressure on a scenario already sketched out by Bayle. According to Bayle, the attraction to younger men was Sapho's central passion, one she grew increasingly incapable of controlling. He believes the "marry a younger woman" fragment predates the Phaon episode and is from a period when she was more rational: "She was [at the time of Phaon] no longer capable of listening to reason. . . . The younger Phaon would have been, the more he would have been to her liking." D'Auvigny eliminates the initial period of rationality, abandoning the "young widow" to her lust for younger men. In so doing, he fulfills the promise of the fiction that can be glimpsed in the intersection between Racine and Ovid, making explicit for the first time in the history of Sappho's family romance the identification between the adulterous mother and the oedipal mother. And once the contours of this fiction were made plain, male writers followed D'Auvigny's lead as though he had succeeded in establishing his example as fact, in their eagerness to demonstrate the literary mother's passion for her first male heirs.

After this incestuous interlude, D'Auvigny's novel settles into the already familiar routine, as Sapho, abandoned by jealous friends and fickle lovers, first pleads incessantly for Phaon's return and then leaps to her death. By closing with this plaintive, saccharine figure, D'Auvigny reminds us of his second contribution to the fictionalization of Sappho. He stands as Gacon's counterpart in fiction, the reinventor of Sapho as a heroine of his century's equivalent of dime-store novels. In D'Auvigny's wake, the perils of Sappho crop up again and again in the kinds of novels and plays that went through multiple editions in their day but have long since disappeared from the annals of literary history. In France, Sappho enters popular fiction as the faintly libertine young widow who was one of the century's most durable stereotypes.

Toward the end of the century, "les malheurs de Sapho" had so thoroughly infiltrated the public domain that the teenage Germaine Necker (future baronne de Staël) could consider Sappho's tale, as she knew it, appropriate subject matter for the naïvely simple popular song that is one of her first literary efforts: "Romance to the tune: We loved each other from childhood."[18] In the late eighteenth century, *romance* could signify "a simple poetic effort, a folk song, on a sentimental subject that fills one with pity [*attendrissant*]" (*Robert*). For her *romance,* the young Germaine Necker essentially follows Ovid's plot, but the influence of the "tenderized" Ovid promoted by Barrin, L'Héritier, and others, as well as the "pitiful" (*larmoyant*) Sapho that originates with Gacon and D'Auvigny, is evident throughout. Her Sapho is thus a far cry from Ovid's figure consumed by wild passion and raw sexuality. She is a piteous creature, abandoned by the women jealous of her talents and, of course, by Phaon. The fledgling writer explains that she sings of "this sad story" in order to "touch" her listeners' hearts with Sapho's "miserable destiny." Germaine's *romance* demonstrates that, once Sappho's sexual "makeup" is removed and her passion "tenderized," the original woman writer eventually becomes no more threatening than the humble *grisette* of nineteenth-century popular fiction who fulfills her "miserable destiny" in abandonment. In France, the fictionalizing tradition generated by the *Heroides* ends once Ovid's female heroic, thoroughly declassed, is installed in the domain of folk songs.

With so little energy left in the heroine, the machinery churning out *images d'Epinal* of Sappho might have ground to a halt, had not the fictionalizing process been revitalized with the appearance of the pseudo-Greek novels that are an important literary strain in late eighteenth-century neoclassicism. Just four years after Germaine Necker penned her Sapphic folk song, a novel was published that was destined to energize her déclassé vision of the original woman writer, to chart a new course for popular fictions of the tenth muse, and even to inspire trends in Sappho scholarship that lasted well into the twentieth century. Indeed, this novel is easily the most influential fiction of Sappho in the entire French tradition. The abbé Barthélemy's multivolume *Voyage du jeune Anacharsis en Grèce* is one of those works whose immense contemporary popularity and authority seem inconceivable today. The unqualified admiration reserved for Barthélemy's scholarship until at least 1815 establishes the reliability and the longevity of the formula crudely applied by D'Auvigny: the marriage of thorough documentation and totally unfounded fabulation.[19]

In his preface, Barthélemy reveals the fundamental drive behind all fictions of Sappho firmly grounded in scholarship: "I composed a voyage rather than a history because everything is in motion [*en action*] in a

voyage, and one is allowed details forbidden to the historian. These details
. . . are often only hinted at by ancient authors" (vii). The repeated
eighteenth-century attempts to narrativize the fragments of Sappho's
biography found in ancient sources, the desire to set Sappho "in action,"
are motivated by the sense that if only the man of letters can successfully
read between the (often broken) lines of ancient texts, he will outstrip the
historian at his task. More than anyone else, Barthélemy was to
demonstrate the truth of this axiom.

The travelogue that sets Barthélemy's Sapho in motion is a description
of the island of Lesbos as a forerunner of decadent late eighteenth-century
Paris, corrupt and dedicated to pleasure: "Lesbos is the home of pleasure,
or rather of unbridled license. Its inhabitants bend their moral principles
at will, and adapt them to all circumstances. . . . There reigned in this
new world great freedom of ideas and of emotions" (2:58–59). He
continues D'Auvigny's policy of characterizing Sappho's poetry as typical
of whatever school of poetry the commentator wants to promote, in this
case, a sort of pre-Romantic nature poetry: "She paints all that is most
cheerful [*riant*] in nature. . . . She knows so well how to nuance its colors
that she always finds a happy mixture of light and shadow" (2:72). The
explanation for this incongruous deformation becomes clear when
Barthélemy cites fr. 31 in a translation by the abbé Delille (2:74), in which
the translator attributes to Sappho the picturesque nature poetry for which
he himself was known, and Barthélemy thereby appropriates for his fiction
the "dominating authority" of the Boileau of his age (Canat, 1:15).

After the death of her husband, Barthélemy's Sapho gathers the women
of Lesbos about her to promote poetic activity, a propagandist gesture
that precipitates her downfall.[20] Barthélemy motivates Le Fèvre Dacier's
"slander" scenario in a fiction destined to leave its mark, most prominently
on Staël's Sapphic novels. He explains that the Greeks' "extreme
sensitivity" (*sensibilité*) led them "to borrow the language of love for the
most innocent relations," and that Sapho, by nature "violently passionate"
and therefore "excessive" even by these already excessive standards, takes
this potentially ambiguous discourse to new heights. Her too evident
"superiority humiliates a number of powerful women," and they express
their "hatred" by willfully misreading her innocently passionate discourse
about other women. Sapho counterattacks with an "insight" and an
"irony" that "put the finishing touch to their malice" (2:69–70).
Barthélemy's Sapho is slandered and ostracized because she has attempted
to promote her poetic message, to convert other women if not to

passionate relations among women at least to a passionate language characterizing those relations.

Barthélemy follows the then standard heterosexual scenario, but he introduces innovations, the importance of which can only be evaluated when the entire span of their influence is visible. Seventeenth-century commentators had already theorized that the "Ode to Aphrodite" was composed, in a last attempt to win back Phaon, in Sicily where Sappho had followed her inconstant young lover. By the eighteenth century, the Sicilian journey is an accepted element in Sappho's biography; Barthélemy contributes both a new narrative to explain it and a source from antiquity to justify it. He also imagines an elaboration of the context for Sappho's final leap. However, in both cases Barthélemy introduces his innovations only elliptically, by juxtaposing familiar and unfamiliar elements without commentary, as though he sees no possible link between them—or as if he wishes prudently to avoid drawing potentially controversial conclusions. Since his successors make explicit what the abbé prefers to leave hidden in plain view, I will defer discussion of his revisions of Sappho's plot until the implications of his elliptical suggestions are realized.

Barthélemy's most apparent heir, writing less than a decade after him, is Etienne Lantier. His *Voyages d'Anténor en Grèce et en Asie* (1797) was described by contemporaries as a lower-class *Anacharsis,* "the *Anacharsis* of the boudoirs" (Canat, 1:152), by which Lantier's detractors meant that he had increased the amount of fabulation and decreased proportionally the quantity of erudition in the novelistic blend, thereby creating a less pedagogically reliable text. However, as is evident in the example that interests us here, on occasion, rather than adding unauthorized elements, Lantier simply outstrips his precursor at his own game of setting biographical details "in motion" when he supplies the narrative Barthélemy had refused to develop.

For his fiction of Sappho, Lantier elects the most dramatic presentation heretofore imagined. He begins with the story of the White Rock of Leukas, then recounts Sapho's life as a flashback, a retrospective explanation of her suicidal leap. Furthermore, even his presentation of her suicide is oblique. Lantier opens not on Sapho's jump, but on that of a precursor, a certain Queen Artémise. She is identified as the queen of Caria known for her courage at the battle of Salamis, but the anecdote that preoccupies Lantier, just as it had Barthélemy before him, concerns the death of this military woman: when she is abandoned by her younger lover, "drunk with jealousy and vengeance, she . . . surprised him in the arms of sleep and, armed with a sharp blade, she put out his eyes" (1:228). In despair, she then leaps from the White Rock. When Barthélemy recounts this anecdote, he relates the two women—"Such was also the fate of unhappy Sapho, abandoned by her lover Phaon" (3:403)—but so hastily that he fails to bring out the story's real pertinence for Sapho's plot. Lantier makes the parallel more explicit. His heroes, Anténor and Phanor, reach the White Rock the day before Sapho was scheduled to jump. They first see her wandering on the edge of the cliff, given over to madness: "With an agitated air, her face inflamed with anger, she gesticulates and looks at the heavens, which she accuses of her misery. There she is, stopping in front of Artémise's tomb; . . . what a subject of meditation for Sapho! How similar their sensibilities, their destinies!" (1:231).

Neither voyage novelist provides the kind of identification of Queen Artémise that would allow the reader to understand why she and Sapho are singled out for "similar destinies." According to Herodotus, Artemisia was an admiral who led the Persians in a crushing defeat against the Greeks at Salamis. In antiquity, this battle was a celebrated example of male humiliation at the hands of a woman. While Barthélemy and Lantier allude to the exploits grounding Artémise in history, they present her as a prototype of the murderous revenge of the older woman scorned by the younger man. They never mention that they bring about this radical shift in Artemisia's exemplary status by shifting the status of their own discourse and moving into the realm of fabulation. Herodotus does not describe Artemisia's end; the variation on a romance theme seems to be Barthélemy's invention.[21] By allowing violence to impart final meaning to a classic tale of female authority in a domain usually closed to women, Barthélemy issues an explicit warning about the threat to the very survival of the patriarchy that woman's invasion of the male heroic sphere poses. Barthélemy and Lantier reconfigure the male child's oedipal fantasy by projecting the child's desire onto the mother. The mother figure burns for the young male, who rejects her advances. She demonstrates the consequences of this monstrous desire by enacting, "with a sharp blade," the symbolic castration Oedipus performed on himself, before she is made to punish herself for this emasculation and her desire.

Lantier's Sapho confides her autobiography—"the manuscript on which are engraved my story and my misfortunes" (1:234)—to his heroes, Anténor and Phanor, and they pledge to publish it if she should perish. According to Lantier, Sapho seeks the posthumous satisfaction of having "deposited in the bosom of posterity her wretchedness and Phaon's crime"

(1:234). However, when he has the original woman writer deliver control over her story to two young men who could be the doubles of her treacherous lover (one of whom even bears a name uncannily close to "Phaon"), Lantier inscribes into his text an authorization of the process, to which he is contributing, by which male writers reconfigure Sappho's plot.[22]

Fugitive Erotics

Pleasure is always allowed.
Let our evanescent existence
Be frittered away on frivolities.

— Parny, "Délire"

At the same time that novelists were manufacturing a heterosexual Sapho with a tenderized voice, a series of translators were reinforcing this vision of the original woman author by remaking Sappho's *oeuvre* in the image of her new biography. The most irresponsible of all Sappho's French translators worked to eliminate her poetry's erotic force and to replace the originality of her voice with a vision of textual promiscuity that makes Sappho virtually indistinguishable from numbers of far less memorable poets. Sappho's descent into poetic mediocrity repeats the pattern of the heterosexual Sapho's reduction to popular fiction. The inspiration for this rewriting of Sappho's corpus may have come from the appropriation, just after the middle of the century, of the *Heroides* by a group of writers who came of age through Ovid. Their strategy may have encouraged the breakup of the long-accepted union between Ovid and Sappho.

Three writers are most intimately associated with the subgenre that splinters off from the *Heroides:* Jean de La Harpe, Claude-Joseph Dorat, and Adrien Blin de Sainmore.[23] Because they were producing the so-called new heroides in great quantity at a time when Ovid's original was not being retranslated, their Ovid, at first freely reinvented and later frankly ersatz, began increasingly to be substituted for the authentic heroic epistles. Their favorite subjects are updatings of Ovid's woeful outpourings, tales of women more recently abandoned by famous men: Louise de la Vallière to Louis XIV, Anne de Boulen to Henry VIII. In addition to his *Héroïdes nouvelles* (1759), La Harpe contributes a slight variation on this scenario in a number of poems he refers to as "romances" rather than "epistles" (hence, perhaps, Germaine Necker's choice of this term for her Ovidian poem). In La Harpe's complaints of unrequited love, the favorite scenario has the woman scorned writing her unfaithful lover to ask why he prefers his new love. Dorat brings the Ovidian plot closest to the eighteenth century's obsessions with a masculinized oedipal epistle from the comte de Comminges (the hero of a novel by Claudine de Tencin) bemoaning his fate not to an unfaithful lover but to his mother.

No writer put the term "heroides" to more extreme or varied use than Blin de Sainmore, whose heroic letters include Ovidian updatings such as Gabrielle d'Estrées to Henri IV, but also verse epistles for which the term heroic takes on a very different sense, for example, Jean Calas to his wife. In this collection, Sappho plays a role as anomalous as that reserved for her in Ovid's original grouping. Except for the mythical Biblis (borrowed from Ovid's *Metamorphoses*), Sappho is Blin de Sainmore's only epistolary heroine from antiquity. In the company Ovid forces Sappho to keep, she acquires mythic status. When Blin de Sainmore surrounds her with unfortunate "moderns," Sappho by juxtaposition becomes an average heroine for his age.

The frontispiece to the 1766 volume he entitles *Lettre de Sapho à Phaon*, engraved by Gravelot, is a perfect illustration of this transformation. In Chauveau's frontispiece for Marolles's 1660 translation of the *Heroides*, the wretched heroines who wail as the ships bearing their unfaithful lovers sail out to sea all wear the loose robes that are the seventeenth century's equivalent of antique garments (fig. 1). Gravelot's Sapho is also dressed in a flowing gown, but the only reference to ancient dress is the sandal on her outstretched foot (fig. 2). Sapho is clothed in eighteenth-century garments, down to the pearl bracelet on her wrist. The portrait is completed with a touch worthy of Fragonard: her dress has slipped, artfully revealing her right breast. Also in modern garb is the handmaiden who supports her as she swoons, with one arm indicating the ship pulling out to sea.

The caption to the frontispiece—"Your ship is fleeing across the sea with the wind's help, / The breath of death freezes my senses"—could apply to any victim of heroism. So thoroughly modernized is Gravelot's Sapho that his illustration seems more appropriate for a reedition of the *Lettres portugaises* (whose heroine received bracelets from her inconstant lover before he put out to sea). And this image stands at the end of the *Heroides'* extraordinary presence at the birth of French epistolary fiction. In the second half of the seventeenth century, Ovid's model generated masochistic novelistic outpourings like those of the hapless Portuguese nun. Not quite a century later, all distinction had vanished between such

F<small>IG</small>. 2. Hubert François Gravelot, frontispiece, Blin de Sainmore, *Lettre de Sapho à Phaon* (1766). Reprinted by permission of the Rosenbach Museum and Library, Philadelphia.

fictions and what were passed off as translations or adaptations of the *Heroides*. Ovid had been so thoroughly assimilated that his authentic voice was no longer necessary. Reeditions of the *Heroides* in French remained infrequent until twentieth-century critical editions. And Ovid's authority over his pathetic heroines, most notably Sappho, came increasingly into question—a process that is initiated, if only indirectly, in volumes like the one prefaced by the Gravelot engraving.

Gravelot's engraving serves as frontispiece to a volume by Blin de Sainmore that contains far more than his Sapho epistle in a vaguely Ovidian mode. The disparate elements assembled under the title *Lettre de Sapho à Phaon* provide an early example of the most important development in eighteenth-century French editions of Sappho: the creation of a new fiction of Sappho's *oeuvre* as if by implication, through the elliptical juxtaposition of unrelated poetic samples. In this manner, her Enlightenment editors use Sappho's poetry as the centerpiece in a project of editorial promiscuity. They make her work literally promiscuous when they put together collections that illustrate the term's primary meaning: "consisting of members or elements of different kinds grouped or massed together without order; of mixed or disorderly composition or character" (*OED*). By including Sappho in increasingly indiscriminate associations, eighteenth-century translators gradually succeed in creating the literary equivalent of the sexually promiscuous Freudian mother. Blin de Sainmore's accumulation opens, traditionally enough, with a "life of Sapho." This, however, is followed by what appears to be a pure non sequitur, an "epistle to Rosine," a juxtaposition that suggests a link between the déclassé Sapho and the textually promiscuous Sappho. Rosine is identified as a novice actress aspiring to greater things. The verse letter, with no resemblance to the Ovidian model, is a straightforward attempt at her seduction, in the best *carpe diem* manner. Blin de Sainmore makes an attempt, so vague as to be totally unconvincing, at relating this epistle to the one that follows it, the volume's title piece: "Sapho wrote verse; Rosine improves the verse she recites. Sapho felt love; Rosine feels and inspires it. Therefore, ushering in a letter from Sapho, the homage I give to Rosine is natural" (7).

His construction seems "natural" only according to the Poète Sans Fard's sense of the term: that which remakes Sappho along lines more acceptable to the directors of the cultural order. Once Blin de Sainmore turns to the Sappho epistle, he maintains no pretense of accuracy. Rather he explains that his "Lettre de Sapho à Phaon" only resembles Ovid's epistle in that in both works "Sapho is supposed to be writing before leaving to rejoin her inconstant lover." His warning is well advised, since he thoroughly remodels Ovid's original to offer instead a perfect mid–eighteenth-century period piece. By 1766, therefore, Ovid's authority is weakened to such a degree that his Sappho is no longer needed and can be replaced, in a work that borrows the title and format he devised, with a version of the heroine as déclassé as Staël's romance Sapho. In addition, this ersatz Ovid is followed by what Blin de Sainmore labels a "free translation" of the Aphrodite ode. He thereby opens the door to the sort of wholesale tampering with the Sappho corpus that was about to become widespread in a series of increasingly promiscuous editorial minglings.

Blin de Sainmore is the only eighteenth-century "translator" to revise Sappho through association with contemporary figures of Ovidian heroinism. The more commonly adopted strategy is first employed in the seventeenth century by Du Four de La Crespelière, when he includes Sappho in a volume not simply with Anacreon but with a number of poets, loosely associated under the heading "amorous, charming and Bacchic." In this association, Sappho is almost lost in the crowd of increasingly diverse poets. In the final analysis, all poets included are subjected to a sort of leveling process and become subordinate to the style or type of verse they are said to represent, which is at the same time a style they are *made* to represent. True to his pseudonym, the Poète Goguenard homogenizes the poetic voices he jumbles together to create a sort of bantering light verse.

Two eighteenth-century "translations" of Sappho, both first published in 1773, perfect the technique initiated by Du Four de La Crespelière and Blin de Sainmore.[24] These are the most frequently reprinted translations until about 1815: they therefore establish the image of Sappho that is dominant in France until the next wave of French translations in the 1830s and 1840s. The ultimate eighteenth-century vision of Sappho's *oeuvre* completes the process by which the original woman writer is made over to fulfill the conventions of the day. Both the life and the work of the Sapho the nineteenth century inherits from the eighteenth would have been unrecognizable to such early French reconstructors as Tanneguy Le Fèvre.

In his preface, J.-J. Moutonnet de Clairfons claims to have consulted Wolff's 1733 Greek-Latin edition, a gesture that in late eighteenth-century French work on Sappho is synonymous with an absolute disregard for even minimal standards of editorial fidelity. Moutonnet de Clairfons's work in no way introduces the French public to recent German scholarship. On the contrary, his edition is entirely predictable from the eighteenth-century French tradition I have been describing. He opens with a version of the "Hymn to Venus" perfectly standard for the day. The second ode is altered in accordance with Moutonnet de Clairfons's stand in the preface (in which he outlines all the proofs of Sapho's heterosexuality): called simply "ode," the poem is sexually undecidable, since its female signature has been erased. Then, Moutonnet de Clairfons makes a gesture which, like his borrowing of Wolff's authority, at first glance appears revolutionary: he opens up the Sappho corpus to include a significant number of the fragments (including some not found in seventeenth-century French editions, thereby indicating at least some familiarity with recent German scholarship). However, his elaborate staging of the fragments works to set back rather than to advance knowledge of her *oeuvre*.

Moutonnet de Clairfons is another representative of the promiscuous editorial school: he presents Sappho in the company of Anacreon, Bion, and Moschus. He then supplements this process of supplementation by introducing eighteenth-century poets into his presentation of each Greek poet. On the title page, the edition is said to have been printed "in Paphos (that is, Paris)." It is fitting that the collection be placed under the sign of Venus's favorite city on her native island, for the volume proposes the equivalent in poetry of an "embarkment for Cythera," rococo revisions of the Greek poets classified at the period rather vaguely as "pastoral," into whose company Sappho has been forced to fit.[25] Moutonnet de Clairfons divides Sappho's fragments into two categories established on the basis of factors external to her work. The first section includes those of her poems he feels have been imitated by seventeenth- and eighteenth-century French authors, enabling him to place the successors on an equal footing with their alleged "model." Thus, after a fragment about the rose's beauty long attributed to Sappho he includes a poem by Voltaire on the young rose.[26] A number of his pairings are hardly convincing; his translations are uniformly artificial and saccharine—and through his manipulations Sappho is thoroughly assimilated into perhaps the least appealing poetic tradition in a century not known for the quality of its poetry.

Moutonnet de Clairfons's second category is entitled simply "diverse fragments." The section is devoted in large part to one long poem composed of unrelated fragments he has strung together. (He marks the division between fragments with three dots, but because he has ordered them so that their sum total has a meaning of its own, the independent works blend together in the reader's mind to form a collective.) Moutonnet de Clairfons further complicates his ersatz Sappho by calling the reader's attention from time to time to footnotes in which he cites lines from recent French poets that could be seen as vaguely inspired by Sappho. As if this were not enough, he concludes his Sappho section with a collection of disparate poets, selected seemingly at random, which includes a long section, "The Vigil of Venus's Fête," the most trifling sort of rococo amorous drivel. The final touch is material he presents as an anthology of classical love poetry, but which never rises above the level of the most colorless, the most derivative, pastoral verse.

In the engravings by Charles Eisen that illustrate Moutonnet de Clairfons's edition, image and text are in perfect alignment. In the plate that faces the translation of the "Hymn to Venus," for example, the goddess is perched atop a mass of billowing tiny clouds, rather like a giant feather bed (fig. 3). She reclines on a bizarre piece of furniture that only an artist of the late eighteenth century could have imagined as the equivalent of the "chariot" in Sappho's ode: a cross between a chaise longue, a gondola, and a cradle, it resembles the lavishly decadent daybed said to have been designed for Marie-Antoinette so that she could appear at the theater in Versailles after the difficult birth of her first child in 1779.[27] Sapho, dressed in a flowing robe, holds up her arms in supplication to this theatrical apparition, this *dea ex machina*. Eisen's image is all soft swirls, ripples, and curls. He blurs the passion out of the scene, allows the complexity of the interchange between patron goddess and poet gently to float away. Eisen's illustration of Sapho's suicidal leap similarly conveys a surface unified by a continuous flow of gently swirling rococo forms, a surface whose elegance is not even ruptured by Sapho's falling figure (fig. 4). In the background, a plump little Cupid digs his fingers into his eyes either to stop his tears or to avoid looking at Sapho. In Eisen's vision, Sapho's suicide is either gently tearful (*larmoyant,* in the parlance of the day), or not really visible against the rippling background. Attention directed at Sapho is displaced onto her vast robes, billowing softly about her, all the more so because the shapes designed by her garment repeat the gentle undulation of the sea, the swirls of the cliff, and the spiraling tendrils extending from the elaborate frame that surrounds the vignette. Even the lyre that falls from Sapho's hand functions primarily in the decorative ensemble, echoing the curving elements of the frame. It could also be argued that, in the image's overall economy, the size and ornateness of the frame serve further to distract attention from the leap.

Fig. 3. Charles Eisen, illustration, "Hymne à Vénus," Moutonnet de Clairfons, *Anacréon, Sapho, Bion, et Moschus* (1773). Reprinted by permission of the Rare Book Collection, Princeton University Library.

FIG. 4. Charles Eisen, Sappho's suicidal leap, Moutonnet de Clarifons, *Anacréon, Sapho, Bion, et Moschus* (1773). Reprinted by permission of the Rare Book Collection, Princeton University Library.

The alleged subject of the illustration, proportionately tiny, seems lost in an elaborately appealing aesthetic complex.

Eisen's avoidance of passion is the artistic equivalent of her translators' move to make her *oeuvre* but one in an association of unrelated elements forced into stylistic similarity. But his iconographic silence may also result from timidity in the face of innovation. As Judith Stein points out, the scene of Sappho's suicidal leap was first depicted in a Roman fresco (only discovered in the twentieth century), subsequently to disappear from the iconography of Sappho until its resurrection in the 1760s in France (21). Eisen's failure to realize the potential of his innovation might indicate his inability to imagine a scene then largely without visual precedent. The jump is also outside the narrative of *Heroides* 15 for when we leave Ovid's Sappho, she has pledged to die only if her letter brings no response from Phaon. Eisen's illustration and the rare suicide images of the preceding decade were actually providing a visual record of a scene recounted only in French popular fiction starting with D'Auvigny, and in the biographies of Sappho provided by her treacherous eighteenth-century translators. In France, Sappho thus enters painting as a construct of popular fiction. From this point on, visual images of her proliferate. Without exception, when Sappho is given plastic form, she is enshrined in the visual imagination in poses taken from the popular tradition of Sapphic speculation.

The most unreliable eighteenth-century edition first appeared in 1773, along with Moutonnet de Clairfons's attempt to saccharinize Sappho's verse. In the first volume of *Le Parnasse des dames*, Billardon de Sauvigny includes a translation of Sappho's poetry which he advertises as the most complete to date. He claims not only to have consulted Wolff's edition but also to have had access to a German source "about to be made public" (Brunck's 1772 *Anthologia Graeca*, which must have come into print as he was writing). In the context of what follows, however, his parade of erudition seems a mockery. To begin with, there is nothing routine about the obligatory biographical sketch with which he begins: Billardon de Sauvigny proposes the most fanciful fiction of the century by embroidering on every element mentioned by previous biographers, reliable and unreliable. I will go over his chronology in some detail since its influence is crucial on the most popular Sapphic fictions of the late eighteenth century and is still evident in the first quarter of the nineteenth century.

According to Billardon de Sauvigny, Sapho was "married just on emerging from childhood," had a daughter immediately, followed by "a prompt widowhood." She was, therefore, still a very young woman when she began writing and knew "such dazzling and immediate fame that she forgot to be on guard against envy." Sapho was surrounded on the one hand by "the most famous women in Greece" who were her "disciples" and on the other by "a crowd of ardent admirers, among whom could be counted the three greatest poets of her century, Archiloque, Hipponax, and Alcée" (1:64). Sapho's "first misfortune" was to attract the attention of such illustrious men, for when she rejects each of them they, and Alcée in particular, begin to slander her reputation. Initially, there is female solidarity and the women of Mytilène stand behind Sapho. But this alliance ends when Phaon appears on the scene: all the women are after him, and Sapho "had the dangerous good fortune of being preferred" (1:66). The scorned poet-lovers renew their attacks and Sapho's female disciples, now also the victims of rejection, turn against her: "Damophile, one of her favorite pupils, dealt her the most painful blow; she tricked Phaon into doubting his beloved's fidelity, and because of this doubt he became estranged from her" (1:67). From this point on, Sapho is able to write only about Phaon's betrayal. Her fickle lover returns to her briefly because he is seduced by the "immortality" that she is giving him by making his name familiar to all Greeks, but he soon abandons her a second time and leaves for Sicily. Sapho, by then "the object of public hatred and scorn," writes to beg him to return and then follows him there (1:67). When all efforts fail, she makes the fatal leap.

Billardon de Sauvigny then unveils his translation, in which he presents a Sapho even more composite than Moutonnet de Clairfons's concoction. He proclaims that the translator faced with a corpus of fragments must "adopt [the] manner [of his original] and . . . become imbued with its genius" (1:73, n. 1). The promiscuous translator, in other words, invests himself with Sappho's authority over her work. Billardon de Sauvigny assumes Sappho's authority and invents poems in two ways. First, he literally makes up verse not by Sappho. He also strings together some of the fragments German scholars had been editing, interspersing them with bits of his own invention, in order to create composite poems that, when read together, add up to a vision of Sapho that confirms every phase of the biography he constructs for her. Billardon de Sauvigny rearranges what he knew of Sappho's poetry into a series of eighteen odes, the majority of which are labeled with a title and a caption, so it is easy to situate the ersatz odes in their proper place in the biographical sketch. In the first ode—"made up of three fragments" (1:69, n. 1)—Sapho explains that because she's lost her "innocent happiness" (presumably with her husband), she'll never know "the peace that would have been dear to her" and so, under the influence of her "blood so quick to catch fire," she intends to "dedicate the days of her springtime . . . to glory and pleasure" (1:70). The initial definition of his heroine culminates in the fourth ode, "The Dream," with the caption: "Sapho feels for the first time the need to love. A dream teaches her" (1:73). "Nature was filling her heart with calm" when "love came to trouble the sweetness of her naive peace." "It's time, love told me, to give yourself up." At this point, Sapho falls asleep: "I was alone, and I belonged to Venus." In her dream, she recognizes the island of Cythera where she disembarks and breathes "a contagious fire" under "a burning rain." A god pursues her and she is "expiring" and "yielding to rapture" when she awakens (1:75–76). Sapho thus defined in all the lasciviousness of her nature, the stages of her amorous career can be unfolded.

Billardon de Sauvigny cites as ode 6 Boileau's translation of fr. 31, inaugurating the period during which Sapho is surrounded by "the most famous women in Greece" who are her "disciples." In a series of composite odes, she is made to praise Athis's beauty and demonstrate in various ways the centrality of the feminocentric phase of her existence. Ode 15 shows that our "translator" will introduce any evidence, however spurious, in support of his idea of a period during which Sapho was sought after by many men, all of whom she scorned. The "dialogue between Alcée and Sapho" reproduces an often repeated apocryphal exchange (cited originally by Aristotle) in which Sappho was alleged to have rejected Alceus's indecent overtures. From then on, the plot unfolds quickly, perhaps because Billardon de Sauvigny is almost entirely on his own. Ode 16, "Sapho tries to cure Phaon of his jealousy of Alcée," is completely his creation. How could Phaon, "adorned with the graces of springtime," Sapho asks, be jealous of "an amorous old man"? Ode 17 is his version of the Aphrodite ode, which he contends was written during the period (of his invention) when Phaon was still in Mytilène but his passion had "cooled off": "With this ode Sapho was trying to reawaken his love and flatter his amour-propre" (1:111).[28] The final ode, he contends, was written just before the suicide, a place prior French editors had assigned the Aphrodite ode. Billardon de Sauvigny concludes with a work that roundly reaffirms his absolute authority over Sappho's poetry: "Here's the ode to which Sapho contributed the least," he proclaims almost proudly; "I tried to imitate her manner" (1:112, n. 1). Sappho contributes exactly nothing to this ode, invented by her most treacherous translator to establish his idea that Phaon's final departure and therefore Sapho's suicide were provoked by the betrayal of a female confidante: "too trusting I loved my unfaithful rival [*ma rivale infidelle*]" (1:116), Sapho wails.

Billardon de Sauvigny's counterfeit Sapho initially ended at this point. However, four years after his original edition, he reissued his translation, this time supplementing his composite odes with techniques borrowed from Blin de Sainmore and Moutonnet de Clairfons. He takes advantage of his second chance to invent more evidence in support of his view of the end of Sapho's life. He adds a second version of the Aphrodite ode, labeled, like Blin de Sainmore's, "free translation of Sapho," a translation both so free and so different from his original effort that the reader relying on this edition as an introduction to Sappho might take it for a separate ode. He also includes a "Letter from Sapho to Phaon," his own version of *Heroides* 15, which is even more illegitimate than Blin de Sainmore's ersatz Ovid. Billardon de Sauvigny's aim in including Ovid in his package is to win acceptance for his version of the last phase of Sapho's life. To do so, he must complete the erasure of Ovid's authority initiated by the creators of the "new heroides." He therefore tries to pass off this verse epistle, too, as part of Sappho's *oeuvre:* the coda to the first half of his edition, "end of Sapho's poetry," appears only after the second Aphrodite ode which follows the spurious letter. By including this Ovidian fiction under Sappho's name, and by restyling it in the same language and tone from which his composite Sapho is constructed, Billardon de Sauvigny takes what proves to be the penultimate step in the erosion of Ovid's authority over Sappho's plot.

His tactics won for him a measure of the authority over Sappho's plot that had been Ovid's in the early eighteenth century. Proof that Billardon de Sauvigny succeeded in supplanting the poet of heroinism for a generation of readers is provided by the late eighteenth-century counterpart of the anonymous early eighteenth-century "Lettre de Sapho à Phaon." The version of Sappho's life and work included in the 1787 *Bibliothèque universelle des dames,* a vast compilation modestly priced for wide circulation, shows us the popular view of Sappho the poet on the eve of the Revolution. The anonymous presentation teaches us above all that a decade after the publication of his most complete edition, Billardon de Sauvigny's fiction reigned supreme. Virtually all the information in the biographical sketch reproduces his; much of the spurious verse attributed to Sappho is of his invention.[29]

The second part of Billardon de Sauvigny's 1777 edition stands as the final gesture in the total assimilation of Sappho's voice into a tapestry of eighteenth-century poetic discourses. To his composite Sapho, Billardon de Sauvigny appends first of all a twenty-five-page poem, "Les Tourterelles de Zelmis," in tone and imagery often similar to the odes he attributes to Sappho. However, since this is a poem about the loves, misfortunes, and jealousies not of humans but of turtledoves, its juxtaposition with Sapho's "heroic" complaint makes her plot, in precisely its eighteenth-century formulation, seem promiscuously absurd. The verse tale of quarreling turtledoves is followed by the edition's final section, nearly fifty pages of which are entitled simply "poésies érotiques," whose authorship is established only in a note: "The poems that end this volume are by M. Parny" (103, n. 1). The reader might simply dismiss this final gesture as an editor's desire to market a fatter volume, were it not for the fact that the work's title, "Poems by Sapho, followed by other poems of the same type [*dans le même genre*]," clearly indicates that Billardon de Sauvigny intended to express a bond between his version of Sappho's *oeuvre* and the poetry appended to it. His characterization of Sappho's poetry reinforces this notion further. "The genre in which she excels is immediately obvious," he proclaims with the confidence of someone stating a self-evident truth. In case Sappho's genre is not immediately recognizable by all, he clarifies this with the most succinct of notes: "the erotic genre" (62). In fact, in the genre as he seems to understand it, the Parny poems he includes are no more or no less "erotic" than what he attributes to Sappho.[30]

Billardon de Sauvigny uses another adjective to characterize the poetry of his day, an adjective that casts light on what he means by "erotic." Speaking of a poem by Jean-François Saint-Lambert, he declares: "This piece is considered by connoisseurs one of the finest occasional poems [*pièces fugitives*] that we have in our language" (71). "Fugitive poetry" differs from its English counterpart, "occasional verse," in the first place because it has a particular association with the eighteenth century, an association foregrounded in the Robert dictionary's definition of the term: "little works in verse on inconsequential subjects. *Fugitive poems were very much in vogue in the eighteenth century.*" In addition, fugitive verse is without the primary connotation of occasional poetry, that of having been "produced on, or intended for, a special occasion" (*OED*). The category fugitive poetry, as its name indicates, connotes above all the instability just below the surface of occasional verse. Fugitive verse is perhaps the ultimate self-consuming artifact, written, as it were, haphazardly, seemingly without authorial design or intention, and it is therefore intentionally a thing of little substance, destined to disappear almost as soon as it sees the light of day. The eighteenth-century Trévoux dictionary defines it thus: "works that escape, sometimes on purpose, from an author's portfolio, and that can be turned into only a slight volume."

This transient, ephemeral literary territory was the terrain of choice of the age's foremost poets: Saint-Lambert (to whom Barthélemy compared Sappho), Delille (who translated her), and Parny (with whom Billardon de Sauvigny paired Sappho)—all were promoted as fugitive poets.[31] Their choice of genre undoubtedly explains why their names are of so little consequence today. In the age of Enlightenment, poets chose to be viewed as fugitives on the literary scene. In this context, it is hardly surprising that, in the hands of Sappho's eighteenth-century interpreters, from Gacon and D'Auvigny to Moutonnet de Clairfons and Billardon de Sauvigny, her poems are turned into classics of a genre that in the history of French poetry has become synonymous with their age, "fugitive" poetry. By the end of the eighteenth century, her poetry is no longer "erotic" in any definition of that term acceptable today. In fact, the anonymous editor of the *Bibliothèque universelle des dames* repeats Billardon de Sauvigny's magisterial pronouncement, "the genre in which she excels is immediately obvious," only to name the genre not "erotic," but "tender" (8:95). By that, he means something close to Barthélemy and Delille's "cheerful" nature poetry, for he leads off the selection from Sappho's *oeuvre* with her (spurious) pastoral side: "Rose," "Etoile du soir."

The heterosexual Sapho fashioned by eighteenth-century novelists could never have been the author of truly erotic verse. Her contemporary translators presented her poetry as worthy of the authorial fiction, as superficial, inconsequential, fleeting. It is as though the famous "phobeitai" from fr. 31, one of the signatures of Sappho's sublimity, had been scaled down semantically from what Le Fèvre Dacier describes as a "convulsive trembling," a tremor that sends shock waves to the core of one's being and a cataclysm that marked literature indelibly, to a gentle ripple fluttering prettily across the surface of literature without leaving a trace of its passage. By the time of the French Revolution, Sappho's authentic poetic voice had apparently disappeared from the face of French literature.[32] An unspoken critical axiom seems to have governed this revision: female homosexuals might compose troubling poetry, but heterosexual women could only write calming, "tender" verse.

Fugitive Sappho: Sappho as *émigrée*

A man must know how to defy public opinion, a woman to sub-
mit to it.
— Suzanne Curchod Necker,
Mélanges

At the same time that her poetry is being reduced to the status of
fugitive verse, Sappho herself, for the first time in her history, is gradually
being assigned an increasingly complex and detailed role in the political
life of her day, a role that presents revealing parallels with the key
developments in the French political arena of the late eighteenth century.
Once the pattern is imposed on Sappho's poetry, the progression from
promiscuous to fugitive, with a concomitant loss of erotic energy, is also
inscribed in her biography. The same novelists and commentators who
promote the fiction of a heterosexual Sapho and a saccharine version of
Sappho's *oeuvre* are also responsible for the creation of a political Sapho,
an invention that revitalizes the Sapphic plot by shifting its energy from
sexual promiscuity to political sedition. One of the traditional stereotypes
of the unnatural woman is the woman who attempts to play a political
role. Those who politicized the heterosexual Sappho replaced one form of
unnatural female behavior with another, as if to guarantee that Sappho's
biography would never be free of menace. Indeed, during the Napoleonic
period commentators respond to this politicization of Sappho with a
renewed attempt to contain the muse of Mytilene within the limits of a
sexual scenario even more stringently normalized than that imagined for
her at the beginning of the century. Sapphism's invasion of the political
arena may also be one cause of the complex and extended nineteenth-
century German backlash against Sappho centered on the theory of
Sapphic chastity.

In the course of the eighteenth century, Sapho's political life crystallizes
around her alleged Sicilian voyage. By the early eighteenth century, it was
universally admitted that Sapho had followed Phaon to Sicily, where he
had fled to escape her importunate passion, and that it was there that she
composed the "Ode to Aphrodite" in a final attempt to win back her
inconstant lover. No authority from antiquity is ever cited in support of
this theory. Le Fèvre Dacier proposes it; other commentators follow her
lead; and the fiction eventually gains acceptance simply by virtue of
repetition. In the course of the eighteenth century, however, a new
explanation for Sapho's travels gradually takes shape. By the time this

theory is fully articulated, the fugitive poet has become a political fugitive.

D'Auvigny, the original novelist of Sapho's heterosexual promiscuity, also initiates the bond between Sapho and political unrest. In his novel, he fits Sapho's biography into his version of the political situation in Mytilène. At the time when her future husband is away and Alcée is trying to win her hand, "a storm rose up in the Republic of Mytilène" (212), and Alcée becomes involved in "a plot to take the government from the senate and is imprisoned by the dictator Pittacus, who has been brought in to bring the situation under control" (213). Alcée escapes and begins to stir up trouble from outside the country (218). D'Auvigny's Alcée is a Greek *frondeur*, a revolutionary against the just rights of dictators (or monarchs). His Sapho never participates in these activities, but Alcée is her father's relative and her suitor during this period. D'Auvigny admits that there is no evidence to support his political supplement but justifies it in novelistic terms: "I couldn't remain silent about the civil wars of Mytilène since they took place under Sapho's eyes" (440). Then came Barthélemy, and subsequent commentators never again needed to justify their speculation about political affairs.

Barthélemy, you will remember, characterizes Sapho's contemporaries on Lesbos as precursors of the late eighteenth-century Parisians whose lives were dedicated to pleasure. He suggests a second implicit comparison, either an accidental foreshadowing or an accurate prediction of the evolution from den of iniquity to den of revolution that his first readers would witness in the months that followed the publication of the *Voyage d'Anacharsis*. Like D'Auvigny, he uses Alcée to introduce political questions. Barthélemy's Alcée, who "in his earliest writings had given vent to his hatred of tyranny," is a patriot who "professed loudly his love of liberty." He first joins forces with Pittacus to free Lesbos from the tyrant Mélanchrus, then takes part in an unsuccessful uprising against Pittacus. "He was banished from Mytilène; he returned some time later at the head of the exiles" (2:66–67). Alcée thus becomes a foreshadowing of a familiar French figure of the period, an individual who takes up arms against a series of rulers not simply to prolong a period of unrest but because he feels that each has been corrupted by power and begun to deprive his subjects of their basic rights. Even Barthélemy's vocabulary encourages this premonitory identification: in the section on Lesbos, he employs "tyrant" not according to the usage of Sappho's Mytilene, a ruler who wielded force to come to power, but in a prophetic anachronism that allows the term to take on the meaning that would be crucial in the wake of the French Revolution, a head of state who abuses his position to deny his subjects their freedom.

Barthélemy does not immediately make apparent the link between Alcée's revolutionary activities and Sapho's Sicilian sojourn. In the body of his novel, he describes Sapho's exile as self-imposed, the result of a desire to avoid the persecution of women blindly faithful to a social code and threatened by Sapho's independence from the conventions they enforce (2:70). At this point, Barthélemy breaks off his narrative to refer his reader to his source, "Marm. Oxon. epoch 37," and then to a note at the end of the volume: "The place where the Parian chronicle [Marm. Oxon., the Parian marble] speaks about Sapho is almost entirely effaced on the marble, but one can read distinctly that she ran away and set out for Sicily. It was not therefore, as has been said, to follow Phaon that she went to this island. It can be presumed that Alcée got her involved in the conspiracy against Pittacus, and that she was banished from Mytilène along with him and his partisans" (2:539–40).

By the late eighteenth century, the chronicle of early Greek history carved into a stone called the Parian marble had been known for decades. If previous Sappho commentators had never cited it in their discussions of her biography, it is because, as even Barthélemy is forced to admit, it cannot unlock the mystery of her voyage. The decipherable part of this section of the marble reads, in a recent translation: "When Critius the First was archon of Athens Sappho fled [Barthélemy's 'was banished'] from Mytilene and sailed to Sicily" (Miller and Robinson, 56). This part of the Parian marble (epoch 37) is primarily devoted to chronology, and only the sentence's second verb hints at a motivation for Sappho's voyage. Barthélemy's reading is made possible by the ambiguity of what he alleges to be his source: the Greek verb means both "to flee" and "to be banished." The text surrounding this elusive fragment is mutilated, leaving Sappho once again in the position of being interpreted on the basis of a single word.

Barthélemy's most recent critic declares that the abbé "refuted" the opinion that Sappho followed Phaon to Sicily and "demonstrated on the basis of indications on the Parian marble that she was sent there in exile" (Badolle, 271), but this is to fill in the blanks in the abbé's carefully elliptical note. Barthélemy explains that his source is illegible in the crucial spot, then proceeds to read this absence as a presence: "It was not therefore"; "It can be presumed." Barthélemy proceeds by promiscuous juxtaposition rather than deduction to introduce his novel interpretation.

Thus he moves from his initial "Sapho ran away," a self-imposed exile such as he describes in the body of the *Voyage,* to "Sapho was banished," an officially ordained exile, without any indication that the two positions are not synonymous.

In Barthélemy's wake, Sappho was enshrined as a political exile, a revolutionary who had fought alongside Alceus to overthrow tyranny. This reading won acceptance despite the fact that Sappho's poetry, unlike Alceus's, is resolutely apolitical. According to C.R. Haines, the only reference in Sappho to "the political parties or affairs of Mytilene" is found in the fragment in which the poet criticizes a certain Mica (or another of her students) because of her affection for "a daughter of Penthilus," generally accepted as a reference to the family of the wife of Pittakos, Alceus's enemy (Haines, 109; Mora, 44)—a fragment, furthermore, unknown in the eighteenth century since it was only brought to light in the twentieth-century papyri discoveries.[33] Even in the absence of evidence, internal or external, to support the image of an *engagée* Sapho, Barthélemy's artfully suggested portrait so successfully captured the imaginations of numerous Sappho commentators that it was quickly assimilated as historical fact, eventually even by serious scholars. Barthélemy's and Lantier's direct heir, Chaussard, affirms with confidence the fiction of a political Sapho: "[The poet Alcée] involved her in the conspiracy against Pittacus, for which she was banished from Mytilène" (4:242). Subsequently, Claude Bréghot Du Lut, a major figure in the early nineteenth-century "recovery" of Sappho, figures the new image of an exiled Sapho into his biographical sketch where earlier translators speak of her pursuit of Phaon to Sicily, and he simply cites the relevant passage from Barthélemy in support of this view (162, n. 5). Barthélemy's theory of Sappho's political involvement has remained stubbornly alive. Even a noted twentieth-century philologist, C. M. Bowra, in the entry on Sappho in the first edition of the *Oxford Classical Dictionary,* an entry still reprinted, contends that "no doubt owing to political troubles, she went into exile in Sicily" and cites as supporting evidence the same passage in the Parian marble, even though he admits that "no traces of this are left in her fragments."[34]

No writer plays a more active role in the exploitation of Sappho's exile than Germaine de Staël. The *Voyage du jeune Anacharsis* was at the height of its enormous initial success when the twenty-two-year-old baronne de Staël improvised a long poem eulogizing its author in the course of a banquet in his honor (*Correspondance littéraire,* February 1789). Barthélemy is identified as having taken up "Homer's golden lyre," and Staël, whose own career as a published author was just being launched, asks him to lend it to her so that she might "sing his praises." Twelve years would pass, and she would herself live the life of an exile for a decade, before she took up that lyre to play Sappho to Barthélemy's Homer and create a new Sapphic fiction informed by the abbé's vision of the original woman writer.

A continuously evolving identification with Sappho as intensely personal as Scudéry's is revealed at the major intersections of Staël's literary career. So durable, in fact, is her obsession with Sappho's plot that it can be considered the primal story from which her most important fiction is generated.[35] We have already seen how Germaine Necker came to writing through a romance of Ovid's heroic fiction. By the time she begins her first major literary effort, *Delphine,* she no longer accepts a purely Ovidian scenario for the original woman writer. Curiously, although Staël was in her day the leading proponent in France of German literature and scholarship, her fictions reveal no awareness of the efforts of contemporary German Hellenists to broaden the Sappho canon and eliminate the most outrageous biographical fictions. The influences that complicate the Ovidian plot she originally dictates for Sappho are first from the French popularizing tradition and later from French translations of the even more distorting Italian tradition that developed late in the century. However, Staël sets herself apart from her contemporaries, in this case all male, by rescripting their constructions with a feminist twist. The plot she slowly elaborates for Sappho—beginning in *Delphine,* and continuing in *Corinne* and in her final literary effort, a tragedy *Sapho*—can be seen as the fulfillment, but more properly as the disclosure of the goal, of the eighteenth-century French Sappho tradition. According to Staël, Sapho's suicidal plunge is inexorably, irrevocably dictated by the laws governing the patriarchy's family romance. In her major fictions, she uses a series of Sappho figures to explore the consequences of woman's rejection of the plot dictating her promiscuity.

Delphine occupies a pivotal position in the history of French prose fiction: it is the last major epistolary novel. In it, Staël returns to that genre's origin in France in the "heroic" outpourings of Saphos and Sapphic figures and goes against the grain of epistolary development to antiquate her fiction. She introduces first a series of confessional letters, miniature autobiographies (madame de Vernon's is a particularly developed example). Madelyn Gutwirth aptly characterizes these epistles as "portraits de femmes" which collectively constitute a "plaidoyer," a plea in favor of women's rights ("La *Delphine* de Madame de Staël," 155–56). They are complemented by the texts that open the novel's fifth part, "fragments written by Delphine during her journey." All these first-person cries from the heart by women wronged are regressive, out of step with the quick-paced, plot-oriented final phase of French epistolary fiction as represented by the work usually taken for its masterpiece, *Les Liaisons dangereuses.* They are in form intimately related to the outpourings of heroinism, as though Staël had plotted a volume of heroinical epistles within her letter novel. In subject matter, however, they break radically with the plot of heroinism. Staël develops the modifications codified by Barthélemy to make Sapho representative no longer just of the woman wronged in love but of a more comprehensive vision of the female condition.

When we measure *Delphine* against traditional fictions of Sappho such as Staël's own youthful *romance,* the importance for her of the new Sapphic plot becomes clear. Delphine is related to the eighteenth century's Sapho in two important ways: she has been an orphan since a very early age and she finds herself a widow while still very young. These factors make her, like the Sapho of the popular tradition, a free agent in the patriarchal order at a time when she is still a coveted object of exchange. Staël's novels are traditionally read as projections of the author's own, apparently blatantly oedipal, family romance with her illustrious parents. However, in both *Delphine* and *Corinne,* Staël carefully disengages her heroines from their parental ties at an early age, and even more carefully displaces the scene and alters the content of her novelistic family romances. The heroine's genealogy, and this is especially true in *Delphine,* is impoverished in order to privilege the genealogy of the man who becomes the object of her affections. It is that family rather than her own that serves as an obstacle to her passage into the cultural order: in Staël's fiction, the father's interdiction is the rejection of the heroine by the hero's family, a rejection designed to make permanent her exclusion from the community of families. When she makes her Ur-heroine a female child trying, unlike her male counterpart in Marthe Robert's typology, not to reinvent the world but to win a place for herself in the family of men, Staël's fiction may be pertinent to that blank in Freud's schema, the allegedly "weaker imagination" of the female child. Staël suggests that the scene of the female child's family romance may be elsewhere in that for her the crucial rite of passage involves not her own family but that in the name of whose father she will accede to the patriarchal order.

For her illustration of the female orphan's family dilemma, Staël is heavily indebted to Barthélemy's definitive version of the story of Sapho's exclusion from society. Both Barthélemy's Sapho and Staël's Delphine attempt their rites of social passage on an island of conformity and propriety in a sea of relaxed standards, corruption, and threatening new ideas. In a milieu where assimilation and total allegiance to accepted standards are the highest virtue, both distinguish themselves by their too evident superiority. *Corinne* has often been preferred to *Delphine* on the grounds that in the later novel Staël concerns herself with the plight of women of genius, but Delphine corroborates perfectly the model for the woman of letters established by popular fictions of Sapho. As proof of Sapho's genius, Barthélemy, like his precursors, cites only her prodigious "sensitivity" (*sensibilité*) and her equally magnified "passionateness," both qualities with which Delphine is also gifted to an exceptional degree. Delphine displays her talents in the same arena as the seventeenth-century Sapho, the salon, thereby giving the women who set the codes of propriety ample occasion to become jealous of her "superiority."[36] Both heroines are models of personal virtue and high moral standards, yet both commit the socially unpardonable sin of what Barthélemy terms "indiscretion" by living according to their own laws. Delphine "scorns the accepted maxims" in favor of "her own ideas about personal behavior" (1:2:26). Like Sapho, she thereby "exposes herself to blame" and becomes a subject for gossip (1:11:68; 2:3:195). The two heroines seal their fates by taking the offensive against the rulers of the social order. Sapho points out behavioral "truths" they would have preferred to avoid and answers their defenses with "irony" (2:70). Delphine introduces a similar dose of sarcasm into her attempts to make the representatives of the "world and the city"—in Staël's fictions, the guarantors of the patriarchal order have either "monde" or "ville," if not both, embedded in their family names—confront the hypocrisy and ignorance that govern their discussions of new ideas (1:25:115–16).

In similar fashion, the heroines set themselves up to serve as illustrations of the one social truth that Staël neatly packages as a maxim—the citation from her own social arbiter mother, the noted *salonnière* Suzanne Curchod Necker, that stands as the ominous epigraph to *Delphine:* "A man must know how to defy public opinion, a woman to submit to it." Because these

Sappho figures elect the male plot and "defy public opinion," they must be driven out of the society whose foundation they threaten. The women "humiliated" by Sapho's superiority and high-handed independence spread rumors about her sexual preferences, until Sapho is obliged to flee their continued persecution. Staël is more precise about the nature of that persecution. When she fills in Barthélemy's ellipses, she develops a plot that parallels the biography devised for Sappho by Billardon de Sauvigny, whose often reprinted edition was the dominant French translation at the time of *Delphine*'s composition. Staël's heroine first is betrayed by the women who spread the rumor that her "innocent" passion for her cousin's husband, Léonce de Mondoville, is a "guilty" one. Her plight is exacerbated by the gossip about her improper conduct with regard to him generated by a rejected suitor, M. de Valorbe, like Alcée a political fugitive. The superior woman has no recourse against those who discipline the social order and keep the patriarchy safe from excess and indiscretion: Delphine, like Sapho, flees into self-imposed exile.

Like Barthélemy, Staël turns flight from social ostracism into political exile. On the surface, she seems also to echo his elliptical juxtaposition of these two scenarios. Delphine is often in conflict with the rulers of the social order because she rebels against their dictate that a woman's place is outside the political arena, and because she publicly defends such Revolutionary ideals as "the love of liberty" (1:25:118). However, Delphine would remain a sentimental fugitive rather than a political exile if Staël had not filled in, as it were, the obliteration in the Parian marble by bringing her Sapho figure into the eighteenth century and pinpointing the kind of political activity that the superior woman might appropriately undertake. Writing just prior to the events of the eighteenth century's final decade, Barthélemy was unable to be specific about the shape of political unrest: he defines Alcée and Sapho's activities with vague slogans like "opposition to tyranny" and "love of liberty." Staël, however, writing in 1801–2, knew where such ideals could lead. In view of this hindsight and of Staël's own continuously active involvement in political affairs, the presence granted the Revolution in *Delphine* appears at first surprisingly limited.

Delphine's action is set in the period April 1790–September 1792. There are references throughout to the events of the Revolution and to the positions of the novel's characters with regard to these events. However, Staël never makes a systematic attempt to come to terms with the Revolution, a fact that continues to disappoint critics today.[37] The total political context remains underdeveloped, not simply because this was a dangerous subject for literature at the turn of the nineteenth century but because Staël's real political subject lies elsewhere. The only Revolutionary issue systematically addressed in the novel is the question of divorce. Divorce, indeed, is the determining factor in the novel's chronology: the story moves by fits and starts—on several occasions, hopes are raised, only to be dashed—ever closer to a law allowing divorce. This momentum explains Staël's choice of *terminus ad quem*. The novel's final letter, from Léonce to Delphine, is dated 8 September 1792, which allows enough time for the drama's last scenes to unfold and still make its final action, Delphine's suicide and Léonce's execution, approximately simultaneous with the culminating event in the divorce saga, the decree of 20 September 1792 establishing civil marriage and divorce.[38] That Delphine and Léonce die far from Paris and so are not informed, any more than are the novel's readers, of the ultimate victory in the struggle for marital freedom, and that they no longer stand to benefit from such a decree since Léonce's wife Mathilde is already dead, are not tragic ironies but clear indications that, for Staël, the drama of divorce is bigger than the saga of her two lovers. Divorce, she suggests, is a crucial step in establishing the legal code essential to women's independence from the dictates of the patriarchal order.

Delphine ultimately clarifies the ellipses with which Barthélemy moves Sapho from social fugitiveness to political exile. From her exile, Staël's heroine defines with perfect clarity her threatening situation: "What a chain of affection, from century to century, binds families together! And I, poor woman, I am outside that chain; I have lost my parents, I will not have children, and all the emotions of my soul are focused on a single being, from whom I am separated forever!" (5:16:229). Staël creates a heroine who, like Sappho, represents a pure challenge to what she terms the familial "chain of affection," the patriarchal order. Since she is not bound by the patriarchy (she is "outside that chain"), she must be outlawed from its domain. Because Delphine goes out fighting for the right to her exceptional status, and for all women's right to legal independence from families into which they have been adopted not by choice but by exchange, she is not merely a fugitive but a political exile. In one of the vast novel's most powerful scenes, Delphine is first publicly and universally ostracized by the most prominent members of society because of Valorbe's rumors, and then rushes out into the night to flee her persecutors. Her mad exit immediately evolves into a march into political exile. Fleeing, like Barthélemy's Sapho, "in the face of ill will and hatred," Delphine "finds herself in the square Louis XV"; before she knows it, she is "already on the bridge Louis XVI," and when she realizes that this political review will end for her, as for the ancien régime, in death, she considers a Sapphic leap into water (4:29:124). "I must leave the world forever," she cries (4:29:125), linking the ancien régime to the voice of public opinion—in Staël's idiom, the dictates of her heroine's enemies, "monde," "ville," "orbe," the Mondovilles, mother and son, and Valorbe.

Sappho's first nineteenth-century translator, Bréghot Du Lut, comments that Barthélemy's influential "conjecture" was inspired by the expression "fugitive" or "exile" still visible on the the Parian marble (162, n. 5). In view of his close proximity to a time when such terms had been of central importance, Bréghot Du Lut's failure to distinguish between them is curious. He echoes the ambiguity of Barthélemy's own pre-Revolutionary usage of "exile" to denote both an individual struggling to liberate his country from oppressive rule and someone fleeing from malicious gossip aggravated by his attempt to preserve an individual code of behavior. Staël maintains this equivocal usage, and makes it more equivocal still, by linking *exilé* to *émigré*, a neologism that enters the French language in 1791, *Delphine*'s central year. The word was created to refer to "an individual who took refuge outside France during the Revolution," and therefore to someone "who left his native land [*s'est expatrié*] for political reasons" (*Robert*). It was understood at the time that those "political reasons" could only be monarchist, that all who left were enemies of the Revolution and of the the new shape it was giving the fatherland. Delphine falls outside this category, too, because she supports the Revolution, even if she does not fight for it. However, Staël's heroine, like all superior women, is "outside the [familial] chain," a natural enemy of the patriarchy, literally an expatriate, ex-patria. Staël's counterfiction of Sapphic exile indicates that since revolutions do not overthrow the Law governing woman's place in the social order, for a woman flight from the patriarchal Revolutionary order is both a political and a revolutionary act. She also, perhaps inadvertently, suggests what will be the French tradition's response to the politicization of Sapho. Her female revolutionary activity will be rejected by both sides in the political conflict, and *émigré* and *exilé* will be, for once, legitimately synonymous.

Critics often deny that *Delphine* is a political novel. Yet because of this novel Bonaparte, alleged inheritor of the Revolution, forbids Staël access to Paris, prolonging her exile and her expatriate status.[39] Staël's resolutely ex-centric heroine is too clearly a threat to the values of the patriarchy, pre- or post-Revolutionary.[40] In Napoleonic France, Sapho is also made to pay a price for her politicization in fictions that reinstate the superior woman ever more firmly within the patriarchal law.

Sapho in (Napoleonic) Italy

The maxim that was carved in gold letters by her wise parents above the door of our Saffo's study: work keeps the soul peaceful, just as exercise maintains the health of the body.

—Alessandro Verri,
Le Avventure di Saffo

The chronology of Sappho's presence in France highlights the eighteenth century's most important production of Sapphic fictions during the 1770s and 1780s, the decades in which growing political unrest prepared the Revolution. The existence of a link between Sappho's unsettling presence and revolt against tyrannical rule was posited explicitly for the first time by her last pre-Revolutionary interpreter, Barthélemy. However, at no point during or after the events of 1789 was Sappho's potential as a classical revolutionary exploited by the dominant French tradition of Sapphic speculation, despite the fact that, especially under the Empire, Barthélemy's success and authority were uncontested. On the contrary, at the turn of the century Sappho became the almost exclusive property of writers with close ties to Napoleon's immediate entourage. These writers rejected both Barthélemy's revolutionary Sapho and the earlier political fiction by Sappho's first French biographer, Scudéry, who makes the original woman writer, like Alcée, a political poet, but a protomonarchist poet who writes occasional verse in celebration of Pittacus's military victories (*Artamène,* 10:461). The creators of Napoleonic fictions of Sappho remove her from the political arena and assign her a role in a plot limiting heroism to activities even more passive and more demeaning than those dictated by the Ovidian plot, as if to guarantee against the threat of all female political activity, either conservative or revolutionary: they become thereby the first true precursors of the nineteenth-century German tradition of Sapphic commentary.

The eighteenth century's idiosyncratic vision of Sappho finds its fullest realization in a series of fictions that honor the Napoleonic presence in

Italy. These texts have one main precursor, among the most curious of all fictions of Sappho, whose influence is felt in the most unexpected places, Claude de Sacy's *Les Amours de Sapho et de Phaon* (1775).[41] Sacy offers a true fairy-tale Sapho, a heroine who is a cross between an orphan and a bastard but who, unlike Marthe Robert's novelistic heroes, is never allowed to remake or conquer the world. Initially, Sapho is dramatized as a superwoman who comes into the world in a literary variant of the divine birth. Sapho's parents are childless until Cleis has a dream in which she is first "torn apart by a thousand shooting pains" and then comforted by the nine Muses, who gather around her bed "to take in their arms the fruit of my suffering . . . ; the child seemed sensitive to their caresses." One of the Muses announces their plans for the child: "We are adopting this girl as our sister; we want to nourish her with our milk; one day she will be the honor of her sex and her fatherland [*patrie*]" (17–18). The girl Sapho follows the scenario of the archetypal hero. She is so tough that even if she feels pain, she reveals no sign of her suffering: "a child whom nature seemed to have freed from the common law, the tears ordinary to childhood never dimmed the fire of her eyes" (19). In addition, a true intellectual superchild, "she was already formulating her ideas at an age when other children are barely able to make their needs known" (20). As soon as Sapho begins to perform her verse, her genius is so powerful that all other poets simply "break their reed-pipes" in recognition of her mastery (21). Shortly after she achieves dominance over the literary scene, Sapho is freed from her pseudoparents: when they become lost in the forest while returning home one evening, first the father and then the mother are eaten by a raging lioness (28).

Sacy's fiction might initially appear a feminist revision of the virgin birth, in which the Muses replace the Holy Spirit's agency to guarantee that the female literary savior comes into the world without male participation. However, once the divine child loses her human foster parents, she embarks not on the career of heroism for which she had apparently been destined but on a downward course even more humiliating than those previously imagined for Sappho. The telltale mark of Napoleonic or proto-Napoleonic fictions of Sapho is the heroine's uncontrollable attraction to male physical beauty. In this tradition, a revitalized Phaon is the agent of Sapho's reduction to markedly unheroic status. Sacy's heroine falls in love with Phaon's physical beauty when she sees a painting of him in Mytilene's temple of Apollo. Like Sapho, this Phaon is protected by a fairy godmother: when he is orphaned at birth, "nature alone became his mother and watched over his childhood." Like Sapho, he is a poet, taught, like her, by the Muses to excel in what is defined in Sacy's day as Sapho's genre, pastoral poetry (39).

Phaon lives alone in the forest because, like Racine's Hippolyte, he is a "wild man" (*farouche*) who "has sworn an eternal hatred to [Sapho's] sex" (47, 50). Unlike Hippolyte, however—and this is Sacy's most durable contribution to the fictionalization of Sapho—this Phaon is no effeminate child-man. He is the same age as Sapho, and he is a paragon of masculine physical strength, destined, like Sapho, for heroism and exemplarity. Sapho makes their rivalry visible when, in order to be allowed into Phaon's company, she has recourse to cross-dressing.[42] Attired as a shepherd, she pretends to be a man until she wins Phaon's confidence. However, when the revolution breaks out, Sapho is captured by an enemy general and must be rescued by her lover. Phaon then leaves her for Aglaë, a rich *older* woman. When Sapho makes her suicidal leap, the Muses' prophecy that she would become "the honor of her sex and her fatherland" seems a poor joke indeed.

For the patriarchal fictions created in the wake of Sacy's novel, the moment of Sapho's divine birth and entry into heroism is an always repressed primal scene. In the fictions I call Napoleonic, there will never again be the slightest hesitation as to whether Sapho should be entrusted with "the honor of the fatherland." The next phase of French Sapphic fictionalization will be activated outside of France, in Italy just prior to the French presence there. These Italian fictions begin to function as part of the French tradition when they are translated into French by writers who realize their complicity with the Napoleonic ideology.

Alessandro Verri begins his *Le Avventure di Saffo* (1780) with a chapter entitled "Phaon Transformed." The opening title calls attention to the fact that, following Sacy's example, Verri exaggerates Phaon's masculinity in order to put a revitalized Phaon at the center of the Sapphic plot. He continues the normalization of their ages: Phaon is older than Saffo who, even at the time of her suicide, is a mere girl. They meet at the annual games held in Mytilène for the feast of Minerva. Saffo falls in love at first sight when she watches Phaon in the wrestling contest. What Verri has his reader admire through her eyes is less Phaon's physical prowess (although he does repeatedly refer to his strength and agility) than the sheer beauty of his body. Surely few, if any, fictional scenes available in 1780 afforded the novelist the possibility, in which Verri luxuriates here, of narrating the moment at which a handsome young man "stripped off his garb . . . and appeared perfectly naked, having only the usual wrestler's girdle." He then dwells on "the action of his muscles" (Nott, trans., 39)—all this for the seduction of an adolescent female.[43] Saffo is so enraptured with this display of male flesh that she is moved spontaneously to embark on her poetic career. After the wrestling match, she presents Phaon with a bunch of flowers and, "framed in sudden poetic frenzy," in his honor she improvises her first poem (47).

Eloquent confirmation of this interpretation of Verri's proto-Napoleonic romance is provided by a 1784 volume of aquatints inspired by it. In a series that contains some of the most powerful pictorial representations of Sappho ever, the Irish painter Henry Tresham portrays the key scenes of Verri's Sapphic romance. Tresham's plates 1 and 7 provide the most succinct illustration of the transfer of power to Phaon that is the central message of Napoleonic fictions.[44] Plate 1 depicts the scene in which Saffo, transfixed by the beauty of the nude Faone, hands him a nosegay (fig. 5). Tresham's caption, "Saffo si accende per Faone," means most obviously simply that she falls in love with him. However, the verb's primary sense of "to inflame" or "to ignite" leads us to the heart of the matter: Verri and Tresham steal the fire that is the most vivid image in Sappho's largely imageless fr. 31 and make Faone the cause of Saffo's burning poetic sublimity. Tresham's plate 7 completes the transfer of power (fig. 6). His title "Faone narrates his transformation" refers to the legend of Phaon's rejuvenation by Aphrodite, but it also highlights Phaon's "transformation" into the magnetic *literary* presence in the Sapphic romance: Faone tells his story "with a tongue inspired by the gods", in Verri's words, and, upon hearing him, "all motion was suspended in [Saffo]; even her respiration seemed to cease" (103, 101). The power of the verb to captivate one's audience has been transferred to the object of the poet's unrequited passion, who had only previously been endowed with a literary gift by Sacy.

The original edition of Verri's novel predates the Napoleonic presence in Italy. However, no sooner had Italy been brought under French control than the novelist seized the opportunity to capitalize on his fiction's potential to find favor with the new regime. In 1797, Verri reedited his *Saffo* with a dedication to Napoleon's sister Caroline, to whom he refers as "our Saffo." In a dedicatory preface, he details the ideology that he feels will appeal to the new ruling family: "Such a truth is too well understood by you, fairest Citizen [*Cittadina*], for you have engraved upon your mind the maxim that was carved in gold letters by her wise parents above the

Saffo si accende per Faone

Gia si presento recandogli i fiori, e cantando all improviso Versi allora in lei formati dall impeto del miglior estro: cioè l'Amore.

FIG. 5. Henry Tresham, plate 1, "Saffo si accende per Faone," [Verri], *Le Avventure di Saffo* (1784). Reprinted by permission of the Bibliothèque Nationale, Paris. Phot. Bibl. Nat. Paris.

FAONE narra La sua trasformazione.

Intanto la Vergine bevea a larghi sorsi il veleno, ed inebbriata dalla soavità di quelle parole, si stendeva verso del narratore con volto ansioso.

FIG. 6. Henry Tresham, plate 7, "Faone narra la sua transformazione," [Verri], *Le Avventure di Saffo* (1784). Reprinted by permission of the Bibliothèque Nationale, Paris. Phot. Bibl. Nat. Paris.

door of our Saffo's study: that work keeps the soul peaceful, just as exercise maintains the health of the body" (my translation). At the height of French imperialism and the new militarism on which it is founded, the story of Sappho is deployed as an alleged moral tale worthy of the citizens of the new republic, because it justifies the work ethic and glorifies physical fitness. Furthermore, the syntax of Verri's overblown dedication leads us to read into it more than undeserved praise. Caroline Bonaparte is addressed in both the second and third persons, and that pronominal split allows the reader to see the passage not as a eulogy of a woman who was hardly a Sappho figure in any usual sense of the term, but as an indication of the moral presented by Verri's novel, a warning to "our" true Saffos. Had Saffo followed "parental wisdom," she would have kept busy and fit, a source of no trouble to the patriarchal order. It would be a mistake to dismiss Verri's ingenious self-promotion as simply an attempt to make his fictionalization palatable to the future wife of the Napoleonic general Murat. For Verri is far from unique in his attempt to put a revitalized, masculinized Phaon at the heroic center of Sapho's plot.[45]

Lantier's *Voyages d'Anténor* appeared the same year as the repackaged *Saffo,* and it contains a first encounter that develops the implications of Verri's earlier fiction. In the manuscript she entrusts to Lantier's two heroes so that they can take charge of her posthumous reputation, Sapho recounts in the first person her initial vision of Phaon. This time the scene is set in Athens, in the temple of Jupiter: "[Phaon] had just attracted attention in the noble exercises of the Gymnasium; the unctuous juices of the olive still glistened on his bare breast. A fine down, softer than new grass, was just beginning to appear on the blush of its tint" (244). This vision of what has recently come to be known as baby beefcake drives Sapho to an ecstatic outpouring, Lantier's own blend of the two odes with bits of Phèdre's monologue to Venus mixed in. In light of Verri's preface, the overblown sensuality of Lantier's "unctuous" lingering over Phaon's young flesh can be seen as a protofascist iconography of the male body, a hymn to the male body as well-oiled machine for the domination of all forces that threaten, in Verri's terms, "the peace of the soul," the ability of each man to play his proper role in the patriarchal order. In this Napoleonic plot, a vision of glistening male flesh awakens both Sapho's sexuality and her poetic voice. The writer who makes Phaon the origin of Sappho's poetic gift fulfills the Ovidian fiction: the beautiful young man now inspires, in addition to destroying, Sapho's poetic voice. The Sapho who comes to life at the sight of the male body stripped for battle is, predictably, feminized into bourgeois respectability. When Lantier's Phaon asks her to give up her glory in Athens, she follows him into obscurity in the country, where he abandons her for a beauty named Théagène.

Lantier might well have known Verri's novel in Italian. Subsequent French readers no longer had to make a linguistic detour in order to understand the proximity between his brand of Sapphic speculation and the nascent Italian tradition. In 1801, Chaussard gave his *Fêtes et courtisanes de la Grèce* a subtitle designed to establish his status as heir apparent to Barthélemy and Lantier: *Supplément aux voyages d'Anacharsis et d'Anténor*. Then on the title page of his fourth volume, he advertises the status of his "Aventures de Sapho" as a translation of Verri's canonic version of this plot. This gesture, highly unusual for a translator of his day, may have been intended to win a share in the favor of "our Saffo," Caroline Bonaparte. Such a strategy would have been characteristic of Chaussard, a fanatical Napoleonic loyalist who gradually rose to political prominence during the Directory: *Fêtes et courtisanes* would establish the plot developed by Verri and Lantier as the official fiction of Sappho of the French empire. Chaussard's lush, overblown rhetoric consistently maximizes the erotic charge of Verri's original to exaggerate the already caricatured portrayals of Sapho as virtual nymphomaniac and Phaon as the unctuous object of her desire.

Despite the fact that Lantier's and Chaussard-Verri's plots closely parallel Barthélemy's in many aspects, they contain no mention of Sapho's exile and her political activities. In addition, in the clearest indication of the new fiction then taking shape, Sapho also loses her sexual promiscuity, the ability to attract a series of rival poet-lovers. Any potential for an active plot is denied her in the fictions that allow Phaon to bask in glory at her expense. Perhaps the most flagrant example in this tradition is another Italian entry, by a Neopolitan general, Vincenzo Imperiale. Imperiale presents *La Faoniade: Inni ed odi di Saffo* as a translation of a previously unknown work by Sappho, newly discovered in true Ossianic fashion by "the famous Russian scholar Ossur," who was visiting Cape Leukas and found some papyri in a stone box.[46]

Although Imperiale's fiction, like Verri's, antedates the French presence in Italy, it was frequently republished later in the century, often in the same volume with Verri's *Saffo*. The preface to the 1803 edition ends with a passage that can perhaps be clarified with the aid of Verri's dedicatory preface: "Who would ever have guessed that for a Princess from the north, a legislator and a warrior, protectress of knowledge, would be reserved the glory of discovering, after twenty-four centuries, the work of a Greek Poetess?" (xi). The reference to a "Princess from the north" could also apply to Caroline Bonaparte, by then the wife of Imperiale's fellow general Murat and a member of a family ever more royal. If this is the case, the Napoleonic clan would have found in this fiction the same qualities that made Verri's work worthy of its attention. When Imperiale presents what he claims to be "the only complete work that we have of Saffo" (xv), he is attempting to replace the Sappho corpus with a "faoniade," an epic poem to the glory of Aphrodite's fickle boatman. The *Faoniade* is actually a collection of poems, all of them about Saffo's love for Phaon, "hymns" addressed less frequently to the gods than to the physical beauty of the perfect young male.

Imperiale's literary fraud fooled many of his contemporaries. Predictably, it was discovered by the French tradition just in time to suggest a textual basis for the developing Napoleonic fiction. Imperiale's hoax was reactivated in 1796 when J.-B. Grainville presented his translation as a newly discovered manuscript of Sappho's verse. Grainville-Imperiale realizes the goal of the eighteenth-century French tradition of Sappho "scholarship": her *oeuvre* appears to confirm the destiny decreed for her in fiction when Imperiale makes Saffo announce her own suicidal leap. He also heralds the shift in focus that is the logical outcome of the presentation of Phaon as a locus of "mental peace" and "bodily health": the promotion of the Leukadian leap as the dramatic center of Sapho's life.

We have already seen how the Leukadian leap first figures timidly in Sappho iconography during the 1760s, in illustrations to French translations of her poetry. The full exploitation of the scene's dramatic potential begins outside France only once spurious suicide poetry has been implanted in Sappho's corpus. One of the first artists to capitalize on the leap's emotional force is Tresham, whose aquatints illustrating Verri's proto-Napoleonic romance reinforce exaggerated sexual normalization by promoting Phaon's physical beauty in illustrations, such as Tresham's view of the scene when Sapho presents flowers to the victorious wrestler, centered on Phaon depicted nude and with the powerful body of a Greek warrior (fig. 5). Tresham joins Verri in the concomitant promotion of Saffo's emotional and physical disarray, by including melodramatic portrayals of her running to the cliff and then leaping from it. However, the exploitation of Sapho's suicide achieves its full potential only when the scene is liberated from any link to textual illustration. The episode is first depicted in oil and independent of any relation to a literary fiction in 1791 by Jean-Joseph Taillasson in his *Sapho se précipitant à la mer.*

The pictorial representation of the suicide destined to have the greatest impact on the literary tradition was exhibited in the salon of 1801 by a painter whose ties to Napoleon are well known, Baron Gros. Moreover, Gros's *Sapho au cap Leucade* is the first fiction of Sappho whose inspiration is directly traceable to the future emperor's immediate entourage. After Gros was presented to Joséphine in Genoa, she brought him to Milan to meet Napoleon, who quickly commissioned a painting from him. They then introduced him to General Dessoles, who in turn commissioned the painting of Sapho. The origin of the painting's subject has not been determined, but, whether it came from painter or patron, the idea of focusing attention on Sapho at the moment of her alleged solitary leap to the death and of couching the representation in agitated, dramatic rhetoric was formulated by someone intimately linked to Napoleon. In addition, both patron and painter were closely involved with the new militarism that was the foundation of the Napoleonic myth. Gros was primarily a military painter: in the 1801 salon in which his *Sapho* was exhibited he was also represented by a more typical canvas, *Bonaparte Crossing the Bridge at Arcola,* a tribute to Napoleon's courage and daring in a 1796 battle that had won for him both the gratitude of the Directory and the loyalty of his troops, helping prepare the coup d'état that had made him consul in 1799. In 1801, Gros was already an official maker of Napoleon's superhuman legend, a recorder of the events that were the foundation of the new patriarchal order. He took time off from these essential tasks to depict a tormented Sapho leaping to her death, even though representations of suicide were violently criticized on moral grounds in Napoleonic France. (The suicide with which Staël originally ended *Delphine,* published the year after Gros's *Sapho,* came under such persistent attack that she eventually composed a new conclusion for the novel.) Gros's gesture suggests that France's new regime may have had a stake in the violent self-destruction of the original woman writer, a conjecture that finds support in the most developed Sapphic fiction of the turn of the century, Germaine de Staël's *Corinne.* In *Corinne,* the battle lines between literary women and the forces of the (Napoleonic) patriarchal order are drawn as nowhere else.

Corinne reinstates, literally with a vengeance, the writer in the Sapphic plot. We first encounter Corinne on the morning she is to be crowned at the Capitol as "the most famous woman in Italy, poet, writer, improvisatrice" (2:1:49).[47] In the course of this ceremony it becomes clear that Staël wants her heroine to be seen as not only a Sappho figure, but as the direct successor to Sappho: sonnets of praise are read to her, "a pleasing mixture of images and mythological allusions that could have been addressed from century to century from Sappho to our day to all the women celebrated because of their literary talents" (3:1:54). By choosing "Corinne" for her heroine, Staël elects a name with Sapphic associations—Korinna was, after Sappho, the most famous Greek woman poet—but a name, unlike Sappho, bound neither to an *oeuvre* nor to a biography. Before the twentieth-century papyri discoveries, almost nothing remained of Korinna's work, and even today all that is known of her life is the story of her rivalry with Pindar, over whom she was allegedly victorious in poetry contests. In the only fiction of Korinna prior to Staël's, Barthélemy claims that "Pindar, younger than Corinne, made it his duty to seek her advice" (3:317), making her, like Sapho, a literary older woman.

Perhaps following the lead of Barthélemy/Homer, to whom she as a fledgling writer had wished to play Sappho, Staël multiplies the resemblances between Corinne and the eighteenth-century French Sapho.[48] Corinne has the physical features traditionally attributed to Sappho—both are dark, with unusually expressive eyes, and so on. Like Sappho, she performs her poetry to musical accompaniment. Like Sapho, she gives up glory, a circle of admirers, and eventually even her poetic gift when she falls hopelessly in love with a younger man, who abandons her to sail across the sea to an island where he prefers the charms of a woman even younger than he, Corinne/Sapho's former pupil. In a preface to Staël's last literary work, a tragedy *Sapho,* her son (who was publishing it posthumously) explains that "it is easy to see that [my mother] drew its original idea from *Corinne.*"[49] Given that the play exploits virtually all that was believed known about Sappho in France at the turn of the nineteenth century, it is just as "easy to see" that the original idea for Staël's *Sapho,* and for her *Corinne,* was "drawn from" the eighteenth century's fictions of Sapho. In *Corinne,* as in *Delphine,* Staël's personal contribution to that tradition of fictionalization is a modernization of the Sapphic plot to stress its implications—legal, political, and this time literary as well—for the "superior woman" of her day.[50]

When the reader first encounters *Corinne*'s Phaon, he is, as Staël remarks of his counterpart in *Delphine,* "surrounded by all the prestige of danger" (1:20:100): Oswald has barely arrived in Italy when he engages in a fierce battle to rescue the inhabitants of Ancona from a raging fire. Staël's presentation of the scene differs in essential ways, however, from the Italian tradition of Phaon the athlete. To begin with, the scene is staged to demonstrate Oswald's courage rather than his physical attributes. In addition, Corinne is not present to ogle the hero in the making: she only learns of Oswald's "selflessness" (1:1:31) secondhand. Most important, Staël's heroine owes nothing of her own self-constitution to this vision of the male in his glory. Indeed, *Corinne* reverses the model established by Napoleonic Sapphic fictions, in which the obscure young woman is irresistibly attracted to the handsome strong man. Oswald and Corinne only meet when he arrives in Rome, a foreigner totally out of his element, and is caught up in the immense crowd celebrating the coronation of female literary genius: the unknown young man falls under the spell of the celebrated writer's literary glory. Staël's reversal of the dominant contemporary plot exposes its origin in the threat to patriarchal fictions that the woman writer's exercise of power over the physically vigorous hero represents.

Oswald is no sooner "dazzled" by Corinne's brilliance than he pulls back from her, overcome by "a sort of terror at the emotion that was carrying him away." This terror leads him to question the source of his "captivation": "Was [Corinne's] charm the result of magic or of poetic inspiration? Was she Armide or Sapho?" (3:1:77). The sentence reads literally "was it [*était-ce*] Armide or Sapho?", as though such a powerful female figure could not be essentially human.[51] The equation Staël has her hero voice, between Sapho and Armide, succinctly defines the "woman problem" in *Corinne*. In Tasso's *Gerusalemme liberata,* Armida is the seductive princess who uses her charms to lure the crusader knights away from the quest to which they have been assigned. Like an Armide, a Sapho or a Corinne employs "poetic inspiration" as a "magic charm" to cast a spell over the defenseless young innocent: Oswald is "captivated," "blinded," "carried away," "subjugated"—all by the glorious spell woven by Corinne at their first encounter.

This same vocabulary of enchantment is indissociably linked to the particular literary domain in which Corinne displays her genius, improvisation. Even today, in all the examples of "improvisatrice" given in the *OED,* Corinne's official title is attached to words like "bewitching" and "generating enthusiasm," with the sense of being transported outside of oneself that they imply. This association is already present in Staël's novel, as it undoubtedly was in the Italian context from which she drew both this vocabulary and her sense of its referential context. In all the early references for "improvisatrice" and "improvisation" cited in the Robert and Littré Dictionaries, one author's name predominates, Staël's. The vocabulary of improvisation is in large part her gift, in *Corinne,* to the French language. The inspiration for these neologisms dates from Staël's travels in Italy, where she heard some of the legendary improvisatrices.[52] These improvisatrices, like Corinne and like the late eighteenth century's Sapho, are geniuses of a more sublime type of fugitive passion, women who can abandon themselves to the transport of their gift so that their poetic voice issues forth in apparent spontaneity. In *Corinne,* improvisation is the Sapphic language, the "phobeitai" as the origin both of literary genius and of its threat to the patriarchal order. For as the improvisatrice is transported outside of herself, so she also has the power to sway her audience. Staël's Sappho figure is a literary enchantress, a Circe who sings an improvisation designed to lure the protector of his country outside the boundaries of his family plot.

Oswald ends his meditation on the origin of Corinne's terrifyingly seductive charm with what initially seems a non sequitur: "O my father . . . if you had known Corinne, what would you have thought of her?" (77). At the beginning of the next chapter, his traveling companion, the comte d'Erfeuil, says to him, equally unexpectedly: "You were made to live in the happy time of the patriarchs" (78). What both young men know instinctively, and what Oswald will spend most of the novel trying to articulate, is the irrevocable unacceptability of the literary sorceress to the representatives of the Paternal Law. As Vallois points out, just as in Greek tragedy, Oswald ignores until very late in the work (book 13) Corinne's genealogy and the way in which she is forbidden to him. However, Staël replaces the adulterous mother of the oedipal plot with her Sapphic fiction in order to pinpoint the particular taboo against literary women. The novel builds up to the scene at Cape Miseno, Corinne's most Sapphic moment: from the top of the cliff, she looks down at the sea; dressed in flowing, antique garments and accompanying herself on her lyre, she improvises her last song (13:4:348).

At this moment, the turn-of-the-century iconography of Sapho and what was to become the archetypal vision of Staël's heroine (and eventually also of Staël as her heroine) intersect. Gros's 1801 *Sapho* depicts the poet atop Cape Leukas, eyes closed, poised for a passive self-abandonment rather than a leap into the sea. Stein suggests that the canvas is perhaps most remarkable because of "the powerful presence of moonlight" (180). Staël also chooses a moonlit setting for her heroine's last stand on a seaside promontory, and her choice is ratified by the other official Napoleonic court painter to produce a Sapphic canvas, the Baron Gérard. (Gérard is better known for his battle scenes and his portraits of the emperor and the imperial family, including Caroline Bonaparte and her husband Joachim Murat.) After Staël's death, he produced a posthumous homage to author and heroine, *Corinne au cap Misène,* also known as *Madame de Staël en Corinne au cap Misène* (1822). Dramatic lighting, billowing draperies, the lyre in hand—all point to the fact that Miseno is Leukas, just as Sapho is Corinne (is Staël). The canvas and the novel also have in common their portrait of the artist as melancholy and no longer moved by the transport of poetic inspiration: both improvisatrices still hold onto their lyres, but their instruments, like that of Ovid's Sappho, are "mute for grief."[53] After this clifftop pause, Corinne does not leap to her death in the waters below as Sapho did, but, after a last brief display of her poetic brilliance, she does go off to accept the destruction decreed for her by the patriarchy. Before accepting her sentence, however, she reveals her past in the form of a written document she leaves for Oswald to read.

The text of Corinne's "avowal" is a double reversal of the family romance, the story authorizing and recounting the hero's passage into the social order. She tells of the fictions others project onto a young girl in order to exclude her from "the chain of [familial] affection." Staël follows the most recent plot for Sapho's childhood, found in the Italian romances, in which she loses first her mother and her father only when she is no longer a child: after the death of her Italian mother, Corinne's father takes her to England where he remarries and has another daughter before his death leaves the budding improvisatrice without parental protection in a country suspicious of the charms of literary women. When we first meet Staël's heroine the day of her crowning in Rome, we learn that "no one knew her family name" (2:1:50). In her story, we learn why she was obliged to abandon her father's name when she became an expatriate from his native land. When she announces her intention of embarking on a literary career, her stepmother, fearful that Corinne's reputation as an "extraordinary person" would affect her chances of "establishing" her own daughter, declares that she "owes it to her family to change her name and to pass for dead" (14:3:382–83). So Staël's heroine baptizes herself "Corinne" (14:4:386), the name that simultaneously signifies her birth as a literary woman and her death to the patriarchy.

After he learns of Corinne's past, Oswald attempts to win forgiveness for her so that they can be married. But her stepmother explains that "a person who fled the paternal home, . . . abdicating her rank, her family, the very name of her father" is a permanent source of scandal and can never be readmitted to the social order (16:6:459). Oswald persists in his intention of making a new "Lady Nelvil" out of the woman he calls "Corinne Edgermond" (459)—an onomastic impossibility forged by linking the sign of the heroine's existence in the world of literature to the name under which she had refused to be bound to the Paternal Law. But he learns that by decreeing her stepdaughter's exile from the fatherland and the father's house, Lady Edgermond had simply been following the wishes of the dead father whose spirit holds sway over Oswald's existence as an incessant voice of guilt recalling him to the destiny from which Corinne threatens to seduce him.

Corinne's stepmother reveals that Lord Edgermond had proposed a union between their children to the previous Lord Nelvil. In response, Oswald's father called his friend to order in the name of all fathers, that is, of public opinion—the forces of "the world and the city" to which their names proclaim their allegiance. In a letter to Corinne's father, Lord Nelvil objects to her because of the very qualities that define her literary gift: she "pleases," "captivates," "enchants." He compares her to "one of those beautiful Greek women who cast a spell and subjugated the world," suggesting, as Chaussard had recently done, that literary women threaten the family in the same way as the celebrated courtesans of antiquity (16:8:466). Under the power of such an unnatural woman, Lord Nelvil theorizes, his son would abandon the patriarchal values—"soon he would lose that national spirit, those prejudices that bind us together and make of our nation a body, a free but indissoluble union that can only perish with the last of us"—and finally be lost to the patriarchy—"he would go establish himself in Italy, and this expatriation, if I were still living, would make me die of grief" (467). Since Lord Nelvil is already dead when his son reads this letter, he does not have to carry out this threat. But Oswald understands perfectly the blame he is meant to feel for his father's death, and he soon fulfills the wish with which his father closes the letter by marrying the woman his father terms "the true English wife," Corinne's blond, demure, dependent half-sister Lucile (468).[54] *Corinne* explains that the Sappho figure must be kept ex-patria, outside "the chain of [familial] affection," because she would threaten its continued functioning by preventing a dutiful son's passage into his rightful place in the social order. And the female child must not be allowed to remake the world, to offer a counterfiction to the family romance of the patriarchy in which the woman of the son's dreams resembles his mother.

"Italy alone suits [Corinne]" (467), Lord Nelvil declares, decreeing the country of her exile. He has in mind the contrast his son recognizes immediately upon setting foot on English soil again, between a country where the coronation of the reigning improvisatrice is considered more important than the concern for "prosperity and commerce" that rules the fatherland (16:4:447). Writing in 1791, he could not have foreseen that by the time his decree took effect, the Italian political situation would have evolved dramatically. It is easy for the reader to overlook this evolution for, as Simone Balayé points out, the increasingly dominant French presence is mentioned only in passing, and the situation is not developed even at the end of the novel when Oswald returns to Italy in 1803 (119). Staël's lack of an overt political context for her romance should not be taken for an omission, however, any more than *Delphine*'s discretion about the link between divorce and the story's chronology should. Staël began *Corinne* in the summer of 1805, the month after Napoleon, already emperor of the French, had been crowned king of Italy, and directly upon her return from travels in Napoleonic Italy, where the original improvisatrice had become the Saffo of Verri, Imperiale, and Baron Gros. It is impossible to imagine that, writing from such a vantage point, Staël chose her novel's chronological and geographical situation in innocence of any reference to her archenemy, a man whose opinion of woman's role in the patriarchy, and in particular of the literary woman's complete lack of value in the social order, ratified perfectly that of Lord Nelvil *père*.[55]

Staël makes the ruling improvisatrice of Italy the kind of revolutionary poet who would have merited exile in the occupied state Italy actually was at the time she chose for her novel's action, the political Sapho of Barthélemy's dreams. Gutwirth shows how Corinne's extended improvisations can be read as meditations on Napoleon's annihilation of Republican values (*Madame de Staël*, 236). Her spontaneous literary outpourings can also be seen as a plea for passive resistance to military oppression. Corinne's first improvisation is a eulogy of the forms of Italian domination across the ages: "Italy, empire of the sun; Italy, mistress of the world; Italy, cradle of literature, I salute you. How many times has the human race submitted to your authority, dependent upon your arms and your fine arts?" (2:3:59). The renaissance of slave as free woman is followed by a justification of the durability of Italian influence even more threatening to the social order of Staël's day: "Rome conquered the universe with its genius, and was queen by means of liberty. . . . [Italy] continued as queen because of the scepter of thought" (2:3:60). Corinne's dominant political value is that of Barthélemy's Sapho: rule by liberty. Staël sets what she portrays as an inherently female reign—Italy was "mistress," "queen"—in resolute opposition to the patriarchal militarism of the empire that controls the Italy of her day: the cornerstone of the empire of liberation is literary genius.

Staël's awareness of the utopian quality of such political meditation is clear from the contrast between Italy and England that Oswald makes upon his return to his father's house. The daughter of the celebrated Genevan financier and banker Necker surely agreed with Lord Nelvil's son's assessment that "commerce" and "industry" and not "fine arts" would dominate the politics of the dawning nineteenth century. Nevertheless, she devotes Corinne's final improvisation, in her Sapphic pose high above Cape Miseno, to a consideration of the transience of political authority and of the relative unimportance of all human power. Turning her gaze from the "lake of Avernus, an extinct volcano which formerly inspired terror" to the still awe-inspiring Vesuvius, she speculates that, like volcanoes, so do civilizations and governments succeed each other: "The masters of the world, in turn slaves, subjugated nature to console themselves for their own oppression" (13:4:349, 351). Staël's meditation on the fugacity of militaristic oppression, composed in 1806, the year that witnessed many of Napoleon's most spectacular victories, is also the swan song of her heroine's Sapphic gift. When Corinne comes down from the mountain, she begins her final march toward suicide. However, Staël scripts the scenario of her death so that, like the passive resistance Corinne urges on the citizens of the occupied Eternal City, it contains an element of revolution against the patriarchal plot.

Oswald spends almost no time with his "true English wife" before his regiment is called up for active duty (undoubtedly against the French, although this is never said) and he sets his private life aside for the good of the English nation, as his father would have wanted. He leaves Lucile with child and under Corinne's spell so that, when their daughter Juliette is born, "the little girl looked more like Corinne: Lucile's imagination had been strongly preoccupied with the memory of her sister during her pregnancy" (19:4:542). Oswald returns from the army to find a three-year-old perpetual reminder of his involvement with poetry's fugitive transports. As soon as the peace is signed, he returns to Italy with his family, ostensibly because of his health, but really to figure in Corinne's carefully shaped suicide.

Probably because Delphine's suicide had been so vehemently attacked, Corinne does not technically take her own life. She simply begins to pine away as soon as Oswald abandons her. However, Corinne is able to time her death to extract from it the maximum amount of punishment for the man who betrayed her. She controls her end to the smallest detail, making it for all intents and purposes a suicide, yet a suicide that would leave her creator protected from the tight censorship of the Napoleonic literary order. The iconography of Sappho's suicide originates in France in the late eighteenth century, and some of its most influential images, such as Gros's 1801 canvas, were actually generated from within Napoleon's entourage.[56] It is, to say the least, curious that these representations of suicide were encouraged by the same regime that objected to the suicide of Staël's earlier Sapphic heroine as a threat to the new Catholic orthodoxy promoted by the emperor. In this regard, Foucault's definition of suicide as a manifestation of the individual's power over the state (the Father) proves useful: "[Suicide] was formerly a crime because it was a means of usurping the right to death that the sovereign, the one here below or the one in the beyond, alone had the right to exercise" (*La Volonté de savoir*, 182). From the difference in official response, we can infer that "the sovereign here below" approved of a representation such as Gros's, in which Sapho's death is the acceptance of her exclusion by the woman who had threatened the patriarchal order.[57] Such a suicide functions implicitly as an officially ordained sanction, in the manner of Boileau's ritual murder of literary women.[58]

Unlike previous representations of the end of the *improvisatrice*, however, Corinne's end is not passive self-abandonment, submission of personal will to the collective Law, but rather a final gesture of independence from the forces of public opinion, an act of self-possession. She thereby fulfills the potential of Staël's reading of the Sapphic plot. Commenting on Delphine's suicide, Gutwirth concludes that "through her death, Delphine becomes heroic" (*Madame de Staël*, 141). Even in Staël's original fiction of Sappho, the *romance* she composed as a teenager, she portrays the suicide as a liberating gesture: "From your unhappy destiny / Sapho you must set yourself free" (d'Andlau, 130). Unlike a man, a woman cannot "defy" public opinion, according to the maxim of Staël's mother that serves as *Delphine*'s epigraph. She can, however, refuse to "submit" to it as the mother advised. Staël's own reflections on suicide explain how it can be a means to that end.

In an early work, *De l'influence des passions,* Staël rehearses various justifications for self-termination, the most personal of which might be termed suicide as escape route: the individual courageous enough to live the perilous "life of passion" to the fullest must have the possibility of recourse to suicide in order to maintain "self-control" (*l'empire de soi-même*) throughout "the storms of passion" (*Oeuvres complètes* 3:123 n.; 3:121–22). In Staël's vision, suicide as self-possession can also be suicide as self-repossession, a gesture of revenge against the individual who, after having accepted power over another's destiny, betrays that trust. For the woman abandoned, the goal of suicide is to make her memory more powerful than the woman who has taken her place and thereby to attain "that immortality so necessary to sensitive souls," to win immortality as a reincarnation of the Eumenides.

When Staël's heroine meets Oswald and Lucile's daughter and finds that Juliette is, in Oswald's terms, "her miniature" (20:4:575), she begins to instruct the child to take over the life she is about to relinquish. Corinne first transmits to her future double her accent in Italian and, as Juliette explains to her father, "she promised to teach me all she knows. She says that she wants me to resemble Corinne" (575). And that she does: Oswald walks by one day during a music lesson, and sees his daughter learning to place her arms in Corinne's manner around a miniature lyre. Corinne teaches her double to sing to the lyre's accompaniment. Unlike her teacher, however, Juliette will not improvise: Corinne teaches her the song she played for Oswald on a visit to her villa at Tivoli, and she extracts from her miniature a promise to play the same air for her father every year on the anniversary of that visit.

The subject of the song reveals that, by taking revenge on Oswald/Phaon, Corinne/Sapho is also resisting her ostracism from the social order. The song is identified as "a Scottish air that Corinne had played for Lord Nelvil . . . in front of a painting inspired by Ossian" (20:4:576). Corinne interprets the canvas for Oswald while giving a tour of her villa: "Caïrbar's son sleeping on his father's tomb. He has been waiting three days and three nights for the bard who is to pay homage to the memory of the dead. The bard can be seen in the distance . . . ; the shade of the father broods over the clouds" (8:4:237–38). Both the date chosen for the recital and the subject of the painting associate the scene of the father's death with the woman writer and her exclusion from the paternal order. The bard who will come to sing the air associated with the father's death is female, the reincarnation of the woman writer ostracized by patriarchal veto. Once a year, Juliette will ensure that no representative of the Paternal Law remains at rest: the only homage the dead father receives is from a bard whose creative genius was so threatening to him that he ordered her exclusion from the genealogy he controlled.

In *Corinne,* Staël takes the desire for revenge on the unfaithful lover evident in earlier fictions of Sapho to its logical conclusion. Her most evident precursor, Billardon de Sauvigny, for example, imagines Sapho turning her poetry into an arm for revenge: "I will follow you everywhere; everywhere my weak verse / Will make public my love, your flight and my misfortune" (*Poésies de Sapho,* 72). With Juliette, the adoptive daughter trained by the woman writer to carry on her poetic tradition, Staël transforms the Sapphic image of the poet and her disciples into a flawless revenge fantasy, in the name of all women writers forbidden to reproduce under the Father's Law. When Staël stages Corinne's suicide as a work of art, she transforms it into an authorial act that rescripts the Napoleonic plot of the passive suicidal abandonment of a demurely feminine Sapho.

Restoration to the Patriarchy

You know that at the party M. Talleyrand gave for me on my return from Italy, when [Mme. de Staël] asked me which woman in modern times I most admired, I told her "the one who has had the most children." She was stupefied by my response.

—Napoleon Bonaparte,
Cahiers de Sainte-Hélène

In *Sexe et liberté au siècle des lumières,* Théodore Tarczylo describes diverse manifestations of "the fear of depopulation" that he uncovers as an increasingly widespread phenomenon in late eighteenth-century France, from the 1760s to the end of the century. He believes, for example, that the investigation of the possible causes of depopulation, especially Moheau's *Recherches et considérations sur le peuplement de France* (1778), forms "the basis for a new science, demography" (168, 170). In Tarczylo's work, the promotion, really the glorification, of marriage and motherhood that is still central to what Lord Nelvil *père* considered "those prejudices that . . . make of [the French] nation a body" is traced to the growing concern, in the second half of the eighteenth century, that there might soon no longer be a critical mass of French citizens, and that depopulation posed therefore a threat to the solidity of the French nation itself.

In the realm of sexual politics, the question of homosexuality, and of female homosexuality in particular, is inextricably tied to the complex of issues Tarczylo raises. His study of police and judiciary archives leads him to the following account: "To judge from the number of trials, [homosexuality] seems less widespread in the eighteenth century than in the sixteenth century. . . . It is symptomatic that the number of sodomy trials and the number of witchcraft trials followed the same decreasing curve. As for female homosexuality, it is totally absent from the archives, or nearly so. Does this mean that it was not practiced?" (146).[59] Tarczylo, perhaps prudently, does not attempt to answer his own question, thereby leaving tentative his hypothesis about the direct correspondence between criminal proceedings and illegal sexual activity. I will likewise defer speculation, except to repeat that the relation between what the seventeenth century termed propriety and Staël public opinion and the degree to which homosexuality could be admitted is undeniable, and yet this cannot mean that homosexuality simply ceased to exist when the word could not be spoken.

It is surely no accident that the texts Tarczylo considers milestones in the investigation of depopulation are exactly contemporaneous with translations like Billardon de Sauvigny's that transform Sappho's *oeuvre* into an unrecognizable exemplar of fugitive heterosexual erotics. It seems logical, in a period when marriage and motherhood were being promoted as antidotes to depopulation, that Sappho would be a powerful threat to the official propaganda campaign. When the state and the scientific establishment were asking that women be evaluated according to their reproductive potential, the woman who does not reproduce and makes therefore no contribution to the patriarchal order, would be either eliminated, or brandished, à la Staël, as the ultimate symbol of revolt against a repressive society. (Remember that, in the rare eighteenth-century fictions in which Sapho has a daughter, the child usually dies very young.) The development in the late eighteenth century of an iconography of Sapho's suicide may be the projection onto literature and painting of the public punishment for homosexuality that Tarczylo found missing.

The interrelated phenomena Tarczylo discusses in turn interact with a development whose effect on the fictionalization of Sappho we have already considered, the militarism at the foundation of Revolutionary,

Republican, and Napoleonic doctrines. In France, all the major articulations of the modern nation-state were associated with wars to enlarge the French territory and to define its borders, conflicts that could only further aggravate the fear of depopulation. By 1810, this fear had invaded the very home of the emperor of the French himself, to such an extent that he had annulled his marriage to Joséphine, of whose quintessential womanhood he had so proudly boasted, because the alleged total woman was unable to reproduce and thereby gain value in the patriarchal order. The annulment was quickly followed by his remarriage with Marie-Louise of Austria and the birth of his first son and heir, the beginning of Napoleon's personal contribution to the campaign against the anti-French forces of depopulation.

This crucial period for the emperor's posterity, sandwiched in between the war in Spain and the disastrous campaign in Russia, was also the time during which Germaine de Staël was putting the final touch to her vast *oeuvre,* in the form of a series of short plays and a five-act tragedy. Her last work, composed the year that the emperor finally received an heir, marks a return to Staël's *oeuvre de jeunesse* for, like her youthful *romance,* it is devoted to Sapho's betrayal and suicide. *Sapho, drame en cinq actes,* concludes nearly three decades of speculation by Staël on the fate of the original woman writer. The play's title demonstrates that Staël remained as aware of generic fashion as when she wrote her *romance:* "drame bourgeois," "drame révolutionnaire," "drame romantique"—these were the classifications elected by those who sought, during the period to which Tarczylo traces the fear of depopulation, to revitalize the French theater by replacing what they considered the outmoded aristocratic model of French classical tragedy with more popular prototypes that could speak to the increasingly domestic concerns of their day.

By giving her final story of Sappho theatrical expression, Staël predicts the first important generic evolution in Sapphic fictionalization since the tradition's inauguration in France in the mid–seventeenth century. At the turn of the nineteenth century, the tradition shifted course dramatically and the theater (and opera) replaced the novel as the scene of continued speculation for nearly a century to come. With *Corinne,* Staël had transplanted Sapho's plot into the domain of the third-person novel, long the chosen format for pulp fictions like Verri's but previously explored by only one novelist of note, Scudéry. She also updated it to a contemporary setting, thereby moving Sapho into what was to become the most influential domain of nineteenth-century French literature, the historical/

realist novel in the third person with a contemporary milieu. But this figure so threatening to patriarchal values was once again denied a place in the literary mainstream. As long as the novel was considered a minor genre, it served as literary home to fictions of Sappho. As soon as the novel was accepted as a major genre, however, Sapho was relegated to a domain no longer of vital importance in the literary patriarchy.

Often the Sapphic playwrights return to the origin of Sappho's presence on the French stage and introduce, at least implicitly, Racine as the model for their tragedies. Staël's reconnection of Phèdre and Sappho is plain as soon as Sapho enters, like Phèdre, in the third scene of the first act. As she is approaching, Alcée tells us that, like Phèdre, she is so weakened from her struggle with passion that she can hardly support herself (*Oeuvres complètes*, 16:288). Yet Sapho's first words are a reference not to Phèdre, but to *Phèdre*'s precursor Sappho: "The Pleiades are already appearing . . . and Diana reigns in the sky" is a reversal of the nocturnal chronology of one of the first two of Sappho's poems to be edited in France by Henri Estienne, "La lune a fui," in which the moon and the Pleiades have just left the sky. Staël's heroine goes on to speak of her hope, that of Ovid's Sappho at the end of the fifteenth epistle, that Phaon is about to leave Sicily to return to her. The reader familiar with Sappho's poem remembers here its ending and sees it as a prediction of the fate of that hope: "the moon has fled, . . . and I sleep alone."

Staël's decision to take up Sappho's plot where Ovid puts an end to it allows her to provide a commentary on the relation between woman writer and posterity explored by both Ovid and Racine, a commentary that evokes the dilemma surrounding maternity at the time of the play's composition. The generic placement of Staël's final Sapphic fiction is subversive, for her *drame* condemns the ideology motivating that family-oriented theatrical tradition. Staël transfers attention from the issue of biological posterity to the question of literary posterity. This is not to say that her last Sapho is no longer a mother. The adoptive daughter scenario familiar from eighteenth-century fictions is repeated here: Cléone, the daughter of her closest friend Diotime, is like a daughter to Sapho, a younger, nonliterary version of the poet, and it is for her that Phaon betrays the poet who had "inflamed his mind" with her brilliance (323). "I want to possess myself myself [*Je voudrais me posséder moi-même*]" (337), Staël's last Sapho declares, and the double reflexive indicates the degree to which Staël views her suicide as an act of self-reclaiming. Yet Sapho's vision of immortality is centered neither on a revenge fantasy involving the daughter figure as in *Corinne,* nor on a murderous plot against the filial lover as in *Phèdre.*

"It seems as if she is already preparing the monument that posterity will erect in memory of her," Cléone remarks upon observing Sapho's strange behavior (286). What Staël attempts, once again, is to reunite what Ovid had put asunder, the two Sapphos, woman and writer. Lantier's filicidal Sapho, you will remember, confides her autobiographical manuscript to two men so that they can make her side of her story known to posterity. Staël's Sapho shares this concern with posterity's image of her, but as a writer rather than a notorious woman. Staël's Alcée is a fellow poet and erstwhile lover who, even after Sapho rejected him, remained a faithful friend. It is to him that her heroine turns at the end when she seeks a literary executor. Sapho explains in their last conversation that, because the language of poetry ("the language of the favorites of the gods") "is only understood by a small number of mortals," she is obliged to choose someone who will accept the responsibility of "teaching the centuries to come what Sapho was" (351). Note that she says "what" and not "who": as in *Corinne,* the pronoun indicates that posterity should look at the writing and not for the woman. "You saw me," she says pleadingly to Alcée, "when Apollo conspired in [that involuntary inspiration] behind the hymns that I addressed to Olympus; You saw me! You will tell what I was, and the inhabitants of these countries will preserve the memory of my songs" (290).

In proper post-Revolutionary fashion, Sapho refers to Alcée as her "co-citizen in the fatherland of the arts" when she gives him what amounts to power of attorney over her literary production: "To you alone do I confide my name among the Greeks" (351). Sapho frames her literary testament as though her given name, like Corinne's, had been shrouded in secrecy. Her bequest is only comprehensible if "name" is understood to mean "author's name," in the sense of a legally binding signature by means of which an author both assumes responsibility for his or her fiction and claims authorial rights over its transmission. With this gesture, Staël reminds us of both the striking presence of the signature in Sappho's poetry and the beginning of the fifteenth epistle, in which Ovid has his heroine take possession over her writing with "my author's name Sappho," her official, public signature.

Ovid inscribes this signature to indicate the ambivalence of his Sapphic ventriloquism. Staël rehearses Sapho's transfer to Alcée of the power to control the publication of her textual legacy to signal her awareness that the Paternal Law would not allow women's writing to circulate in the "patrie des arts," the literary patriarchy, without male protection, without a Father's name to guarantee its ideological orthodoxy. Staël may also have intended to indicate her acceptance of the fact that without male authorization, the plot she had dictated for Sapho would not be passed down to posterity. She did not publish her tragedy in the six years before her death in 1817. In the preface to the work's posthumous first edition, we learn that it was the only one of her plays not even staged for a limited public at her private theater. In view of its meditation on literary property, the manner in which the work was finally presented to other readers has a fine irony: the 1821 (still authoritative) edition of Staël's *Oeuvres complètes* is marked "published by her son," as if to confirm Staël's intuition about the circulation of women's writing in the patriarchy.

Staël may have felt that making still another of her Sapphic fictions public would be a superfluous gesture, for, by 1810, there were already indications that her attempts to reject the most conservative readings of Sappho's plot were not taking root. The clearest indication of the return to the dominant eighteenth-century vision was the publication of a tragedy that had been staged in 1794. *Sapho, tragédie mêlée de chants* is the first sign of Sapho's complex association with opera in nineteenth-century France. However, the play's careful packaging for publication presents the work as a Revolutionary, and therefore popular, production. The author is identified as the "citoyenne Pipelet," the composer as the "citoyen Martini." Moreover, the title page states that it was first staged in 1794, amidst the renewed patriotic fervor of the months following the end of the Terror, at a theater whose name is a perfect translation of the play's ideology: Theater of the Friends of the Fatherland.[60] Pipelet's version is centered on an exploration of two elements contributed by the eighteenth-century tradition: Sapho's betrayal and her revenge. Pipelet uses the name traditionally given to Sappho's daughter by proponents of her motherhood, Cléis, for Sapho's favorite student, whom the poet had taken in when she was a very young child and raised as though she were her own (48). Since those familiar with the then accepted reconstruction of Sappho's life would have recognized in "Cléis" a reference to the Greek poet's motherhood, citizen Pipelet was thereby able to hint at, without actually affirming, the suggestion of mother-daughter sexual rivalry that lies just below the surface of the eighteenth-century male fictions of Sapho in which Phaon betrays her for a daughter figure.[61] Since the friends of the Fatherland composed the play's first audience, it is no surprise that the unnatural mother is betrayed by her adoptive daughter. Cléis is aided in her attempt to run away with Phaon by Damophile, the woman whom Sapho believes to be her closest friend, but who has never forgotten that Alcée left her for Sapho. When Cléis and Phaon feel remorse, that false friend has them kidnapped. As a result, Phaon deserts Sapho on what was to have been their wedding day. She is waiting for him at the altar when she hears that he has sailed from Lesbos with Cléis. When Sapho also learns of Damophile's treachery and finally glimpses the boat with the three individuals who have betrayed her being tossed about at sea in a storm and about to go down, the stage is set for the tragedy's culminating vision.

Her dedication informs us that Pipelet's play is a first work, presented to the person "to whom I owe my talents, my father." Predictably, a father figure is assigned the only noble role in the tragedy first performed before the assembled Friends of the Fatherland. Alone of Sapho's friends, Stésichore remains faithful to her, the man whom Sapho addresses as "my friend, my father . . . to whom I owe the day that enlightens me" (18). She refers to his attempts to have her return to poetry as an antidote to her unhappy love, an effort he renews, once again unsuccessfully, to dissuade her from her leap. Sapho hurls herself from the cliff just before the unfaithful crew out at sea drowns, in an apparent attempt to save them by having the gods accept her death in exchange: "I should be the one to die," she cries as she falls to her death (77). Her leap inspires Stésichore's transformation from a simple protector to a cross between a patriarch and a prophet: "with the greatest indignation, his arms raised to the sky," he bellows

> Avenge the heavens, avenge the earth,
> Avenge love, humanity;
> O gods, why has not your lightning
> Already exploded? (79)

On command, lightning bursts forth and "strikes the temple; the bark which is carrying Phaon, Cléis and Damophile reappears thrown about by the waves and is swallowed up; the temple catches fire and crumbles; a fiery rain begins to fall" (80). In Stésichore's last speech, he represents more than a voice familiar to readers of the late eighteenth-century Sapho tradition, the vengeful outpouring of the unnatural mother and the woman betrayed. The play culminates in a holocaust orchestrated by its sole survivor, the character who signifies paternal guidance in the play and who, as a poet, is remembered in literary history for the introduction of epic traits that brought lyric poetry more in line with patriarchal values. Pipelet's "fiery rain" denotes the will to destroy, in the name of the father and the fatherland, Sapho, the threatening Sapphic plot, and even the fugitive erotic verse into which her poetry has degenerated.

Pipelet concludes the packaging of her tragedy for publication with a preface, a "summary of Sapho's life," in which, for the most part, she repeats the "facts" familiar from earlier eighteenth-century biographical sketches. Two details, however, make the ideological placement of her fiction clear. When Pipelet contends that "Sapho saw Phaon for the first time in a public fête" (4), she signals her acceptance of the Napoleonic plot of the poet inspired by male beauty. In a related move, citizen Pipelet refuses to make Sapho her counterpart, a friend of the Revolution. She explains that Sapho left Mytilène for Sicily "to follow her unfaithful lover there" and then adds a note to complete her rejection of Barthélemy's Revolutionary heroine. When Pipelet refuses the suggestion that made Sapho a freedom fighter struggling against a tyrant's usurpation of the Father's Law, in order to write her back into that Law as a slave of love, she brings to an end the brief moment during which Sapho was portrayed as an active heroine in political fictions. This politicized Sapho provided thereby an alternative to the tradition becoming dominant at the turn of the century, in which, in Stein's terms, Sapho becomes the passive "embodiment of debilitating artistic melancholy" (145).[62] From this point on, political fictions of Sapho disappear from literary texts and are banished to scholarly commentaries.

The play that at once marks the culmination of the eighteenth-century French tradition and sets the norm for nineteenth-century Sapphic theater is Franz Grillparzer's *Sappho,* a tragedy that recapitulates the ideology of the entire Napoleonic tradition.[63] Grillparzer's tragedy provides the most eloquent testimony to the power of the French fictive tradition to win out over the German scholarly tradition, even among German writers. At the same time, it is the first clear indication of the next major phase of Sapphic speculation, in which German scholarship finally begins to generate fictions of the original woman writer, a development whose impact only becomes clear in France in the 1830s. The scene opens as Sappho is returning home from the Olympic games where she has been crowned for her victory over Anacreon and Alceus (9). She is accompanied by Phaon, who explains how he fell in love with her when she recited her verse (10). Phaon is beginning to feel shame because of this love for which he "forgot myself, and my parents," and is worried that they may have learned that the son "they sent a champion to Olympia, / Has sunk ignobly in the arms of Sappho" (19). He describes Sappho as a Circe who with her "captivating songs . . . drew her magic circle of enchantment around me . . . until I felt my neck bowed down beneath her yoke" (48). He soon falls in love with Melitta, a slave girl and Sappho's attendant, whom the poet has raised like a mother from the time she was a baby. The love of these two child figures turns Sappho into the murderous mother. She threatens Melitta with a dagger, provoking their attempted flight to a neighboring island. When Sappho learns that they are trying to escape her, she calls on the gods to "launch your avenging bolts on the betrayers," and orders her "slaves and peasants" to bring Phaon back so that she might "dart [her] eyes like daggers in his soul" (64). In the end, Sappho turns her violent rage upon herself and crafts her suicide in a manner that departs from the path of eighteenth-century fictions. Her slave Rhamnes has already described to the child lovers what would have been their fate according to the tradition that highlighted Sapho's vengefulness:

> The world contains no corner to protect you:
> Even from your footsteps would a sound come forth,
> And cry aloud, "Lo, Sappho's murderer comes!"
> ....
> Yes, you will roam an outcast through the world. (79)

Grillparzer, however, makes a bold new move and scripts his Sappho's suicide as her renunciation of sexuality and a gesture of penance necessary to gain poetic immortality. "Such light as beams from the Immortals plays around her brow" when Sapho assumes the role of demigod Staël reserves for Stésichore. Before hurling herself from the cliff, she "stretches her hands over the pair, and blesses them" with these words: "Love be for man; be reverence for the gods! . . . Bless them, O gods! and take me to yourselves" (85). The last words belong to Phaon who, "raising his hands," proclaims: "She has returned to her native skies" (86). Grillparzer transforms Sappho's plot into the tragedy of a deity who tried to live as if she were a mere mortal woman: "Why did I resign / The bright and sunny heights of Helicon, / . . . Why came I down into the vale of life?" (39). His heroine comes to realize that this descent into human emotions must be expiated by means of another descent, a fall that will allow her to rise up from the dead immortal, cleansed of the human frailty of sexuality. When Grillparzer has Sappho exchange "love" for "reverence," he indicates, for the first time clearly in literature, the major way in which the nineteenth century justified its reexaltation of her poetry: by denying her sexuality. The suicide that ends this tragedy is an effort to disengage Sappho from all sexual scenarios, so that her poetry could be revered as a monument of classical purity, and Sappho the poet could finally be granted unconditional canonic status—a development that was just gaining momentum at the time of the triumphal success of Grillparzer's new tragic scenario.

His *Sappho* was first staged in Vienna in 1818. Grillparzer's earliest English translator says of the author, "though but a young man, [he] has made considerable progress in public opinion" and traces that approval by the forces of the "world and the city" to the brilliant reception immediately accorded his play:

> Such was the applause with which it was received in Vienna that its representation was extended to nearly a hundred successive nights. The Emperor of Austria . . . honored one of the early representations with his presence, and testified to the pleasure he had received by conferring on the author a handsome mark of his approbation. The enthusiasm of the public was such that the youthful poet was crowned with laurel on the stage and accompanied to his home with torches and music. (v–vi)

Grillparzer realizes the dream of all writers who stage a fiction of Sappho as a rite of initiation: he receives the laurel crown and is honored by a triumphal procession through the city. Grillparzer, like Ovid's seventeenth-century "secretaries of ill-fated loves," makes a name for himself and wins an authorial signature by killing Sappho, or at least the Sappho that, for two hundred years, authors following the Ovidian plot had been constructing bit by bit. To take proper advantage of Grillparzer's intuition, it would next be necessary to kill Ovid in his relation to Sappho, a move already being contemplated by German Hellenists.

Clearly, Grillparzer had found the scenario for his age. Staël's Sapphic *drame* hardly caused a stir, either at the time of its publication just three years after Grillparzer's triumph or later in the century, perhaps indicating that the newly restored monarchy had as little use for an exploration of the exceptional woman's struggle for control over her posterity as the emperor of the French. Grillparzer's tragedy, however, was translated into all the major European languages and reedited throughout the century. Even

Pipelet's tragedy was reissued and continued to enjoy a limited success, but this may have been due to the fact that she was successful in repackaging herself for the Restoration, under which the former *citoyenne* reappeared as the Princesse de Salm-Dyck. Her new relation to the patriarchal order is parallel to Sappho's situation in the early decades of the nineteenth century: both post-Revolutionary politics and a new wave of Sappho scholarship made a revitalization of Sapphic fictions inevitable.

*

In 1791, Fabricius's monumental *Bibliotheca Graeca* was reissued in an updated edition: his continuators, when necessary, added numerous lengthy footnotes into which they compressed a summary of the contributions of eighteenth-century Hellenists to the body of knowledge originally compiled by Fabricius. One of the articles in which the ratio of footnotes to original text is particularly disproportionate is the entry for Sappho. The revised entry pays eloquently succinct testimony to the revolution in scholarly geography that had taken place in the course of the century. Whereas Fabricius had originally featured the work of French Hellenists, his continuators include not a single French contribution in the long section (141–42) devoted to Sappho scholarship since the *Bibliotheca Graeca*'s first edition, a discussion that features the erudition of German Hellenists, most prominently Fabricius's student Wolff. Nevertheless the new footnotes do bear witness to the fact that the French eighteenth-century fabulators had succeeded in putting two questions on the agenda of all Sappho scholars, even the punctilious Germans. First, Fabricius's continuators devote the longest of their footnotes to the question of which famous male poets could have been Sappho's contemporaries, and eventually her lovers, an issue initially made controversial in the tradition of French Sapphic romances (137–38). Second, they raise, if only timidly, the question of Sappho's flight or exile to Sicily and quote as the source of additional information the intensely overread passage in the Parian marble (137).

However, the revised Fabricius predicts as well as recapitulates the course of Sappho scholarship and speculation. The continuators introduce, once again only timidly (137), an issue that German Hellenists will develop out of scattered references in antiquity into a full-blown theory in the early decades of the nineteenth century. This issue will prove so explosive that it will finally provoke French Hellenists to enter into a debate originating abroad and thereby to take a step in the direction of rejoining the international scholarly community: they include a reference to what will become known as the theory of the two Sapphos when, in the course of the nineteenth century, it comes to dominate the scene of Sappho scholarship.

From this point on, the battle for Sappho is characterized above all by the nationalism that motivates its principal opponents. At Staël's salon-in-exile at Coppet, the French and German intellectual traditions were probably more closely aligned than at any time in early modern history. However, just when Staël was presiding over this Franco-Prussian unification, the modern vocabulary of nationalism was entering her native language. The differences between the French and the German Sappho traditions may not have seemed irreconcilable when Staël was composing her Sapphic production, but this situation was not destined to last for long. In an atmosphere of rising nationalism, national schools would soon part ways: at the same time that they ended the eighteenth-century tradition, Staël's passionately political Sappho and Grillparzer's purified poet inaugurated the century of greatest divergence among national scholarly traditions.

3 *Sappho Revocata (1816–1937)*

Sappho retrouvée (Louis Planchon, 1846)

Sappho retrouvée (Louis Planchon, 1846)
Sappho revocata (J. M. Edmonds, 1928)
Sappho réhabilitée (Jym, 1937)

The fictions of Staël and Grillparzer stand at the crossroads of the eighteenth- and the nineteenth-century Sapphic traditions. They also mark a crossroads of nationalisms, both scholarly and political.

At Staël's home in exile in politically neutral Switzerland, she gathered around herself a pan-European intellectual circle.[1] In a famous *mot,* Stendhal referred to Coppet as the "Estates-General of European opinion." In this uniquely diversified community, intellectuals of numerous nationalities and of all points on the political spectrum exchanged ideas: Swiss, English, French (either official political exiles or self-exiled *émigrés*), Italian (displaced from their occupied homeland), and what we today would call German and Austrian, though at the turn of the nineteenth century the movement that would lead to the modern definition of these nations was still in its infancy. In the discussions of this international intellectual conglomerate, presided over by Staël (herself a national mongrel, the daughter of Swiss parents, married to a Swede, considering herself French), questions of nationhood and nationalism must have been hotly debated, all the more so since the very vocabulary basic to such considerations is one of the period's linguistic innovations: according to the Robert Dictionary, "nationalisme" entered French in 1798, "nationalité" in 1808.

The largely nation-less group at Coppet can be associated with the dissemination throughout Europe of a number of concepts central to the last phase of this study: first, nationality in the sense of national identity, and, second, philology as the intellectual arm of nationalism, the science that defined national identities (and that would help constitute German nationalism). Because of the enduring obsession of Coppet's mistress with

198

the poet of Lesbos, Sappho's presence can also be established at the fountainhead of modern Franco-Anglo-Prussian nationalism. In fact, for the next century, Sappho is disseminated throughout Europe simultaneously, and often jointly, with philology and nationalism.

Evidence of this semantic and intellectual collision is provided by the near simultaneous composition not only of the Sapphic tragedies of Staël and Grillparzer (1816, 1818), but also of the volume that launched the modern tradition of Sappho scholarship, Friedrich Gottlieb Welcker's 1816 study of Sappho—just at the time when philology, newly implanted in Germany, is being transplanted to France. (Under "philologie," the Robert Dictionary lists as the first entry an 1818 text by Friedrich von Schlegel, brother of Staël's longtime protégé and intellectual collaborator, Wilhelm August.) Had this collision between Sappho and nationalistic theories taken place earlier in Staël's life and before the dissolution of the Coppet circle, it might well have resulted in a scholarly tradition independent from nationalistic interests. As it was, however, the individual schools went separate ways: for example, the Schlegels, who had collaborated with Schiller as well as Staël, went on to pursue literary issues, such as the importance of folklore to national identity, which the philologists hoped would help hasten the unification of the German nation. And until the eve of World War II (which would force a new redefinition of national unity), the issue at the heart of pan-European Sapphic speculation is Sappho's place in the nation-state, the role she can be assigned in the development of national identity.

*

One hundred and twenty years is a long time in literary and intellectual history. I could easily have subdivided this somewhat unwieldy expanse into more manageable units. To do so, however, would have meant running the risk of obscuring the continuity that I came to perceive throughout the entire span of post-Revolutionary Sapphic history. Moreover, the modern construction of Sappho is geographically as well as temporally complex. In the following pages, I will be presenting my vision of the relation among documents published during the course of more than a century and in three different countries. I will therefore ask for my reader's patience while I explore developments that may seem at times to stray from my central subject.

Prior to the nineteenth century, Sappho scholarship is fragmentary and unstable. Its history is presented as the sum of its great moments— Estienne's edition, then Le Fèvre Dacier's, then Wolff's—and only rarely, most notably in late seventeenth-century France, does it resemble and is it perceived as a true scholarly tradition. Filiations and influences are of course visible, but there is no sense of continuing progress, little sense of knowledge definitively gained. This is what makes possible the almost total regression throughout the eighteenth century in France. By the early nineteenth century, however, the course of erudition is permanently transformed. In the generation after Winckelmann's extraordinary pan-European success, German scholars began to present themselves, and to be received, with a seriousness not previously encountered in the annals of scholarship. Two and a half centuries after its origin, the modern reconstruction of Sappho at last moved forward with the kind of intensity that would shortly make it impossible for any translator, however eccentric, to ignore the progress being made in textual reconstruction and to counterfeit his own ersatz Sappho. Finally, the publication of the papyri discoveries at the turn of the twentieth century, first in Germany and then in England, was a fitting conclusion to a century that had witnessed the establishment of individual Sappho texts and of Sappho's corpus. The recovery from Egyptian papyri of what were called the "new fragments," the only subsequent addition to the corpus already available to German philologists at the beginning of the nineteenth century, provided the impetus for the establishment of the twentieth-century editions of Sappho that are still considered definitive.

This study will conclude in 1937, the year of the publication of the Belles-Lettres edition, the first truly scholarly French version of Sappho since the Le Fèvre Dacier and Longepierre volumes of the 1680s. However, this *terminus ad quem* should not lead readers to believe that the French moved back into the scholarly mainstream at any point in the period under consideration. In fact, throughout the nineteenth century philological authority over Sappho's *oeuvre* is an uncontested German province, whereas in our century this same control has been inherited by English scholars. But despite this shift, at no point does the French involvement with Sappho abate. On the contrary, it reaches several moments of almost frenzied obsession—most notably in the mid–nineteenth-century pattern of involvement centered on Baudelaire, and in the fin-de-siècle movement referred to as "Sapho 1900."[2]

The two modern traditions of Sappho speculation—German philological solemnity and French sexual sensationalism—appear so far opposed as to be mutually exclusive. Indeed, I will not often project a pattern of direct influence between the domains of scholarship and fiction as I did for the

Enlightenment Sappho. I hope rather to expose a phenomenon that I find more intriguing than the earlier mutual contamination of high and low culture. In the modern period, the erudite and the popular images of Sappho followed a parallel evolution, although it is rarely evident that the most influential commentators and fictionalizers were aware of developments outside their own domain. Even though the practice is often attacked—witness the objections to Foucault's *Histoire de la sexualité*—fiction is still interpreted as a barometer of a period's zeitgeist or episteme. It would appear from the commentaries we will examine here that scholarship can almost as easily be used to measure the overriding preoccupations of the period in which it was produced.

Modern scholarship makes it evident that prior to 1816, Sappho's sexual potential had not yet begun to be tapped. Nineteenth-century speculation quickly made the eighteenth century's saccharine, heterosexual fiction seem a mild response to Sapphism. Nineteenth-century scholars at last definitively extend Sappho's corpus beyond the limits prescribed for it at the end of the seventeenth century. Contemporary translators gradually revive the power of the Sapphic voice. At the same time, all those involved in the definition of their century's Sappho transformed the tenth muse into an archetype of the period's tortured vision of female sexuality: Sappho is presented at times as virgin, at times as whore, at times even as the union of Freudian paired opposites, a sort of virginal whore or prostituted virgin.

At key moments, the century's progressively more intense involvement with Sappho is synonymous with her Christianization. By this I mean that her restoration is no longer presented solely in literary terms, as the simple reclaiming from textual oblivion practiced in earlier periods. Instead, Sappho is now *redeemed*. Her recovery is often viewed as her salvation, if not from sin, at least from accusations of sinfulness. Writers like Baudelaire, who do not portray Sappho's chastity, at least have recourse to religious terminology to characterize her as a virgin of perversity, as though sexuality could not be expressed outside the dominant moral vocabulary of the day. Even the establishment of texts is consistently presented as a moral tale. Editors claim to have access to the truth about Sappho: their version will restore her to lost integrity, will finally make the entire Greek moral system apparent. What I describe as a Christianization is a direct result of the new prominence won for erudition. Sappho's most important nineteenth-century commentators restore her to grace as part of a grandiose effort that promises no less than the purification of

201

contemporary society if it can be restructured according to what were presented as the ideals of ancient Greece. "Sappho revocata," "Sappho réhabilitée": this vocabulary, so prominent during over a century of Sappho commentary, signifies her elevation to the role of virgin priestess of any one of a number of religious cults that could save mankind from the loss of value, from the mediocrity of modern life.

The origins of Sappho's reincarnation as patroness of modernity can be traced to the presentation of her biography and her poetry in the first truly scholarly commentaries to be devoted to her since Christian Wolff's 1733 edition. These commentaries all appear in Germany. I will consider them in some detail because, without them, it is impossible to understand the seriousness and the persistence with which the theory of Sappho's chastity was promoted, and is still promoted today by representatives of every scholarly tradition. The theory of Sapphic chastity is by far the most important single invention in the history of Sappho scholarship to date. In fact, it can be seen as the move that founds that scholarly tradition. It was evidently what commentators were waiting for, because they latched onto it with gusto, promoted it with enthusiasm for over a century, and in many cases still refuse to abandon it even today.

German scholars immediately link the interpretation of Sappho to what was destined to become one of the most hotly debated issues in Hellenistic studies, the phenomenon now most frequently referred to in German as *Knabenliebe* (boy love), and in English as "ideal love," "Socratic love," or "Greek love." I will begin this chapter by considering at some length the way in which that link is established. This connection reveals that a major strain of what is commonly known as "*the* tradition" (that is, the tradition of commentary on classical texts) illustrates repeatedly the phenomenon Luce Irigaray terms "hom(m)osexuality": all their discussions of sapphism refuse to admit the existence of a female variant of the male same-sex love that is the actual center of their preoccupations. Which is to say that well over a century of the alleged German preoccupation with Sappho's sexual difference is just what Irigaray would have predicted, sexual indifference, the inability to imagine a second sex. Hence the necessity of decreeing Sappho's chastity in commentaries that perform a rite of scholarly coming of age, an initiation of the individual into an order where the importance of culture as a foundation for society is always recognized.[3] Without this double excursion, into German erudition and into perhaps the first scholarly commentary on male homosexuality, the terms in which Sapphic virginity was formulated are incomprehensible. Those terms in turn determine the formulation by French Hellenists of a countertheory, Sappho as courtesan. In addition, the place accorded sapphism in discussions of male homosexuality helps define the role played by Sappho for the French and English decadent amateur Hellenists who were the first to attempt to produce editions establishing Sappho as a lesbian poet. Finally, each scholarly presentation of her sexuality generates a wave of fictions either reinforcing the erudite vision, as is the case with the numerous poems and plays featuring a chaste Sappho, or offering a challenge to it, as does the wave of fin-de-siècle antilesbian fictions.

As in previous chapters, I will alternate between erudition and fictionalization and between scholarly and popular variants in each category. My initial discussion of the contribution of German philologists and the relation they establish between Sapphic chastity and Greek love will be followed by a review of nineteenth- and twentieth-century translations in order to demonstrate the range of interpretations with which the reader was confronted throughout this period. I will then discuss the fictions of Sappho as virgin and as prostitute before concluding with a figure inconceivable without the virgin-whore dichotomy, the decadent, lesbian Sappho, whose formation originates in the Racinian tragedies and Baudelairean poems of the mid-nineteenth century and who is still alive in Marguerite Yourcenar's 1936 collection *Feux*.

Sex and Philology

We want the truth, only the truth. Besides one doesn't usually hang the devil's portrait in a salon.

—M. H. E. Meier,
Paederastia

At the beginning of his scholarly autobiography, the theoretician of "mother right" proclaims "I was drawn to the study of law by philology" (3). J. J. Bachofen's placement of philology at the origin of his theory of sexual ethics also applies to virtually all the influential intellectual systems to come out of nineteenth-century Germany. In the beginning, there was philology. As the keystone of law and ethics, and also of history and the history of art, stood the study of language and of literature. Never has further-reaching importance been attributed to literary texts, especially to founding literary texts like Sappho's. And never has literary commentary appropriated with such confidence the right to apply its conclusions to other domains, even to assume that textuality was at the center of all knowledge. The philological science, as it was defined by its founders in the late eighteenth and early nineteenth centuries, was an intellectual totality, a world unto itself, the study of language redefined to give philologists access to the essence of nations. In particular, philology was the science of antiquity, the tool German scholars would use to rehabilitate antiquity and reveal the Greeks as the standard for beauty, grandeur, and national genius. In the process, German scholars would guarantee for themselves a role as privileged interpreters of the essence of Greek genius. The dimensions of the mission philology assigned itself explain why the reader of nineteenth-century German Sappho commentary must expect to follow arguments that lead well beyond her corpus, to begin with Sappho's sexuality and conclude with the foundations of Greek nationalism and the source of Greek artistic power.[4]

Already in the decade before the Revolution the rising prominence of German scholars was making itself felt in France. As a result, information on Sappho and her contemporaries that contradicted the fictional excesses of a Barthélemy or a Lantier was already being made available at the time of their immense popular success. Sapphic fictionalizers were therefore soon obliged to put an end to the plot that had made her an eighteenth-century novelistic heroine. The eighteenth century had reduced Sappho's *oeuvre* to literary triviality by making it over in the image of the pale heterosexual heroine. The nineteenth-century tradition is inaugurated with the attempt to resurrect Sappho's poetic genius by severing the poet's ties to the woman.

We left the eighteenth-century tradition with the closing lines of Grillparzer's 1818 tragedy: "Her home was not upon the realms of earth; / She has returned to her native skies" (86). The transformation of the suicidal plunge into an expiating ritual that frees Sappho from the flesh and completes her translation into immortality might well indicate a familiarity on Grillparzer's part with either a tradition we will consider later, the century's first French Sapphic poems, or with the opening salvo of German philology's attack on Sappho's carnality, Welcker's 1816 treatise. If Grillparzer did intend a reference to the contribution of the nascent philological science, however, he failed to include the second element essential to the philologist's pathbreaking new conception of the tenth muse, the revitalized masculinity Welcker makes a necessary correlative of her purification. This element may well have been suggested to Welcker by the Napoleonic Sappho fictions in which Phaon is transformed into a young Greek god. This new image of Sappho's mythical lover is still powerful in the opening decades of the nineteenth century—witness Anne-Louis Girodet's 1829 illustration of Sappho under Phaon's spell, in which the poetess, fully clothed, bows her head and lets her hand fall from her lyre, rendered mute by the vision of the perfect male body that Phaon, reclining on an Empire day bed and holding his drapes carefully away from all the essential parts, exhibits as artfully as one of Ingres's odalisques (Girodet's plate 11, figure 5).

There is little doubt that Girodet, student of that chronicler of imperial glory, David, knew the fictions of Sappho humbled by raw male physicalness that proliferated during the empire; his volume of illustrated translations is prefaced with a "notice" on Sappho and her work by P. A. Coupin, whose formal experience was in the imperial army rather than as a classicist. Even Welcker, who had fought against Napoleon's army, knew at least Verri and Imperiale (Wilamowitz, 18, n. 2). It also seems likely that Welcker knew Staël's countertradition of a pacifist, antinationalistic Sappho, and that the new politics of "the tradition" as he defined them were designed to put an end to such speculation. We should not forget that anyone writing on Sappho in 1816 had few erudite precursors to cite.[5] Whether by accident or by design, the pattern was formed: at the time of the French Restoration and in a period of rising German nationalism, Welcker posited an essential bond between male physical beauty, militarism, and patriotism on the one hand and Sappho's chastity on the other. The prodigious respect that his theory wins among Hellenists, even including some of the scholars most respected today, makes it seem more than mere historical coincidence that the official consolidation of philology—"philologie" in the modern sense enters French in 1818, two years after Welcker's treatise and the year of Grillparzer's tragedy—is simultaneous with the decree pronouncing Sappho's virginity. This partnership formed, philology and female chastity remain inseparable for over a century. In addition, aesthetically justified militarism, though it eventually is eliminated from modified views of Sapphic purity, remains at least until World War I an active ingredient in the formula philologists propose as a foundation for German nationalism and as a means of countering Sapphism's threat to that nationalism.

The translation of values, or at least the homogeneity of values, that I note in imperial fictions and early philology may seem less startling if one considers that Phaon's idealized masculinization coincides with the dissemination throughout Europe of Winckelmann's aesthetic system. Surely Winckelmann's most influential contribution was his definition of

Greek ideal beauty and his success in promoting the equation between the cult of that ideal beauty and the essence of Greek national identity.[6] The most recent German philologist to situate Sappho in the context of Greek ideal beauty and love, Hans Licht (Paul Brandt) proclaims Schiller's slogan, "at that time nothing was sacred but the beautiful" (from *On Naive and Sentimental Poetry,* 1795), "the key to the understanding of Greek life in general."[7] Certainly these words are "the key to the understanding" of what Greek life represented to the nineteenth-century German intellectual and, after the success of philology, to European intellectuals in general. And certainly in their contemporaneous volumes Schiller and Winckelmann laid the foundation for the powerful influence of philology by guaranteeing that Greek culture would play a privileged role in the creation of German national identity and values.[8]

Key terms of Winckelmann's definition of the Greek aesthetic ideal, accepted and passed down by the philologists who set the standard for Sappho commentary, can help us understand the tenaciousness of the most influential presentation of Sappho to date. Most notable is Winckelmann's absolute privileging of the athletic young male body as the measure of the Greek aesthetic ideal. He states repeatedly that "beautiful virile youth" provides the almost exclusive model for the masterpieces of Greek art (*Histoire de l'art,* 374). He treats in great detail the types of male beauty glorified by the ancients, while he dismisses the value of the female body as an artistic model in summary fashion. ("Few observations can be made about the beauty of women" [*Histoire de l'art,* 395].) Winckelmann repeatedly lingers over descriptions of the nude as the summit of Greek art, and especially over the evocation of naked youths in what he terms "schools of beauty," the gymnasium where they exercised and the stadium where they competed. He even contends that the extraordinary sensitivity to beauty that he puts at the origin of the greatness of Greek art resulted from the fact that Greek men were so often exposed to the sight of the naked young male body.[9]

The fact that Winckelmann's theory is prescriptive as well as descriptive helps account for its importance in an age of rising nationalism. He resurrects the glories of ancient art and society as a model for a new nation-state: "The only way to become great and, if possible, inimitable, is to imitate the ancients" (*Recueil,* 95). The people who would become the new Greeks must begin by cultivating an awareness of "ideal beauty," that is, beauty that is "more" than "the most beautiful nature," beauty "in a Platonic sense" (99). The new Greeks will be led to this ideal by "the true connoisseur," he who is "capable of judging the works of the Greeks." This guide to aesthetic and civic greatness cannot simply be "knowledgeable about beauty in general." Winckelmann stops just short of saying that the beauty of female forms must be ignored; he does say that the program to national greatness must pay no attention to "beauty to which woman is sensitive." The true aesthetic leader can only be "touched by the beauties of our sex," that is, by the male body, "the statues of men" (*Recueil*, 244). National greatness will only be achieved if the young male body is made the exclusive aesthetic ideal—and if the gaze admiring and objectifying that body is exclusively male.

The philologists who rose to prominence in Winckelmann's wake had mastered this lesson in the ethics of aesthetic doctrine. Certainly the bizarre structure of the work that inaugurates the modern tradition of Sappho interpretation is incomprehensible considered in isolation from it.[10] Friedrich Gottlieb Welcker's *Sappho von einem herrschenden Vorurtheil befreyt* (1816) has most often been read simply as the original formulation of the theory of Sapphic chastity. However, this work, and all the volumes that build on Welcker's project, present their philological argument only through a complex detour of desire, a seemingly inevitable excursion no longer into Winckelmann's primary subject, Greek art, but into the subjects he had annexed to it—the origin of Greek nationalism, the primacy of a male aesthetic model—and also into a subject only hinted at in Winckelmann's privileging of the erotic gaze of male upon male, *pederastia*. The reader of Welcker's volume comes to wonder if the acceptance of male homoerotic relations somehow *required* the female to be asexual.

Of the members of the generation that codified philology, Welcker is hardly the most celebrated today. But in the genealogy of philology, Welcker is a true founding father with a career that covered the first half of the century and a long tenure as editor of the *Rheinisches Museum für Philologie*. He is also the dominant influence on Ulrich von Wilamowitz-Moellendorff, whose work spans the nineteenth and twentieth centuries and still commands considerable authority today.[11] This history must be remembered if we are to understand how his arguments won such widespread acceptance. In the annals of Sappho scholarship, Welcker was known for more than a century as Sappho's "defender," a position to which Welcker appointed himself when he, as he termed it, "freed Sappho from a reigning prejudice." Welcker himself never explains where or when the prejudice from which Sappho required salvation was dominant, a first unfortunate omission, since at no point in classical commentary or in modern interpretations before his day had a homosexual Sappho "reigned." Welcker also generally avoids naming the "prejudice" in question, although he on occasion speaks of "female homosexuality" (*hetärisstrien*). This avoidance points to the truly crucial omission in his text, that of any real discussion of either Sappho's homosexuality or of female sexuality in general.

Indeed, the logic behind Welcker's chastity argument is so convoluted as to defy reconstruction. Welcker admits that Sappho's poetry shows love for women, but disclaims the existence of any "basely sensual," "punishable," or "reprehensible" element in that love. This claim, on which his entire chastity theory rests, is based on no evidence more concrete than his personal conviction that "no educated Greek would have thought these were beautiful love poems if something monstrous and disgusting had been going on in them" (*Sappho*, 69). For Sappho herself, Welcker promotes the standard fiction "reigning" at the dawn of the nineteenth century as much because of the influence of hack novelists of the previous century as of Ovid's. (After an early marriage, Sappho became a young widow with a daughter. She was virtuous until she met Phaon, who betrayed her and whom she followed to Sicily.) Yet Welcker never suggests—and this is the only point on which he is subsequently attacked—that Sappho composed poetry of heterosexual passion. It is as if Sappho's passion finally engaged him as little as the forms of female beauty had interested Winckelmann.

The subject that really does engage Welcker, the issue for which the study of Sappho serves as a pretext—whether consciously or unconsciously it is impossible to tell—is male homosexuality. Ironically, while *Sappho von einem herrschenden Vorurtheil befreyt* really offers no new fiction or knowledge about Sappho, it does formulate what seems to be the first modern defense, even eulogy, of male homosexuality—or at least of the Greek practice of *pederastia*.[12] Sappho is really necessary in Welcker's argument to permit a reformulation of a Platonic concept important to philologists throughout the century, the distinction between a completely sensual eros and an eros that is "if not completely devoid of sensuality, at least blameless" (*Sappho*, 15). Woman, Welcker claims, can only know the baser, sensual eros and never its higher form. The Greeks understood this and hence never evoked the possibility of Sappho's homosexuality. He implies that moderns are so feminized that they no longer know the purer, masculine eros, and hence have difficulty understanding this concept of an erotics without sensuality, "not just a difference of degree but a complete break" (15). Here Welcker resurrects the argument Winckelmann developed to demonstrate the uncontested primacy of male aesthetic values, the philologist as seer, alone able to decode the language of the lost utopia and therefore competent to lead his contemporaries in a return to greatness. "Only a few men," Welcker admits, will understand what he is saying. But that select few, like Winckelmann's connoisseur, keep alive the knowledge of a phenomenon that ennobled mankind.

Welcker shares this almost forgotten knowledge by composing a detailed rehabilitation of Greek love. Two points of his argument—that this love was so widespread that it should be understood as "an inclination particular to the Greeks," and that this bond was ennobling because it "assumed part of the character of fatherly love and took over the pedagogical role" (*Sappho,* 52)—are often simply repeated by Welcker's followers. But on at least two points Welcker is bolder than any scholar was willing to be for well over a century. First, he speaks not solely of "love of boys" (*Knabenliebe*), but interchangeably of "love of boys" and "love of men" (*Männerliebe*). He thereby implies that his argument is applicable not only to the particular phenomenon associated with Greek society—the bond between a mature man and a younger youth—but to the larger context of all homoerotic relations. Second, unlike many of his followers, Welcker refuses to deny completely the sensual content of "love of men" by claiming that the phenomenon existed solely for pedagogical purposes.

The boldness of his formulation is especially important in view of the conclusion that he suggests. Welcker repeatedly stresses the status of male homosexuality as an essential part of what he terms the Greek "national character" (see, for example, *Sappho,* 52). He was making this claim only some twenty years after Winckelmann and Schiller had sounded the rallying cry that would echo throughout the philological tradition: the Germans will be the new Greeks and will become thereby inimitably great. Implicit in Welcker's polemic therefore is the conclusion that the Germans, in order to become the new Greeks, should adopt not only their male-centered aesthetic model but also the sexual orientation that could explain such an aesthetic ideal.

And Sappho in all this? Remarkably, the scholar known as her "champion" and credited with founding modern Sappho scholarship remains consistently unconcerned with the tenth muse. His implicit reasoning is that women could never have participated in a national project as great and ennobling as "love of men." Welcker wants to demonstrate that Sappho does not offer a female variant of *Männerliebe*. This said, he never bothers to grant her a sexual orientation: she is left simply a blank, a blank Welcker's immediate disciples soon began to fill in with attempts at characterizing just what Sappho was.

I want to stress that no German scholar ever pointed out any deficiency in Welcker's argument: the master had spoken, and his disciples simply took his title at face value and set about continuing to "free Sappho from prejudice." In the process, they developed the initial set of arguments for Sapphic purity. Within less than a decade, Johann Christian Neue provided the first edition of the fragments designed to illustrate what he imagined to be Welcker's position. In his discussion of the variants to the "Ode to Aphrodite," Neue dismisses the homosexual reading of the poem that some German scholars were beginning to propose: "we would embrace this [reading of line 24] if the accent were moved back" (27)—as though his objection is purely technical and the question purely an affair of metrics uncolored by sexuality.[13] In his introduction, Neue enshrines the myth of Welcker. Before Welcker, he claims, all had believed the "calumny" that Sappho was a "tribade," but Welcker demonstrated that "this monstrous desire was . . . detestable to the ancients." Neue concludes his eulogy by adding a new "proof" in the Welckerian tradition of demonstration through absence of evidence: if the ancients had believed such "slander," they would never have held up Sappho, along with Diotima and Theano, as part of the "complete image of the perfect woman" (7–8). The notion of Sappho as example for womankind was soon Christianized by Welcker disciples, among them Johann Richter, who speaks of Sappho's "virgin purity" (*jungfräulicher Reinheit*) (22). The interpretive tradition, thus launched, had defined its central goal: the establishment of Sappho's chastity, her purity, her virginity. By the end of the century, in England, these interpretations would reach full flower. For the moment, however, let us follow German developments and the expansion of Welcker's logic concerning the link between Sappho and Greek love.

This is my reconstruction of the history of this linkage: Welcker's central scholarly project (not only in his work on Sappho, but in his entire corpus) is the resurrection of *pederastia* in Greek literature. He is afraid that Sappho will be labeled a homosexual—not, however, because he fears this stain on the reputation of a great woman, but because he fears that *pederastia* will be contaminated and weakened by a female presence. He cannot go so far as to add a new "calumny" by strengthening Sappho's association to the basely sensual heterosexual eros, but he does not intend to proclaim her chaste. His followers are guilty of a double misreading when they demonstrate Sappho's "virgin purity" and when they proclaim the completely spiritual nature of *pederastia*. In other words, the association forged between Sappho and Greek love leads to a double overreaction that eventually cuts off both Sapphism and *pederastia* from sensuality.

Indeed, after Welcker only one influential German theorist dares proclaim the physicality of Greek love. In his 1837 *Paederastia*, M. H. E. Meier attacks both those who condemn homosexuality *and* "those singular minds" who have invented "apologetic theories in order to idealize and glorify" this love.[14] Meier does not deny either the central role played by *pederastia* in Greek society or the particular character of Greek love. On the contrary, he contends that "the strange mixture of materiality and spirituality" has never existed elsewhere (7). However, Meier refuses to see idealization as the price of glorification, sublimation as the cost of sublimity. He alone offers a pragmatic reading of the Platonic version of *pederastia*. Homosexuality existed, so Socrates gave it a central role to play in his project of "perfecting human nature." This meant neither that, as post-Welckerian philologists habitually contend, Socrates saw eros only as "a method of moral instruction," nor that he felt that pederastic relations could be sexually chaste (123–25). "It is wrong to believe that, even in its noblest forms, the love that the Greeks had for boys was something exclusively spiritual, a purely aesthetic satisfaction in the presence of beauty." Meier alone develops the hint of sensuality present in Welcker; Meier alone refuses to have recourse to the connoisseur theory that those without special knowledge of the Greeks are unable to understand this; Meier alone refuses to divorce *pederastia* from modern practice: "The spiritual elements of this affection were always mixed with a highly sensual element, the pleasure inspired by the physical beauty of the beloved; lovers then did not evaluate this beauty any differently than they would judge female beauty today" (18).

In this debate over the nature of male erotic experience in antiquity, some readers will undoubtedly recognize the opposing positions in the currently active controversy about the existence of a pre–nineteenth-century tradition that can be characterized by the nineteenth-century word, homosexual. The issue, in David Halperin's formulation, is "first of all, how to recover the terms in which the experiences of individuals belonging to past societies were actually constituted and, second, how to measure and assess the differences between those terms and the ones we currently employ" (38). The opposing views in today's debate are represented most notably on the one hand by K. J. Dover and John Boswell, who believe that pederasty should be considered part of a homosexual tradition. On the other hand, Jeffrey Weeks and his followers like Halperin contend that, in Weeks's words, "clear lesbian and gay identities" have recently been developed for the first time, a development that has its roots in late nineteenth-century capitalism, at the time when the sexologists' commentaries gave homosexuality "potentially the embryo of an identity" (92).

However, if we take a long-range view of the current controversy and situate it in the context of the speculation that led to the development of the sexologists' position on homosexuality, it may be possible to mediate somewhat between the two positions. At the very least, an examination of key texts in the nineteenth-century German tradition of ideal love commentary illuminates the origin of the widespread fin-de-siècle medical curiosity, verging on the obsessional, about homosexuality. The terms in which German philologists defined the concept of ideal love set both Sappho scholarship and commentary on Greek homoerotic relations on a resolutely binary course that has recently been the subject of debate, but from which we have not yet escaped. Before returning to the history of this development, let me make the terms of this debate somewhat clearer.

Foucault argues that the relationships between sexuality and access to truth and between sexual abstinence and access to truth were always formulated by the Greeks with reference to "boy love," whereas Christianity reformulates these questions with reference to heterosexuality, and the nineteenth century—he gives the example of Goethe's "eternal feminine"—finally links them to "love of woman, her virginity, her purity, her fall, and her redemptive power" (*L'Usage*, 27, 251–52). Goethe's contemporaries, the founding philologists, however, formulate "boy love" as the male counterpart of the eternal feminine, purified of the fall. They thereby decree, as it were, the existence of the countertradition that will define homosexuality as a sin, a perversion. The medical tradition that originates in Germany in the mid-nineteenth century and that culminates in such syntheses as Krafft-Ebing's *Psychopathia Sexualis* (1888) and Havelock Ellis's *Studies in the Psychology of Sex* (1897) defines homosexuality, male and female, as a "rare and possibly diseased form of access to pleasure" (Lanteri-Laura, 32), an illness it rebaptizes "sexual inversion."

The increasingly abundant recent literature on homosexuality considers this the original tradition of scholarly commentary on the subject. Those who grant the greatest power to the literature of perversion—I think most notably of Lillian Faderman and Weeks—trace the creation of the modern notion of homosexuality to the late nineteenth century and attribute a formative role to the commentary on sexual inversion. The dictionary conspires to lend credence to this view: the *OED* credits C. G. Chaddock with having introduced "homosexual" into English in 1892 in his translation of Krafft-Ebing.[15]

But the dictionary is wrong. "Homosexual" appears to have first been used in English by John Addington Symonds who speaks of "homosexual relations" in *A Problem in Greek Ethics,* a text available at least as early as 1883.[16] This detail is of significance only because, though his study is subsequently included as an appendix to Ellis, Symonds really writes as a representative of the ideal love tradition. It is surely no accident that this tradition has almost been effaced from the history of homosexuality. Its exponents' insistence on proving that the Greek phenomenon was without sensual content may explain why *Knabenliebe* has been dismissed as *not* homosexuality by many recent historians. This dismissal forces Boswell to develop at some length an argument that concludes "if the term 'homosexual' has any significance at all, it clearly includes relations between men and boys no less than between men and men or boys and boys" (*Christianity,* 28). It leads Halperin to conclude that it is still to be decided whether "Athenian pederasty is primarily a matter for philological investigation" (44). But I have gotten ahead of myself. Let us return to the giants of the nineteenth-century philological tradition to see how they succeeded at the same time in decreeing the virginity of both *pederastia* and Sappho and in making them "primarily matter[s] for philological investigation," and how in the process they pushed those who refused to deny the sensuality of all homoerotic phenomena to view these phenomena as diseased.

With the generation of 1820, philology came into its own and was able to consolidate some fifty years of work, to make good on its claim of being an intellectual totality, that is, of using the study of language to reach the essence of nations. At the forefront of this generation stood Karl Otfried Müller, Welcker's successor at Göttingen, whose syntheses of Greek culture were quickly translated and whose influence was especially keen in France. Müller establishes all the patterns that dominate the nineteenth-century scholarly vision of Sappho: he devotes separate studies to the tenth muse and to *pederastia,* and he uses parallel arguments when decreeing their chastity. Yet when read together, Müller's history of the Dorians (1820–24), a foundation of the ideal love tradition, and his history of Greek literature (1841) make it plain that when both become "matters for philological investigation," Sapphic passion will be purified but never glorified like *pederastia.*

Müller's scholarly reputation was established by his history of the Dorians, in which he proposes this civilization as the model for the Greek genius and *pederastia* as the origin of that genius.[17] Müller contends that he will not examine Greek love from a "moral point of view" (*The Doric Race,* 2:306), but he then attempts to prove that it is a phenomenon without moral content: *pederastia* must not be confused with "the vice to which in its name and outward form it is so nearly allied" (2:310). The custom he is characterizing belongs to the domain of nationalism and pedagogy—precisely, therefore, to the domain of philology. Müller provides the kind of detailed description of the pedagogical function of *pederastia* as a tool for civic and military values that is missing from Welcker's polemic. He traces the origin, the spread, and the official "encouragement" of Greek love "in the race of all the Greeks the most distinguished for its healthy, temperate, and even ascetic habits" (2:311), and he does so with a moderation absent from Welcker's more propagandistic text.

But when Müller subsequently turns to literature, the eulogy begins. Furthermore, in what is probably the most influential history of Greek literature in the nineteenth century, he also strengthens the bond between Sapphic purity and *pederastia.* Müller has hardly begun his presentation of Sappho before he launches into a discussion of a poem then still unknown except for a reference in Herodotus (it subsequently turned up in the papyri discoveries [Edmonds, *Lyra,* 141]), in which she scolds her brother for his relation with the courtesan Rhodopis. It quickly becomes evident why Müller elects this aberrant introduction: Sappho's alleged moral "severity" in the conjectured poem "allows us to determine the principles that she followed in her own life. . . . The conscience of a young girl of *immaculate* honor raised with modesty is just as plainly evident in the lines concerning her relationship with Alceus" (*Histoire,* 1:356, my emphasis). Sappho's immaculateness thus established on the basis of an unknown poem and lines whose attribution was already in question in his day, Müller proceeds to unveil the "innocent artlessness" in poems of more certain provenance. The "Ode to Aphrodite" is a youthful effort and, even then, she wrote to the goddess rather than the man; when she was older, she sent men away. The fragments addressed to women were composed for the "association" she directed whose object was to promote music and poetry.

Müller resurrects the theory of Sappho the schoolteacher as a means of evoking *pederastia*.[18] The comparison seems initially to assimilate Sappho to the passionately chaste pedagogy already documented in Müller's earlier history: she wrote to her students in "exactly the same exalted style used by the Dorians for an officially sanctioned relation between men and adolescents whereby the young men learned noble and manly virtue" (1:367–68). However, as soon as the comparison is put to the test, it is revealed to be without content: all Müller has to say about fr. 31 is that, in it, the language of *pederastia* is used to paint "a simple friendly affection for a young girl" (1:368).

Just how uninspired this reading really is becomes evident as soon as it is compared with the treatment of Alceus, a figure Müller flagrantly privileges. He expresses at length his regret that we do not have more of Alceus's erotic (homosexual) poetry: "What charming thoughts . . . natural and true, the poetry Alceus addressed to beautiful adolescents must have contained. . . . These erotic poems revealed no trace of an effeminate sybarite, a libertine only thinking of sensual pleasures. One saw throughout them the vigorous man, . . . and the tumult of war and political struggle formed their background" (1:349–50). The passage ends with Müller's strongest explicit formulation of his admiration for *pederastia* as "noble love." Indeed, much of his consideration of Alceus is really a Welckerian eulogy with greater emphasis on the bond between Greek love and military capabilities. The pretext of describing what must have been the content of poems now lost to us allows Müller to define *pederastia* as a militaristic, virile relation cleansed of eroticism because it offers instruction in manly virtue.

The problem with the vision Müller halfheartedly suggests of Sappho as pederastic professor is that she provides no instruction in the acquisition of virility. The content of her poems is therefore unworthy of the official sanction of either the Greek state or the German philologists who are its modern interpreters. This means finally that, beyond perfunctory remarks about her candor and ingenuous frankness, Sappho's poems will in effect not be read by the philologists who claim to understand her essence. A brief look at two of the most respected philologists of the early twentieth century is sufficient to demonstrate how Müller's conjectural reading is preserved intact for the next century.

Paul Brandt, like Müller, devotes separate studies to the tenth muse and to *pederastia*. His 1905 *Sappho* is remarkably close to Müller's 1841 presentation. Sapphic friendship is initially justified with a description of "the noble bonds of friendship" between men and boys that "are bound up with the essence of the Greek being" (9). Brandt takes Müller's insistence on Sappho's naive innocence to its logical conclusion and infantilizes Sappho in her erotic relations. He makes Sapphism not the love of girls but love among girls: "Who will blame the Aeolian girl if she formed a bond of friendship with a like-minded girl? . . . Who would blame this girl if she openly . . . proclaimed her happiness?" (10). This "Greek girl" is, of course, Sappho, "who in the final analysis remained a child all her life" (10). Brandt never explains how this perpetual child could have made "virtue and morality" "the basis of her friendships." He is content to leave Sappho in that state of ill-defined virginity to which "Welcker's great book" had consigned her (45). Indeed, the status of this chastity is so vague that Brandt's strongest ethical pronouncement—"The Greeks loved the beauty of the body. This had nothing to do with sin because from the point of view of the Greeks bodily beauty pleased the gods" (47)—exposes the confrontation between antithetical moral systems ("sin" and "the gods") that subtends the German Christianization of Greek nationalistic aestheticism. Throughout his study, Brandt reserves high praise for Sappho, yet his only justifications of how the love of beauty found in her poetry plays a role in the ennobling enterprise he is describing are his vague claims that her poetry is full of "delight in nature" (47) and that her "songs" to Atthis are "higher hymns full of majesty" (35). Brandt never confronts the difficulty of reconciling a poetry that praises female forms with the type of sublimating aesthetic his work glorifies, that is, one that sees the male body as the aesthetic norm: "The Greeks knew nothing of the tyrannical law that saw beauty only in women," Brandt proclaims at the outset (9).[19]

When Brandt publishes his full-blown eulogy of *pederastia* some twenty years later, he does so only under cover of the pseudonym "Hans Licht," even though his position in *Sexual Life in Ancient Greece* is no bolder than that earlier expressed under his own name, but only more likely to attract attention because of his work's announced subject matter. Brandt's project therefore raises the possibility that Sappho may have functioned as a smokescreen against censorship for the apologists of ideal love. His second study is initially puzzling because of his refusal to recognize his precursors. He contends that to date the Greek pederast has been less studied than the hetaera, so that the reader unfamiliar with Greek sources would have the idea "that Greek homosexuality was a subsidiary phenomenon," whereas Licht, the initiate, the connoisseur, knows it to be on the contrary "*the* key to the understanding of the whole of Greek culture" (412–13).

Indeed, Licht's monumental study is geared less to the presentation of an overall sexual history than to the demonstration of this sweeping axiom. Witness his concluding sentence—"But anyone who is able to set himself free in the spirit from modern views, and to penetrate with unprejudiced mind into the thoughts of these ancient peoples, will comprehend the lofty ethics of the Hellenes, whose highest ideal expresses itself in 'the beautiful both in body and soul' " (525). This is the most common defense of *pederastia* used throughout the ideal love tradition. It is only in the chapter devoted to "Perversions of Greek Sexual Life" that the explanation for Licht's attempt to divorce himself from the philological tradition becomes clear: here he contests the view that Greek homosexuality "at least" (Licht's expression, indicating a timid attempt to defend homosexual relations in general against the charge of perversion) should be considered part of the domain of *psychopathia sexualis* (499). Licht provides the only evidence that the philologists were aware that the school of medical morbidity was usurping their power over the history of homosexuality.

Licht responds to the German medical tradition with perhaps the strongest formulation ever made of ideal love as virile nationalism, an argument of seemingly guaranteed appeal in Germany between the wars. Licht's rhetoric seems directed at those who sought to renew Germany's prestige by restoring its military capabilities: "Everything that created for the Greeks a civilization that will be admired as long as the world exists has its roots in the unexampled ethical valuation of the masculine character in public and private life" (440). "The love of boys was not persecuted, but fostered, to become the power that maintained the State and upheld the foundation of Greek ethics" (441). "We are indebted to their heroic lovers . . . for Europe's freedom" (434). And once "the unprecedented ethical valuation of the masculine character" becomes the clearly formulated goal of the ideal love tradition, Sappho's usefulness is over.

The culminating work in the philological representation of Sappho which carried the nineteenth-century vision over into her depiction in the twentieth century exposes Sappho's fate once it is divorced from that of ideal love. Wilamowitz-Moellendorff's 1913 *Sappho und Simonides,* dedicated "to the memory of Friedrich Gottlieb Welcker," shows how far the heir of the nineteenth-century tradition is prepared to go in order to reduce the story of the tenth muse to her chastity. Even though by the early twentieth century Phaon had been dismissed by most scholars as a legendary figure whose fate had, by mistake or by design, been entwined with Sappho's, Wilamowitz is almost willing to resurrect Aphrodite's boatman as what he clearly considers the ultimate proof of Sappho's chastity, that is, her freedom from the sin of lesbianism. The love she felt for the beloved girls who were pupils in her school did have a sexual component, but it was never realized since it was understood that the girls were to be married. Sappho herself led the way for them by falling for Phaon (60). No sooner has he evoked Phaon than, as though sensing the outlandishness of this scholarly backsliding, Wilamowitz retreats into a position already proposed by Müller: "Whoever first spoke of Sappho's love for Phaon conveyed her nature so truly and so beautifully as though in a picture" (60). The philologist is free to act as though Phaon had existed because he is the fulfillment of the philological science's privileged understanding of Sappho's nature, the "true" and "beautiful" image of her heterosexuality.

In fact, Wilamowitz is not content simply to promote Sapphic heterosexuality. He sees marriage, the ceremony that would seal the respectability of her pedagogical establishment, where it had never been suspected before. Thus fr. 31 becomes a poem about the preparations for the wedding of one of Sappho's beloved students, and the man in the ode is presented as the girl's husband (see 54). And with the accumulated authority of a century of philology behind them, Wilamowitz's views come to dominate the twentieth-century official vision of Sappho, to such an extent that in 1955 Denys Page still feels obliged to devote the single most extensive section of his commentary on fr. 31 to a scornful dismissal of the scenario imagined by Welcker's heir (30–33).

Thus Wilamowitz finally manages to confine Sappho to the kind of status philology had been trying to craft for her for a century. The purpose of her pedagogy is to prepare girls for marriage, to fuel the official institution whose existence interests the philologists only insofar as it is necessary in order to produce new citizens.[20] Witness the conclusion of Licht's *Sexual Life,* in which he presents *pederastia* and marriage as unions whose complementarity was recognized by the state which sanctioned "love of boys" as a "necessary supplement" to marriage, a supplement undoubtedly made necessary by the inability of any union with a woman to ennoble her partner and make him thereby the heroic warrior citizen who can lead the state to greatness. Philology's passion for Sappho can be laid to rest once a place has been found for her in the nationalistic program for civic virtue. Wilamowitz finally manages to take account of the similarity first formulated by Maximus of Tyre—"The love of Sappho . . . was surely the same as the art of love practiced by Socrates" (Edmonds, *Lyra*, 155)—without according her any share in the unique and essential Greek pedagogical enterprise. Sappho is granted status as "an immortal woman" (71), if it is accepted that she won immortality by defending the modern patriarchal view of the importance of virginity, by watching over in her role as "teacher of the Lesbian virgins" (71) the chastity of future mothers of beloved boys.

Thus for Wilamowitz the greatest threat is any interpretation that would cast doubt on the bond he forges between Sappho and marriage. From his notes it is clear that he has scoured even the most obscure and even the most blatantly fictionalized visions of Sappho to police them on this score. Thus Verri and Imperiale are mentioned but, because their readings are politically correct, their fictions do not come under heavy attack (18, n. 2). However, Wilamowitz levels a full measure of his scorn at an even more obscure volume, J.-M.-F. Bascoul's 1911 *La Chaste Sappho* which, as its title indicates, does not even take issue with philology's founding Sapphic principle. But Bascoul presents Sappho as a precursor of turn-of-the-century feminists and Wilamowitz cannot let this theory stand. She "was no *mascula Sappho* and she would not have joined the suffragettes," Wilamowitz proclaims (16), driven by his conviction that no suggestion, however humble, that Sapphic chastity would have freed women from the bonds of marriage can remain unanswered.

Wilamowitz realized that the most serious challenge to philology's continued control over Sappho was being mounted by those "outside of Germany" who refused to accept Welcker's "triumph" (71). He is therefore prepared to put not only his intellectual authority but his "heart" behind the "defense of this great woman" against the threat of Pierre Louÿs's *Chansons de Bilitis* and its portrayal of Sappho's rapaciously sensual homosexuality (63). So great is Wilamowitz's rage against Louÿs that he sacrifices the very structure of *Sappho und Simonides* to it. At the center of this volume still considered a standard reference, he reprints, in its original format, his seventeen-year-old review of *Bilitis,* in which he levels considerable critical overkill against a fiction no one could have taken for an attempt to invade the by then carefully defined territory of erudition. One sample is sufficient to measure the philologist's sense of outrage: "In order for Pierre Louÿs to be correct, one would have to think that the teacher of Lesbian virgins could acknowledge perverted feelings before the gods and men" (71). Wilamowitz's anger can only result from his fear that philology's victory would never be total, that Sappho's poetry would continue to be seen as "tribade poetry" (70), and especially that this would no longer be viewed as a sin. As we will see, Wilamowitz is correct to pinpoint the origin of this threat "outside of Germany." However, the two most interesting attempts at reviving, and even glorifying, a homosexual Sappho came from within, if not always Germany, at least the ideal love school.

Long before Louÿs reveled in his tales of lesbian turned temple prostitute, Bachofen's 1861 *Mutterrecht und Urreligion* had attempted to resensualize the virginal Sapphic body. From his vantage point outside the philological tradition, Bachofen is able to create a theory of Sapphism that avoids some excesses of the official view of idealizing sublimation. Among nineteenth-century German thinkers, Bachofen alone seeks to establish a real parallelism behind the recurrent pairing of Sappho and ideal love by making Sapphism the result, and in some sense the fulfillment, of *pederastia*. The goal of the sexual political history Bachofen traces often seems a familiar tale of the ennobling powers of a politico-aesthetic institution: the "ultimate form" in the development of classical history is the "Apollonian purity" of "the paternal system of Athens" (76). Even his "Lesbos" section initially appears to be only the ideal love theory enriched with exotic elements. He recounts the legend that traces the poetic genius of Lesbian women to the friendly welcome they gave Orpheus's head when it arrived singing on Lesbos. Orpheus, prophet of Apollo, had proclaimed the importance of "masculine loves"[21] as "an ethical transcending of the lower Eros" that "raises man . . . to a higher stage of existence" (203). When the women of Lesbos begin to follow "the Orphic life," they initiate "a higher spiritual development which culminated in Sappho and her circle." Bachofen pronounces this "love of women for their own sex" "equivalent" to the Orphic masculine love by which it was inspired (204). Since he alone grants Sapphism equal status, it is in his description of its function that we can measure Bachofen's independence from the ideal love tradition.

After a familiar beginning—"Here again the sole purpose was to transcend the lower sensuality, to make physical beauty into a purified psychic beauty"—we find a new pedagogical justification for same-sex love, when Sappho is portrayed as a protofeminist: "her task was to elevate and educate her sex" (205). We also find a new vocabulary of religious "enthusiasm," almost of spiritual frenzy: Sappho's "enthusiasm" "*seized* upon the sensuous*,*" "Eros *drove* her to all [the Lesbian maidens]"; "wherever she found physical beauty, Eros *impelled* her to create spiritual beauty as well" (204–5, my emphasis). The cool sublimation of Müller's heroic lovers has been replaced by Bachofen's vision of Sappho as a wildly driven, mad priestess of Aphrodite—and of doctrines more mysterious still. He reinterprets the ancient description of ideal femininity as a composite of Theano, Diotima, and Sappho, which for Neue proves Welcker's theory, to mean that the Sapphic muse was anticlassical, pre-Hellenic in spirit. He stresses the three women's links to Pythagoreanism, the force Bachofen views as combating Hellenism with a revival of old maternal cults.

Bachofen ultimately offers a reading that, because of the place accorded Sappho and female powers, goes against the grain of the philological tradition. The Lesbos section of *Mutterrecht und Urreligion* culminates in a eulogy not of the powers of sublimation but of the force of "woman's sublimity," "a consequence of her relation to the hidden doctrine," and "the source of her enthusiasm." Sappho becomes a repository of these secret mysteries and attains immortality not for her chastity but for her access to the doctrines hidden from men. Bachofen alone illustrates the reading, so often proposed by the philologists, of Phaon and the leap as poetic fulfillments of the Sapphic spirit: "Singing both nature and womanhood, Sappho encompasses all sides of the goddess she serves, and in the popular legends of Phaon and the Leukadian leap, she becomes one with her" (206–7).

Bachofen transforms philology's vision of the leap as the baptismal gesture by which Sappho frees herself from her base female corporeality into the poet's initiation into the ranks of the great female mystics. He thereby announces the wave of Pythagorean interpretations of the suicide that occurs after a Roman fresco depicting the scene is discovered during World War I in a subterranean building near Rome's Porta Maggiore, identified by some as a center of Neopythagorean activity. In this view, Sappho becomes a "burning," transported female mystic.[22] Bachofen is the first to reembody, as it were, the disembodied functionary of the state's marital service in order to reempower Sappho as a prophet of female supremacy and the voice of Woman's initiation into the mysteries of the universe. His reading finds echoes only at the turn of the century, after Wilamowitz's dreaded suffragettes had put substance into Bachofen's vague dream of female power. The homosexual, feminist Sappho that would first be actively promoted in France at that time is a pan-European production influenced both by Bachofen and by the renegade commentator on ideal love, John Addington Symonds.

Symonds follows the philological model in a number of ways, the most obvious being his composition of parallel studies of Sappho (in *Studies of the Greek Poets*) and *pederastia. A Problem in Greek Ethics,* written in 1873 and gradually made public over the next twenty-five years, parallels Bachofen's attempt to add mysticism to the philologists' concept of ideal love as sublimation.[23] For the most part, Symonds merely replicates the arguments proposed by the philologists to portray *pederastia* as a program for noble virility, in his formulation, "closely associated with liberty, manly sports, severe studies, self-sacrifice, self-control and deeds of daring" (44). However, Symonds refuses to follow them in their denial of the sensuality of what his near-contemporary sensualizer Bachofen calls "male loves": he distinguishes at some length between what he terms "heroic love" on the model of Achilles and Patroclus which, he contends, "existed as an ideal rather than as an actual reality" (4), and what he terms "Greek love," defined as a mixture of "heroic and vulgar" love (7–8). Furthermore, Symonds decisively parts ways with the German scholarly tradition in his conclusion, when he moves remarkably close to Bachofen.

Like other commentaries on ideal love, Symonds's has a strange structure, as though it bore conscious marks of its author's fear of censorship, or unconscious marks of his self-censorship. This perhaps most exhaustive eulogy of Greek love ends with three brief sections: "The Relation of Paiderastia to Greek Art" is followed by a discussion of female homosexuality in Greece and then a final section in which Symonds reviews the development of history, and not just the history of homosexuality, from Greece to "modern times" in three short paragraphs. Symonds's discussion of the centrality of Greek love to the Greek "esthetic morality" (69) is still straight out of the philological tradition and in no way hints at the surprises he holds in reserve for his last four pages. The second-to-last section has become such a commonplace in subsequent histories of Greek homosexuality that it would be easy to skip over it, too: Symonds explains that it is difficult to assess the importance of "homosexual love between females," not because it did not exist, but because "feminine homosexual passions were never worked into the social system, never became educational and military agents" (71). Symonds does not state, as more recent authors do, that the absence of institutional status would explain the absence of documents; he seems only interested in separating, in the best philological manner, female sexuality from male and in classifying it as less important, "unhonored" (72). Rather than explain this section away on the basis of its similarities with subsequent commentary, however, I would like to explore the strangeness of Symonds's brief innovation—which may well contain the first usage in English of the female form of "homosexual."[24]

On several occasions Symonds points out what he considers the "parallelism" between "the two Platonic conceptions of love," that is, *pederastia* and the "chivalrous enthusiasm for women" (see, for example, 54–55). The notion that chivalry marked the continuation of ideal love becomes more than an implication only in the enigmatically elliptical final section: "Greek love did not exist at Rome—Christianity—Chivalry—The *modus vivendi* of the modern world." Throughout his study, Symonds develops his arguments with great care, more carefully than any member of the ideal love school. At the end, however, he adopts the jump-cut progression of his precursors for this review of the history of sexuality after Greece: the Romans of the Decadence corrupted Greek love to mere "lust" and thereby provoked the early Christians to cut man off from tainted "nature" by pronouncing a mind-body dualism, and to confine Woman to "the convent." But escape to the convent was not the answer, for Redemption was to come this time from Woman, a "truth" "for the first time truly apprehended" by "the Teutonic converts to the Christian faith." This idea was a nineteenth-century commonplace, but Symonds's final sentences reveal the innovation of his *pederastia*-chivalry comparison: "The mythology of Mary gave religious sanction to the chivalrous enthusiasm; and a cult of woman sprang into being to which, although it was romantic and visionary, we owe the spiritual basis of our domestic and civil life. The *modus vivendi* of the modern world was found" (73). With this flourish, the work that has been referred to as "the first thorough account of [homosexuality in ancient Greece] in English" (Boswell, *Christianity*, 17), the work that seems to have made "homosexual" an English word, comes to an abrupt halt.

Symonds's study marks at once the ne plus ultra of the ideal love tradition and the revitalizing of the Sappho tradition. The price eventually paid for the recuperation of Greek homosexuality as ennobling love is to deny homosexuality any life after classical Greece. Outside the Greek ethical aesthetics, Symonds implies, homosexuality can only be corrupted to "lust." Unlike the philologists, Symonds has no message about the implicit revival of male same-sex love necessary to create a race of "new Greeks"; he proposes only the relatively innocuous recuperation of Greek homosexuality as a "noble synthesis" that can never be made to function as it once did. Yet Symonds does implicitly suggest a modern continuation of the idealizing sublimation necessary for *pederastia*. In an act of homage more reminiscent of Bachofen than of any other nineteenth-century German thinker, Symonds implies that the modern pederast-homosexual worships at the shrine of the ultimate in female mysticism or chivalric womanhood, the Virgin Mary.

Moreover, the strange unfolding of Symonds's argument suggests a second way in which the potential of the ideal love tradition may be realized. When he glides from the aesthetic value of *pederastia*, to sapphism, to the Virgin Mary, Symonds establishes a rhythm whereby Sappho—chaste in a Bachofian rather than a Welckerian manner—finally assumes the role that the philologists had implicitly assigned her all along, as precursor of the Virgin Mary. By the same progression, "homosexual passions among females," in a move the attentive reader of the philological speculation on ideal love has anticipated for some time, become central to "the *modus vivendi* of the modern world." I believe that the possibility of this conflation of the ancient and the modern formulations of the relation between sexuality and access to truth had been all along at the root of philologists' attempts to dissociate Sappho from homosexuality: in the age of the "eternal feminine," Sappho, and no longer those Symonds calls "the heroic lovers," was the logical center of a cult of sublimated homosexuality. The enormously elliptical presentation of Symonds's final sections makes it impossible to determine just how far he intended to carry this line of reasoning. But we must not forget that, unlike more recent commentators on male homosexuality in ancient Greece who must feel that at least a nod in the direction of women is mandatory, Symonds was not obliged to recreate the philological bond between Sappho and *pederastia*. Furthermore, the structural juxtaposition of the only two female figures in his study invites the reader to compare Sappho and the Virgin Mary.

With *A Problem in Greek Ethics,* Symonds becomes part of an unexpected transfer of knowledge by which the philologists' theories, so marked by the German nationalism that crested during World War II, were coopted—and feminized—by an interconnected group of fin-de-siècle decadents in England and France whose aim is to realize Symonds's conclusion that Sapphism is the *"modus vivendi* of the modern world." Thus for his defense at his 1895 trial, Oscar Wilde turns to the classic topoi of ideal love theorists—David and Jonathan (the "modern" Achilles and Patroclus) and Plato. Pierre Louÿs, who corrected the French for Wilde's *Salomé,* dedicated the fiction that tormented Wilamowitz for over twenty years "aux jeunes filles de la société future," a dedication that soon became a battle cry for the first female commentators of Sappho to proclaim both their feminism and their homosexuality.

This milieu also generated what Bram Dijkstra terms a "relatively rare explicit early treatment of lesbianism" (153), the 1864 *Sappho and Erinna in the Garden of Mytilene* by Simeon Solomon, who moved in the same circles as Swinburne and Symonds (fig. 7).[25] This lush garden scene is among the few unequivocally homoerotic depictions of Sappho at any time, the only visual representation, to my knowledge, of the poet actively initiating an embrace with another woman. Judith Stein cites William Gaunt's testimony that Solomon's drawings of Antinous and of Sappho decorated the Oxford rooms of the initiates in the 1860s (296–97). This suggests that, perhaps under Symonds's influence, Sappho had already assumed the role of patron saint of modern (homo)sexuality that is forecast for her at the end of *A Problem in Greek Ethics,* and that the peaceful cohabitation that Symonds predicts between the ideal beloved boy and the poet who immortalized her beloved girls had already become at least an iconographic reality. The juxtaposition of Sappho and Antinous in Symonds's circle may also imply an invocation of her patronage for a modern renewal of *pederastia.* Sapphism, as Dover correctly stresses, differs from the pederastic model in a major way: it replaces "the usual distinction [in *pederastia*] between a dominant and a subordinate partner" with "a marked degree of mutual eros" (177). This mutual eros could explain Sapphism's attraction for Symonds who, as the finale to *A Problem in Greek Ethics,* rather than evoking once again the redemptive value of sublimation typical of ideal love commentary, might have wanted to suggest its attraction for a homoerotic "future society."

The proof that this position is implicit in the philological presentation of Sappho was supplied some seventeen years before Symonds wrote by

Fɪɢ. 7. Simeon Solomon, *Sappho and Erinna in the Garden of Mytilene* (1864).
Reprinted by permission of the Tate Gallery and of Sotheby's, London.

no one less than the man who forged the link between Sappho and ideal love, Welcker. For decades, Welcker had received only praise for the "salvation" of Sappho and his simple rejection of female homosexuality had been amplified into a theory of Sappho's "virgin purity," when he suddenly came under attack from an outsider, an Englishman always identified as "the Colonel" Mure. In his history of Greek literature, Mure devotes a major part of the entry on Sappho to a refutation of the ideal love-chastity theory on the grounds that its proponents were naively trying to cover up the existence of female homosexuality in general and Sappho's double homo- and heterosexual promiscuity in particular. In his response, Welcker disdains Mure for having tried to attribute to German scholars opinions which "even in England no one could ever believe they had expressed" ("Oder der Sappho," 236). Welcker is prepared to deny that any German had ever even implied, much less openly argued, that Sappho was chaste. He feels obliged to jettison this by-product of his 1816 study in an effort to win an absolute victory for what is now shown to be the essential proposition for him, the chastity of *pederastia*. He is prepared therefore to condemn Sappho to heterosexual lust—anything to keep her off the territory of heroic male sexuality and to guarantee the sublimity and the sublimation of that sexuality[26]: "Surely a task far more difficult than the theologian's of converting someone who cannot believe in God and immortality is the task of the philologist of bringing over to his own views someone who is determined not to believe in that state of falling-in-love which does not dream of unchastity" (236).

The theologian-philologist resorts to a triple negation to retain his power over the mysteries of ideal love, a syntactic weakness that exposes the extent to which philology had allowed its authority to become bound up with the definition of this concept. Behind Welcker's determined resistance to Sappho lay from the beginning the realization that she was endowed with the power to become the mystical, redemptive Virgin who would preside over much of fin-de-siècle decadence. Once Sappho had been empowered by a connection to chastity, the relation between sexuality and access to truth formulated by the Greeks and the philologists with reference to "boy love" could be transferred to her. Chastity was a powerful attribute for the century that finalized the cult of Mary's absolute purity when the Immaculate Conception became dogma in 1854.

The most original and compelling late nineteenth- and early twentieth-century visions of Sappho are all related to this rebellion against philology, which created the chaste priestess of sensuality. This does not mean, however, that philology's authority was broken. On the contrary, until virtually the mid-twentieth century, the most respected Hellenists everywhere preach the pure doctrine of German philology, despite the decreasing frequency of powerful philological statements on ideal love after the mid-nineteenth century.[27] Let me evoke briefly just two examples from different national traditions. In 1863, Léo Joubert pronounces Sappho's poetry free of sensuality ("the storm takes place entirely in the region of the soul" [*Essais*, 180]) and declares that the Greeks "would have punished with death a woman capable of a crime . . . that was a direct attack on the family" (181). Joubert claims the protection of "all modern criticism" for these views, covering up thereby dissenting voices like Mure's, whose book he is allegedly reviewing in the article in which these citations appear (187). Like all chastity proponents, he stakes his own authority on acceptance of this vision of Sappho: her two odes are "completely misread" by those who do not accept their "philological peculiarity," that is, the fact that in Sappho's day "Greek didn't yet possess the nuances necessary to express the distinction so clear today between love and friendship" (179).[28]

Like the French, the English, after Colonel Mure's skirmish with the formidable Welcker, fell into the German line, so that by the time the turn-of-the-century papyri discoveries made Sappho the object of renewed attention, her purity was universally decreed. The English tradition follows from the German without missing a step, supplying proofs for the chastity theory with a zeal that went far beyond that of its alleged originator. J. M. Edmonds's commentary is a perfect example of the English tradition of reading Sappho's poetry to show why it could not have been produced by a "bad" woman. But my favorite examples of this interpretative style are from the work of an American, David Robinson, in his 1924 study of Sappho. In a volume still widely cited today, Robinson—and I hasten to stress that his reasoning is only slightly more ludicrous than that common for decades in all national scholarly traditions under the influence of the chastity theory—devotes page after page to a demonstration of why homosexuality and Sappho's poetry are irreconcilable. Exercising utmost restraint, I will permit myself only one pared-down example from a vast stock:

> It is against the nature of things that a woman who has given herself up to unnatural practices which . . . throw the soul into disorder . . . should be able to write in perfect

obedience to the laws of vocal harmony. . . . Sappho's love of flowers, moreover, affords another luminous testimony. A bad woman might love roses, but a bad woman does not love the small and hidden wild flowers of the field as Sappho did. (44–45)[29]

Robinson finally makes explicit the often implicit philological position that sexuality is an affair of metrics: moral corruption (homosexuality) is incompatible with metrical perfection.

Not the least of Welcker's dubious accomplishments is the way in which he set the terms according to which the history of Sappho scholarship was written. By this I mean that, in his wake and at least until the 1930s, all those who follow his point of view and proclaim either Sappho's chastity or her lukewarm heterosexuality are known as Sappho's "defenders," while those who believe in her homosexuality are known, if not as her attackers, as those who "calumniate" her. Those reviewing the history of Sappho's interpretation also place Welcker at the summit of the defense tradition, which is seen as originating with Le Fèvre Dacier in 1681 and continuing at least as far as Reinach and Puech in 1937 (see, for example, Larnac and Salmon, 6). Under the influence of the myth of philology—that the study of Greek, made scientific, would permit the perfect recovery of Greek genius—Sappho's modern history is reduced to that of her chastity and "*the* tradition" of Sappho scholarship allows into its ranks only those who proclaim this doctrine. If the French humanists and their homosexual Sappho are forgotten, and the German neohumanists are portrayed as the ultimate authorities, then the problem of Sappho seems resolved.

The chastity's theory's success story corresponds perfectly to the paradigm for sexual politics articulated so famously by Luce Irigaray in *Speculum de l'autre femme:* men found a cultural order through the creation of a shared discourse of female sexuality. This discourse conveys no information about the actual reality of women's lives, in this case that of a female intellectual in antiquity. The discourse fulfills its mission of male bonding because it purveys instead a fiction of the feminine convincing to men at the time of its articulation because it corresponds to their desired fantasy of woman's place in the sociocultural order. This is not to say that the Sapphic fictions imagined by women writers are necessarily more accurate renditions of experience: Scudéry's contains more facts and many fewer idiosyncratic inventions than, say, Barthélemy's, but it remains an idealized, idyllic view of Sappho's experience. The major difference between these uses of Sappho is a question of influence: prior to the early twentieth century, no Sapphic fiction promoted by a woman succeeded in founding a tradition of commentary.

The tradition inaugurated by Welcker demonstrates that the overwhelming modern scholarly preference in fictions of Sappho is for the vision of chaste handmaiden serving the interests of what Staël termed "the world and the city." The total inability on the part of its proponents to deal with the issue of female homosexuality and their concomitant desire to speak only of male homoerotic bonds provides further confirmation of Irigaray's paradigm. But this is only logical. The inspiration for Irigaray's theory is Freud's treatment of female homosexuality: for example, she presents his "Psychogenesis of a Case of Homosexuality in a Woman" as a detour of desire in which the woman serves only as a pretext for the creation of a male homoerotic scene (*Speculum,* 122–23). When read in the context of the nineteenth-century German philological position on Sappho, the original psychoanalytic treatment of female homosexuality seems perfectly compatible with the then authoritative view of the original female homosexual. In this area as in others, Freud can be seen as a product of a specific historical moment. His theories, as well as those of the sexologists and proponents of the "medical morbidity" school (those most often cited as Freud's historical precursors), bear the mark of the discourse that reigned over the German nineteenth century, philology. These late nineteenth-century theories, now thought to have played a formative role in the creation of a modern homosexual identity, should not be read in isolation from the ideal love commentary so privileged by philologists. No more than the contemporary dual Sapphic image (virgin and whore), these opposing visions of male homoerotic relations cannot be dissociated from each other.

At the eve of World War II, the debate on Sapphism must have seemed to the reigning philologists finally to have been concluded. In fact, the heterosexually virginal Sappho was dominant for barely more than a century. Even in the nineteenth century, outside scholarly circles, the theory of Sapphic chastity was constantly under attack. Contemporary fictions of Sappho show how the virgin generated the two emblematic nineteenth-century French figures, Sappho the courtesan and Sappho the (mad) lesbian. Before we can understand the development of modern fictions of Sappho, we must review the presentation of her poetry in the period during which chastity dominated scholarly theory.

De Rerum Natura

On prétend que Sapho fit d'admirables vers. Dans tous les cas, je ne crois point que ce soit là son vrai titre à l'immortalité.

—Guy de Maupassant,
"La Lysistrata moderne"

L'apparition soudaine de notre médaille résout enfin cet *imbroglio* historique, et c'est un nouveau service que la numismatique rend aux lettres.

—L. Allier de Hauteroche,
Notice sur la courtisane Sapho

Sappho's textual history in the nineteenth century is a story of slow acquisition coupled with determined avoidance of diversity. The approximately one hundred and twenty poems and fragments made available in the first nineteenth-century German editions (Volger 1810, Neue 1824) increased in early twentieth-century English editions to nearly two hundred. Whereas the expanded corpus published by Edmonds in 1922 was made accessible to French readers fairly rapidly in the 1937 Reinach-Puech edition, however, their nineteenth-century counterparts waited some ninety years (Lebey 1895, Vivien 1903) to profit from the first advances of German philologists. And while French scholars complained loudly of their deprivation during the fifteen years that separated Edmonds and Reinach-Puech, the far more scandalous delay in transmission during the previous century was hardly mentioned. Nineteenth-century complacency originated in large part in the continuing influence of the eighteenth-century French tradition: Sappho's translators, for the most part political conservatives, continued to disseminate the reduced, watered-down corpus they had inherited from their precursors. They introduced the new fragments published by German philologists only gradually, and generally only when these fragments could be made to conform to their vision of Sappho as a poet even more chaste than her contemporary German counterpart.[30]

This said, I will begin with the most important exception to the rule of right-wing politics and retrograde scholarship. Jean-François Boissonade was fired from his position in foreign affairs when he was suspected of having participated in the royalist insurrection of Vendémiaire an IV. He went on to attain unequaled critical authority as a promoter of the superiority of German erudition. His election to the Collège de France in 1828 rewarded both a decade (1803–13) of involvement with the *Journal de l'Empire* as a contributing editor, during which his efforts to bring Greek literature to a broad public helped spark a major revival of Hellenism, and his scholarly work, especially his *Lyrici Graeci* (1825), long recognized as the best edition available in France and the only French contribution cited by the foremost German authority of the century, Theodore Bergk (see Canat, 1:25–26). In 1812, Boissonade chose the very public forum of the *Journal de l'Empire* to lambaste French ignorance of Sappho. His chosen target is equally visible, Jean de La Harpe's pronouncement in his *Lycée*, the multivolume literary manual published exactly at the turn of the century that is the best guide to the canon the nineteenth century inherits from the eighteenth: "We have only a dozen lines by the famous Sapho" (1:521). The bulk of Boissonade's attack proclaims what he himself establishes only later and only in an all-Greek edition, an expanded Sappho corpus (seventy-seven fragments in his 1825 edition).

Boissonade sneaks into a note what remains the boldest proposal for textual revision formulated by any scholar before Bergk. In his commentary on his translation of the "Ode to Aphrodite," Boissonade declares: "I didn't want to write *if he flees;* I didn't dare write *if she flees.* I decided to use *one,* which reproduces the ambiguity of the Greek" (4). This suggestion by the most respected authority of the day that the orientation of the only poem in which Sappho identifies herself as the desiring subject is homosexual provoked none of the outcry one would have predicted, probably because Boissonade does not offer, either here or in his edition, a solution to the troubling twenty-fourth line.[31] Nevertheless, his polemic proves that on the eve of the philologists' campaign, Sapphic sexuality seemed (at least to one authority), for the first time in one hundred and fifty years, undecided. However, when the very masters whose authority Boissonade proclaimed spoke, they put an end to speculation. After Welcker, French commentators scrambled to replace the promiscuity constructed by their eighteenth-century precursors with a vision of heterosexual chastity.

While the details of the German chastity package were still being worked out, the cornerstone of the corresponding French construction was laid in a quaint 1822 contribution, *Notice sur la courtisane Sapho, née à Erésos, dans l'île de Lesbos.* Its author was no Hellenist, but a former officer in Napoleon's army in Egypt who had begun an important collection of medals while serving at the French consulate in Turkey. Although he does not mention any precedent, Allier de Hauteroche in fact simply resurrects Aelian's theory that there were two Sapphos in Lesbos, the poet and a courtesan, a theory amplified in the ancient lexicon, the Suda, to make the courtesan Phaon's lover (see Edmonds, *Lyra,* 151, 153). The former soldier of the empire allies himself with modern sciences, iconography and numismatics, to demonstrate that it is no longer possible to believe, as "for a long time everyone has, that only one woman existed with that name" (3). He credits E. Q. Visconti, author of *Iconographie grecque,* with having identified what both herald as the coin mentioned in antiquity as having been struck by the Mytileneans to honor their famous citizen (despite the fact that Sappho's name does not figure on the coin whose authenticity they so confidently proclaim). Allier de Hauteroche announces the completion of the Sapphic iconography with his discovery of another coin, this time with the name "Sappho" on it but with Eresos as the city where it was struck. This he offers as proof of the existence of a second Sappho, born not in Mytilene like the poet, but in Eresos. He is even able to conclude his "notice" with a final discovery so recent that it is announced only in a postscript dated 5 August 1822, the discovery of what is now known as the Munich vase which bears portraits of Alceus and Sappho (with finally the name "Sappho" attached to a portrait of the poet).

Our numismatist dwells at length on the advantages of his Sapphic doubling, which in essence allows him to hold onto all legends and simply divide them up between the two Sapphos: the poet, for example, is exiled to Sicily, while the courtesan follows Phaon there. It all works out so neatly that, if only Ovid hadn't made a "mistake" and created a composite heroine, thereby leading all moderns into a "historical imbroglio," no one would ever have thought otherwise (14–15). The real advantage, never made explicit, is that the creation of another Sappho makes possible the true realization of the chastity theory: the entire sexual biography can simply be shoved off onto the other Sappho of Eresos. So insistent is Allier de Hauteroche on desexualizing the poet that he maintains the identification of her double as the incarnation of female sexuality for his age, the courtesan, even though he is finally obliged to water down his own typecasting: "courtesan, *if you will,* even though this profession can hardly be reconciled with the amorous despair that drives one to self-destruction" (13, my emphasis).

The reasoning behind the entire argument is not only flimsy; it is also lifted in its entirety from Visconti.[32] Yet in the decade after Welcker's pronouncement the time was ripe for the theory of the two Sapphos, so an ex-soldier was able to win for it a virtually unchallenged acceptance for nearly a century. Moreover, since allegiance to this theory was also at the same time a reaffirmation of Barthélemy's authority—his political exile hypothesis conveniently eliminated Phaon—the Hauteroche-Barthélemy alliance in effect created the signature of the nineteenth-century French school and served as an acid test of nationalistic scholarly fidelity. Thus, in the preface to the next translation of Sappho (Girodet, 1827), P. A. Coupin (also a former soldier in the imperial army) declares: "It is now recognized that there were two Sapphos" (3), and most subsequent translators fall into line—Bréghot Du Lut (1835), Veïssier Des Combes (1839), Redarez-Saint-Remy (1852), up to and including Jym (1937). They are joined in proclaiming this hypothesis historical fact by writers like Gautier, historians like Michelet, and even Hellenists like Deschanel.[33] The theory comes full circle when a modern iconography of the other Sappho develops, most notably in Barrias's 1847 *Sapho d'Erèse,* where the languid, Ingres-like display of sensuality has been shifted from Phaon, where it originated in Napoleonic representations like Girodet's, to the courtesan double.[34] French allegiance is matched by a concomitant rejection of the doubling theory on the part of philologists (see, for example, Neue, 8) and their French disciples alike (see Joubert's dismissal of the two-Sappho theory as an "infantile operation" [*Essais,* 187]).

The Germans, of course, had to reject both political involvement and doubling since they wanted to keep Phaon alive, to resurrect him at will as the proof of Sapphic heterosexuality. Ironically, they thus found themselves unable to jettison a work whose authenticity the fledgling philological science was prepared to reject, *Heroides* 15. Indeed, before Welcker, philology seems to be moving toward Allier de Hauteroche's position. In 1794, A. G. Raabe attributes the love for Phaon to Sappho of Eresos and declares that either Ovid was confused or the fifteenth epistle is "spurious and completely suspect" (5), a position to which Wolff already leans (i–ii, 65), and in both cases the writers call on Heinsius's testimony that "the letter from Sappho to Phaon is in none of the earliest manuscripts of Ovid's *Heroides*" (123).[35] Logically, if Sappho is to be made chaste, Ovid has to be pronounced spurious.

The French are, for once, able to follow scholarly logic and sever at last the bond between Ovid and Sappho forged in the early seventeenth century, at the time of her entry into the modern literary imagination. And, just as interest in a Sapphic discourse prompted Ovid's rise to prominence, once the Ovidian version of Sapphism is cast aside, the *Heroides* falls from grace in France: immediately after the inauguration of the two-Sappho era, two new translations of Ovid appear (Saint-Ange 1824, Crestin 1826), but then the rhythm falls off, for the first time in centuries, and only Pichot (1871) and Miroux (1919) precede the still standard 1928 Bornecque edition. Whereas in Germany nineteenth-century Sappho scholars continue to cling to a text rejected by Latinists, in France the fifteenth epistle inhabits a no-man's-land until twentieth-century scholars accept once again its authenticity.

Nineteenth-century French translators, partisans all of the two-Sappho theory, piggyback each other's efforts to purify her *oeuvre*. Under their guidance, not only is the homosexuality evoked by Boissonade kept at bay until the very end of the century, but the sphere of Sappho's heterosexual activity is severely restricted. Long before the corpus is sufficiently expanded to warrant this move, the first French editions devoted solely to Sappho appear (Girodet 1827, Planchon 1846). The dissolution of the partnership with Anacreon, reinforced since the mid-seventeenth century, begins as soon as the French wish to do away with Sapphic promiscuity.[36] French translations appear steadily throughout the first half of the century, most frequently from 1852 until 1855 (the period Henri Peyre associates with the renewal of Hellenism after the political and financial crises of 1848–51 [38–39]). Rable's 1855 edition marks the turning point, the completion of the textually chaste Sappho. When the tradition is renewed with Lebey's 1895 volume, Sappho has been reembodied.

In the notice that accompanies his 1835 translation, Claude Bréghot Du Lut—one of the first nineteenth-century commentators to return the long excised second *p* to "Sappho"[37]—provides what remains for twenty years the standrd biographical scenario: the poet was a teacher and political exile; the courtesan committed suicide when abandoned by Phaon.[38] This distribution once agreed upon, over the next sixty years translators contribute to the fictionalization of Sappho only through the ordering and presentation of the fragments. This is in fact the major development in nineteenth-century editions: since for the first time editors have to deal with a corpus and not just a half dozen fragments, the presentation and the construction of the corpus become essential. Henceforth, the accent will be placed on certain poems to indicate a specific reading of Sappho. As Louis Planchon (1846) correctly remarks of the role he assigns fr. 31,

"The place alone that we have given it in the collection [i.e., after the poems to a *male* Athis] changes its meaning" (205).

Jules-Henry Redarez-Saint-Remy (1852) compares the translator to the jeweler who sets stones to bring out their brilliance (18). Each of Sappho's translators in the first half of the century highlights a different aspect of the fiction of Sapphic chastity as it had been recently drawn up by the philologists. In 1839, for example, Louis-Alphonse Veïssier Des Combes gives a selection of twelve fragments whose biggest surprise is its conclusion, a poem entitled "A une jeune fille":

> If honor had always made your heart quiver,
> Would your proposals be afraid of violating its laws?
> Would your eyes shine with an immodest flame?
> Honor would speak through your voice. (235)

The poem is a perfect example of defamiliarization: readers of the eighteenth-century French tradition would recognize it as what had previously been presented, on Aristotle's authority, as Sappho's rejection of an indecent proposition by Alceus (Reinach-Puech, 305–06, n. 2), a poem that philologists foreground as still another proof of Sappho's high moral standards. Veïssier Des Combes's version is the perfect chastity poem; the professor at the collège royal de Henri IV has Sappho speak with the very vocabulary ("honor," "immodesty") used to banish the specter of female same-sex love, on the grounds that such a high-minded woman could never have conceived a criminal passion. Furthermore, by eliminating the male role in the exchange and by adding a new title, "A une jeune fille," he implies that the poem is actually the true philologists' dream, an openly antilesbian poem.[39]

Sappho's next translator is also a professor, but a professor of rhetoric and the future author of a strange exercise, *Méthode pour transformer presque tous les mots français en mots italiens* (1851). In 1846, Louis Planchon already claims to be interested only in systems: Sappho has been "retrouvée," his title implies, because she has been translated into "sticometric verse." Indeed, this edition is so weighed down with its technical apparatus (such as a "summary of sticometrics") that Planchon seems to echo Neue's opinion that sexuality is really an affair of metrics. His "sticometric" rendering inaugurates a minitradition in which Sappho will be dished up, first in "imitative," then in "equirhythmic" verse.[40] However, each system of metrics merely camouflages still another packaging of sexuality, as Planchon's edition demonstrates admirably.

Sappho retrouvée prefigures the essence of both Edmonds's and Wilamow-itz's theories of Sapphic chastity. Planchon puts his awareness of the importance of disposition to good use, presenting first the poet of nature (he puts in second and third position, after "Aphrodite," "Rose," and "Etoile du soir") and then the poet of marriage (he creates a nucleus of nuptial verse by assigning completely unjustified titles like "Le Portrait de la vierge, épithalame," "Conseils à la fiancée mourante," "Epitaphe de la fiancée"). A true proto-Wilamowitz, he next has Sappho set an example for her students by grouping together the then available poems of the Atthis cycle to which he assimilates the ode he calls "A l'objet aimé," in a masculinization justified by his identification in the biographical dictio-nary that concludes his volume of "Athis" as "jeune homme aimé de Sappho" (204). He wraps up his edition in proper French chastity fashion by combining several fragments to form "La Vieillesse de Sappho," whose message is anti-Phaon, antisuicide: Sappho lived to old age, rejecting suitors, and preaching marriage to the "fiancées" under her protection.

With Planchon's contribution, Sappho was "rediscovered" in a perfect fulfillment of the two-Sappho theory. There would have been no need to continue the effort, if this virgin Sappho had not come under attack the following year in the second most influential contribution by a nineteenth-century French Hellenist, Emile Deschanel's demonstration (to be discussed more fully below) that the poet was herself a courtesan. This attack provoked in quick succession the double apex of the chastity tradition. An appropriate representative of the post-1848 climate of political conservatism, Redarez-Saint-Remy identifies himself as a "mem-ber of the Legion of Honor"; he was also a frequent orator at the Société de Saint-Napoléon. His response to the socialist Deschanel—by this time in exile for his political writings and activity—is vintage Welcker: "Sapho was on the contrary severe in her morals" (11). In his presentation of her poetry, he develops Planchon's male Athis into the model "fickle lover." His principal innovation is to place stress on evocations of virginity: witness this transformation into a eulogy of chastity: "Everything is deserting me! . . . I have lost my virginity! . . . Where to recover that crown, the only bloom of beauty?" (60). Redarez-Saint-Remy is so staunchly conservative that he sides with the German tradition against the French and rejects Barthélemy's politicization of Sappho: "[A poet] does not conspire. A great poet always has a place under any régime" (12). Once exile became the fate of the political left, Sappho had to be dissociated from it.[41] From this point on, Barthélemy's authority is no longer automatically reaffirmed by each translator; the political Sappho will be resurrected only when exile can be dissociated from left-wing politics. Redarez-Saint-Remy "rehabilitates" Sappho by presenting her as a *salonnière* receiving "the most distinguished men of letters and the arts," who serve as models for her female students (15).

His worthy successor, Paul-Pierre Rable, who presents himself as the inventor of the system of "imitative verse," uses metrics once again as a science of sexual dispassionateness. He claims to have attained perfect "exactitude" with his method of "metric concordances" that can be applied to all poetry "since Anacreon, Sappho, Homer, and Dante are all about one and the same subject . . . curbing rather than exciting passion" (12–13). Indeed, his system has only one restriction, "relative to behavior whose depravity shocks nature and religion" (40). This means simply that, when faced with poetry like fr. 31 that does not "curb passion," Rable simply omits it: he cuts off his translation abruptly after the fifth line and, faithful to metrics to the end, replaces each amputated syllable with a dot. 1855 thus marks the nadir of Sappho's repression in France, the first and only moment when the poem that was for centuries the foundation of her reputation was wished back into modern oblivion.[42]

Having thus been taken beyond articulation, the French theory of Sapphic chastity disappears from the mainstream to resurface only sixty years later and in a manner in every way eccentric. From turn-of-the-century Algiers appear two volumes devoted to "the chaste Sappho" (1911, 1913) that attempt to revive a tradition that, in France at least, had already known its great moments and even in Germany would be a casualty of the Great War. The amateur Hellenist Bascoul tries to bridge the distance separating him from the European theater by feverishly denouncing the existence of "an imposture that has lasted for twenty-four centuries," "a plot against Sappho" in which all Hellenists beginning with Estienne have wittingly or unwittingly conspired to publish "vulgar" versions of Sappho's "sublime" poetry (1:2, 30).[43] Bascoul pronounces them all guilty of having misread as tales of passion what are in fact narratives of the anxiety of influence. In an argument so detailed that I cannot begin to reproduce it, Bascoul devotes separate volumes to fr. 31 and the "Ode to Aphrodite" in which he transforms them into accounts of the threat that a rival poet's developing talent posed for Sappho. Fragment 31 thus becomes for him a poem detailing the terrible effects produced on Sappho when she hears a new poet, perhaps Stésichore, whose talent is so great that it menaces her dominance (1:30). The poem is addressed to her daughter in an effort to make her understand the gravity of this rivalry. By the second volume, Stésichore has been positively identified as "the subject and the object" of the "Ode to Aphrodite" (2:10). Here, Bascoul attacks the then recently proposed notion that all the names of Sappho's female students in what was by then known as the "Atthis cycle" are parodic inventions of later comic playwrights.[44] The medical doctor from Algiers thus offers the purest realization of a century of chastity speculation by offering one of the few completely original fictions of Sappho: Sapphism as the absence of all sexual desire, the passion for absolute poetic greatness. Like all totalizing Sapphic fictions, it came too late to provoke any response; by 1911, the vision that Bascoul, like Welcker, feared most was finally becoming dominant.

In France, the homosexual Sappho originates in the only fiction formulated from the political left, Deschanel's courtesan Sappho. His 1847 "Sapho et les Lesbiennes" was perhaps only possible in the pre-1848 upheaval. It is the first fiction in any tradition in two centuries that reembodies Sappho with a decidedly nonconventional sexuality. So powerful is Deschanel's vision that it alters the entire course of Sappho's history in nineteenth-century France. It provokes a long interruption in new translations which occurs well before the weakening in the influence of Hellenism that Peyre situates in 1870 (67). Immediately after its publication, the center of speculation shifts not only from chastity to sexuality but also from erudition to fiction. The first half of the century had produced almost no powerful fictions centered on Sappho. In Deschanel's wake, however, writers from Baudelaire to Daudet, from Louÿs to Vivien, gave Sappho a hold on the French literary imagination more powerful than any she had exerted before. With Sappho the courtesan, Deschanel touched the pulse of his century.

His fiction has its roots in the decadence of the eighteenth-century tradition. Billardon de Sauvigny closes the first volume of his *Parnasse des dames* (in which his translation of Sappho initially appeared) with a dictionary of "famous Greek Courtesans." Sappho is not included, but throughout the eighteenth century the most tenacious arguments are originally simply hinted at through juxtaposition. In 1801, J.-B. Chaussard repeats this structure by inserting his translation of Alessandro Verri's *Avventure di Saffo* in the volume with a "general table of Greek courtesans" in which he immediately makes plain Billardon's suppressed logic, comparing Sappho to the *baladères* (5). In the entry on Sappho in his "Dictionary of Courtesans" we first encounter the logic that explains both

239

the terms of Deschanel's theory and its eventual importance for the "Sapho 1900" movement: Sappho belongs in the class of courtesans because her poetry reveals her to have been a homosexual. And so it will remain for the next century: virgin and lesbian are paired opposites, and the lesbian is a courtesan-prostitute.

In an argument that moves forward in bursts of lyrical élan, Deschanel heads toward the conclusion that Sappho was a courtesan because she could not have been anything else. Sappho's life is pronounced "inseparable from that of the Lesbiennes," and Lesbos is defined as a "seminary of courtesans" (330–31). This justifies a long digression on the training of Greek courtesans, in which the socialist Hellenist lingers voluptuously over details such as the "beauty contests" during which their perfect bodies were "adored" (333). This initial outburst is what passes for proof of the article's central conclusion: "In ancient society [courtesans] alone could play the role of what we call today society women [*femmes du monde*]; . . . they alone could be musicians, literary women, philosophers" (336). Only a courtesan, in other words, could have had the freedom and the advantages necessary to become a great writer. Rather than situate Sappho in this context, however, Deschanel goes off on another tangent on the "principal" courtesans. In all, he devotes nearly a third of this work—one of the most frequently cited contributions to French nineteenth-century Sappho scholarship—to courtesans with no relation to Sappho, none of whom were poets.

When Deschanel finally takes up his announced subject, he immediately twists the two-Sappho theory to suit his obsession: there were two Sapphos, *both* courtesans, Sappho of Eresos only a lowly lyre player, and the poet a member of the highest rank. With them now classified as neatly as the prostitutes of his day, Deschanel proceeds to enrich his characterization with another nineteenth-century cliché of prostitutional behavior: homosexuality flourished in assemblies of prostitutes. Sappho was trained in a "school of Lesbiennes"; she in turn formed another such school: she was therefore "Lesbian in every sense of the word. . . . In vain is it objected that this opinion was only expressed by writers who lived long after her; this only proves that, in her day, this corruption was too widespread to be noticed" (343).

There is no great merit in Deschanel's argument—indeed, Théodore Reinach easily offers a refutation on the grounds that his precursor had "ingeniously confused periods, places, civilizations" ("Pour mieux connaître," 54). Nevertheless, "Sappho et les Lesbiennes" revitalized

Sapphic interpretation by returning, with a vengeance, sensuality to the poetic body chastened and purified by decades of scholarly decrees. Thus Deschanel lambastes the cornerstone of the theory of *pederastia:* "ideal love or sensual love? In her day such distinctions weren't made" (353). He accepts the principle of Sapphic doubling only on the condition that *both* Sapphos be allotted a full measure of sexuality. Finally, Deschanel's lyric tribute to the civilizing influence of courtesans contains a translation of Sappho so broad-minded that it paved the way for editions of the future. He works into his commentary new versions of thirty-seven fragments in a presentation designed to give a sense of diversity rather than a denial of sexuality. Deschanel does not try, with the exception of fr. 31, to use the poems to prove his theory: he simply concentrates on establishing the range and the overall quality of the corpus.

His sensualization of Sappho, at the height of the age of chastity, was the bold move needed to keep the French tradition alive. And his boldness should not be underestimated. Only one previous nineteenth-century French edition gives even a hint of Sapphic eroticism, Anne-Louis Girodet's 1827 volume, which seems to confirm Welcker's fear that if Sappho is allowed sensuality, she will be pronounced homosexual. This is a packaged edition in which poem, image, and biographical commentary allegedly work together to tell the story of Sappho. Girodet contributes a series of spectacular engravings (perhaps the most impressive of all visual images of Sappho), each of which illustrates (and therefore foregrounds) a fragment. The edition was published posthumously with the addition of biographical commentary by Girodet's executor Coupin that is supposed simply to weave together the artist's translations into a narrative. However, either the two disagreed on the interpretation of Sapphism (as later happens in the 1937 Reinach-Puech volume), or censorship was tightening as the 1820s progressed, for Coupin's commentary is really a denial of the design still evident in the engravings.

Girodet begins with a marginal fragment, but one that immediately positions his edition in the thick of Sapphic ambiguity. "Sapho scorns the occupations of her sex" (plate 1, fig. 8): she has dropped the symbols of weaving, the most traditional woman's work, but "occupations" is plural and the only other possible pursuit of the female sex visible in the image is the naked youth in the background. Girodet's plate 2— "Sapho rejects the husband her parents have chosen for her"—implies that their intended is the man in the first scene. When the spectator-reader reaches plate 3,

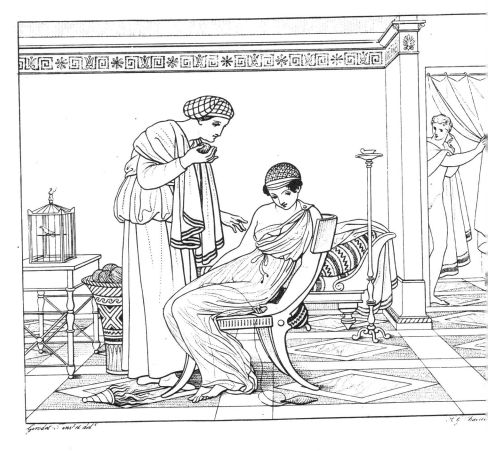

"Sapho dédaigne les occupations de son sexe"

Fig. 8. Anne-Louis Girodet, plate 1, "Sapho dédaigne les occupations de son sexe," illustration, Girodet and Coupin, *Recueil de Compositions dessinées par Girodet . . . avec la traduction en vers par Girodet de quelques-uns des poésies de Sappho* (1827). Reprinted by permission of the Spencer Collection, The New York Public Library/Astor, Lenox and Tilden Foundations.

"Sapho's dream" (fig. 9), Girodet's vision appears clear: the image seems so explicitly homoerotic that it is hard to imagine its publication in 1827. Coupin's commentary, however, makes the reader feel blind: he explains that Sappho simply didn't like her parents' candidate; plate 3 shows her in the arms of Venus dreaming of the man of her choice, her husband-to-be (5).[45]

Yet Coupin's reading, unlike Girodet's image, does not respond to still another instance of the erotic ambiguity of the Sapphic corpus. The fragment that inspires this scenario reads, in Girodet's translation,

> I yield, my tender mother!
> The needle escapes my fingers:
> Under the power of Venus and her laws,
> *Love* preoccupies me entirely.
>
> (4, my emphasis)

He leaves the door open to either a homo- or a heterosexual reading by eliminating the phrase in the original that modifies "love", a phrase rendered literally by Lobel and Page as "love for a child" (LP 102). Girodet's calculated hesitation prefigures the dilemma that the declaration inscribed here, of a woman's desire for a youth, still poses for Hellenists one hundred and fifty years later. The Greek *pais* can be male or female and translated either as "maiden" or "slender youth" according, of course, to the sexual orientation the translator prescribes for Sappho.[46]

The only contemporary reaction to the Girodet-Coupin volume I have found is as blind to any note of homoeroticism as is Coupin.[47] This confirms my suggestion that the chastity theorists' active repression of sapphism was premature: the audience of the 1820s may not have been ready to detect female homosexuality. Witness as well the response twenty years later to Deschanel: chastity critics protested with outrage Sappho's definition as a courtesan, but no one mentioned her definition as a homosexual. Yet in France the level of public awareness was rapidly being raised, as sapphic fictions multiplied in the decade that followed Deschanel's contribution. Within this same decade — during which, for example, Baudelaire announced his forthcoming volume under its initial title, *Les Lesbiennes* — the first truly outstanding Sappho edition since Wolff's 1733 volume appears, supporting Deschanel's view.

Bergk's 1854 *Anthologia lyrica* bridges the gap between Wolff and the still definitive Lobel and Page.[48] His edition of 109 fragments consolidates all the textual knowledge possible before the papyri discoveries.

Songe de Sapho

FIG. 9. Anne-Louis Girodet, plate 3, "Songe de Sapho" (1827). Reprinted by permission of the Spencer Collection, The New York Public Library/Astor, Lenox and Tilden Foundations.

Surprisingly, none of those who pay homage to Bergk's authority comment on the most startling innovation of his Sappho edition. He inaugurates modern practice by placing the "Ode to Aphrodite" at the head of his edition: Bergk then coolly reverses all previous readings of the poem by removing the final letter of line twenty-four and making the object of Sappho's desire female. Bergk neither calls attention to his reading nor makes any of the usual attempts to justify it through metrics: he simply offers previous normalizing readings as variants. In the absence of evidence, I am inclined to think that Bergk decided simply to follow the same intuition that Boissonade ultimately rejected for his edition and to provide the text that decrees the femininity of the object of desire.[49] Scholars eulogized his edition, but almost no one maintained his reading. When Bergk is reedited at the end of the century, Hiller and Crusius simply erase the version originally proposed. They bracket the last two letters of line twenty-four, offering thereby as their primary text the variant generally favored in seventeenth and eighteenth-century editions. This punctuation makes it seem as if the only variant would add both of the last two letters, thereby normalizing once again the ode's sexual orientation. Bergk's "deviant" reading is thus swallowed up between the two acceptable versions. Furthermore, Hiller and Crusius do not even note this fundamental reorientation; in the annotations that preface the reedition they simply refer the reader to Wilamowitz's 1896 contribution.[50] Chastity had won another round. And so it will go, back and forth—Wharton homosexual, Lebey heterosexual, Lobel and Page a draw. Sappho's textual fate in post-Bergk editions is the most recent, but surely not the last, act in the drama of her sexual definition.

In France, Sappho really becomes a homosexual poet only after the vocabulary of "homosexuality" had been developed, when female same-sex love had been renamed. However, this statement should not be taken as confirmation of the theory that the homosexual in the modern sense only recently came into existence: the relation between word and sexuality is more elusive than my first sentence reveals. Dictionaries note "saphisme" 's existence in the sense of "female homosexuality" as early as 1838 (when only Boissonade and Girodet had hinted at Sappho's homosexuality), that of "lesbienne" in the sense of "female homosexual" as of 1867 (post-Deschanel), and the entrance of "homosexuel" only in 1906. This evolution is reversed in English, in which a vocabulary for female same-sex love develops later than in French: "sapphism" and "lesbian" seem to have been associated with same-sex love only shortly after "homosexual" 's implantation.[51] For the scholarly sexualization of Sappho, English usage is more important than French: two years after Symonds introduced "homosexual" in his commentary on ideal love, he provided the first translation of Bergk's homosexual Sappho into a modern language, a translation that, as we will see, inspired the same revision in French.

André Lebey, the editor credited with first having made Bergk's advances available to the French public (see Mora, 175), in fact refuses to follow the German's lead for the interpretation of Sapphism—thereby suggesting that without the influence of the English Sappho, French editors would have continued to withhold the homosexual text. Lebey's 1895 volume is easily the best French edition of the century: he includes all the fragments in Bergk, and he respects their fragmentary status, resisting the impulse, to which almost all his precursors had succumbed, of sewing them together into ersatz complete units. Yet this socialist sympathizer[52] apparently did not share his precursor Deschanel's position on Sapphism. Nor is Pierre Louÿs's influence (the edition is dedicated to "my friend Pierre Louÿs" [18]) evident in anything but the heavy dose of local color.[53]

Lebey's preface opens with an attack on Müller for having tried "to absolve her conduct by establishing the falsity of that of which everyone was aware" (10). But Lebey will set the record straight: "I cannot fail my duty to certify that [the philologists] are wrong: Sappho was very beautiful" (10). After having thus toyed with his reader by withholding the declaration of sexual preference he had seemed ready to announce, Lebey launches into local color, like the mist on Lesbos, before finally offering this portrait of Sappho: "If her morals were infamous, her inaccessible ideal must be blamed. As soon as Phaon appeared, she abandoned them" (15). To avoid controversy, Lebey is prepared to resurrect both Phaon and the leap from Leukas (11). He is even prepared to reject the authority of Bergk, whose edition he allegedly follows: he leads off with a normalized "Ode to Aphrodite," never mentioning Bergk's female variant. At the close of the nineteenth century, French editions had still not deviated from the philological line.

At least one contemporary Hellenist was not so reluctant to continue Deschanel's reasoning. Alfred Croiset's 1898 reading of Sappho remains, to my mind, unrivaled in any scholarly tradition for its critical modernity. Croiset explains why he believes both the love for Phaon and the suicide to be legends grafted onto Sappho's story (230, 232). He opposes any theory that would make Sappho either virgin or whore: Sappho was neither "a vestal concerned with maintaining poetry's sacred fire," nor "a fallen woman" (233). He concludes his commentary on Sappho with a prose translation of the "Ode to Aphrodite" that, for the first time in French, feminizes the object of desire. In the note Croiset appends to line 24, he offers the most direct explanation of his position possible. According to the reading found in the manuscripts, "the poem is addressed to a man." Bergk offers a revision and "it follows from it that it deals with a woman. Bergk's correction seems evident to me, no matter what one may think of the heart of the matter" (234, n. 3).

Now whereas Croiset's defense of Bergk's "correction" cannot be unrelated to his view of "the heart of the matter," he nonetheless does not offer a simple replacement of heterosexuality with homosexuality. Croiset's most striking innovation, the essence of what I would term his critical modernity, is his insistence that readers maintain a distinction between Sappho and her poetic voice. Such an opinion may seem to today's reader so evident as hardly to bother repetition. However, in the history of Sappho scholarship prior to Croiset no one, to my knowledge, had bothered to make this point at all clearly; even today, it is hardly ever reiterated, and even less often heeded.

> It is perfectly idle to discuss the quality of her love [for her young friends] and to determine with precision limits that her very language seems so often to undertake to blur; friendship more or less aesthetic and sensual, love more or less platonic, these are nuances very difficult to disentangle; without considering that in such matters one must avoid making conclusions about acts on the basis of words. (235)
>
> Sappho . . . surely often expressed in her songs sentiments that were not personal, and one cannot see a declaration of her love in all the lines in which she happened to make a woman in love speak. (232–33)

I let Croiset speak for himself at such length because I find both his appreciation of Sappho's ambiguity and his refusal to use her poetry to define her (sexual) nature refreshing in the midst of repeated efforts to proclaim the truth about Sapphism. He implicitly offers the only argument in favor of Bergk's "correction" that he (or Boissonade, or Bergk, or anyone who shares their "intuition") will in all likelihood ever be able to offer: he prefers to think that the object of desire in the "Ode to Aphrodite" is female because this seems to him more compatible with the portrayal of eroticism in Sappho's poetry, without drawing any conclusions about the sexual orientation of the author of that verse. Such a modified view of the sapphic significance of Sappho's corpus might have seemed less threatening and therefore might have been able to gain authority—many scholars in the early decades of the twentieth century do indeed proclaim their loyalty to Croiset's views, although they do so without modifying their own reading to follow his model—had not Sapphic interpretation immediately and suddenly been thrust just as violently in the direction of (homo)sexuality as Welcker had pushed it in that of chastity. This next revision took place under the aegis of the English realignment of ideal love commentary.

Henry Thornton Wharton's 1885 edition is one of the most influential of the past century; he is Lebey's counterpart in the English tradition and is indeed the first to render Bergk accurately in a modern foreign language. Nevertheless, his edition replicates the deep-seated ambivalence with regard to Sapphism already noted in Lebey's, to such an extent that one has to wonder just what image was conveyed to the numerous fin-de-siècle literary figures whose Sapphic vision was based on these two translations. Wharton's ambivalence is a mirror image of Lebey's. Lebey's preface opens with a rejection of chastity theorists, Wharton's with an expression of admiration for "Welcker's defense," a defense which still stands despite "the onslaughts of Colonel Mure" (viii). However, it is no easier to decipher his homage to Welcker than Lebey's dismissal, for Wharton never defines that theory for the uninitiated. His refusal to pronounce the word chastity creates as much confusion about the view of Sapphism he is promoting as Lebey's sudden praise of her beauty does—especially in view of the text that follows, which opens with the first translation into any modern language of the "Ode to Aphrodite" with a female object of desire. The homosexual translation Wharton publishes is a famous one by John Addington Symonds done especially for this edition and dated 1883, the year Symonds also proclaims as that of the first edition of *A Problem in Greek Ethics* with the inaugural appearance of "homosexual" (see my n. 16). Thus, whereas Lebey follows an implicit homosexual placement with a heterosexual translation, Wharton leads into homoerotics with an implicit affirmation of heterosexuality: these companion volumes inaugurate the twentieth-century reign of Sapphic bisexuality.[54]

The Wharton edition may be at the origin of what eventually came to be known as the "Sapho 1900" movement: on a trip to London at the turn of the century Natalie Clifford Barney came across the volume (see

Souvenirs, 50). The very nature of that edition, its open expression of female homosexual passion tempered by a biographical sketch compatible with a chastity defense, can help explain the passion with which her longtime companion and fellow Sapphic poet, Renée Vivien, sought to rewrite the presentation of Sappho's life and to eliminate all the contradictions with which Bergk's followers had burdened it.

Vivien learned Greek in order to become only the second woman to translate the greatest woman poet. Surely the irony of the distance that separates her from Anne Le Fèvre Dacier cannot have escaped Vivien: while Le Fèvre Dacier is always cited as the origin of the chastening heterosexualization of Sappho, Vivien gives the public a Sappho, in Mora's words, "far more lesbian than she was in what was then known of her verse" (200). Her "more lesbian" Sappho is a product of both a written biography and an amplified corpus. The biography that opens Vivien's 1903 edition is above all an overturning of previous scenarios, which reads as a hostile dialogue with previous commentators when Vivien's text is compared with the views standard in her day.[55] I will give a few examples. Others: the poet's name is written either "Sapho" or "Sappho". Vivien: "the Dorian and correct form of the name Sapho is 'Psappha' " (iii, n.).[56] Others: various theories of her sexuality, most often heterosexual. Vivien: "We can only glimpse Psappha through the lines that remain of her. And in them we do not find the faintest tender thrill [*frisson*] of her being for a man" (x). Others: Sappho respected the family and promoted marriage. Vivien: "She expresses her scorn for marriage" (xi).[57] Vivien subsequently ridicules the scenario of Sappho as mother of a daughter Kleis.[58] Vivien also rejects the existence of Phaon, the suicidal leap, Barthélemy's political theory, the portrait of Sappho as ugly—the essence of all previous biographical scenarios.

Vivien offers instead, first in this edition, then in a series of fictions of Sappho (which we will consider with the "Sapho 1900" movement), the most radical revision of the poet in the two and a half centuries since her biography and her corpus had first become the object of modern speculation. Her edition is Welcker's obsession finally realized, a version of Sappho that puts philology's advances at the service of a flagrant display of female homosexuality. Furthermore, as if to defend her edition against those who would seek to dismiss it, Vivien expands the usual critical apparatus to provide for each poem the Greek text, then a prose translation, followed by a verse translation, and finally poems inspired by Sappho's original, such as Swinburne's imitation of the "Ode to

Aphrodite." Her model for this multilayered edition is Wharton; however, Vivien eliminates virtually every trace of the profound ambiguity characteristic of his volume, the bisexuality of his edition. (Only unavoidable exceptions, like Catullus's ode, break the unity of her vision.)

Vivien makes one important departure from her stance of scholarly respectability, a departure which is largely responsible for her edition's notoriety. For her verse translations, she expands, often greatly, the Greek text, making the briefest of fragments into full-fledged poems. Thus, the fragment she renders in prose as "Atthis, my image is hateful to you and you flee towards Andromeda" is transformed into this quatrain:

> You hate the thought of me, Atthis, and my image.
> That other kiss, which persuaded you,
> Burns you, and you flee, breathless and wild,
> Toward Andromeda. (21)

Her amplifications tend to become ever more ample as her vision of the corpus unfolds, until the broken line "Why, daughter of Pandion, lovable swallow, me . . ." explodes into a verse "translation" twenty lines long, devoted to the poet's abandonment by Atthis, a description of Atthis's lips, and so on (50–51).

Unlike her precursors, Vivien makes no attempt to camouflage her infidelities: a comparison with the prose translation makes plain where Sappho stops and she takes over. Susan Gubar has described the edition as a "fantastic collaboration" with the precursor poet (47), but this description does not give a sense of the unsettling quality of these "translations." Because her expansions so greatly overburden the often fragile remains, Vivien seems to assume Sappho's voice, to try to replace the original. And because her additions are often graphic and explicit, reminiscent in fact of the decadent antisapphic fictions we will examine at the end of this chapter, Vivien's doubly Sapphic poetry ultimately seems designed only for an initiated public. Even a sympathetic reader can hardly avoid being brought up short by the inevitable realization of Vivien's morbid identification with Sappho, her desire to intercept, as it were, the "burning" kisses from Atthis's lips. At the very least, this text—Psappha fulfilled by the new Sappho, Vivien—is so violently different from other editions available to fin-de-siècle readers (in which, until very recently, Atthis had been presented as a man) that it must have been easy to dismiss it as an invention. The scholarly tradition, for example, remains prudently mute on the subject of Vivien—remember that it is Pierre Louÿs who provokes Wilamowitz's abundant wrath, not Vivien—as if for fear of spreading her message. And, with one exception, the next generation of French translations bears no trace of her influence. At the dawn of the twentieth century, Sappho's interpreters were not yet ready for a flamboyantly lesbian Sappho.

By 1911, the foremost Hellenist of the day, Théodore Reinach, sounds again the call of chastity in the purest notes. In a discourse to the Académie des Inscriptions et Belles Lettres, Reinach demands resoundingly that "Sappho's trial" be reopened on the basis of the "new evidence" of the papyri fragments. For this self-proclaimed disciple of Le Fèvre Dacier, Welcker, and Müller ("Pour mieux connaître Sappho," 59–60), the enemy is named Deschanel and Croiset, not Vivien, and the recently discovered fragments are the definitive proof that "in order to find a stain on this poetry, one must begin by putting it there" (68). Of the "Atthis cycle," source of Vivien's most ecstatic expansions and enlarged with papyri discoveries, he concludes: "Flowers and more flowers, perfumes and more perfumes, finally sweet tears. . . . In this outpouring of delights, not a single drop of sensuality can be found" (68, 70). Sappho trained her pupils to become "real women, understanding, as she did, life's duties" (70).

Mora considers Bascoul's 1911 chastity fiction the end of "Sappho's legendary period," from which scholarship escapes "finally to embark upon the era of her authenticity," that is, the period in which scholars at last started searching out "the truth of Sappho" only in her verse (203), but I cannot share her optimism. If indeed—and this is far from certain—legend has by now been replaced by truth, the substitution was not complete in 1911. Reinach's authoritative pronouncement simply succeeds in provoking a wave of editions as consciously bisexual as Lebey's and Wharton's ambivalent volumes. Also in 1911, Mario Meunier published the original edition of a translation that he would revise and republish in 1932, when it becomes the first French translation to include the new fragments. In the 1932 volume, he adopts Vivien's ordering, the two odes followed by the now expanded Atthis cycle, the structure that best supports a homosexual reading. Although he only alludes to the fact in passing in a note, for several of his translations in the first section Meunier even provides reconstructions à la Vivien, thereby awarding privileged status to the most sapphic Sapphic verse. However, the preface to Meunier's 1932 text still reprints long sections of Reinach's 1911 purity oration; Meunier even pronounces himself a partisan of "the chaste

Sappho" (whom he compares at length to "the Virgin of Avila" [47])—even though such a pronouncement is ill-served by his own, implicitly lesbian, presentation of her poetry (39, 49) and can only be understood as a eulogy, à la Symonds, of lesbian virginity as the "*modus vivendi* of the modern world."[59]

And so it goes even in the last pre–World War II editions. Jym's 1937 *Sappho réhabilitée* is bisexual in the manner of Wharton and Meunier. The preface announces an edition that will make the reader understand how "high-minded" Sappho's emotions were and therefore "how odious were the reproaches made against her by men with dirty souls" (9). What follows is, however, hardly a chastity text: it opens with a feminized "Ode to Aphrodite" following Bergk's original "correction" and it goes on to provide a complete and faithful version of the corpus. Jym's volume is published in Angers, just down the Loire from Saumur where Tanneguy Le Fèvre played his pivotal role between humanist scholarship and modern fictionalization. Nearly three centuries later, the standards he advocated had at last become the norm for the edition of Sappho's corpus, if not for the presentation of her biography.

This conclusion is reinforced by the other edition published in 1937, what remains today the definitive French text, Reinach and Puech's *Alcée Sapho*. Reinach had been charged with the Belles Lettres edition; after his death Aimé Puech supervised the publication of Reinach's text and used the master's notes as the basis for a preface. Their edition, organized in an attempted reconstruction of the nine books believed used in Sappho's day, remains the most complete in French. It would simply repeat the bisexual structure already present in Meunier's, if Puech had shared Meunier's unquestioning acceptance of Reinach's authority to decree the truth about Sapphism. The text is a surprise for any reader familiar with Reinach's views: it gives, most notably, Bergk's "corrected" "Ode to Aphrodite" and a feminized French translation, simply listing previous variants in a note, and is, therefore, more unhesitatingly homosexual than the definitive English edition.[60] The preface only adds to the confusion. The body of the preface obviously reproduces the master's notes faithfully, for the argument is vintage Reinach: "It is difficult for us to imagine . . . the exact nature of the relations [Sappho] maintained with the young girls whose charming names adorn her verse. There is no doubt that we must reject with scorn the obscene interpretations that come from Attic comedy" (169). His student Puech obviously doesn't agree, so he explains in a note: "See in particular the reading of Théodore Reinach [his 1911 chastity speech], Wilamowitz's *Sappho und Simonides,* and correct the excessive optimism undoubtedly found in both with the composed [*froid*] and delicately measured judgment of Croiset" (169, n.).

The standard French edition transmits, therefore, a confusing double message for which several explanations seem possible. Puech might simply have taken the liberty of altering Reinach's text for the "Ode to Aphrodite" to provide an edition more in line with Croiset's "delicately measured" views—although such editorial subterfuge seems totally out of character. Reinach could have been following the example of Edmonds who had for his recent edition reproduced Bergk's "corrected" text without modifying in the slightest the chastity arguments he himself had previously expounded with fervor, even though text and preface were thus in contradiction. One final, even more hypothetical, possibility remains: at a time of worsening relations with Germany, Reinach—member of a prominent Jewish family whose scholarly career was equally divided between Hellenism and the history of Judaism[61]—could, without backing down on his own chastity stance, have published Bergk's text, the reading rejected by Welcker's heirs, as a gesture of his own independence from the increasingly threatening militaristic nationalism at whose service the philologists had placed their erudition. Shortly after World War I, another member of the Reinach family, Joseph, at a conference presided over by Alfred Croiset, had argued that "Hellenism must be erected as an indestructible barrier against the ambitions of Germany, which, even though vanquished today, has not given up" (54).

Even as the French public still awaited the Reinach-Puech edition, a volume appeared in which Sappho is assigned a role in a nationalistic enterprise more important than protecting matrimony. Jean Larnac and Robert Salmon's 1934 biography concludes the political trajectory Barthélemy first decreed for Sappho with implications that even Germaine de Staël could not have foreseen. The authors proclaim at first a middle-of-the-road stance, taking issue with both Sappho's "defenders" and Deschanel (6–7). The strangeness of their own theory becomes apparent only when they spell out its foundation, an assumption for which they offer no proof: Sappho was religious because all the Greeks of her day were. Because her poetry makes it evident that "Sappho had the morals that one knows [Sappho eut les moeurs que l'on sait]," they decree that the only way to reconcile "Sappho's piety" (always a given for them) and her morals is to define her as a priestess of Aphrodite. As proof of their conclusion, they point out the headband she wears in all known portraits—a "mystical insignia," sign for the Greeks that the wearer was "possessed by a god"—as well as Sappho's poetry which shows that she was "possessed" by Aphrodite (7–8).

Unwitting disciples of Bachofen and Symonds, Larnac and Salmon dwell on "Sappho's quasi-superstitious piety, the piety of an adherent of the archaic matriarchal religion," of a "saint of Pythagoreanism" (66, n. 1; 69). Like Symonds, they make Sapphism an integral component of the poet's sainthood: "As priestess, she followed the orders of her divinity. . . . In abandoning herself to love with her companions, Sappho in no way sullied her reputation; on the contrary she extended it" (8). Larnac and Salmon use this piety theory to offer a new totalizing fiction of Sappho. Fragment 31 becomes a "religious hymn" because, unlike a "Christian poetess who must sing of purity to please the Virgin, to please Aphrodite, a priestess . . . must not only sing of love but practice it" (34). Their reading of the "Ode to Aphrodite" is more startling still: Sappho begs the goddess for help in the "torments" of her indecision over whether to follow Alceus in his revolt against Pittakos (42–43).[62] The link between piety and politics thus established, they take to new heights Staël's transfiguration of Barthélemy's exile into an *émigrée*.

Larnac and Salmon turn Lesbos into a foreshadowing of pre-Revolutionary France: for centuries, the Lesbian aristocracy had resisted the assimilation of new peoples, provoking many "class struggles." After a "troubled period" of popular revolt, the aristocrats are driven from the island (12). In this biography, Sappho becomes a conservative proto-restorationist faithful to the ideals of the monarchy and the rights of the aristocracy: she belongs to one of the noblest families, one of the few that had "shared for centuries the privilege of providing priestesses of Aphrodite" (18). Armed with her "pride," she holds out against change, "firmly attached to her privileges" (37). The revolution over, Sappho returns home, still the *émigrée,* to find her family estate and her old world in ruins. Ever faithful to the old values, she returns to the service of her deity as a "choral instructor," the head of a school where young girls remain until their marriage.

The reader should not be fooled by the resemblances into taking this for simply an aristocratic version of Wilamowitz. Larnac and Salmon's bibliography privileges to an outrageous extent English and American works at the expense of German scholarship. When they want to resurrect such conservative theories as Sappho's marriage, motherhood, and early widowhood which Croiset and Vivien had rejected, they do not refer to the obvious sources like Welcker and Wilamowitz. Instead they cite as authorities such obscure, and generally flagrantly fictionalized, volumes as Arthur Weigall's chatty 1934 biography (the origin of much of their political expansion), and even Lucy McDowell Milburn's 1902 epistolary novel about Sappho's love for a Pharaoh's son who uses the pseudonym Phaon, *Lost Letters from Lesbos* (the source of their ideas on her widowhood).[63] Larnac and Salmon's desperate desire to replace German erudition is only comprehensible in light of their own political enterprise. They explain that the new fragments could not at first be properly evaluated because they were commented on "at the beginning of the war," and "it was then necessary to support martial valor" (77, n. 2). The implication of their revision is that in the aftermath of the Great War, it is time to support the old, aristocratic values.

At the eve of World War II, then, scholarly battle lines were drawn as clearly as military. To the politics of *pederastia* proposed by the philologists, French commentators opposed a doctrine that realizes Welcker's worst fears, the union of religion and conservative, aristocratic nationalism with female homosexuality. More explicitly than Symonds, Larnac and Salmon suggest that "the *modus vivendi* of the modern world" is founded on a recognition of the mystical power of the woman they characterize as the lesbian "hypostasis of Aphrodite," the poet thought to be, like Christ, simultaneously human and divine and, like Mary, "at the same time virgin and mother" (71–73). Purged of its Napoleonic elements only as World War II was drawing near, the French tradition finally makes a place for Sappho at the origin of the city state.

Thus the message of Barthélemy and Verri, first disseminated throughout Europe just as the boundaries of modern nationalism were being established, followed a complicated trajectory for the next century. At three moments of its unfolding, female homosexuality seemed close to acquiring a *droit de cité,* an openly admitted existence: 1819–27 (Boissonade-Girodet), 1847–54 (Deschanel-Bergk), and 1895–1903 (Lebey-Vivien). On the eve of the conflict that would force a definitive reexamination of modern nationalism, however, the last stage of Sappho scholarship culminates in a singular final manifestation of the dualism that Welcker's decree had made inevitable. On the one hand, there is the hetero(a)sexual Sappho, handmaiden of the state founded on militaristic *pederastia,* and on the other, her mystically homosexual counterpart, the potential savior of those faithful to the old ways of the aristocracy.

The Pure and the Impure

A bad woman as well as a pure woman might love roses, but a bad woman does not love the small and hidden wild flowers of the field. . . . The nature of things does not admit of such an inconsistency.

—David Robinson,
Sappho and her Influence

With the birth of a scholarly tradition intent on establishing its scientific seriousness, fictions of Sappho finally can be assigned to an independent sphere. From the early nineteenth century on, scholarship is no longer practiced in fiction, according to the model of Scudéry and Barthélemy. In addition, fictions like Barthélemy's are never again generally taken for scholarly fact. This repartition of territory seems to have liberated fiction, setting it onto a more adventurous course: for example, Sappho becomes a homosexual in fiction long before scholarship admits this possibility. Indeed, the most conservative, least interesting fictions are those that can be most directly related to the dominant scholarly tradition. Whereas in the decades before the Revolution Sappho becomes a heroine typical of contemporary French fiction, in the nineteenth century Sapphic heterosexuality never again knows a continuous development. The best creative energy is henceforth channeled into the slow creation of a homosexual Sappho. Almost without exception, whenever the post-Revolutionary Sappho is heterosexual, the fictions divide up according to the dichotomous vision of female sexuality that Freud describes, and Sappho is portrayed as either virgin or whore.

I evoke Freud in this context rather than the appropriate Sappho theorists (Welcker and Deschanel) because this heterosexual vision seems to have remained virtually untouched by erudite theories. (Ironically, the influence of both Welcker and Deschanel is present instead in sapphic fictions.) Nineteenth-century heterosexual fictions are at first fed by the late eighteenth-century theatrical tradition and are subsequently nourished by their century's fascination with fictions of feminine virginity and prostitution. In fact, the counterpart in literature of the philologists' chastity theory develops so early and so steadily that it is clear evidence of the nineteenth-century's obsession with female virginity and indicates the

256

extent to which the philologists were influenced if not by French Sapphic fictions, at least by a shared zeitgeist.[64]

The story of Sappho's "virgin purity" dominates all theatrical and poetic fictions for over fifty years, despite the fact that these fictions immediately reveal chastity's narrative limitations. For this reason alone, playwrights can never follow the rigid scenario championed by scholars. The tradition's originator, Vénard de La Jonchère, realizes that he can hold onto Phaon only if he introduces a closing "apotheosis" which he describes as "the spectator's recompense for [Sappho's] indiscretions" (290). Consequently, after his heroine has been rescued in mid-leap by Apollo, the last three scenes of his 1772 *Sapho* take place on Parnassus. Sapho arrives there on a cloud, assumed into heaven like the Virgin Mary. With Apollo pleading her case, she is granted immortality as though she were being pardoned for her sins. This scenario of suicide as expiation followed by divine pardon is still adopted by Hippolyte Cournol in 1819: Sapho "ascends on a cloud" and this time Venus pleads the case for her immortality (46).

By far the most elaborate chastity fiction is an immense (two-volume) 1805 poem that can only be described as the epic of Saint Sappho. Its author, L. Gorsse, is the only true precursor of chastity fanatics like Bascoul. In extensive notes, he details the crimes against Sappho committed by editors intent on accusing her of homosexuality (for example, the manuscripts of both Ovid and Longinus were altered). Predictably, Gorsse stages the grandest assumption ever in which the leap becomes a "divine victory" and Sappho is granted immortality by her "eternal master," Jupiter (2:84).

Contemporaneous with these assumption dramas is a series of plays and long poems in which the price of Sappho's redemption is her transformation into a "victim of love." Just as in the works that culminate in an apotheosis, Venus is jealous of Sappho: in his 1815 poem, Joseph-Joachim-Victor Chauvet explains that, because of her "scorn" for Venus's "cult," Sapho made the maidens of Lesbos pledge their lives to Apollo and the Muses (9). Her mad love for Phaon is thus presented as Venus's revenge for this attempt to spread chastity, and in each play Sappho struggles to win back her reason: in M. Touzet's 1812 poem, for example, before resorting to suicide, Sappho offers herself to the goddess dressed as a sacrificial victim (6).[65] Only in 1824 does the appropriately named Hippolyte de La Morvonnais make clear that this redemption scenario is the last step in the joint process by which Racine displaces Ovid as the ruling Sapphic authority and Sappho comes to dominate the nineteenth century's vision of the Racinian plot.[66]

La Morvonnais prefaces his "drame lyrique" with a manifesto for a new French "drame" in which it becomes clear that this chastity tradition, too, is anchored in nationalism, although the French variant is an openly royalist (literary) nationalism. Proposing an anticipated alternative to Victor Hugo's soon-to-be articulated literary nationalism, he calls for an end to the "monstrous Anglo-German dramas" and a return to the Greek model, "the best tradition of French tragedy" (86). All the chastity and redemption poems contain numerous Racinian echoes, but none more than La Morvonnais's. For his version of Sappho's tragedy, he borrows heavily from the structure and the poetry of *Phèdre,* most notably for Sappho's avowal of her love to her confidante which begins "Je le vis," and in which La Morvonnais, in order to make his mark on French theater, pillages Racine and is thereby obliged to return Sappho's own formulation of the force of desire to her fictional double.

Thus, decades before 1843, where Henri Peyre situates the revival of Racine (25),[67] a series of playwrights turn to him as the theatrical standard for the Restoration. This gesture by which the plot of Sappho's heterosexual passion and suicide are brought under French control repeats the scenario so frequently encountered in Sappho's history in which a group of fledgling authors comes of age by appropriating simultaneously Sappho's voice and that of a male precursor. The plays are veritable echo chambers in which Racine alternates with Sappho and sometimes fuses with her in near comedy—"Songe, songe, Sapho" (Touzet, 6).[68] Once the philologists had destroyed Ovid's authority, Racine had to be resurrected to guarantee the literary son's successful rite of passage.

In a conservative political atmosphere, the early Racinian playwrights pass over Barthélemy's scenario—which Staël, clearly inspired by the beginning of this redemption tradition as well as the *Voyage d'Anacharsis,* had begun to develop—and center their chastity dramas around the suicide.[69] In fiction, Sappho is repoliticized only after the events of 1848, when she is portrayed as a revolutionary rather than an *émigrée.* Paul Juillerat's *Reine de Lesbos* (1854) is the last of the "drames" that blend Racine and Sappho. Here, Phèdre and Barthélemy's revolutionary Sapho are combined to produce a mockery of women's capacity for political action. Juillerat's creation is easily the most contemptible Sapho ever: she plots with Alcée against Pittacus without political motivation but solely to exploit Phaon's alleged dreams of power. When the tyrant abdicates in her favor, Sapho-become-Phèdre is sure she will seduce her lover with the offer of a throne. But when Phaon rejects her with all the chaste horror of his Racinian precursor, the queen for a day takes her life.

All but two of the nineteenth-century fictions that portray a heterosexual Sappho can be linked to the theatrical tradition. Of these misfits, the first is a mere curiosity, while the second is perhaps the most influential Sapphic fiction in modern times. Emile Augier's libretto for Charles Gounod's 1851 opera—certain aspects of which come into their own in the early twentieth century—is both the most resolutely political nineteenth-century fiction and the most melodramatic. Despite the fact that it is a product of the repression that followed 1848, the Augier-Gounod scenario is openly prorevolutionary opera: Phaon and Alcée are engagé Republicans, co-conspirators plotting to kill Pittacus; they cry out for the people's freedom and circulate manifestos against tyranny. With this, the authors invent a totally new plot for Sappho, making her thoroughly bourgeois, a typical heroine of nineteenth-century opera. Sappho is Phaon's true love; the woman he had abandoned for her, Glycère, learns of his conspiracy and threatens to reveal it to Pittacus unless Sappho gives up Phaon. The poet declares that she no longer loves him, and he goes into exile with Glycère, leaving Sappho to her suicide.

The Augier-Gounod scenario is an attempt to reenergize the Sapphic plot by giving it a contemporary setting in which the principal characters are raised to bourgeois respectability: for the first time in Sapphic fiction, they are truly victims and not responsible for their fate. The other maverick nineteenth-century fiction also integrates Sappho into contemporaneity, although hardly into respectability. Sappho goes *bohème* for Alphonse Daudet's 1884 novel, the work that seems to come most frequently to mind when modern readers think of Sapphic fictions. This seemingly inevitable association can only be understood as a reenactment of the eighteenth-century phenomenon whereby a fiction captures the popular imagination because it remodels Sappho into a heroine familiar from contemporary literature. In this case, she becomes a type immediately recognizable from Balzac, Sue, and virtually every other popular novelist of the first half of the century. She is the exemplary male fantasy of woman in Daudet's day, a prostitute—not Deschanel's homosexual, intellectual courtesan, but an uneducated, lower-class kept woman, the streetwalker whose alleged heart of gold makes her all the more dangerous to the young men who become entangled with her.

Those potential victims are ever in Daudet's thoughts. His dedication, "to my sons when they turn twenty," is the sign of his recognition of his volume's function: to reproduce a stereotype of female behavior to enable a male rite of passage into the social order. This *Sapho* serves as an extended warning to all the sons of the bourgeoisie that such women threaten to destroy their careers and their family ties. Daudet's hero Gaussin is a model provincial youth, come to Paris to prepare a diplomatic career, until he meets an older kept woman, Fanny Legrand, who initially reveals only her heart of gold: for Gaussin, she gives up her life of dissolute luxury to become a model homemaker. Only gradually does the young man learn of her Sapphic past from her former lovers: the poet La Gournerie, author of "cries of despair to Sapho" for whom he "gave all the blood in [his] veins" (14–15), and especially the sculptor Cadoudal who used Fanny as the model for his statue of Sapho, so widely circulated in cheap reproduction that even Gaussin himself as a little boy was familiar with the intimate details of his future mistress's body from having observed the statue on the mantlepiece of his father's study (36, 66). But Gaussin suffers most acutely from the revelation of his mistress's sapphic past, from the realization that Cadoudal's description of her as "Sapho toute la lyre" referred not to her poetic soul but to her having experienced "the full sexual gamut" (92). The young man then feels that she has been "completely revealed as a skillful courtesan, in all the horrible glory of Sapho" (103).

But then Fanny's heart of gold is fully revealed—she even goes to work to pay off his uncle's gambling debts—and she becomes a "virtuous Sapho," "a saint" (158, 155). For this virgin and whore combined, Gaussin breaks off with his family, refuses the marriage arranged for him, and abandons his chance for a brilliant career. At the novel's end, Gaussin is sitting in Marseille in the "hôtel du jeune Anacharsis" waiting for his Sapho to join him, before sailing off—not, however, like Barthélemy's hero, into a voyage of initiation, but into the dead end of a third-rate diplomatic post. He receives a letter from Sapho (modeled on the text then viewed as her Greek precursor's rejection of Alceus) announcing that she's abandoning him: because she will age faster than he, she is sure he will soon tire of her.

Daudet's novel achieved immediate success—it was reprinted five times in the first two years alone. This most successful of all nineteenth-century

Sapphic fictions before *Bilitis* owes both its success and its importance in the Sapphic tradition to Daudet's definition of Sapphism as a variant of prostitutional circulation. By naming his common streetwalker "Sapho," Daudet reduces the poet's name to what his hero calls "the nicknames of public women in the grotesque Almanach-Gotha of gallantry" (72), completing the process initiated by the writers who made Sappho promiscuous. However, Daudet's book is not, as his dedication might make one think, still another fantasy of revenge against the menace of female sexuality—the behavior the sculptor urges on Gaussin: "Take revenge for [all men] on those wenches" (296). Rather it is a commentary on Sappho's fate in what Walter Benjamin, speaking of another of Sappho's nineteenth-century poet-lovers, Baudelaire, called "the era of high capitalism."

Sappho is enshrined in Daudet's novel in the form of a "commercial bronze," a cheap reproduction destined for wide circulation. In this guise, she passes from hand to hand, simultaneously the inspiration for slightly pornographic thrills for fathers and sons, and a banal artistic accessory defining the bourgeois interior: "Attractive, the bronze of Sapho . . . a commercial bronze that is found everywhere, as banal as a street-organ tune, like that name 'Sapho' which, by rolling through the centuries, has encrusted its original grace with vile legends, and from the name of a goddess has become the label of an illness" (77). Daudet's icon of Sappho's commercialization is modeled on the saga of the most celebrated Sapphic sculpture of his day, Pradier's 1852 statue in which the melancholy poet is seated with her lyre put to the side. The sculpture, widely hailed as worthy of Pradier's classical models, was quickly vulgarized into commercial bronzes and became the image of Sappho for its age, the role Daudet's heroine would fulfill in literature. (Pradier's *Sapho* now proudly stands over the entrance to the Orsay museum, once again enshrined as the dominant Sapphic image, and a crucial fiction of the female, of its age [fig. 10].) A contemporary reviewer claimed that the essence of Pradier's genius was his complementary ability "to carry the antique type over into modern times and expose the modernity of ancient times."[70] For his female figures, Pradier looked for the antiquity of modern life among the *grisettes* of the quartier Bréda (see Mora, 185). Indeed his *Sapho* appears to be the product of just the recipe Daudet follows: woman of the streets blended with artist's mistress creates the modernity of Sappho. (Flaubert's mistress, Louise Colet, is rumored to have posed for Pradier's *Sapho* [see Stein, 230].) Daudet, the Ovid of the

Fig. 10. James Pradier, *Sapho* (1852). Included in a view of the interior of the Musée d'Orsay in Paris. Reprinted by permission of Giraudon/Art Resource, New York.

age of department stores, figures the commodification of Sappho, the process by which writers like himself profit from the commercial attraction of the "vile legends" encrusting her name. This commercial bronze among Sapphic fictions presents Sappho as a true creature of the sexual marketplace, exactly the kind of vision Deschanel's detractors believed him guilty of promoting.[71]

Indeed, 1884 marks Sappho's second complete descent into popular fiction, as well as the first time she enters pulp fiction as a homosexual. The lead volume of the new series "les grandes amoureuses" was devoted to Sapphô (this may be the first appearance of that popular fin-de-siècle spelling, a spelling almost always used for homosexual Sapphos).[72] The series' title and the volume's overblown frontispiece (fig. 11) prime the reader for a fiction reminiscent of Daudet's, so the portrayal of the heroine comes as a shock. The volume, by Jean Richepin, opens on the feast day of Aphroditâ (a scene and a spelling popular in decadent fictions). When Sapphô's beautiful young girls enter the temple, they are identified as "her students and her lovers" (16). She is every inch "la mâle Sappho," with a body whose masculinity is detailed at great length. Thereafter, the volume quickly charts a standard Ovidian course, although the suicide for a man is qualified as "absolutely unexpected" (29).

Richepin's sapphic fiction is framed by publicity for the series it was inaugurating: a more appropriate original figure, Eve, was assigned the second volume, with subsequent titles devoted to, among others, La Fornarina, La Belle Hélène, even the wives of Sardanapal. However, since the introduction by the general editor follows Richepin's text, the reader may not realize until the end that Sappho's story is a totally inappropriate inauguration for this series. The editor explains that the series will teach a powerful lesson in history because so many decisions of famous men were motivated by their passions for these "grandes amoureuses." One wonders what could have motivated Sappho's selection, especially in a version that privileges her homosexuality, as figurehead for this multivolume celebration of the political power of female heterosexual wiles. The frontispiece (fig. 11) gives it away: her name floats inside a heart-shaped ornamental wreath which serves as a cushion for a beckoning female nude; the figure dominates a composite of fragments of nineteenth-century romance, such as the cavalier suspended from a rope ladder to kiss his lady on a balcony. By 1884, "Sappho" had become a brand name advertising a package of lush amorous adventures, risqué yet acceptable for wide circulation. She could even be portrayed as a lesbian, for the actual content of Richepin's

Fig. 11. Hector Leroux, frontispiece, Richepin, *Sapphô* (1884). Reprinted by permission of the Department of Rare Books and Special Collections, University of Michigan Library.

fiction does not matter. "Sappho" was the name of a "grande amoureuse," that is, the kind of woman who poured out her passion in operas and pulp fiction.

Even as it appeared enshrined, however, that situation was changing. Within a decade, the majority of Sapphic fictions would be sapphic. This altered vision is often explained as the consequence of a new sexual climate, specifically, of the highly visible, often militant, lesbian presence in fin-de-siècle Europe. However, this historical interpretation seems at odds with the just as visible, and probably more militant, repression of homosexuality, what Boswell characterizes, for the early twentieth century, as the most "vehement intolerance" in Western history (*Christianity*, 23). The history of Sapphic fiction casts new light on the history of homosexuality in "the era of high capitalism." The lesbian Sappho comes to prominence as the most open practice of female homosexuality in modern times begins. Yet the sapphic textual development owes far more to fifty years of literary speculation than to the political environment for sexuality at the time of its creation. Even a leader of the lesbian community like Renée Vivien creates fictions of Sappho heavily indebted to Baudelaire and the Sapphic configuration that formed around him, a milieu attracted to sapphism purely as an intellectual or an aesthetic force and generally vehemently antisapphic in actuality. The progressive aestheticization of female homosexuality culminates in a fiction of Sappho as the alter ego of the male decadent outsider, a fiction thus in resolute opposition to the commercialized bronze designed by Pradier and Daudet for easy circulation in the marketplace. Literary homosexuality, as we will repeatedly observe, most often seems strangely out of sync with all historical phenomena, be they economic or sexual.[73]

"The Pagan School"

Why is this name, Sapho, . . . like a self-reproach and like a menace in the depths of all anxious souls? Why is the Muse of Mytilene now the phantom of all our insomnias?
—Théodore de Banville,
18 November, 1850.

The anticapitalist Sappho has her roots in the period 1845–50. At that time Sappho is truly launched on her career as patroness of modernity when her legend acquires some of the trappings of romanticism. It may be impossible to decide how this happened and to recreate a chronology and assign degrees of responsibility. All that is certain is that a number of interrelated factors—a historically documented contemporary lesbian presence, the political climate surrounding 1848, and a campaign among rival young authors to win a sort of popular copyright over the Sapphic plot—culminated in three nearly contemporary works: the embryonic version of *Les Fleurs du mal* and two additional Sapphic "drames" by members of Baudelaire's circle, Arsène Houssaye and Philoxène Boyer.

The story begins sometime around 1845. Referring to this period in a chapter of his *Confessions* entitled "Où il n'est pas question du Rocher de Leucade," Houssaye remarks, "At this time Sapho was resuscitated in Paris, not knowing if she loved Phaon or Erinne" (2:13). The remark is typical of the usage that became current during the half-century covered by his memoirs (1830–80), a usage that originates in the more or less bohemian milieu of fledgling writers, according to which "Sapho" becomes a synonym for "female homosexual": Houssaye's chapter has nothing to do with Sappho and is only an account of the scandal-mongering that surrounded the George Sand-Marie Dorval relationship. And his is but a more decorous version of the scandal literature—notably that frequently expanded poem *Les Lesbiennes de Paris*—that circulated in Paris around 1845 with the goal of denouncing the well-known women of the day suspected of having homosexual liaisons. Among the names regularly evoked were all the women important in Baudelaire's early amorous life, notably his long-term mistress Jeanne Duval.

Anyone trying to found an argument about literature on this vaguely certifiable history does not have an easy task. To cite but the most obvious example: Baudelaire first announced the volume that would eventually appear as *Les Fleurs du mal* several times in print during 1845–48 under the title *Les Lesbiennes,* but this does not mean that the poems that can be associated with this first stage of his project, as we will see, have anything in common with *Les Lesbiennes de Paris*—or that he, like Houssaye, used "Sapho" purely as a substitute for "lesbienne." And this is also true of Houssaye's Sapphic fiction: he carried none of his appreciation for sexual gossip into his literary exploration of Sapphism. The most that can be said is this: these young literary lions might not have sought inspiration in Sappho's story without the contemporary fascination with female homosexuality.

Once it is established that they were aware of the distinction between Sapphic fictionalization and sapphic speculation, it must be added that these young writers sometimes blurred the line between the two genres, always, it seems, in an attempt to capitalize on the sensationalism of "amours lesbiennes" to promote their literary efforts. Long before Daudet, they concluded that "Sappho" was a brand name with the potential to commercialize texts. Hence Baudelaire's choice in the mid-1840s of a promotional title that mimics scandal-sheet appellations. Hence also Théodore de Banville's advertisement for Boyer's *Sapho* in the newspaper *Le Pouvoir*'s column, "La semaine dramatique": "Art obeys the supreme and fatal law of painting its period and its lacerations. And . . . Sapho's madness is the raving lunacy of the women who surround us." Hence finally Houssaye's chapter title, which denies the connection between the muse of Mytilene and contemporary sapphism, even as it links to that very contemporary context his own Sapphic production and the controversy that surrounded it. "In which the Rock of Leukas isn't mentioned " is an ironic reference to a notice published in the *Corsaire-Satan* in 1845, allegedly an account of Houssaye's first reading of his *Sapho,* in which the anonymous chronicler mocks the play by claiming (erroneously) that Houssaye's only innovation is his conclusion, a dialogue between Sapho and a personification of the Leukadian leap.[74]

Houssaye published his *Sapho* only five years later and then only in the relative privacy of the journal he himself edited, *L'Artiste.* The premature parodic preview in the *Corsaire-Satan* remains anonymous, but I am tempted to attribute it to the authors of another parody of Houssaye, published several months later in the *Corsaire-Satan,* a group of young authors led by Baudelaire and Banville.[75] This parody is presented as a citation from Houssaye's play, a fragment of a "love scene between Phaon and the famous Lesbienne," even though it has no more to do with the text Houssaye later published than the alleged dialogue with the leap personified. The poem is, however, a quite evident parody of fr. 31, addressed by Sapho to Phaon to describe the effects of her love. It is such a clumsy, schoolboy effort—"I suffer all day long the pain of your absence, / But that's nothing like the happiness of your presence"—that it is easy to dismiss the authors' conclusion: "these short citations . . . will excite the public's attention" (Baudelaire, ed. Le Dantec, 1:207, 1592).

It seems just as easy to write off this burst of Sapphic activity in 1845–46 as a struggle between two rival factions, with Baudelaire and Banville taking exception to Houssaye in order to protect the territory of their friend Boyer. However, there is no explanation of what could have motivated Baudelaire, who published many of his early poems in *L'Artiste* and later dedicated *Le Spleen de Paris* to Houssaye, to humiliate him publicly. Furthermore, there is no evidence that any of these Sapphic productions existed in 1845. Certainly, after this wave of publicity, they all seem to disappear, to resurface, amazingly enough, at exactly the same moment in 1850—but at this point they really exist. In the meantime, a great deal had happened, most notably the events of 1848. Deschanel, who had proclaimed a lesbian Sappho in 1847, was suspended from his duties as professor of Greek at the Ecole Normale Supérieure in 1850 because of his article, "Catholicisme et socialisme." As for Houssaye, his nomination to the chair of aesthetics at the Collège de France was about to be signed when he presided over some of the reformist student banquets of 1847, and his appointment was canceled.

Against this backdrop of risk and repression, and before literary activity had really taken off again in the aftermath of 1848, our authors release the Sapphic fictions they had been hatching quietly for five years, as if in a sudden frenzied need to publish. Baudelaire leads things off when "Lesbos" appears in Julien Lemer's anthology *Les Poètes de l'amour* in July 1850.[76] The first act of *Sapho* is included in *L'Artiste*'s October 15 issue, the second in its November 1 number. Boyer's *Sapho* (Banville is sometimes considered its coauthor) is staged on November 13, only two days before the publication of the final act of Houssaye's. Finally, at the time when the two apparently rival Sapphic plays were being staged, Baudelaire was often asked to recite his other famous sapphic poem, "Delphine et Hippolyte," in public, as though it were a miniature play in the same tradition. Predictably, critics frequently make sense out of this Sapphic outpouring by pointing to the influence of one *Sapho* on another: Boyer's alleged influence on Baudelaire has been noted, for example, and Baudelaire has been proposed as a model for Banville's Sapphic poem "Erinna" which, in his 1861 volume *Les Exilés*, really concludes this extended group effort (see *Les Fleurs du mal*, 435–36, 412). Such theories seem to me vastly to underestimate the complexity of this multiple coming-of-age through Sappho. Let us begin to tug on the threads that bind these texts together with the two works whose similarities are most striking, the simultaneous Sapphic dramas.

When Banville—who, in view of his close participation in the play which he may have coauthored and whose rehearsals he supervised in Boyer's absence, should probably not have been reviewing the Boyer *Sapho*—announces that "the novel of Sapho is *our* history. . . . M. Philoxène Boyer's *Sapho*, like that of Pradier, like that of Clésinger, is a profoundly *contemporary* work" (my emphasis), his words apply equally well to Houssaye's play. These are Sapphic fictions deeply rooted in contemporaneity, and in a male "ourness" that reveals itself most prominently in the most completely redefined and revitalized Phaon since the militaristic Napoleonic hero. Of the two, Boyer's was the more successful, receiving wide public acclaim, most prominently from poet laureate Victor Hugo.[77] According to Banville and to Boyer himself, this praise is a result of his having recast "the novel of Sappho" along the lines of a recent success by George Sand, whose alleged sapphism inspired Houssaye's chapter: Banville calls Boyer's Sapho a "modern Lélia"; Boyer pronounces his Phaon "a classic Sténio" (30). While the (misleading) comparison with the heroes of Sand's novel *Lélia* allows the young writers to continue to exploit the commercial value of sapphic scandal, it also distracts attention from the broader contemporary meaning of this Sapphic revision.

Boyer—the son of a noted Hellenist and, according to Daudet, "the Frenchman who, in his day, knew the most Greek" (*Trente ans,* 102)—admits that he set out to write the "poem" of modernity rather than a recreation of antiquity (32). This means most obviously that Phaon has become that standard Romantic male lead, the superfluous man afflicted with "the disease that *we* all suffer from in our hearts" (32, my emphasis), what Banville describes as "the incurable boredom that he has promenaded across all the seas." In fact, Boyer and Houssaye give an identical vision of Phaon as "modern man": for the first time, he does not simply abandon the poet for a younger woman but is torn between Sapho and her student Erinna. These are really "two Sappho" dramas, with Erinna cast as the sexual double (Banville calls Boyer's version a "courtesan," but she is really only a woman defined exclusively as a source of physical pleasure) and Sapho as one facet of "the impossible" that the modern Phaon searches out in an effort to ward off boredom (Boyer, 8; Houssaye, 2:2). In both plays, but more completely in Houssaye's, the translation Phaon-Phaethon-Icarus, already initiated in the seventeenth century, is finally made explicit (Boyer, 8; Houssaye, 1:7).

The Sapho finally, if only fitfully, desired by this superfluous Phaon is Houssaye-Boyer's most influential innovation. Rather than simply plagiarize Racine like their precursor Sapphic playwrights, these writers recast Sapho as a neo-Racinian, neo-Romantic figure who stands at the intersection between the chaste Sappho and the Baudelairean tradition of the "femmes damnées."[78] Houssaye gives us "l'altière Sapho," that is, a figure of darkness who defines love as "a bird of prey" and binds Phaon with her "somber," "infernal love" (2:8, 1:7). Boyer's heroine, described

232223

by Phaon in an unmistakably Racinian flashback, is darker still: guilty of adultery and political insurrection, she is condemned as an "infinite abyss of monstrosity" (14–15). More important, his is the first Sapho of the century to give a hint of the demonic sexuality that she will increasingly come to represent. "Virile by virtue of the vices of the soul," Boyer's heroine is a "strange androgyne" (15).

Thus, even though these Saphos are heterosexual, they indicate the translation from the chaste Sappho, "mascula" because of her intellect, to the homosexual figure who is about to come to prominence. Houssaye revises the assumption scene that is the signature of chastity plays when he has Sapho's *dead* body borne away by a group of sirens: from the protection of the saintly muses, she passes to that of the classic *femmes fatales*. The reference to Orpheus's end, only implicit in Houssaye, is made clear by Boyer. He does away completely with the apotheosis scenario in favor of a brief epitaph pronounced by Anacréon: "The muse of Lesbos has perished like Orpheus" (30). The young writer is thus first to point out what Bachofen would soon call "the Orphic quality of the Sapphic muse" (206), and, in so doing, he shows the way toward the final portrait in the nineteenth-century Sapphic gallery, Sappho as the female Orpheus. That image, what Mario Praz calls "the lesbian *femme fatale,*" was just then being inaugurated by Boyer's friend Baudelaire.

Because of the close similarity between the two plays, and because of the wide discrepancy between the original description of Houssaye's, as announced in the early parodies, and his finished product, I am tempted by a series of hypotheses. These *Saphos* may have been hardly more than ideas when they initially became the object of literary gossip in 1846. Boyer and Houssaye were not Sapphic rivals. Instead they seem to have been co-conspirators, along with Baudelaire and Banville, in a well-organized effort to use Sapphism to commercialize themselves as men of letters before, in Boyer's case at least, they had done anything to deserve the title. This authorial self-invention through Sappho might be seen as the equivalent for the age of capitalism of the seventeenth-century neo-Ovidians who came of age through their new *Heroides*: these fledgling writers—Boyer was only seventeen when their self-promotion began—became literary commodities able to circulate in the marketplace solely on the strength of Sapphic, and sapphic, notoriety. It may have taken them nearly five years to assume their Sapphic voices and to come of age as writers with the help of the muse of Mytilene. By the time the Sapphic playwrights had become men of letters, their co-conspirator Baudelaire had already begun to move Sapphism more squarely into the mainstream of modernity and, in the process, to render obsolete their attempts to modernize the plot of Sappho and Phaon.

For all the actuality and the male "ourness" of their *Saphos,* Boyer and Houssaye are situated in the time-honored French neoclassical tradition. In 1852, when their Sapphic fictions were still fresh, Baudelaire lashed out against that very tradition in "L'Ecole païenne," an extended meditation on an often repeated phrase of the day: "Who will deliver us from the Greeks and the Romans?"[79] He presents a number of figures from antiquity as too worn out to serve as artistic inspiration, among them "the burning Sapho, that patroness of hysterics" (Baudelaire, ed. Le Dantec, 1:625). "L'Ecole païenne" is interpreted as an attack on Banville (833)—on, therefore, the very tradition from which Baudelaire's own Sapphic identity initially seemed inseparable. He had to mark his distance: in *Les Lesbiennes* become *Les Fleurs du mal,* Baudelaire's coming of age through Sappho is still visible, but it is also completely distinct from that of his former co-conspirators.

As Benjamin remarks in his brilliant analysis of the sapphic presence in *Les Fleurs du mal,* "Baudelaire by no means discovered the lesbian for art" (90). He did, however, completely realign literary lesbianism. Consider the example of his illustrious precursor in this domain, Théophile Gautier. With *Mademoiselle de Maupin,* Gautier contributed perhaps more than anyone to the lesbian's reduction to androgyny, simple source of sexual scandal and prurient interest. Despite the fact that he popularized the theme of lesbianism, we know from Gautier's notes for a projected article that he believed in the two-Sappho theory, and therefore in a chastely heterosexual muse of Mytilene.[80] This fact alone should make us realize that a distinction must be made between the fiction of Sappho and that of *the* lesbian. Baudelaire's portrait of Sappho is most striking because, alone among contemporary men of letters, he makes her sapphic. And this homosexual Sappho is the key to Baudelaire's redefinition of literary lesbianism.

Benjamin points out that only once does Baudelaire allow a figure from Greek antiquity to intrude on his fascination with Roman antiquity (90). This exception made for Sappho may help us understand Benjamin's judgment that "Baudelaire wanted to be read like a classical poet" (90). Of all the nineteenth-century Sapphic poets, only Baudelaire reveals something of the uncanny identification that resonates in Ovid and Racine. Witness the portrayal in "Lesbos" of his poet-double as heir to the muse of Mytilene and sole keeper of the secrets of Lesbianism: in Baudelaire's Sapphic scenario, she dies after (because of?) the "blasphemy" of having "insulted the ritual and the cult" of the Lesbian "religions" by giving her body as "fodder" to a "proud brute." The island then proclaims and trains her successor, someone to preserve the Lesbian mysteries and to keep watch in case one night the sea should carry to Lesbos, Orpheus-like, "Sappho's adored cadaver." This role, still found in the poems of Baudelaire's followers among the "Sapho 1900" poets, but always confided by them to a woman, in "Lesbos" is not only carried out by a man but can only be entrusted to a man:

> Car Lesbos entre tous m'a choisi sur la terre
> Pour chanter le secret de ses vierges en fleurs,
> Et je fus dès l'enfance admis au noir mystère
> Des rires effrénés mêlés aux sombres pleurs;
> Car Lesbos entre tous m'a choisi sur la terre.
>
> (*Les Fleurs du mal*, 167–68)[81]

And with this inheritance, Baudelaire makes, in Benjamin's words, "the lesbian . . . the heroine of modernism." In particular, he makes Sappho the "heroine of modernism," a role she still plays for English decadents like Swinburne and Symonds and their French counterparts like Louÿs—and even for an heir to decadence, Proust, who must have felt he shared Baudelaire's calling to "chanter le secret de ses vierges en fleur" and who pronounced the "Femmes damnées" "the most beautiful [long poem] that Baudelaire wrote" (125–26). My glissando the lesbian → Sappho → the lesbian is intentional: Baudelaire not only gave his readers a homosexual Sappho; he also made Sappho synonymous with the "femmes damnées," redefining thereby the literary lesbian in her antique image. Witness the order he established for the homonymous "Fleurs du mal" cycle for his collection's original edition: "Lesbos" was the third poem, followed by the two "Femmes damnées" poems. Orpheus-reincarnate, Sappho would thus have presided not only over the initiation of the *poète maudit* but also over modernism's new literary lesbian.

She is defined in the two poems that originally followed "Lesbos." Of those two, the poem anchored in Greek antiquity, "Delphine et Hippolyte," came first, establishing a progression from Greek to modern times while maintaining the primacy of the classical model. Traditionally, Baudelaire has been assumed to be indebted to Boyer for the local color in "Lesbos" (see *Les Fleurs du mal*, 435–36), but these elements had been common in the French tradition even before Barthélemy's canonical fiction. However, Baudelaire's sapphic vision does borrow the essence of Boyer's modernity: like Boyer's Sapho and Phaon, his "femmes damnées" are "chercheuses d'infini" driven by "unquenched thirsts" ("Femmes damnées"). The poet figure in *Les Fleurs du mal* is a fitting stand-in for the Lesbian virgins: like them, he is pulled toward "the vacuum," "the abyss," "the chasm" ("Delphine et Hippolyte").

Benjamin stresses the union of paired opposites that he sees as fundamental to Baudelaire's attitude toward lesbianism—" 'Lesbos' is a hymn to lesbian love; 'Delphine et Hippolyte,' on the other hand, is a condemnation of this passion" (92)—and he explains this contradiction as a result of the poet's complete unconcern for actual lesbians—"he had no attitude towards [the lesbian] in real life, as it were"; "he did not recognize her in reality" (93). While I agree with Benjamin that these opposing visions ultimately cancel each other out, it is also nonetheless obvious that Baudelaire's actual readers have often been sensitive to only one of the warring voices in his Sapphic verse. However, before we explore the readings of Baudelaire that portray him as the origin of either subsequent celebrations or condemnations of lesbianism, let us first consider the background for Benjamin's view. Baudelaire's modern heroines are anchored in their literariness, most evidently in a variety of Sapphic plots from Ovid's to Boyer-Houssaye's, but also in allusions to less obviously related pieces of the immense Sapphic fiction in which Baudelaire and his confrères had found their literary initiation. Hence, for example, the two modern sapphic names. "Delphine," the name of Baudelaire's masculine heroine, is generally thought to evoke Staël's heroine, "mascula," like Barthélemy's Sapho and Boyer's, because of her involvment in political sedition.[82] "Hippolyte" is always identified only as the name of the queen of the Amazons, mother of a son by Theseus. But the name Baudelaire gives to his "frail" sapphic lover seems, especially in the Sapphic tradition in which his poems are so thoroughly grounded, a more likely reference to the effeminate young male, named for his warrior mother, emasculated by Racine's Phèdre-Sappho.

Given Baudelaire's detachment from lesbianism as anything but a lure useful as a promotional device, it is hardly surprising that one tradition inspired by his Sappho portrays her as pure literariness, the absolute in art for art's sake. The most striking example of this inheritance is Banville's poem "Erinna" in *Les Exilés* (1861), a cross between the German chastity plot and a proto-Mallarméan rhetoric of the absolute. Banville dedicates the poem to Boyer, "who resuscitated the figure of Sapho" (99), but this implied relation is misleading. "Erinna" unites Baudelaire's intuition that Sappho had become a literary artifact and the chastity theory to portray Sapphism as the cult of art for art's sake. Banville feminizes the role of Sappho's heir that Baudelaire had imagined for his poet-narrator: Erinna explains Sapphism to young poets, "vierges en fleur." If they do not marry, they must remain "chaste and virginal" in order to give themselves to the "arid cult [of rhythm]." "Victims of lyric fury," "they will become drunk with voluptuousness," yet they will never be "offended by matter's impure ugliness" (99–101).[83] This is precisely the "immoderate taste for form" which Baudelaire in "L'Ecole païenne" terms "art's madness" (ed. Le Dantec, 1:628), yet that "plastic" madness is present in his Sappho—as is the obsession with her chastity that resurfaces much later throughout "Sapho 1900" poetry.

Obviously, Banville's version of chastity cannot be equated with Vivien's, just as his sense of Sapphic plasticity is different from Baudelaire's. Yet Banville, no more than Vivien, does not misread the precursor poet. Baudelaire's divergent heritage may be explained by the contradictory ideological charges that resonate in his Sapphic verse, what Benjamin terms "the profound duplicity which animates Baudelaire's poetry" (26). For the example of Sappho, we have just seen the evidence that supports a reading of her pure literariness. But it is also possible to "prove" Baudelaire's contempt for the "bétail pensif" ("Femmes damnées") and make him thereby the precursor of the fin-de-siècle decadents for whom Sappho becomes an object of lush, overblown vilification (Faderman's view of Baudelaire). It is even possible to "establish" his sympathetic solidarity with the "poor sisters" ("Femmes damnées") whose poetic cult of Sappho he shared (Le Dantec's position).

Baudelaire is the first French lyric poet to reject simple adaptation of the Sapphic original, à la Catullus or Ronsard, in favor of a highly original personal fiction of Sappho. He presents Sappho as the classical model for his ideal of modern heroinism: female mannishness (*mascula Sappho*), woman devoting herself to intellectual creativity, woman perpetually virginal because she refuses men access to her body. Such a woman was "lamentable," was of necessity "damned," that is, would, in his fiction of her, inevitably be ostracized. That the "sublimity" of Sapphic "sterility" would be threatening to civic values was inevitable: the notes Baudelaire prepared for his lawyer for the 1857 trial about the *Fleurs du mal*'s obscenity reveal that it did not occur to him to try to contest this.

274

Certainly, the menace of that sterility became increasingly a historically documented fear as the century progressed, and especially when the Franco-Prussian conflict had made the need for French soldiers to counter what were portrayed as the ever-expanding German ranks a subject of acute public concern.[84] During the same period, however, infertility became a highly prized beauty by Baudelaire's spiritual sons, the decadents. In fact, for almost all the remaining Sapphic fictions, the ornamentalism that is part of Baudelaire's legacy proves a stumbling block to interpretation. Unless one has recourse to facile "explanations" like the fact that certain poets were also militant lesbians, it is not always easy to grasp the ideological situation of fictions that seem so similar because of their overly charged decorative surface.

Of the poets who proclaim their debt to Baudelaire for their Sapphic vision, only Paul Verlaine eliminates all of the complexity of the definition of Sapphism that would be dominant for the next half-century. The section "Les Amies" (first published in 1867, then in the 1884 collection *Parallèlement*) reverses Baudelaire's order: rather than an authorizing classical origin, Sappho appears last, in the sixth of a series of sapphic sonnets. Despite the fact that Verlaine openly acknowledges Baudelaire's priority in his "Sappho" when he describes her as "forgetful of the Ritual," his sonnet has nothing of the *Fleurs du mal*'s intellectualization of sapphism and recalls instead the licentious scandal-mongering of a Gautier.[85] Indeed, those who lambaste the nineteenth century's sensationalistic portrayals of lesbianism should choose Verlaine rather than Baudelaire as a target: his fiction marks the entry of nineteenth-century popular vilifications of Sappho into the literary canon.[86] Like Ovid's, Verlaine's Sappho is a madwoman ("furieuse"), but she is overburdened with the trappings of the sensationalistic literary lesbianism of the day (with "sunken eyes" and "bruised eyelids," she runs about "like a she-wolf" and "tears out her long hair by fistfuls"). Verlaine in fact includes more of Sappho's alleged biography than Baudelaire, but he is interested only in her resemblance to a contemporary cliché.[87] Surprisingly, Verlaine's is the only antilesbian Sapphic fiction created in Baudelaire's immediate wake.[88] There is no tradition of such negative fiction associated with Sappho before the turn of the century, and by then a second Sapphic complex will have been formed around Baudelaire.

Baudelaire's modernist heroine stands in resolute opposition to courtesan fictions like Daudet's in which the Sappho figure circulates in the marketplace. In fact, his Sapphic fiction was so obviously ahead of its time that it lay dormant for decades of "the age of high capitalism" before it began to be exploited. In the chronology of nineteenth-century fictions of Sappho, there are only two interruptions. The first occurs in the decade prior to the Baudelaire-Banville-Boyer-Houssaye publicity stunt, and it can be explained by the uninspired translations produced during the general retreat after the Boissonade-Girodet homosexual reading, formulated in the explosive climate of the 1820s. The second interruption is far more impressive: after the poems by Banville and Verlaine in the 1860s, there is no Sapphic production before the works by Silvestre, Daudet, and Richepin in the early 1880s. These are followed by another decade of silence before the *Chansons de Bilitis* announce the arrival of the most active decade of Sapphic production in the entire French tradition. The second interruption, like the first, must have been influenced by the contemporary weakness of the French scholarly tradition: in the second half of the nineteenth century, the only innovative erudition was produced in England (Symonds, Wharton). Like the previous hiatus, it must also have been a backing off, this time after Baudelaire's far more audacious association between Sappho and lesbianism. (The fact that the first works to reveal the imprint of Baudelaire's Sapphic vision are all part of a prolesbian tradition reinforces my view that his "femmes damnées" should not be classified with the century's simplistic, antilesbian propaganda texts.) In the final analysis, at no time in the nineteenth century do homosexual readings of Sappho in either literature or scholarship generate a tradition of sapphic speculation.

The "age of high capitalism" was much advanced when a homosexual Sappho was first actively promoted by a tradition that seems to view Baudelaire as sympathetic to sapphism. She makes her literary debut under the name "Psappha" in Louÿs's 1895 volume, a work destined to serve as a source of titillation for more than one generation of readers. Louÿs's bravado begins with his dedication "of this little book of ancient love . . . to the young girls of the future society," a consecration whose audacity is clear only to the reader familiar with his version of Sapphism. Baudelaire associates Sappho only obliquely with his graphic portrayal of female homosexuality, by making her preside indirectly over the activities in the two "femmes damnées" poems. Louÿs, on the other hand, makes Sappho for the first time an active participant in a fully developed sapphic fiction. In order to do so, he sexualizes Sapphic pedagogy, making Sappho, for the first time in fiction, the absolute female counterpart of the older man who is the erotic teacher in *pederastia*.

Elaine Marks has discussed the prevalence of what she terms "the lesbian fairy tale based on the Sappho model," that is, the choice of "the gynaeceum, ruled by the seductive or seducing teacher" as "the preferred locus for most fictions about women loving women" (357–58). Marks traces both the origins of this model in eighteenth- and nineteenth-century male texts and its continuation in the twentieth century by both male and female authors. Once again, however, Sapphic fictions follow a different course from sapphic fictions. Whereas in scholarship the question of whether Sappho headed a school became an issue in the eighteenth century, and whereas Sappho is evoked as a professor of erotics in antilesbian fiction as early as *L'Espion anglais* (1778), in Sapphic fictions the pedagogical plot is outlined but remains undeveloped prior to Louÿs. From the first Sapphic plays in the late eighteenth century, for example, she is defined as a teacher, but all we know of her pedagogy is that she has produced a single student, the younger woman for whom Phaon betrays her. From all signs, this teacher-student relation is closer to a mother-daughter bond: Sappho has raised the young girl rather than educated her. Furthermore—and this is the crucial difference from the "lesbian fairy tale" model—the relation between Sappho and the pupil-daughter is characterized as affectionate but not erotic.

Les Chansons de Bilitis sets Sapphic pedagogy on a new course. First, Louÿs actually shows us Sappho teaching and defines her instruction. When the Greek peasant girl Bilitis becomes a member of Sappho's circle, she receives an education in "the art of singing in rhythmic phrases, and of preserving for posterity the memory of loved ones" (16). In addition, as the poem "Psappha" explains, the muse of Mytilene herself initiates Bilitis into same-sex love. Psappha thus transformed, as in the original project for the "femmes damnées" cycle in *Les Fleurs du mal,* into the presiding figure authorizing sapphic eroticism, the volume becomes the story of Bilitis, according to what Louÿs claimed were her own recently discovered autobiographical poems. When her story is retold, we observe the first way in which this volume—presented as a translation from the Greek of poems found in a tomb and thus foreshadowing the actual discoveries of papyri fragments which began some two years later—is situated, as it were, in the interstices of Sappho scholarship. Louÿs weaves Bilitis into Psappha's life as her rival for one of the beloved girls actually mentioned by Sappho, Mnasidika. In the classic tradition of French historical fiction, he thereby fills in a historical doubt with his creation: the Bilitis poems, he explains, give us final proof of Mnasidika's name and of her role in Sappho's life.[89]

Louÿs then exploits the Bilitis-Mnasidika connection to implicate Sappho in a homosexual scenario far more graphic than anything contained in her poetry and only surpassed in the history of Sapphic fictions by Vivien's later expansions. (Louÿs's poems are, like Vivien's amplifications, another incarnation of the dream of making Sappho's poetic body whole again.) The relationship takes place between the two young girls but, since they are both Sappho's students, their involvement is identified with Sapphism. Louÿs obviously relishes the type of lush, erotic imagery I had in mind when I described his volume as a popular source of voyeuristic thrills—witness this example from the cycle to Mnasidika: "She was standing against me, completely abandoned to love and consenting. One of my knees, little by little, rose between her hot thighs which yielded as if to a male lover [*amant*]" (131). He also imagines a plot for sapphism that, like the little scene I just cited, portrays female same-sex love as mimicry of heterosexual passion: Bilitis and Mnasidika have a "marriage ceremony" (they aren't allowed to live together before this) with Dika dressed as the bride and Bilitis as her groom. Bilitis gives her a wax doll that she calls her child. This impersonation of bourgeois respectability ends when Mnasidika abandons husband and child. The *Chansons* then veer squarely into heterosexual erotics, because Bilitis goes to Cyprus to become a temple prostitute, a courtesan of Aphrodite. This final phase allows Louÿs to complete the gamut ("toute la lyre," in Daudet's expression) of the sexual scenarios proposed for Sappho in his day. Bilitis acts out the fiction of the courtesan Sappho.

As should be clear by now, *Les Chansons de Bilitis* is steeped in nineteenth-century Sappho lore and scholarship. (Louÿs, you will remember, knew the English decadents in John Addington Symonds's circle.) It often, in fact, has the ring of a parody of Sapphic commentary (an observation I would make about only one other Sapphic fiction, Virginia Woolf's "A Society"). No reader has ever been more sensitive to the threat to the high seriousness of erudition posed by Louÿs's volume than the august Wilamowitz-Moellendorff who, the year after the appearance of its original edition, first published his violent denunciation of Louÿs's literary hoax (even though there is no evidence that anyone had been taken in by *Bilitis*). Louÿs countered with more tongue-in-cheek: subsequent editions of the *Chansons* include a brief (fictive) bibliography of critical works devoted to these poems, in which the German edition is attributed to Prof. von Willamowitz, Goettingen, 1896—the year and the place in which his hostile review had appeared.[90] Of course, for Wilamowitz, the imagined threat of Louÿs's hoax was purely scholarly, that it would encourage a redefinition of Sapphism. It is unlikely that he, or Louÿs, was at all prepared for its most spectacular influence, the role *Bilitis* would play some seven years later as an inspiration for the first tradition ever of openly sapphic Sapphic fictions.

The double posterity of *Les Chansons de Bilitis* is something of a puzzle. Like Gautier, Louÿs profits from the power of sapphism to *épater le bourgeois*. One could hardly have expected, therefore, that his volume would be resurrected by the "jeunes filles" of the "société future" which his dedication slyly predicts. However, the first publication to signal the arrival of what would be termed well after the fact the era of "Sapho 1900" opens with a dedication to "Monsieur Pierre Louÿs" from "une jeune fille de la société future." The pseudonym under which the 1902 volume *Cinq petits dialogues grecs* was published, Tryphê, camouflaged the identity of Natalie Clifford Barney, whose discovery of the Wharton Sappho edition is at the origin of that new society.

Barney and Vivien (née Pauline Tarn), two English native speakers whose often intertwined literary careers would unfold in French, met in 1897. The twist of fate by which Sapphic and sapphic finally became completely united in the French tradition, Barney's trip to London and her chance discovery of Wharton's sexually equivocal translation, took place shortly after their meeting. Witness Barney's assessment of the discovery's importance for them in her *Souvenirs indiscrets:* "This precious volume served Renée Vivien as a comparison with her French translation, became her bedside reading and the source at which she drew the pagan inspiration for several of her future books" (27). Also according to Barney's *Souvenirs indiscrets,* it was at her instigation that the discovery of an equivocal Sappho became the origin of their sapphic movement. She reports this suggestion to the woman about to become Sappho's first female translator since Le Fèvre Dacier: "Why wouldn't we assemble around ourselves a group of poetesses like those who surrounded Sappho in Mytilene and who provided mutual inspiration?" (51). Most commentators efface this double origin to identify the first truly sapphic Sapphic literary creation in France solely with Vivien. Barney, however, if not as powerful a Sapphic influence as Vivien, clearly stands at least as an independent, original voice within the "Sapho 1900" movement. Certainly, she provided an impetus for that movement with her discovery of Wharton and also, one suspects, of Louÿs. When she and Vivien went to

meet Louÿs, it was to her that he inscribed a copy of *Bilitis*. "A Natalie
Clifford Barney, jeune fille de la société future, son admirateur Pierre
Louÿs" (*Souvenirs*, 77)—and she inaugurated the movement's literary
production with her *Cinq petits dialogues grecs*.

The fin-de-siècle French Sapphic fictions appear at a time of transition
in both literary and scholarly conventions. These fictions are part of a
context from within which was mounted a major challenge to the standard
configuration of literary eroticism. In Marks's formulation, "In 1900, for
the first time since Sappho, the narrator Claudine in *Claudine à l'école* looks
at another woman as an object of pleasure and without any excuses
describes her pleasure. A great revolution had begun" (363). At the very
same time, Sappho's corpus was being expanded: the discovery and
publication of the papyri manuscripts that complete and sometimes
challenge the previous vision of Sappho begins in 1897. Since much of the
turn-of-the-century scholarly activity originates in England, the bilingual-
ism of the "Sapho 1900" founders surely came into play once again. In
addition, French readers begin to have access to those discoveries in an
article by Reinach in 1902, the year of Barney's five dialogues.

These dialogues, presented almost as a companion piece to *Bilitis*, read
in part as a continuation of the scenario for Sapphism prescribed by the
male decadents, Louÿs and his precursor Baudelaire. As in "Lesbos,"
Sapphism is a "cult" to which one is "consecrated," an exclusive bond that
the initiate cannot break without being pronounced "unworthy" (12, 13).
From the very opening of her prologue, however, Barney spells out, as her
male precursors never do, what Wilamowitz may have understood as the
menace this female erotic pedagogy posed to the well-being of the polis:

> Alors l'Inconnue—la persuasive et la redoutable,—la terri-
> ble et la douce, me dit: —Si tu m'aimes, tu oublieras ta
> famille et ton mari et ton pays et tes enfants et tu viendras
> vivre avec moi.
> Si tu m'aimes, tu quitteras tout ce que tu chéris, et les
> lieux où tu te souviens . . . et tes souvenirs et tes espoirs ne
> seront qu'un désir vers moi. . . .
> Et je lui répondis en sanglotant: Je t'aime. (vii–viii)[91]

Barney inaugurates the Sapphic fiction of "Sapho 1900" by assaulting
her reader with a definition of Sapphism as a totalizing "cult" experience,
a pseudoreligious experience that requires those who would be believers to
sacrifice everything else to it, to give up all aspects of a traditional "normal"

life, to leave the ranks of their families' genealogies, on whose uninterrupted unfolding the state depends for its security. Not since Staël had a writer taken on the forces of "the world and the city" in the name of Sappho. Furthermore, Barney flaunts the unspoken threat of Sapphism, its potential contribution to depopulation. She sings a hymn of praise to Sappho as a deity cast in vintage Baudelairean terms: "Isolated androgyne / In your perversity cunningly infertile" (2). Barney offers a "cunning perversion" of the standard defense of *pederastia:* the goal of male homoerotic pedagogy had traditionally been presented as the initiation of the young male to civic virtue; she proclaims its female counterpart to be the initiation of the young female to the perversion of all public values.

The *Cinq petits dialogues grecs* also announce the most original, and perhaps the most disquieting, aspect of "Sapho 1900"'s Sapphic fictionalization, its obsessive identification with Sappho. This cult of Sappho's person originates, once again, with Baudelaire, in this case, his revision of Horace's "mascula Sappho." Barney's Sapho is "more man than woman": "Her mind and even her soul, if the soul has a sex, are those of a man" (18). She is "mascula," like Boyer's Sapho, because "she attracts like the abyss"; "mascula," like Houssaye's, because she "dreams of the infinite"; "mascula," finally, like Baudelaire's Sapho, because she reproduces like the modernist outsider: "Her love has the sterility of immutable things. . . . It will outlive those fertile loves that multiply in generations on the earth and then are no more" (21, 19).[92] Thus, at the dawn of the "Sapho 1900" movement, Barney announces the essence of its revision of Sapphism as doubly unnatural love: love that is not inspired by traditional female beauty, and love that refuses its so-called natural function.

The new vision was hardly announced when Vivien produced in quick succession three volumes that form the cornerstone of both her Sapphic production (poems to Sappho and Sapphic doubles can be noted throughout her *oeuvre,* but the essence of her vision is set in these nearly simultaneous volumes) and of the circle she gathered around her: her translation first appeared in 1903, followed the next year by *Une Femme m'apparut* and *La Dame à la louve.* Both these fictional volumes continue the major preoccupations of Vivien's edition—the rewriting of Sappho's biography and the attack on *pederastia* as the unique model for a homosexual erotic—as well as Barney's preoccupation with the cult of Sapphic pedagogy.

In the novel *Une Femme m'apparut,* Vivien's Sapphic polemic is for the most part confided to the poet San Giovanni, the Androgyne (presented as a double for Vivien, since she is the author of a study of Sappho and a volume entitled *Bona Dea,* also the title of the last section of Vivien's other 1904 collection, *La Dame à la louve*). In long, at times overbearingly didactic passages, the Androgyne explains, for example, the sapphic theory of Sappho's chastity: "isn't [this love as ardent and pure as a white flame] a thousand times more chaste than that cohabitation founded on self-interest that Christian marriage has become?" (20). San Giovanni also puts forth a revised (female) homosexual erotic, in which the female body replaces the male body, since Winckelmann the aesthetic standard, while the imitation of nature is replaced by a modernist antimimesis. Male writing has for too long kept literature on a wrong intellectual course, tricking writers into thinking that "coming ever closer to nature" should be their "highest ambition" (150–51). In addition, male aestheticians have proclaimed the imitation of the male body the purest aesthetic model, whereas "adolescents are only beautiful insofar as they resemble Woman" (23). There have been few women writers—and here alone San Giovanni shares Winckelmann's position—because women are not instinctively sensitive to "the inaesthetic par excellence," the male body. Psappha alone became immortal because "she didn't deign to remark the existence of men" (151).

From this assault on the aesthetic foundation of classical Winckelmannian art history, philology, and *pederastia,* Vivien, like Barney, moves to establish a cult of Sappho's person. In *Une Femme m'apparut,* she surpasses the scene imagined by Barney, in which the Unknown Woman invites the "young girls of the future society" to leave their families and join her in a mystical union. In pages in which Louÿs's voice lives on, Vivien's poet-double San Giovanni paints her self-portrait as Bilitis reincarnate: "I was born long ago on Lesbos. . . . An old friend brought me to the temple where Psappha was invoking the Goddess. I heard the odes to Aphrodita. . . . Because of my ugliness and my taciturn uneasiness, Psappha didn't love me. But I loved her, and when I later possessed female bodies, my sobs of desire went out to Her" (24). With this vision of mystical possession and reincarnation, we are at the heart of what Gubar terms Vivien's "interpretation of what lesbianism means as an imaginative force. The fantastic collaboration Vivien . . . enacts through [her] reinvention of Sappho's verse [is] not unrelated to the eroticized female relationships that quite literally empowered [her] to write" (47). There is certainly ample testimony in Vivien's writings to the parallelism Gubar points out between Vivien's expression of Sappho and her homoerotic personal literary friendships—indeed, this is the aspect of Vivien's system that comes most frequently, and most easily, under attack.

Witness what may be the original formulation of this charge in François Jean-Desthieux's 1937 *Femmes damnées,* a volume devoted jointly to Sappho and to Vivien. It marks, on the eve of World War II, the last stage in the contemporary French positioning with regard to sapphism, a complete withdrawal from what must be seen as the French national (although hardly nationalistic) theory, the "Sapho 1900" definition of Sapphism: "Renée Vivien didn't only imitate Sappho: she certainly believed herself to be Sappho reincarnate. . . . She sacrificed everything to her quest for Sappho. . . . She pursued her, even to Lesbos. . . . We realize why she couldn't find her there" (27, 49). Sappho escaped Vivien, even on Lesbos, according to Jean-Desthieux, simply because Vivien misunderstood Sappho. She was in search of a lesbian, whereas the author of this revised view of "femmes damnées" knows that the poet was not sapphic: "Sappho was neither a *gouge,* nor depraved, nor even a lesbian" (10). On the contrary, his Sappho is almost a virgin—on the eve of the conflict that would make them military allies, the Frenchman, who had preached throughout the 1920s the inevitability of a renewal of conflict,[93] promotes a close approximation of the English view of Sappho's chastity, a blend of Symonds and Edmonds. Jean-Desthieux pronounces Sappho's poems to Aphrodite "verse that celebrates impersonally a household divinity in terms destined to be repeated by many other voices after hers" and compares them to "the no less ardent canticles and litanies dedicated to the Virgin Mary by thousands of young Christian girls" (25).

I jumped ahead for a moment to the end of the backlash against Vivien's Sapphism to show the extremes to which a misunderstanding of the principle of Sapphic identification in her work have led—and all because her critics read Vivien too quickly. San Giovanni is not Sappho reincarnate but the would-be beloved girl (hence my identification of Vivien's character with Bilitis). In Vivien, therefore, "what lesbianism means as an imaginative force" (according to Gubar's expression [47]) is more complex than Vivien's reliving with her female companions Sappho's involvement with the beloved girls. Vivien's obsessively repetitive fictions of Sappho are not about becoming Sappho but about a double redefinition: of sapphism as the poetic infinite, an (always impossible) union with Sappho, and of Sapphism as the desire, incessantly emitted by

Sappho across the ages, for the ideal beloved girl, the Atthis or the Dika who will give up without a murmur, in a "sob" of love, father, family, and homeland for the muse of Mytilene.

In Barney's 1910 "Equivoque," the work that closes the explosion of "Sapho 1900" Sapphic fictions, this is the meaning of Psappha's last words before her suicidal leap—a suicide provoked not by Phaon's betrayal but by that of the beloved girl, here named Timas, who has abandoned her to marry Phaon.[94] Psappha reserves her revenge for their wedding night when, although dead,

> *Je serai cette nuit, l'hôte qu'on craint de voir.*
> ....
> *J'occuperai ma place, invisible, à table.*
> ....
> *Comme autrefois, c'est moi qui viendrai vers ta couche,*
> *Ce sera son baiser, mais ce sera ma bouche.*
> *Tu me désireras à travers son désir.*
> *Et tu redonneras mon nom à ton plaisir.* (66–67)[95]

Through San Giovanni and the Psappha of "Equivoque," Vivien and Barney establish Sappho-Psappha as the origin of all sapphic desire and redefine female same-sex love as, "through the desire" of the other, always an attempted union with the woman who gave it her name: "And once again you will give my name to your pleasure." Hence the recurrent theme—to which, for example, the second half of "Equivoque" is devoted—of the mourning of Psappha by the beloved girls she left behind.

The incredible Sapphic outpouring of the years 1902–10 is thus characterized by a nearly equal blend of mysticism and homosexual militancy. One cannot but think of Saint-Simonism, with which so many nineteenth-century feminists were allied and, according to Benjamin, the source of many of Baudelaire's ideas on the lesbian (90–92).[96] Likewise, since Vivien and Barney frequently turned to English sources otherwise ignored in the French tradition, the importance given to Sappho as pedagogue by Anglo-American Hellenists should not be minimized. (For example, Colonel Mure is, in 1854, the first scholar to portray Sappho as teacher of "the art of Love" [*History,* 3:279].) Germans, notably Wilamowitz, preach chaste pedagogy, but the English have always led the way in promoting Sappho the schoolteacher (a position from which the English tradition parts ways only with Page).[97] From these various influences, "Sapho 1900" forged strange alliances, ultimately giving the decadents' outsider lesbian, Baudelaire's *souffre-douleur,* a home in a community for which they, like Louÿs, predicted a brilliant future, status as a real "new society." Hence the enormous importance granted female friendship—and I mean female friendship as distinct from same-sex love—in their works. (It figures most prominently perhaps in Vivien's *La Dame à la louve* in an extended meditation, once again an explicit overturning of *pederastia* defenses, on the superiority of women's friendship.)

If the critic refuses to use biographical knowledge—Vivien was a lesbian, Baudelaire a misogynist with no concern for the reality of female homosexuality—to create differences where there are none, this, then, ultimately seems the point at which Vivien and Barney part company most clearly with the decadents' view of Sapphism. Often, the voices of "Sapho 1900" seem so reminiscent of the clichés about Sappho, the lesbian, and the androgyne circulated by male writers of the previous century that the proximity is disturbing. "[Sappho's] mind and even her soul, if the soul has a sex, are those of a man"—that's Barney, but it might well be Baudelaire, or Flaubert to his mistress Louise Colet (who may have posed for the ultimate commodification of Sappho, Pradier's much reproduced statue). However, beyond this common coin about the masculinity of the sapphic female, there remains a glaring difference: Baudelaire's lesbians are cast off, abandoned to their solitary fate, whereas Barney and Vivien portray a society in which, "in [their] perversity cunningly infertile," Psappha's followers *choose* to ignore the other world. And this must at least partially explain the total avoidance of their work in subsequent Sapphic commentary and fictions.

As is so often the case in literary history, we now refer to this movement with a label, "Sapho 1900," coined after the fact (in 1951) and, perhaps inevitably, by a man. On the surface, André Billy's often cited phrase— "Sapho 1900, Sapho cent pour cent" (227)—seems to translate admiration for these writers who are somehow more Sappho than Sappho. However, this illusion quickly disappears. Like Jean-Desthieux, Billy tries to show that the writers really were "Sapho 0%," because they never understood "the other Sapho, the one from Lesbos" at all. His version of the two-Sappho theory exposes Vivien's rewriting of Sappho's biography, only to undo it in the hope of convincing readers that the traditional life story hidden between the lines of Vivien's text is the true story: (1) "She was portrayed as [*on se la représente*] tall and beautiful, when she was short, ugly, and hairy" (to my knowledge the "hairy" is entirely Billy's invention). (2) "She undoubtedly had little taste for men, but that was because the war had emptied Lesbos of almost all its male population" (a second detail of Billy's invention, undoubtedly inspired by his recent experience of World War II France). (3) "To completely distinguish her from the French Sapho, late in life she fell in love with a young sailor Phaon." Billy's conclusion: "sapphisme" should be replaced by "vivienisme" because Sappho had nothing to do with "sisterly love" (227). I dwell at some length on this critique because Billy succeeded in making his name inseparable from "Sapho 1900," and also because his volume teaches an important lesson about the impossibility of an alliance between sapphic Sapphism and nationalism.

Among the effects of the Second World War on the French publishing industry was the birth of an important series, *Histoire de la vie littéraire,* published just after the war at Tallandier. According to one of its contributors, the series was conceived during a meeting on a train in occupied France between the director of Tallandier (shortly before his arrest and deportation by the Germans) and the author, Billy. Billy's enormously influential *L'époque 1900* was thus written both as a personal act of homage to a fellow intellectual who had died for France, and a nationalistic attempt to inspire his war-torn nation by recreating the period just before the world wars that had interrupted the normal development of its letters.

Nearly at the middle of this long volume is a chapter, "Les Femmes de lettres," mainly devoted to the various ways in which *bas bleu* women of the age had been socially and sexually threatening. The "Sapho 1900" section occurs near the end of this chapter, at the dead center of Billy's study. This Sapphic movement is the major force in what Billy calls "the *explosion* of feminine literature in 1900," an explosion, he tells us, "preceded at the end of 1897 by an *explosion* of feminine journalism," a newspaper, *La Fronde,* run entirely by women (230, my emphasis). Billy's tone in all of this remains elusive, but in a book as antiwar, as opposed to invasion of French national territory as this one, to characterize the sapphic-Sapphic French tradition as an "explosion," a "Fronde" (civil war), is to indicate a critical stance. Just as the original Fronde briefly threatened the smooth succession of the French monarchy—Madeleine de Scudéry, the French Sapho of that day, composed the first full-scale modern biography of Sappho as a parable of women's involvement in that antinationalistic explosion—so the turn-of-the-century uprising menaced the orderly functioning of French domestic life. Billy dwells throughout his alleged chronicle of female literary activities on the authors' broken marriages, rejections of men—"The first man who approached her left her frozen; the first woman set her on fire," he says of Lucie Delarue-Mardrus (225)—and their attempts at seducing often unwilling women.

Then, at the end, order returns. The last section is devoted to the creation of a female literary academy (actually provided for in the will of Billy's ersatz Sappho, Vivien) and a prize for women's literature (now the *prix Femina*). At first, the jury met to deliberate in a "modest room" at the headquarters of the magazine sponsoring the prize. But they were soon transferred to less spartan surroundings, "at the home of Mme. Alphonse Daudet, severe guardian of morals and whose cuisine was excellent" (233). So the sapphic civil war ends in bourgeois respectability. This academy, far from maintaining the marginality of Sappho's original circle or of Vivien's society, meets at the home of a woman known only by the name of her husband (author of the most celebrated, and decidedly antisapphic, Sapphic myth of modern times), protector both of traditional moral values and *cuisine bourgeoise*. "Sapho 1900" finally became no longer one hundred per cent Sappho but one hundred per cent French: Vivien's inheritors, according to Billy, were most concerned with what they ate.

Billy's 1951 volume falls outside the end point set for my study, but there is never a clearer indication of the nationalistic rejection of literary sapphism, even when, as is the case with the French tradition that extends from Baudelaire to Barney, it was the major contribution of its national scholarly-literary school to modern Sappho commentary. To resist the association of a sapphic Sappho with Frenchness, Billy is prepared to go against the better judgment of most of France's finest Hellenists and to collaborate, albeit unwittingly, with the Germans who had driven him to his nationalistic critical enterprise in the first place.

As I said, Billy's reading is typical of what has been until recently the official vision of "Sapho 1900," dismissing this definition of Sapphism as a non-French fantasy of its foreign-born originators. The scholarly rejection of their sapphic commentary and fictions was echoed, in the early decades of the twentieth century, in a number of strange Sapphic novels that are either violently antilesbian or that sensationalize, in a manner reminiscent of the young literary lions of the 1840s, lesbianism via Sappho. At this juncture, I should repeat the warning I gave myself when discussing the Sapphic production of that decade: literary sapphism must always be distinguished from an actual historical phenomenon. In this case, the most violent literary response to the sapphic Sappho appeared in 1901, before any of the "Sapho 1900" production devoted to the muse of Mytilene. Should a novel like Faure's *La Dernière Journée de Sapphô* be seen as a forerunner of what Boswell calls the most "vehement intolerance" of homosexuality in Western history in the early decades of the twentieth century (23)?[98] Is it instead a backlash against decadent fictions of lesbianism, especially Louÿs's, formulated in the very language of decadence? Or should it be considered above all a continuation, in the manner of Verlaine, of the condemnation of sapphism in Baudelaire?

For *La Dernière Journée de Sapphô* is, ideologically and literarily, a bizarre hybrid indeed. Gabriel Faure—Barrès protégé and, like Mérimée before him, Inspecteur Général des Monuments Historiques—is an aberration in Baudelairean terms, a decadent obsessed with the lesbian not purely as a literary force but also in historical actuality. He seems a disciple of Huysmans, because he combines an overtly Catholic ideological stance with the excessively petrified imagistic surface of late decadence. Faure breaks, however, with the decadent position invented by Baudelaire and maintained by such members of the English school as Symonds and Swinburne, whereby Sappho is enshrined as poet-double and patroness of modernity: he uses the muse of Mytilene to legitimate a violent attack on female same-sex love. Faure obviously borrows his Sapphic plot, even to his choice of opening scenes, from Richepin's 1884 volume, the first openly sapphic French Sapphic novel. Despite the "grande amoureuse" setting with which he surrounds Sappho, however, Richepin maintains an antisensationalistic stance on lesbianism: "It's not our place either to blame or to defend Sapphô" (25), whereas Faure's intentions are obviously more inflammatory.

No more ornate fin-de-siècle setting was ever imagined for Sappho; Faure piles on exoticism in the smallest details, encrusting his novelistic surface like a Klimt or a pre-Raphaelite canvas.[99] Sapphô begins her last day under "scarlet draperies" in a bed so "vast" that "several bodies can stretch out on it in comfort in every direction" (31): the most remarkable elements of her interior decoration include "candelabra" in the shape of "naked ephebes" and the "colonnades" of that truly Sadean bed, "sculptures of oversized male organs [*des sexes démesurés*]" (32). She dresses in a series of tunics, the first of which has "three openings [which] leave naked points where Sapphô desires lips to linger" (43). She's outfitting herself for the annual celebration of Aphrodite, for which she is to recite her "last work," an "Ode to Aphrodite," as a prelude to the festival's opening ritual, the deflowering of six Lesbian virgins. This notion inspires an entire chapter, pushing Faure to such phantasmatic heights as a lengthy description of their puberty, culminating in the declaration, "beneath the nascent down is visible the plump flesh of a young quail" (83).

This phantasmagoria of virginity and its loss signals the redefinition of Sapphism. While Sapphô is reciting her ode, she spots Phaon in the crowd with another woman; she breaks down and runs home. This is her conversion experience: from a bisexual who has not given up women for Phaon, she becomes strictly a one-man woman. No one has ever put what has been seen as Ovid's message more clearly: "the smallest caress [from Phaon] would be worth entire days of debauchery [*luxure*]" (114). Faure's choice of "luxure," the religious designation for sins of the flesh, is no accident: as he admits in his preface, he "could be reproached with having made [Sapphô] too modern, too repentant, I don't dare say too Christian" (21–22). For Faure, last of the male Sapphic decadents, modernity is no longer the French celebration of marginality, but a modernity associated in Sappho commentary only with the German Christianizing tradition.

A female Saint Anthony, Faure's Sapphô has to prove her conversion by resisting temptation after temptation: one of the virgins of the year tries to force her favors on her, as does her brother's lover, the courtesan Rhodope, for whom Sapphô had written fr. 31, but she rejects women one and all (107, 128).[100] The conversion from sapphism culminates in an extended dream sequence: Sapphô is in a forest hoping Phaon will come to her, but instead her beloved women appear and she rejects them one after the other, until they arrive in a crowd and file by two by two, kissing each other, displaying their charms, offering her their bodies. When she recognizes them as her "disciples whom she had taken as her lovers," they all join hands and "begin dancing around her in a frenetic round" (193, 195). The dream ends "in a blast of savage voluptuousness," when "bodies come together, are united, interpenetrate, become confused. It became a strange mêlée of faces, of limbs, and of flesh" (197). Sapphô awakens in horror, overcome by this overwhelming, stifling female homosexuality. She then realizes that conversion is not enough: the real sin of her sapphism was to have made disciples. She had taught other women "to ignore love" (defined by Phaon as the total submission of woman to man: "if [man] could, he would destroy even [woman's] ability to think . . ." [174]). She had preached a sexual revolution: "to couple like animals was vulgar and ugly; each sex should find happiness within itself. Women above all, until then slaves and submitted to man's whim, should revolt, no longer belong to a master, and procure themselves for each other every pleasurable sensation" (115).

La Dernière Journée de Sapphô is a first novel. It is possible that this elaborate homophobic outpouring reflects simply the fear of impotence of the writer coming of age in the midst of what Billy terms a female literary "explosion." However, I find this explanation insufficient to account for the virulence of Faure's homophobia. Rather than the beginning of a literature that responds to reality, however, I see this as another moment when fictions of Sappho and fictions of the lesbian diverge. I would situate Faure at the end of a literature that features Sappho as representative of the lesbian threat, less the threat to weaken the nation by an elected sterility, but the threat of seducing ever greater numbers of women away from the love of men. The earliest example of this use of Sappho in France, to my knowledge, is Parny's 1778 "La Journée champêtre," in which the general consideration of homosexuality in the ancient world ends with an exorcism of sapphism:

> Do you hear me, priestesses of Lesbos,
> You renascent disciples of Sapho?
> ....
> Don't look for new sensual delights.
> It's for us that [nature's] hand made you beautiful.
>   (113–14)

Testimonies like Parny's to the concern about "de Sapho disciples renaissantes" have less to do with an actual lesbian presence—they in fact disappear once "Sapho 1900" comes into existence; thereafter, there will be antilesbian literature but none focused on Sappho—than with the development of the erudite theory of Sappho as head of a school for girls. This theory, which the philologists develop in an attempt to revirginize Sappho after the rise of the courtesan fiction, actually makes matters worse, since it is constructed on the premise that Sappho had the opportunity to make disciples, to convert others away from heterosexuality. In the history of Sapphic fictions, Faure's novel is a violent last attempt to strike a blow against Sapphic pedagogy.

In this same history, *La Dernière Journée de Sapphô* is also a beginning: it is the first sign that Sapphic commentary is aware of the medical literature on homosexuality that had grown more abundant in the final decades of the nineteenth century. Thus, when Faure declares in his preface "there is no subject more in fashion, for the last twenty years, than vices against nature" (13), he has in mind the medical "mode" that was just succeeding in implanting the vocabulary of "homosexuality." From this literature, Faure has absorbed only the sense that all lesbians are sick creatures—"the misfunctioning [*détraquées*], neurotics, and all those consumed by hysteria"—from whom Sapphô must be distinguished, since "she was not a sick person." The proof of this? She loved men and so belonged to the class of healthy, "real" women: "there is no real woman who prefers the insipid caresses of another woman to the virile embrace of a man" (16, 20). Under various guises, this same reasoning reappears in all Sapphic fictions that respond to the medical commentary on homosexuality: perhaps there are true lesbians, "depraved" women, but Sappho was not such a mental case. Her biography is refictionalized in an implicit demonstration of the limits of overly complicated medical reasoning on female hysteria and female homosexuality (authors like Faure always link lesbianism to hysteria), and in an explicit demonstration that sapphism has concrete causes and can be stopped with a commonsense approach.

This is certainly the message of Maurice Morel's *Sappho de Lesbos*. Despite its publication in 1903, in the thick of "Sapho 1900" activity, the novel is unmarked by the Barney-Vivien revisions. It is antilesbian in the manner of Faure, although without his violence, because it insists on the pedagogical problem of lesbianism, on the contamination that takes place in a lesbian circle. Sappho is the lone female conspirator in a plot against the dictator Myrsilos. She obtains an interview with him and he propositions her, whereupon she murders him and becomes, almost by accident, a political heroine. But not for long. On her wedding night, the beloved girl who has betrayed her, Cléis, is poisoned by another of Sappho's virgins who had been scorned by the new bridegroom. The young widower, aware of Sappho's passion for the victim, accuses the political assassin of a second murder. In despair, Sappho leaps to her death and out of the sad, sordid life in her sapphic community.

The power of pedagogy and the danger of immoral teaching are subjects that must have been dear to Morel's heart. A lycée professor in Grenoble, he authored a number of works for children, among them, *Violettes et primavères, poésies enfantines; Babette à Paris;* and *Le Mariage du Petit Poucet*. He carries over into *Sappho de Lesbos,* his only work for an adult public, a simplistic vision of character formation: Sappho is married very young to the wealthy Cercolas because of her mother's desire to get her out of their "abject poverty." However, the rich husband is "fat and greasy," so his virginal bride is "disgusted" by men (20). After his death,

291

she refuses all suitors: "Cercolas had disgusted her forever with virile caresses" (27). Despite her desire, she had been unable to have a child since her husband was too old, so she "gradually diverted her affections toward other objects" (28). For the woman afraid of male brutality, sapphism is only a substitute for maternal affection.

The most extreme of these efforts to make Sappho a "real" woman—that is, a down-to-earth heroine, whose hard life makes her worthy of compassion—with nothing in common with those "depraved" clinical cases is Romilly's 1931 novel *Sapphô: La Passionnante—La Passionnée.*[101] Despite the fact that, by this time, it was impossible to ignore the European lesbian community—probably never more visible than in the 1920s and 1930s—Romilly's text for the most part still responds only to medical commentaries, and then only in an effort to find a commonsense alternative to the theories of sapphism proposed by the medical community. His Sapphô is above all a great humanitarian, a defender of the common man against injustice: the opening scene features her ordering one of her father's slaves to give shelter to an old woman being stoned by a mob accusing her of sorcery (13). Nearly a sixth of the novel is devoted to her childhood, to establish her natural innocence and goodness before any piece of his theory is presented. Then, one day Sapphô is in the country, marveling at nature, when she "began to feel herself a bit different from other girls; one would have taken her at times for a very pretty young boy" (30). Just at this moment of "the awakening of her sensuality," Sapphô is witness to the brutal rape and attempted murder of a young virgin just her age: "An incommensurable disgust remained with Sapphô so that for a long time she was repulsed by every strange man" (30–31). From this experience, she derives her definition of heterosexuality: "abjection, anxiety, painful suffering." Then, when she is a bit older, Alcée tries to rape her, and "that incident strengthened the disgust that Sapphô had for all men" (42).

Despite this heavy dose of male brutality, Sapphô simply remains asexual until the day when—orphaned, her faithful slaves dead, her brothers exiled or off chasing courtesans—she is actively pursued by Eranna (84). She gathers a group of young girls around her to form a timidly lesbian enclave, the very presence of which threatens the rowdy, peasant macho types, especially their leader Phaon, who breaks into the compound and tries to seduce Sapphô. She has him driven away by her slaves, but he returns to take revenge with a crowd of fellow ruffians. They rape all the young women, and are only driven off by the priests of Apollo.

Then, Eranna dies of "exhaustion" from too much sapphic passion and, after her funeral, Sapphô dreams that Aphrodite warns her that she will "punish" her for having disregarded "fertility" (120). The goddess elects Phaon as her agent. It is as if Romilly had sensed that he was the last of a dying breed of Sapphic authors, for he heaps the most numerous and the most graphic punishments yet on Sapphô, taking revenge on the ultimate lesbian *femme fatale* in the name of Phaon—and of all the young men who, like Daudet's sons, real and imaginary, felt themselves to have suffered humiliation at the hands of sapphic women.[102] Her degradation goes on and on, culminating in an extended scene during which, tricked by Phaon into a nocturnal rendezvous, he has her stripped naked and displayed as entertainment for his numerous guests lounging around during a banquet. Phaon then forces her to watch while he and his favorite courtesan stage a live sex show. The mutual display ends in a prolonged cat fight, with Sapphô and the courtesan rolling around on the floor clawing at each other. Not since the eighteenth century had Sappho sunk so far into pulp fiction.

The difference here is that while in the eighteenth century, the ludicrous scenarios of a D'Auvigny or a Lantier were invented to make Sappho alone more accessible to a broad public, Romilly's novel is allegedly dedicated to winning comprehension for female homosexuals in general. To this end, he appends a curious afterword with the most blatantly normalizing explanation of sapphism ever set in opposition to theories of medical morbidity:

> In our contemporary Europe, where there are now five women for every man and where polygamy is forbidden, we live in extreme imbalance. And shouldn't the legislator ask himself if female homosexuality, so widespread today (London, Berlin, Paris, New York) and, even though to a lesser degree, male homosexuality, are not natural phenomena? (218)

Thus, for the only time since "Sapho 1900," Sappho is linked to modern female homosexuality. And, despite the absurd context in which it is developed, Romilly's thesis gains credence, in France at least: Larnac and Salmon speak of "Sappho's repulsion for the male sex" as a given and pronounce this "a question that should tempt psychiatrists" (55). This, then, seems to have been the native French view of Sapphism between the wars, before the outburst of nationalism generated by World War II would push a commentator like Billy to resurrect the traditional scenario of German Hellenists, his military enemies but his partners in nationalism: the French commonsense Sapphic response to psychoanalysis at the turn of the century has, by the 1930s, reversed the medical position to portray sapphism as a "natural phenomenon," either a recoiling from scenes of male brutality or a practical solution to demographic imbalance.

But the story is not quite over yet. The lesbian Sappho makes a final appearance in French fiction, this time generated from within the same international sapphic community for whose citizens Romilly sought to obtain naturalization. Marguerite Yourcenar has always controlled the transmission of her biography: she has not, for example, provided the evidence to corroborate Faderman's claim that, at the time of her literary initiation, she frequented Natalie Clifford Barney's rue Jacob salon (370).[103] However, Yourcenar herself links her prose poem (her designation), "Sappho ou le suicide" (from the 1936 collection *Feux*), "to that international world of pleasure from between the wars" (*Oeuvres*, 1044), and her fiction defines that pleasure as sapphic. Yourcenar's "Sappho" is a rarity in the French tradition, the only fiction, with Daudet's, to translate the story of the muse of Mytilene into a contemporary setting.

No longer poet, Yourcenar's modern Sappho is an "acrobat," more precisely a trapeze artist, "because the particular form of her lungs obliges her to choose an occupation that is exercised in mid-air" (*Oeuvres*, 1125). Like her most recent French precursors, she becomes sapphic when, "disgusted" by all manifestations of "virility," she decides that "only the body of young girls is soft enough" (1126). Any resemblance to contemporary male Sapphic fictions ends at this point: the Sapphic affinity here—as Yourcenar hints when she describes her story as "related to Shakespeare's comedies rather than to Greek themes" (1044)—is with that Anglo-French tradition that formed before the war around Vivien and Barney. Rather than try to justify her sapphism, as male writers do, Yourcenar shares the "Sapho 1900" need to explain the existence of the sapphic infractions: Phaon and the suicidal leap. Perhaps in homage to the English origin of that Sapphic community, Yourcenar suggests that the English are the modern Greeks and that an insular heritage is basic to sapphism and the source of sapphic attraction: Phaon is half-Greek, half-English, Sappho and the beloved girl Atthys are one or the other.[104]

Yourcenar explains what Baudelaire terms Sappho's "blasphemy" against the "cult" as the result of an androgynous proximity: Phaon's "flexible and smooth body is almost a woman's body" (1132); Sappho pursues him because "she finds in his features certain characteristics formerly loved in the young girl who has taken flight" (1130). The fascination endures until the young man, realizing the origin of his power, "transvests" himself in a "peignoir" that had belonged to his female double. Once Phaon displays himself thus "à l'aise dans le travesti," comfortable both with his transvestism and with the travesty of this passion, he "is no more than a substitute" for the missing Atthys. Sappho flees in horror "this specter of the flesh" and "the ridicule of having been able to believe that a young man existed" (1132). This, then, is the explanation Yourcenar proposes for the suicide: "this being, tired of being only half-woman [*cet être fatigué de n'être qu'à demi femme*]" is driven to fling herself from the heights of her art by the realization that she could have been tricked by resemblances into believing that the feminine young male body could be female enough to be a standard of beauty, female enough to replace the female missing in her. "[All women] are madly in love with themselves, their own body being ordinarily the only form in which they consent to find beauty. . . . Sappho adores bitterly in her companions that which she wasn't" (1127).

Yourcenar refers the reader to Shakespeare's comedies, even though there is nothing comic about this *chassé-croisé* of transvested androgyny. Yourcenar also insists on the designation "prose poem" (readers would probably spontaneously choose "short story"), which may hide a more useful reference. Yourcenar's most impressive innovation in the Sapphic plot concerns the suicide, which her Sappho miscarries. It begins in a recognizable burst of élan: "Sappho plunges, her arms open as if to embrace half the infinite" (1133). "But those who fail their lives run the risk of also failing their suicide." In her fall, she hits a lamp which throws her back into the net: "And soon the workmen will have to stretch out on the sand the body of pale marble, streaming with sweat like a drowned woman with sea water" (1133). Sappho the acrobat cannot live up to the example of the poet whose pulmonary disposition she shares; all they have in common is the sand on which they are both laid out. The ex-circus attraction will have to carry on, and a fictional model exists that allows us to predict her future.

"Prose poem" sends us back to the poet who both put the genre on the literary map and made the androgynous Sappho the heroine of modernity. In the dedication of Baudelaire's 1869 volume of prose poems, *Le Spleen de Paris,* to his "dear friend" and fellow Sapphic collaborator, Arsène Houssaye, the author explains why this form is particularly suited to "the painting of modern life" (ed. Le Dantec, 229). In one of these scenes of modernity, "Le Vieux Saltimbanque," Baudelaire presents another in the series of marginal figures who, like the *flâneur,* like the lesbian, are doubles for his poet-narrator. Passing by a seedy street fair, as run-down as Yourcenar's provincial circuses, the poet encounters the most "marginal" (*exilé*) of all these pitifully marginal performers, an old acrobat (*saltimbanque*). His career over, he stands there "mute and immobile," "his destiny decided" (248). At this vision, the strolling poet is seized with "hysteria"; in trying to explain his reaction, he comes to this conclusion:

> I have just seen the image of the old man of letters who has outlived the generation for which he was the brilliant entertainer; of the old poet without friends, without family, without children, degraded by his misery and by the public's ingratitude, and in whose shack the forgetful world no longer wants to enter! (249)

And so it is with his future female double, Yourcenar's acrobat Sappho. She who had been the "brilliant entertainer" of a generation "outlives" her public and is not even able to "beat the suicidal record" (*Oeuvres,* 1135) of her Greek precursor. She is condemned to live on, even though, like Baudelaire's acrobat, writers no longer see her as their double. Sappho's failed suicide seems to signify the end of her powerful reign as heroine of modernism: the public no longer seeks amusement in her theater. In one way, Yourcenar was obviously correct, for the decadent Sappho would not survive the Second World War.[105] Yourcenar herself would never return to what she terms the "strained and ornate" style of *Feux,* which she relates to "expressionism" (1047). At the same time as she developed her new style, the petrified, sparse (more Sapphic) neoclassicism of her masterpieces, she replaced Sappho, no longer in vogue (hers is, in fact, the last major French Sapphic fiction) with other figures from antiquity, notably that devout practitioner of the cult of Winckelmannian beauty and erotic *pederastia,* the emperor Hadrian.

But this is to simplify both Yourcenar's chronology and her Sapphic politics. As she reveals in her "Carnets de notes," the conception of the *Mémoires d'Hadrien* goes back to the more sapphic years 1924–29; she was at work on it again in 1934–37, the period of *Feux*'s composition. The first fragments that remain in the novel's definitive version were written in 1937, shortly after *Feux*'s publication (*Hadrien,* 321, 323). These final fragments were composed in New Haven, Connecticut, a fact important only as an oblique signal of *Hadrien*'s political placement. I chose to end this study in 1937, in order to include the French Sapphic scholarship of that year, to include *Feux,* and to include the beginning of Yourcenar's career in America: both her presence here and the novel that would eventually grow out of the research and writing done in the Yale library in 1937 are the most forceful indications of a reaction, on the part of a member of the French Sapphic tradition, to the role reserved for the doctrine of *pederastia* in the nationalistic German ideology that fueled World War II. This is not to say that the cast of characters I have discussed here was implicated in those events: Wilamowitz, for example, died in 1931 (having survived his most powerful adversary, Croiset, dead since 1923).[106] However, the theories of the German Hellenists played their most influential role only after the deaths of their initiators. I also chose to conclude in 1937 in order to avoid dealing more directly with the uses made during the war of the German philological tradition, with its timely blend of nationalism, patriotism, and militarism, founded on the cult of the perfect male body.

Yourcenar says of *Feux* that it was, along with the exploration of fascism in the 1932 *Denier du rêve,* the first of her fictions marked by "the images of the violence and the political disarray of the period" (*Oeuvres,* xix). Her own closest contact with this political violence takes place during her sojourn in Nazi-occupied Vienna late in 1938. She succeeds in leaving Europe a few months later, and in November 1939 it is in New York that she mourns the fall of Paris, "what seemed the definitive end of a world" (xxi). The literary fruit of her self-exile[107] from Nazi-occupied Europe is the novel whose beginnings are contemporaneous with "Sappho ou le suicide." In the *Mémoires d'Hadrien,* Yourcenar invades the territory of philology, to fictionalize no longer Orphic sapphism but *pederastia:* the emperor whose life she so painstakingly reconstructs takes the cult of the perfect young male body and of ideal male pedagogical-erotic friendship to what may well be its highest development. Yourcenar recounts every detail of Hadrian's ideal love for Antinous in a manner that would surely have won the approval of Welcker and his followers. However, she uses the eulogy of *pederastia* to subvert the ideology of conquering nationalism and violent militarism that it had previously been made to serve. She portrays the founder of the cult of Antinous as a spokesman for peace: the *Mémoires d'Hadrien* is a profoundly antimilitaristic novel, a monument — completed after "what seemed the definitive end of a world" — to the need to preserve civilization, Yourcenar's homage to the emperor who tries to break the bond between nationalism and xenophobia, between the empire and the narrow definition of its civilizing mission as the automatic impulse to replace Other (barbarian) with Same (Neo-Greek or Roman).

It is generally considered that this magnificent novel—a meditation on the rise and fall of empires composed far from the limits of the French nation[108] —was the cornerstone of Yourcenar's election to the French Academy in 1980. Her election ended over two centuries of exclusive male control over this ruling body of the French republic of letters. Women were first proposed for membership in the original French Sapphic decade, the 1660s; we do not know the grounds on which they were excluded, only that the list of those rejected was headed by Madeleine de Scudéry, who was awarded instead the Academy's first prize for eloquence in 1670. The French Sapho was widely regarded as the most learned woman of her day. Her reputation was undoubtedly based in large part on the first modern biography of Sappho, her "Story of Sapho," the scope and originality of whose erudition her contemporaries, previously totally deprived of knowledge of the muse of Mytilene, were better able to recognize than today's readers. In a sense, therefore, Yourcenar's election repairs a rift in the Sapphic tradition.

Yourcenar's last work published prior to her election is *La Couronne et la lyre* (1979), a volume of her translations of Greek poets that is just the type of text that might have helped pave the way for her admission to the Academy. (The Greeks were, long before their philological promotion in Germany, the center of French neoclassicism, and classicism has always been promoted as the center of the French tradition.) Included in the volume are a number of Sappho's poems, in free translations that convey more successfully than any others in French the sparse evocative economy of Sappho's verse.[109] Yourcenar also includes a brief biography of Sappho, a text remarkable for the short shrift it gives most of the Sapphic myths by now familiar to my readers. Yourcenar also threatens to start a new myth to replace some of those she debunks. Already at the beginning of her involvement with Sappho, in the opening scene of "Sappho ou le suicide," she reveals her fascination with the aging Sappho. In *La Couronne et la lyre*, Yourcenar dwells with greatest insistence on a Sappho impossible as long as Ovid's authority was accepted: a poet who lived to old age, a poet who gives us "an unglamorized image . . . of her physical degeneration that is probably unique in feminine literature," even a poet "unsettling" because of her "almost maniacal expression of the frustrated desire of an old woman or a woman who appears old" (69).

But I refuse to try from this to predict the future course of Sapphic fictions. I will only add in conclusion that many of the translations in *La Couronne et la lyre* date from 1942: Yourcenar's portrait of the aging poet "maniacally" voicing the desire that has not deserted her even in old age could have been an attempt to "unsettle" the German theoreticians who had sought to decree the chastity of the original woman writer. I will also add that Yourcenar's most controversial translation decision is surely her suppression of the threatening female signature in fr. 31 (75). She also elects a male object of desire in the sexually ambiguous weaving fragment about the poet's passion for "a child" (LP 102). These decisions suggest a variety of interpretations ranging from an attempt to undermine readings based on easy assumptions about the relation between the sex of an author and the narrator's gender, to a desire to consign Sapphic sexuality to indeterminancy, as she clearly hopes to have consigned her own. With her thoroughly undecidable fiction of Sappho, Yourcenar forces us, in the end as in the beginning, to remember that all Sapphic speculation has its roots in Sappho's own rejection of the readerly desire for unambiguous erotic resolution.

Epilogue

The grammarian Didymus wrote four thousand books. . . . The
list includes treatises in which he discusses the birthplace of
Homer, the true mother of Aeneas . . . whether Sappho was a
prostitute, and other questions the answers to which you ought to
forget if you knew them. And then people complain that life is
short.

— Seneca,
Letters to Lucilius

Mother, whore, virgin, *émigrée*—it's true that, as Seneca already
knew, we don't really need to know the answers to certain questions. Yet
somehow we, or at least some of us, for century after century continue to
want to know. I wish I were capable of the optimism that allowed Edith
Mora to end her 1966 study of Sappho with the dual proclamation that
"Sappho's legendary period" had ended with Bascoul's 1911 study of
Sapphic chastity, and that "the era of her truth" had "finally" arrived. By
this she hastened to add that she did not mean to imply a belief in a perfect
reading, uncolored by the prejudices of the period in which it was
formulated, but rather that "we" were now looking for "the truth" about
Sappho "only in her verse, in what has come down to us of her corpus"
(203).

The Algerian Bascoul, writing, as it were, on the fringes of the empire,
may have believed that chastity would reign forever, whereas the theory's
energy was in fact nearly spent: when Reinach in 1911 and Wilamowitz in
1913 showed a united front against sapphism just before their nations
faced off in military conflict, they also sounded the last hurrah of Sapphic
dispassionateness. In France and in Germany, the chastity theory can be
counted among the casualties of the Great War. Philological defenses of
pederastia that use Sappho as a point of departure also disappear after the
war. This joint disappearance seems to confirm that Welcker had only
decreed Sappho's purity in order to protect the nationalistic ideological

301

territory he had reserved for male homosexuality, and also to suggest that the propagandists of ideal love had never desired to establish a connection to any actual homoerotic manifestations. (At no time is the German homosexual movement more active and more open, at no time does it generate more engagé literature, than between the wars, just when German defenses of *pederastia* cease.)

A final scholarly casualty of the Great War is the absolute German control over Sappho commentary. Beginning in the 1920s with Edmonds's *Lyra Graeca* (1922) and Lobel's *Sapphous Melè* (1923), continuing in the 1930s with Bowra's *Greek Lyric Poetry* (1936), and culminating in the joint 1955 publications, Lobel and Page's *Poetarum Lesbiorum Fragmenta* and Page's *Sappho and Alcaeus,* English scholars echo their nation's military victories by conquering the territory over which German reign had been uncontested since 1733. In the beginning (Edmonds, Bowra), the English still pay homage to their German precursors and continue to transmit the chastity doctrine embroidered with native flourishes. Only after World War II do Lobel and Page proclaim the coming of age of English scholarship and its independence from German influence. However, all of this means simply a changing of the guard rather than the beginning of the age of "truth." I will not return to Edmonds's flower-child Sappho, but I will go beyond my terminus ad quem in order to conclude with the major characteristics of the portrait of Sappho presented in what are still today the standard reference works.

C. M. Bowra is responsible for the entry on Sappho in the first edition of the *Oxford Classical Dictionary* (1949), an entry still reprinted verbatim in the edition available for consultation in the library in which I often did research for this study, that of Princeton's Classics department. This standard reference work has by now served as the basis for the received ideas of Sapphism shared by several generations of students all over the world. This account is most remarkable for its erasure of every hint of controversy. The only old chestnut debunked by Bowra is the suicide for love of Phaon; many elements of extremely dubious origin go into his portrait of Sappho as model working mother and solid citizen. He leads off, amazingly enough, with a domestication of Barthélemy's theory: "as a child, no doubt owing to political troubles, she went into exile in Sicily," a variant that clears Sappho of any meddling in the male preserve of politics and makes her only an innocent victim of war's turmoil, like the displaced in the post-World War II Europe of the time of the *Oxford Classical Dictionary's* first edition. Sedition would be out of character indeed for this paragon of bourgeois respectability: Sappho was married, had a child, kept her wayward brother in line, and still—a precursor of today's superwoman—found the time to run a girls' school, "wr[ite] poems about [her students] and celebrate their marriages with songs." The "Ode to Aphrodite" is either part of this production, "written as a hymn for her companions," or must be qualified as "strictly personal to herself" (whatever that is supposed to mean in this rigorously asexual context). Fragment 31, in an exact replication of Wilamowitz's reading, is proclaimed a poem "inspired by seeing [an unnamed girl] next to her bridegroom," a poem which "shows the strength of Sappho's feelings for her." This is the clearest reference to sapphism in Bowra's entry, but it is hard to imagine that it could be interpreted very easily as such by the individual who would turn to the volume for an initiation to Sappho. The *Oxford Classical Dictionary's* crowning homage to philology is Bowra's bibliography, with *Sappho und Simonides* as its lead entry, thereby guaranteeing that English Hellenists would be kinder to German prestige than their country's political leaders: long after the interpretive tradition founded by Welcker at the dawn of the nineteenth century and modern German nationalism actually lost its credibility, its authority still lives on in the standard manual of the national school that dethroned it.[1]

It is unlikely that someone who relied on Bowra's entry would then consult either the edition of Sappho now considered standard, Lobel and Page's *Poetarum Lesbiorum Fragmenta,* or the Sappho commentary that has replaced Wilamowitz's reading as the basic reference for specialists, Page's *Sappho and Alcaeus* (both 1955 and therefore monuments to the end, after World War II, of one hundred and fifty years of German philology's domination of Sappho studies). However, imagine the bewilderment of the reader who would compare these products of the Oxford school's erudition: Lobel and Page strive as energetically to demolish Wilamowitz's reputation as German philology's collaborator Bowra does to buttress it. For example, the overwhelming impression produced by Page's long essay, "The Contents and Character of Sappho's Poetry" (in *Sappho and Alcaeus,* always the first reference cited by Hellenists today), is of a war not yet over, of a national tradition anxious to make certain that it has stamped out every trace of the precursor's infiltration, so that its own authority can be absolute.

> It is obvious to all who read what has been written about
> Sappho in the last century, and particularly in the last
> half-century, that appreciation of the quality of her art and
> judgement of her sentiments has often been distorted by
> prejudiced opinions about her social background and moral
> character. (110)[2]

Page thus opens his second paragraph with sentiments with which I could not be more in agreement. After this, the reader expects commentary focused on "the quality of [Sappho's] art and judgement of her sentiments." However, the following sentence sets matters straight. "The prestige of Wilamowitz gave new and lasting dignity to the old theory that Sappho was a paragon of moral and social virtues. . . ." Page takes it from there to spend the better part of his alleged account of Sappho's poetry (twenty of thirty-five pages) trying to demolish the theories behind which Wilamowitz had thrown all the weight of his "prestige" (Sappho's "virgin purity" [144], Sappho as "principal of a [girl's] academy" [111], Sappho as patroness of marriage). For one after another of the cherished notions of the chastity-*pederastia* school, he offers this rebuttal: "the theory finds no support whatever in anything worthy of the name of fact" (111).

When Page finally gets around to spelling out that in the name of which he so scornfully dismisses the pet theories of the man whose place he hopes to take, "what *is* in evidence in Sappho's poetry" (130), his theory seems somehow slight and slightly inappropriate, a more apt description of the rococo Sapho of Billardon de Sauvigny than the author of the corpus modern scholarship (most recently that of Lobel and Page) had made available: "The principal themes of Sappho's poetry, so far as it is known to us, are her loves and hatreds; the ephemeral pleasures and pains of an idle but graceful society" (133). His reading remains a bit thin, most remarkable for its own new nationalism. As vehemently as Page strikes down Wilamowitz, just as forcefully does he build up his English precursors, in particular Colonel Mure and John Addington Symonds. Indeed, his promotion of Symonds—especially in view of the fact that Symonds wrote relatively little on Sappho in comparison with the major Sappho scholars of his century—is so flagrantly out of line with common scholarly practice that it begs explanation: he cites verbatim and without any interruption nearly three of the five pages Symonds devotes to Sappho in his 1873 *Studies of Greek Poets,* a lengthy quotation in any context, but inordinately so in a thirty-five-page essay. It is as if Page is determined to make readers confront an authority long hidden away, one about to be swallowed up in the oblivion to which he says scholarly texts more than a half-century old are consigned. At the same time, he is resurrecting a link in the English scholarly tradition, one that fleshes it out in a period during which it was not especially powerful, a move essential to his project of assuming the German succession.

The signature of the English school's portrayal of Sappho, to which both this essay and Page's commentary on individual poems provide ample testimony, is the accent it places on Sappho's sangfroid, her poetic stiff upper lip. Page is the foremost authority promoting what seems so far to be enshrined as the dominant twentieth-century view of Sappho, Sappho as genius of "dipassionate[ness]" (*Sappho and Alcaeus,* 18), rather than as primal voice of female passion. This theory provides the clearest indication of why the scholars who unseated the Germans were also worthy heirs to their sublimating chastity, united with them against the hot-blooded, sexualizing French. Thus Page's insistence throughout his interpretations of the major poems on Sappho's "control," her "wit," her "detachment" (18) tends to desexualize her *oeuvre,* in the final analysis to support, once again, a heterosexual reading of Sappho. For example, his reading of fr. 31, even though it culminates in an aggressive mockery of the bridegroom and beloved girl vision (32–33), proposes an interpretive realignment that Wilamowitz could hardly have found threatening, and one with which he could easily have been in agreement. When faced with the interpretive choice as to whether to center his reading on "love of the girl or jealousy of the man" (22), Page, like his German precursor, orders the reader to turn away from the homoerotic bond to concentrate instead on "the *man*": "We must never forget that the *man* was the principal subject of the whole of the first stanza"; "The greatest obstacle to our understanding of the whole is indeed our ignorance of the relation of this man to the girl and to Sappho" (28).

Page does not follow Sappho's early modern commentators in their attempt to normalize the triangle of desire in fr. 31, but he does shift the poem's viewing angle to argue by implication that its female narrator is involved with greatest intensity in the process by which the gaze is used to objectify the girl who is the object of male desire, to suggest, in short, that she desires a woman, like Sappho writes, *as a man.*[3] In the long run, the readings of the poems that Page seeks to impose are most reminiscent, in the entire history of Sappho scholarship, of those quirky chastity volumes by Bascoul: both claim that Sappho wanted to paint the saga of her struggle for artistic control rather than a vision of the woman in love. As Page concludes his analysis of Sappho's "detachment" in the "Ode to Aphrodite": "This everlasting sequence of pursuit, triumph, and ennui is not to be taken so very seriously" (16).

It is in Page's reading of that ode that the ultimate consequence of this critical sangfroid is most evident. For the telltale line 24, he reproduces the same Greek text found in Lobel and Page, that is, Bergk's original emendation, unmodified by his students' camouflaging revision. He maintains this lesson in the English translation provided in *Sappho and Alcaeus:* "For if she flees, she shall soon pursue," Aphrodite advises the suppliant Sappho (4). A reader might conclude from the most evident critical paraphernalia, as have almost all Hellenists whom I questioned about this, that Page presents readers of the second half of the twentieth century with the vision most Hellenists today seem to take for granted, that of a homosexual Sappho. Such a conclusion is, however, hasty, for Page, in the indirect manner characteristic of his argumentation, reveals his colors only in the notes he appends to the text. There, he makes it clear that he continues to reproduce Bergk's lesson only out of loyalty to Lobel: he argues that these scholars simply "expel one anomaly while admitting another" (11). Left to his own devices, Page would obviously have opted for what he refers to as "Knox's conjecture": "Good sense is given by Knox's conjecture . . . : this would reinforce my interpretation of the meaning of the stanza, and of the poem as a whole. I leave [Bergk and Lobel's lesson] in the text, *without the least confidence in it*" (11, my emphasis).

Throughout this passage, Page acts as if the only matter to be decided involved the beginning of the line, "even if," essentially whether it should contain a crasis (ellision), as some readings maintain.[4] (I will not reproduce all his argument; those who read Greek should consult *Sappho and Alcaeus* [11].) Such reasoning makes it sound as if the problem of line 24 is purely technical, strictly an affair of euphonics, a problem of metrics, just as Neue had concluded at philology's beginning in 1824, when he dismissed the homosexual variant with "we would embrace this [lesson] if the accent were moved back" (27). What Page never mentions is that "Knox's conjecture," although buried in a note dealing with problems of ellision, also transforms — with no comment on this far more crucial change — the end of the line, revising Lobel exactly as Hiller had revised

Bergk, and removing the sign of female homoerotic desire: "I have, I confess, always supposed that the poetess wrote ['even if you [Sappho] are no longer willing']" (Knox, 194, n. 3). Surely this change, rather than the metrical technicality of the beginning of the line, is the basis for Page's "interpretation of the meaning of the stanza, and of the poem as a whole"? The next English Hellenist to follow in their footsteps is no longer as shy about retracting Lobel's position. Page's carefully camouflaged hesitation no sooner appears in print, when Beattie devotes articles first to Sappho fr. 1, then to Sappho fr. 31, in which he at last makes sense of all his precursors' talk of "conjectures" and "suppositions."

In his first article, Beattie takes Page's insistence on Sappho's "jealousy" and the centrality of "the *man*" to a logical conclusion: Sappho 31 shows us that Sappho "was in love with the man and envious of the woman who has taken the man from her" ("Fr. 31," 110). Beattie's second article is just as logical a development of the note in which Page undermines Lobel's reading of the "Ode to Aphrodite" 's eternally problematic line 24. Beattie first goes through the motions of discussing the beginning of the line, but he quickly turns to the "further difficulty" of Lobel's reading, the fact that "it would mean that the person whom Sappho loves vainly is a woman or a girl" ("Note," 182). In order to ward off this possibility, he first rehearses the most traditional biographical scenario for Sappho (her marriage, and so on), and then devises a novel arrangement of lines 19–24, which aims to connect line 24 with lines 25–28 rather than 19–23, as the poem had always been read before: "thus . . . we deprive ourselves of the only scrap of evidence for determining the sex of the subject of lines 19–24" ("Note," 183). Beattie is simply the first of the English Sappho scholars to call a spade a spade and allow his personal prejudices a clear place in his scholarship. Perhaps the English school is so vehement in its desire to destroy Wilamowitz's authority because its founders sense their proximity to him. They imagine a Sappho more homebound than his guardian of the marital arts, but they are united by the common goal of "depriv[ing] *ourselves*" of any "positive indication" linking the muse of Mytilene to homosexuality ("Note," 183).

But the English philologist differs from his German precursor in that he appears more concerned with technique, Sappho's artistic "control," than with sexuality. Nor does he appear as terrified of the specter of lesbianism: Page proclaims that "a proper understanding of [Sappho's] personality and poetry is not to be attained as long as we are unaware of [the nature of her relation to her girl-companions]" and insists that the definition of Sapphism must still be left unresolved (142)—but only at the end of the volume in which he has put all his authority at the service of what is ultimately a reheterosexualizing of Sappho. Indeed, for anything like what would be termed a "modern" critical response to Sappho from within the English tradition, one has to wait for Dover's 1979 study of homosexuality in Greece, in which he discusses the metrical difficulties connected to each attempt to forge a lesson that scholars will recognize as "normal": "Among emendations designed to restore linguistic normalcy, some (e.g., Knox, Beattie) have the effect of removing the only indication that the desired person is female" (176, n. 10).[5]

Nowhere in the first generation of English reign do we see even a hint of allegiance to the principles Croiset begged for—*in 1898*—the distinction between speaking subject and biographical individual, and the distinction between word and deed. It is this refusal to admit these basic principles that leads me to go beyond 1937 in order to challenge Mora's judgment about the beginning of an age of "truth." In my critique of Page and company, I am protesting not their backing away from the homosexual view of Sappho's poetry that was becoming dominant in fin-de-siècle Europe but rather their refusal to admit that their readings are more than a question of metrics. Mora's age of Sapphic "truth" is characterized above all by the camouflaging of prejudice behind a front of scientific competence that is even more developed than the similar epistemological cover-up used by the first generation of philologists. As far as changing the course of the actual interpretation of Sappho, the English school's main effect seems to have been the impoverishment of Sapphic fictions. Otherwise, the new rulers seem very much like their precursors, treating sexuality as a subset of metrics, and using their science above all to refuse sapphism a *droit de cité*.

*

It seems even more futile to hold out hope for future change when one knows that earlier attempts to point out these fundamental confusions produced no visible effect. Already in 1921, at the precise transition from German to English rule, no less prominent an English writer than Virginia Woolf provided, to no avail, a veritable exposé of the tenacious blindness at the heart of Sappho scholarship. (Her exposé is also an uncannily accurate prediction of the future evolution of English Sappho commentary, the development we have just traced by which Page ends up sounding like Bascoul.) Woolf's 1921 short story, "A Society," takes place in an England poised on the brink of World War I. Initially, the story is a detailed exploration of the activities of the "young girls" of an intellectual society, a sort of bas-bleu *Chansons de Bilitis*. A group of unmarried young women begins to meet in response to a common anxiety about the changing expectations for women in the modern world, a transition that, in particular, has made it no longer possible for them "to take it for granted that it was a woman's duty to spend her youth in bearing children" (15), to "populate the world," leaving to men the honor of "civilizing" it (16). The members of the new society decide to investigate progress in the male domain: "We vowed solemnly that we would not bear a single child until we were satisfied" that the men produced by women were producing "good books" (16).

Unlike many of their Sapphic precursors, Woolf's intrepid virgins go through only comic misadventures as a result of their decision to defy the state by refusing the function traditionally assigned them. After their vow of infertility, one member, disguised as a charwoman, invades the studies of Oxbridge where she discovers what she proposes to the others as the perfect example of what men consider intellectual activity for the advancement of civilization. The "life work" of a certain Professor Hobkin, an edition of Sappho, is imagined by Woolf in a foreshadowing of the future evolution of scholarship, in which the English become the new Germans: "Most of it is a defense of Sappho's chastity, which some German has denied" (20). The woman pledged to chastity is stunned to learn that the author of an argument defended with great "passion" is in his person only a "mild, old gentleman," a man so dry that he seems the very epitome of infertility: "It never occurred to me that [he] could possibly produce anything" (21). The women decide that someone so driven by this obsession can only be "a gynaecologist," at which point the story begins to explore a question never once posed in all the substantial literature devoted to Sappho's "virgin purity," just what these scholars could have meant by chastity. "Chastity! Chastity! Where's my chastity!," one member cries out just as she is to begin the account of how she became "unfaithful to the cult" (and pregnant). Sappho's fragment on the loss of virginity, so often cited as a proof of the chastity of Sapphism, is here put to zanier use: by "chastity," it appears that the pregnant member, feeling faint, meant simply her smelling salts (22).

Thus launched, their investigation turns into a wholesale debunking of notions dear to all chastity theorists, English as well as German—How can one recognize an "impure" woman? Is a "chaste" woman obliged to chastise someone guilty of immoral behavior? (22)—moving ever closer to a questioning, on the one hand, of arguments central to the defense of *pederastia*—Can eroticism be limited to a cult of perfect beauty and a pedagogical commitment? (25)—and, on the other, of reasoning central to the prohibition of Sapphism—Can official measures be proposed to "dispens[e] with prostitutes and fertilis[e] virgins?" (25).[6] The question of civic control over eroticism once introduced, the society concludes its discussion of chastity by considering whether, in fact, the state should continue to seek to expand its population: the "British Empire" wishes families to grow (28), but should future mothers espouse its interests, when so many of them will die in childbirth, and so many of their children will go hungry or be killed in war (26, 32)?

Woolf never makes explicit the incompatibility between Sapphism and nationalism that is woven in filigree throughout her fiction, although she comes close to doing so at the story's end: it has just been proposed to the membership that the chaste Sappho "was the somewhat lewd invention of Professor Hobkin," when their discussion is drowned out by the din of men shouting at each other in the outside world, broadcasting the news that war has just been declared. "A Society" breaks off at this point, as Woolf allows the Great War to put an end to her virgins' challenge to civic wisdom as neatly as it killed off the German chastity tradition.

Time passes. . . . Woolf concludes with a brief afterword, in which, at the war's end, the narrator and another member review the minutes of their youthful reunions. The baby conceived in the heat of chastity discussions is now a little girl and her mother wonders what values will be left, in a society torn apart by war, to pass on to her. The two former Sapphic conspirators are just reaching a pessimistic conclusion that readers of *To The Lighthouse* will have no trouble predicting when, once again, their voices are drowned out by the cries of men in the street, and Woolf, once again, asks her reader to reflect in tandem about the fate of the nation and that of Sapphism. The men outside are proclaiming the signing of the peace treaty and the end of the Great War; the women inside conclude that the only thing left for a young girl to "believe in" is "herself," whereupon they present the child of chastity with the record of their meetings and elect her "President of the Society of the Future" (35).

Unfortunately, I cannot leave you with even the minimal optimism of a happy end in fiction. When the "jeune fille de la société future" "burst[s] into tears, poor little girl," Woolf makes it impossible to believe that the Pierre Louÿs-"Sapho 1900" model might be revised to provide a blueprint for future Sapphic societies that would be acceptable both to the state and to women intellectuals. By concluding her indictment of over a century of Sappho scholarship with the tears of her reincarnation of the (possibly mythic) Cleis, Woolf suggests that it is impossible to be Sappho's daughter. How can anyone come to terms with a figure whose official history has been for the most part charted by men who, terrified of the consequences of her fecundity, condemn her to sterility? How can a writer dare assume the succession of someone whom literary history has confined to splendid, frozen isolation: " 'Since Sappho there has been no female of first rate-' Eleanor began, quoting from a weekly newspaper" (28). In all that has been written about the original Sapphic society, there is no prototype for the future of Sapphism.

*

Nor was there, it would appear, any lesson for Sappho's critics in Woolf's fiction. We have already retraced Sappho's fate in English hands in the decades following the publication of "A Society." I do not know who her future masters will be: four centuries of erudition make it apparent that each change in scholarly dynasties means only that Sappho is read through the grill of a new set of national prejudices. No one can achieve that impossible dream promoted by the first philologists as the critical ideal: total union with the ancient text, from which the commentator would provide the perfect reading of its message. No critical reading is prejudice-free. The most we can hope for is that an awareness of the history of prejudices past can serve as a warning to pay more attention to the inevitable distortions caused by our own prejudices.

But even so little may still be too much to ask. A review of the recent *Cambridge History of Classical Literature* (*New York Review of Books,* 15 January 1987) proclaims the volume a "monument to the end of an era" (44), a "farewell to innocence" (45). The reviewer, Oliver Taplin, argues that the mark of the Cambridge historians' "innocence" is their belief in the timelessness of criticism, their conviction that criticism has the ability to recover, to transport, as if in a time machine's vacuum, works and authors *intact* from their days to ours (*Sappho revocata, Sappho retrouvée*). However, such scholarship, Taplin contends, is a critical dinosaur: armed with the weapons of philology's heirs, the German reception-critics, today's Hellenists are no longer "blind to the passage of time" and seek instead "to give [literature] a sense of history" (44). If indeed, as Taplin claims, "the fruit of the tree of the knowledge of temporality has been bitten" (45), no writer would better allow the newly fallen classical scholars to show off their postlapserian enlightenment than that paragon of (im)purity, Sappho. All we have to do now is to sit back and wait for the wages of scholarly sin.

Chronology of Sappho's Presence in France*

A. Editions, Translations, and Scholarly Commentaries

1546   "Ode to Aphrodite" published in Robert Estienne's Greek edition of Dionysius of Halicarnassus

1554   "Ode to Aphrodite" and "La Lune a fui" published in Henri Estienne's Greek edition of Anacreon

1556   First French translation of fr. 31 by Belleau (as appendix to his translation of Anacreon)
        Fr. 31 also included in second edition of Estienne's Anacreon

1566   The two odes and nearly forty fragments (in most cases, with Latin translations) in Henri Estienne's edition of Greek lyric poets (second edition)

1612   Déimier, *Lettres amoureuses, ensemble la traduction de toutes les épîtres d'Ovide*

1660   Tanneguy Le Fèvre's Greek-Latin edition of Anacreon and Sappho
        Marolles, translation, *Les Épîtres héroïdes d'Ovide*

1664   Tanneguy Le Fèvre, *Abrégé des vies des poètes grecs*

1670   Du Four de La Crespelière, translation, *Les Odes amoureuses, charmantes, et bachiques des poètes grecs Anacréon, Sappho et Théocrite*

1674   Boileau, translation, "Longinus," *Traité du sublime*

1681   Anne Le Fèvre Dacier, translation, *Les Poésies d'Anacréon et de Sapho*

1684   Longepierre, translation, *Les Poésies d'Anacréon et de Sapho*

1697   Bayle, article "Sapho," *Dictionnaire historique et critique*

1704   Fabricius, article "Sappho," *Bibliotheca Graeca*

1712   Gacon (Le Poète Sans Fard), translation, *Les Odes d'Anacréon et de Sapho*

1733   Wolff, *Sapphus, Poetriae Lesbiae, Fragmenta et elogia*

1758   Poinsinet de Sivry, translation, *Anacréon, Sapho, Moschus, Bion, Tyrthée, etc.*

1773   Moutonnet de Clairfons, translation, *Anacréon, Sapho, Bion, et Moschus*

1777   Billardon de Sauvigny, translation, *Poésies de Sapho, suivies de différentes poésies dans le même genre*

---

*I also include the events in other scholarly traditions that were most influential on developments in France.

B. Fictions

314

1780   Verri, *Le Avventure di Saffo*
1784   Imperiale, *La Faoniade: Inni ed odi di Saffo*
1788   Barthélemy, *Voyage du jeune Anacharsis en Grèce*
1797   Lantier, *Voyages d'Anténor en Grèce et en Asie*
1801   Chaussard, *Fêtes et courtisanes de la Grèce: Supplément aux Voyages d'Anacharsis et d'Anténor*
          Gros, *Sapho au Cap Leucade* (painting)
1805   Gorsse, *Sapho, poème en dix chants*
1807   Staël, *Corinne*
1810   Pipelet, *Sapho, tragédie mêlée de chants*
1812   Touzet, *Sapho, poème élégiaque*
1815   Chauvet, *Sapho, poème en trois chants*
1816   Staël, *Sapho, drame en cinq actes*
1818   Grillparzer, *Sappho*
1819   Cournol, *Sapho, tragédie lyrique*
1822   Gérard, *Corinne au Cap Misène* (painting)
1824   La Morvonnais, *Sapho, drame lyrique*
1836   Hope, *Sapho* (poem)
1850   Baudelaire, "Lesbos"
          Houssaye, *Sapho, drame antique*
          Boyer, *Sapho, drame*
1851   Augier and Gounod, *Sapho, opéra*
1854   Juillerat, *La Reine de Lesbos, drame antique*
1861   Banville, "Erinna"
1862   Dario, *Sappho, élégie antique*
1867   Verlaine, "Sappho"
1881   Silvestre, *Sapho* (play)
1884   Daudet, *Sapho*
          Richepin, *Sapphô* (novel)
1895   Louÿs , *Les Chansons de Bilitis*
1901   Faure, *La Dernière Journée de Sapphô*
1902   Barney, *Cinq petits dialogues grecs*
1903   Morel, *Sappho de Lesbos* (novel)
1904   Vivien, *Une Femme m'apparut*
          La Dame à la Louve
1905   Casanova, *Sapho: Roman de la Grèce antique*
1906   Delarue-Mardrus, *Sapho désespérée* (play, never published, presumed lost)
1910   Barney, "Equivoque" (play)
1912   Vielé-Griffin, *Sapho* (play)
1931   Romilly, *Sapphô: La Passionnante—La Passionnée* (novel)
1936   Yourcenar, "Sappho ou le Suicide"

APPENDIX
Sappho, Fragments 1 and 31: Translations and Presentation

The following is merely a schematic overview of issues important to the history of the reception of Sappho's two most famous poems. All problematic questions receive a detailed treatment in the section devoted to the period during which they were most controversial.

Sappho 1: "Ode to Aphrodite"
1.
O Venus, beauty of the skies,
To whom a thousand temples rise,
Gaily false in gentle smiles,
Full of love-perplexing wiles;
O goddess, from my heart remove
The wasting cares and pains of love.

If ever thou hast kindly heard
A song in soft distress preferred
Propitious to my tuneful vow,
O gentle goddess, hear me now.
Descend, thou bright immortal guest,
In all thy radiant charms confessed.

Thou once didst leave almighty Jove
And all the golden roofs above:
The car thy wanton sparrows drew,
Hovering in air they lightly flew;
As to my bower they winged their way
I saw their quivering pinions play.

The birds dismissed (while you remain)
Bore back their empty car again:
Then you, with looks divinely mild,
In every heavenly feature smiled,
And asked what new complaints I made,
And why I called you to my aid?

What frenzy in my bosom raged,
And by what cure to be assuaged?
What gentle youth I would allure,
Whom in my artful toils secure?
Who does thy tender heart subdue,
Tell me, my Sappho, tell me who?

Though now he shuns thy longing arms,
He soon shall court thy slighted charms;
Though now thy offerings he despise,
He soon to thee shall sacrifice;
Though now he freeze, he soon shall burn,
And be thy victim in his turn.

Celestial visitant, once more
Thy needful presence I implore.
In pity come, and ease my grief,
Bring my distempered soul relief,
Favour thy suppliant's hidden fires,
And give me all my heart desires.

> Ambrose Philips (1711; the first English translation)

2.
Intricate, undying Aphrodite, snare-weaver, child of Zeus, I pray
    thee,
do not tame my spirit, great lady, with pain and sorrow. But
    come to me
now if ever before you heard my voice from afar and leaving
    your father's
house, yoked golden chariot and came. Beautiful sparrows
    swiftly brought you
to the murky ground with a quick flutter of wings from the
    sky's height
through clean air. They were quick in coming. You, blessed
    goddess,
a smile on your divine face, asked what did I suffer, this time
    again,
and why did I call, this time again, and what did I in my
    frenzied heart
most want to happen. Whom am I to persuade, this time
    again...
to lead to your affection? Who, O Sappho, does you wrong?
    For one who flees will
soon pursue, one who rejects gifts will soon be making offers,
    and one who
does not love will soon be loving, even against her will. Come
    to me even

now, release me from these mean anxieties, and do what my
   heart wants done,
you yourself be my ally.

John J. Winkler (1981)

3.
Richly-enthroned immortal Aphrodite, daughter of Zeus,
   weaver of wiles, I pray to you: break not my spirit, Lady,
   with heartache or anguish;
But hither come, if ever in the past you heard my cry from afar,
   and marked it, and came, leaving your father's house,
Your golden chariot yoked: sparrows beautiful and swift
   conveyed you, with rapid wings a-flutter, above the dark earth
   from heaven through the mid-air;
And soon they were come, and you, Fortunate, with a smile on
   your immortal face, asked what ails me now, and why I am
   calling now,
And what in my heart's madness I most desire to have: 'Whom
   now must I persuade to join your friendship's ranks? Who
   wrongs you, Sappho?
For if she flees, she shall soon pursue; and if she receives not
   gifts, yet shall she give; and if she loves not, she shall soon
   love even against her will.'
Come to me now also, and deliver me from cruel anxieties; fulfil
   all that my heart desires to fulfil, and be yourself my comrade-
   in-arms.

Lobel and Page (1955)

   I list these translations not in chronological order but in an order that
summarizes this poem's history. The decision to read the poem as homosexual or
heterosexual has been until the past twenty-five years *the* central issue to be
resolved. Whether or not scholars have been conscious of the centrality they
accord it, this question has dominated all so-called readings of the poem. Philips's
translation represents the reading proposed almost without exception from the
mid-sixteenth century to the early twentieth century, in which fr. 1 becomes the
poet's request to Aphrodite for her help in rekindling the affections of an
unresponsive *male* lover. Virtually without exception, pre−twentieth-century
translations render every instance in which the object of desire is evoked with
"he." Winkler's version is representative of the currently dominant homosexual
view of the poem. It is also one of the rare translations from any period to be
absolutely faithful to Sappho's decision to specify the beloved's gender only
once, in line 24 (of 28), on the last occasion when the beloved is evoked.[1] (Prior
to this line, Sappho uses the indefinite "one.") An improbable twist of what
seems actually to be mere chance has made the end of the line illegible in all

manuscripts. Barring the (unlikely) discovery of a new manuscript, therefore, the one line essential for a definition of the poem's erotic orientation seems destined to remain undecipherable. Philologists allege metrical grounds for deciding whether the participle that assigns a gender to the object of desire is masculine or feminine. But it is evident that such a decision can never be purely technical.

The now dominant reading of the poem began to be proposed only in the late eighteenth century and has gradually gained currency in a context if not always of increasing tolerance for homosexuality, at least of an increasingly visible homosexual presence. This reading is found in most authoritative sources of our day, but this does not mean that it is uncontested. Thus, the third translation, from today's standard edition by Lobel and Page, accurately represents the current scholarly position on Sappho 1: the homosexual reading is contested by a small but influential minority of critics who wish to see reinstated the heterosexual reading that has been dominant since Sappho's rediscovery in the sixteenth century. In a note to line 24, Lobel and Page virtually retract the reading they have just proposed: the note rehearses arguments against the version of this line that makes the poem homoerotic and concludes that the reading has been given "without the least confidence in it." In historical terms, this translation evidently suggests the possibility that the currently prevailing view of Sappho 1 will appear with hindsight merely one phase in the poem's evolving interpretation. With Sappho 1, in other words, we have a flawless barometer of a critic's, and a period's, views on female homosexuality, a poem whose sexual orientation cannot be irrefutably determined from internal evidence, yet a poem that cannot be read unless the critic takes a stand on this issue.

The near consensus on a homosexual reading has achieved something that even a totally uncontested heterosexual view never produced: it has opened up an interpretive space in which critical problems other than the poem's sexual orientation are finally being aired. Among those that have produced the most stimulating readings to date, three stand out. First, there has been discussion of the multiplicity of points of view adopted by Sappho in fr. 1. Even in this poem, which so easily lends itself to literal interpretations because it contains an internal signature "identifying" the poet-narrator with the historical individual Sappho, there is nothing monologic about the poem's voice. The poem is constructed around a double portrait of the narrator, a self-portrait as suppliant and an intercalated revised portrait of the poet as (too) frequent suppliant presented from Aphrodite's point of view (the lines Lobel and Page put in quotation marks). The issue of what I would term Sappho's dialogism is further complicated by the second interpretive avenue recently opened up, in which the poem is discussed as an intricate commentary on the construction of gender in the epic tradition, as a response to Homer, and therefore as a reflection on the space for women's poetry.[2] The third question currently being pursued concerns the nature of the poet's request to Aphrodite. What, in particular, is the meaning of the poem's final lines, especially the phrase whose controversy is not limited to the designation of gender, "even against [her] will"? What do these lines tell us about the nature of (female) eroticism? What exactly does Aphrodite promise in the four lines (21–24) rendered far more elusive by the absence of a direct object? What is the nature of the erotic revenge that Sappho has the goddess design?[3] Recent views of the poem make it clear that the controversy of fr. 1 extends far beyond the mystery of its twenty-fourth line.

Sappho 31[4]

1.
Fortunate as the gods he seems to me, that man who sits
  opposite you, and listens nearby to your sweet voice
And your lovely laughter; that, I vow, has set my heart within
  my breast a-flutter. For when I look at you a moment, then I
  have no longer power to speak,
But my tongue keeps silence, straightway a subtle flame has
  stolen beneath my flesh, with my eyes I see nothing, my ears
  are humming,
A cold sweat covers me, and a trembling seizes me all over, I am
  paler than grass, I seem to be not far short of death...
But all must be endured, since . . .

                                     Lobel and Page (1955)

2.
That one seems to me to be like the gods, the man whosoever sits facing / you and listens nearby to your sweet speech and desirable laughter— / which surely terrifies the heart in my chest; for as I look briefly at / you, so can I no longer speak at all, my tongue is silent, broken, a / silken fire suddenly has spread beneath my skin, with my eyes I see / nothing, my hearing hums, a cold sweat grips me, a trembling seizes / me entire, more pale than grass am I, I seem to myself to be little short / of dead. But everything is to be endured, since even a pauper . . .

                                    John J. Winkler (1981)

3.
. . . Il est pareil aux dieux, l'homme qui te regarde,
Sans craindre ton sourire, et tes yeux, et ta voix,
Moi, je tremble et je sue, et ma face est hagarde
  Et mon coeur aux abois . . .
La chaleur et le froid tour à tour m'envahissent;
Je ne résiste pas au délire trop fort;
Et ma gorge s'étrangle et mes genoux fléchissent,
  Et je connais la mort . . .

                                Marguerite Yourcenar (1979)

4.

Celui-là me paraît être l'égal des dieux, l'homme qui, assis en
face de toi, de tout près, écoute ta voix si douce
Et ce rire enchanteur qui, je le jure, a fait fondre mon coeur
dans ma poitrine; car, dès que je t'aperçois un instant, il ne
m'est plus possible d'articuler une parole;
Mais ma langue se brise, et, sous ma peau, soudain se glisse un
feu subtil; mes yeux sont sans regard, mes oreilles
bourdonnent,
La sueur ruiselle de mon corps, un frisson me saisit toute; je
deviens plus verte que l'herbe, et, peu s'en faut, je me sens
mourir.
Mais on doit tout oser, puisque . . .

Reinach-Puech (1937)

This work, familiarly known in French as "A l'aimée" and in English as "To
a Beloved Girl" or "Peer of the Gods" (an option that stems from the central
debate over the poem's interpretation), has through the centuries generated more
abundant commentary than any other poem by Sappho. Unlike Sappho 1, which
is actively debated only during periods when female homosexuality becomes a
subject for open discussion, Sappho 31 has proved consistently controversial. This
has been the case because, unlike Sappho 1, this poem cannot be read without
confronting in some way a subject to which critics seem irresistibly drawn, often
even as they do their best to undermine its importance—the nature of the female
(homo)erotic experience, especially as it may be distinguished from androcentric
scenes of desire.

Sappho 1 gives us a female narrator discussing her desire for an object whose
gender is identified only late in the poem and only once. This devious structure is
duplicated, but reversed, in Sappho 31: the poem immediately makes plain that the
object of desire is female while the gender of the desiring subject is hidden until
late in the poem, when it is revealed only once, in line 14 (of 17). Since English
does not use feminine forms, English translators are unable to indicate this
configuration. However, translations in any language very rarely recreate accurately the poem's inscription of gender, even when it is perfectly possible to do so.
For example, in French the two feminine participles ("speaking," "laughing") in
lines 3–5 that make the object of desire a woman have since the sixteenth century
almost always been translated as nouns, "voice" and "laughter" (*voix, rire*).[5] This
decision, which can be explained as a translator's convention, has the side effect of
erasing the gender of the object of desire, so that readers who know the poem only
in translation could imagine that the tradition naming it for the beloved *girl* had
originated in a view of Sappho's sexuality externally imposed on the poem. In
addition, the narrator's feminine signature, "*greener* [feminine] than grass," is at
times simply eliminated (Yourcenar), or more often multiplied with the addition
of other feminine agreements (Reinach-Puech is a restrained example of this
tendency) so that the shock of its uniqueness is diluted.

Because most versions hide or displace the elements that define the poem's surprising sexual configuration, readers who know it only in translation may have difficulty in appreciating the tenaciousness and the intensity of the conflict that has characterized its history. Furthermore, translators may only have been following the lead of those scholars who attempted to play down the very elements obscured in translations. And in their commentaries we note the result (if not the goal) of this persistent cover-up. In the past decade, interpretation of Sappho's corpus has often focused on her self-consciousness with regard to preexisting literary models. However, this vision is virtually without precedent historically. Prior to the twentieth century, commentators did not evoke the possibility that Sappho was conscious of her poetic talent and indeed most often hail fr. 31 as a masterpiece of unconscious artistry. While it is inconceivable that the paradigm evident in Sappho 1's history—belief in self-conscious artistry will signal a homosexual reading, whereas a theory of spontaneous genius will signal a heterosexual reading—will reappear in the interpretation of the undeniably homoerotic fr. 31, a desire to rewrite as much as possible Sappho's staging of the scene of desire in more familiar (hetero-sexual) terms is nonetheless evident in all readings of fr. 31 that reveal any reluctance to admit Sappho's artistic awareness.

Thus, even what might otherwise seem an innovative critical gesture for its time (1955), Denys Page's reading of the poem as a manifestation of Sappho's artistic control—"There is certainly no lack of control in the expression, whatever there may have been in the experience" (*Sappho and Alcaeus,* 27)—can be shown to reflect Page's own implicit expectations about the way in which such a scene would be structured. More recent critics try to approximate the viewing angle of Sappho's original audience by defining expectation in purely literary terms closely related to what Jauss terms a "horizon of expectations," and measuring therefore the distance separating Sappho 31 from, for example, the type of song celebrating a marriage traditional in Sappho's day or scenes from Homer. Page, however, closer to commentators who preceded him than to today's critics, is never explicit about the perspective from which he is evaluating Sappho's stance in the poem. This is hardly surprising since he presents the way in which the poem measures up to expectations that are in no way literary but purely personal, his own view of how a scene of desire would be constructed. And, according to this view, Page, without denying the poem's homoeroticism, is able to perform an operation not unrelated to that accomplished by his footnote to line 24 of fr. 1, to make the poem function in ways that are subtly more familiar to readers who share his expectations.

Consider the example of the figure Page refers to as "*the* man." In the terms of his reading, a reading that stands as the culmination of the dominant interpretive tradition of this most celebrated of Sappho's poems, fr. 31 confronts its reader with an option: "We have to choose . . . whether the emphasis falls on *love of the girl* or on *jealousy of the man*" (22, my emphasis). In addition to the obvious attempt to direct attention away from the homoerotic viewing angle, Page's imposition of a choice has other, perhaps more important, interpretive consequences. In particular, Page's desire to establish the narrator's jealous gaze upon "the man" as the poem's visual focus is so overwhelming that he decides that its opening reads "that man," as though there is no question that Sappho is portraying an actual male rival. That individual is so present for Page that he revives a familiar (impossible) dream of Sappho commentary, that of identifying a male figure evoked in her poetry.[6] Thus embodied, the man can function according to René Girard's formulation of triangular desire: his desire for the beloved woman inspires the narrator's mimetic desire. I hasten to point out that Page is in good company when he revises fr. 31 to bring it in line with this time-honored scenario for the birth of *male* desire:[7] since the sixteenth century, commentators, and therefore translators, have acted as though the man enjoyed equal status with the two women.[8]

In a sense Page is correct: interpretation of the poem hinges on the critic's explanation for "[the man's] presence . . . in it." However, the male presence in fr. 31 remains finally elusive, another of Sappho's devious avoidances of a precise erotic configuration. A footnote (once again!) to Lobel and Page (20) lists the real interpretive option facing readers, roughly that between "*the* man" and "*any* man." Translators have always represented the male presence in Sappho 31 with a range of pronouns that would denote an individual of known identity—who, qui, celui-là—whereas the poem features in fact an *indefinite* relative pronoun, "whosoever he may be." Sappho's choice could mean simply that the actual identity of the man sitting opposite the beloved girl is not important in this context, the option that supports the standard reading of this poem since the sixteenth century. But it could also signify a radically different option.

John J. Winkler's translation is, to my knowledge, the first ever to make clear that the man may not be there at all. The famous line could also read "the man whosoever," in other words, "any man who sits opposite you. . . ." In this case, rather than an actual object of one woman's jealousy and another's desire, Sappho would be presenting, as Winkler contends, the man only as a figure of speech, "an introductory set-up to be dismissed" (76). From a central position as origin of female eroticism, the man would be demoted to the status of mere imaginary accessory to a desire that refuses triangulation. Whether or not one agrees with Winkler's theory of male insignificance, it is evident that the doubt immediately cast on the reality of a male presence at the scene of desire should convince us that this poem is not only open to, but openly requests, a plurality of interpretation. At long last, some critics are now moving away from the centuries-old notion that we are not only obliged, but able, to make a choice between the man and the girl.

Certainly, the recently sharpened definition of Sappho's self-consciousness with regard to literary precedent forces just such a realignment of the critical viewing angle. Fragment 31 can thus be seen as anchored in the undecidable, as an allegory of reading if you will, rather than as a recreation of some actual, decidable situation. From this perspective, even the oldest (mis)reading of the poem can be given new life. According to this view, fr. 31 was presented as the archetypal vision of Woman, transported by the frenzy of untamed physical desire, writing literally in the heat of the moment ("burning Sappho"), the archetypal model of women's writing as the spontaneous, uncontrolled outpouring of personal passion. Rather than simply reversing the coin, as do Page and other proponents of the control theory, critics should be able to account for the role played in the poem by the *appearance* of spontaneity. Sappho could be shown once again to have successfully predicted the evolution of a horizon of expectation: the "original" woman writer made her poetry a locus for self-conscious reflections not only on the act of reading (as a woman), but also on the act of writing as a woman, and even on the act of reading women's writing, the process by which we measure the gender-consciousness of literature.

Notes

Introduction

1. I have not systematically attempted to account for the distortions produced by censorship since it seems to me impossible to measure with any accuracy an interference that can vary so widely from country to country and with each change of political regime. In general, therefore, I will be forced to assume that if one author—say Renée Vivien in 1903—was able to publish certain views without fear of prosecution, others could have done so as well and *chose* not to. However, the intentional ambiguity with regard to erotic orientation that I analyze on occasion could, at least in part, be an attempt to skirt censorship.

2. I never address the question of whether authors of Sapphic fictions read Greek and could thus have had direct access to her poems and have bypassed available translations. I decided to eliminate this question once I realized that Racine, among the finest Hellenists in the French literary tradition, was influenced by his contemporary Boileau's translation. It seems natural, after all, that writers would react to the view of a writer promoted by their period, as well as with the writer him- or herself.

A few translations to which I had collected references, such as an 1889 prose translation by Paul Lenois, consistently eluded me. Similarly, no amount of research was able to turn up a number of fictions that I found especially intriguing for a variety of reasons. Three references lurked in corners of my office for years. I fantasized that a novel *Sapho,* allegedly published by a woman identified as "Mme. E. Caro" shortly after Alphonse Daudet's immensely popular 1884 novel, would be a response to one of the principal androcentric French Sapphic fictions. Two works had titles that I found particularly alluring, since they were allegedly published just before my study's *terminus ad quem,* a 1935 play by a certain Baron d'Erlanger, *Le Dernier jour de l'académie de Lesbos,* and a 1936 work by someone named Tristram, *The Burning of Sappho.*

3. See Susan Gubar's "Sapphistries" for a reading of the identification with Sappho that played a formative role for a number of important early twentieth-century women poets. What Gubar terms "sapphistry," the literary woman's "coming to writing" through Sappho, merits further exploration, especially in the form of comparisons that would determine how Sappho's function varied in different traditions and in different centuries.

4. I realize that, while I will appear to be "defending" Sappho against those who make of her an abandoned woman, much of her poetry speaks of her abandonment by her beloved girls. However, I maintain that the abandonment for which Ovid wrote the canonical fiction, by a man (Phaon), the abandonment which Ovid imagines as putting an end to her poetic gift, and the abandonment about which

Sappho herself writes are irreconcilably different: the abandonment Sappho describes generates poetry. In addition, Sappho's focus on love lost but recreated through memory is essential to her, arguably feminine, eroticism.

5. It should be obvious that my criticism of some of the leading Hellenists, especially of the last two centuries, applies only to their interpretive ideology and is not intended as a commentary on their philological skills.

6. Unless otherwise indicated, translations from the French are mine.

7. Croiset contends that the great mid–nineteenth-century German philologist, Theodore Bergk, also supported this opinion (2:232). This seems logical, in view of Bergk's presentation of Sappho. I was not, however, able to locate the relevant passage in Bergk.

8. To help readers keep track of the sometimes complicated chronology of Sappho's presence in France, I have included a chronology of editions, translations, and scholarly commentaries, and a chronology of fictions built around the character of Sappho. See pp. 313–15.

9. Brantôme is one source for Elaine Marks's important delineation of three different fictional topoi whose origin she traces to Sappho's poetry: "the older woman who seduces beautiful young girls, usually in a school or by extension in a convent or bordello; the older woman who commits suicide because her love for a younger man is unrequited; the woman poet as disembodied muse" (356). While I agree with Marks's claim that "Sappho and her island Lesbos are omnipresent in literature about women loving women, . . . whether or not Sappho and her island are explicitly named" (356), I disagree with her illustration of "*the* Sappho model" only with texts that present lesbian relations, most often without dealing explicitly with Sappho's *oeuvre*, or even with Sappho's person.

10. On these issues, see especially John J. Winkler; also Eric Gans's description of the complexity of Sappho's "I" as a primal voice of desire defining itself in opposition to other poetic voices (especially that of the epic).

11. Dover's classical source is Plato's *Symposium*. The word used is "hetairistriai," which, according to Dover, "is not attested elsewhere" (172). In their Sappho commentaries, nineteenth-century German philologists adopt the term without calling attention to its exceptional status.

12. Monique Wittig unhesitatingly qualifies the disappearance of Sappho's poetry and the absence of texts related to Lesbian and lesbian culture as the result of "the most spectacular [persecution] that has been carried out in history" (116).

13. Scholars today commonly refer to Sappho's poems by the numbers assigned them in the standard critical edition—in English, for example, that of Lobel and Page. The "Ode to Aphrodite" thus becomes LP 1, or simply fr. (for fragment) 1. On occasion, LP 1 and 31 are called poem 1 and poem 31 to indicate that they are more complete than other works. Other editions propose many other numbering systems: the French edition by Reinach-Puech, for example, uses a system completely different from that of Lobel and Page.

14. I use homosexual to mean a woman's expression of desire for another woman. I do not wish to take a stand in current debate over the nature of the same-sex relationships in earlier periods. (Lillian Faderman, for example, contends that "most female love relationships before the twentieth century were probably not genital" [18].) As I explain in chapter 3, I agree with Boswell that grave "distortion" can result from "the tendency to exaggerate the differences between homosexuality in previous societies and modern ones" (*Christianity*, 28).

15. This opposition between the configurations of Sapphism and *pederastia* may

be at the origin of the threat Sappho constituted for the nineteenth-century apologists of *pederastia.*

16. In a subsequent (1774) reedition of his treatise, Batteux includes notes that reproduce the objections to his theories formulated by a critic he identifies only as Schlegel. Without additional information, I cannot determine any possible relation between this individual and August and Friedrich Schlegel, two of the most influential figures in the early nineteenth-century turning way from the French classical vision of Sappho, still represented by Batteux, and in the formulation of the opposing vision promoted by early German philologists, a vision whose influence is still widely felt today. Certainly, the confrontation between Batteux and the unidentified Schlegel presents already the key terms we will analyze in this perhaps most important debate about Sappho to date: for example, Schlegel attacks the excessive nationalism of the French view of classical poetry (1:233, n. a) and predicts that this national blindness would inspire only new Anacreons and Catulluses and deprive the French of more sublime poets (1:155, n. a).

17. When I discuss the critical analysis of Sappho specifically as a woman writer, rather than taking sides in the essentialist quarrel about whether writing can be identified as male or female, I will be concerned only with recording those (rare) instances when the issue of a style specific to women became a factor in Sappho commentary. I agree with Nancy K. Miller's view that the anti-essentialist polemic poses an important threat to the continued development of work on women's writing (*Subject to change,* 240).

18. The recurrent tendency to make the lesbian the exemplary figure of modernism—from Baudelaire's day to its most recent reincarnation in the post-structuralist view of the author beyond difference—merits further study.

Preliminaries

1. For additional information on sixteenth-century French translations and adaptations of Sappho, see the articles by Robert Aulotte, Mary Morrison, and François Rigolot, and Henri Weber's book.

2. Aulotte, for example, claims that Du Bellay "imitated" the ode (110, n. 12). However, even with François Rigolot's help, I was unable to track down anything like a clear reference to fr. 1.

3. "If he flees now, he will follow you to live, / . . . / If he doesn't love you now, one day he will love you, / And, to please you, he will do everything."

4. I will consider the interpretation of Sappho's two major odes only as briefly as possible here and will provide more detailed readings of fr. 31 in chapter 1 and of fr. 1 in chapter 2.

5. "A little fire that ferrets a bit / Under my tender little skin."

6. Belleau does slightly displace the mark of the narrator's femininity. Sappho's "I am greener than grass" (in French "plus vert*e*") is extended into "je suis plus pâle et blêmi*e* / Que n'est la tête flétrie / De l'herbe par la chaleur / [I am paler and more blanched / Than the blade / Of grass wilted by the heat.]" I modernize the French in all citations.

7. Gary Wills's analysis of a number of Catullus's modifications of Sappho 31 could buttress the reading of Catullus 51 as a scene of male rivalry and triangular desire (186). This article provides an overview of the history of the comparison of the two poems and useful bibliography.

8. The phrase with which Catullus's narrator reclaims possession over the desiring gaze, "simul te, Lesbia, aspexi [as soon as I looked at you, Lesbia],"

situates the scopic scene in the domain of concrete past action, thereby indicating a greater degree of certainty than does Sappho's more hesitant subjunctive "when I would look at you" (a Greek construction known as present general condition that contains the sense of "on each specific occasion that an action occurs . . ."). Sappho's phrase has troubled translators for centuries. (To give but two examples of their attempts to handle her refusal to portray the desiring gaze: Symonds, "Should I but see thee a little moment"; Mora, "Si je te vois un instant.") Catullus may have tried to suggest the complexity of a construction not available to him in Latin, but his French successors always read his version of the scene of desire as an exercise in the concrete.

9. "For as soon as I see you, / My mistress, before me / Speak, glance or laugh . . ."

10. "I am a demigod when seated in front / of you, my dear care, I hear your chatter, / Chatter interrupted by a gracious smile."

11. It must be admitted that, while Estienne's is by far the most comprehensive early edition, his presentation of Sappho does not make it easy for readers to consider her fragments in their totality, as a corpus. Her poems are scattered throughout the volume in haphazard fashion, so that it would be easy to miss a segment. Poems by Sappho are found in three places in the edition: the most extensive selection is numbered pp. 30–65 (although it is in the middle of this fat volume); additional poems are on pp. 421–22 and 438–41. In addition, the final blocks are no longer translated into Latin, as though they had been included as an afterthought.

12. We cannot know what the Sapphic corpus available in Catullus's day was like; I do not intend to suggest that this speculation might be applicable to his reading of fr. 31.

13. Estienne mentions the anecdote that Aphrodite transformed Phaon into an irresistibly beautiful youth by giving him a plant known as an aphrodisiac; all early Sappho commentators who wish to indicate the legendary status of the individual most frequently mentioned as a male lover for Sappho do so by evoking his involvement with Aphrodite.

14. The Renaissance tradition of reconfiguring "A l'aimée" culminates in the early seventeenth century in François de Malherbe's poem "to a woman who imagined that he was in love with her" (written, in another kind of exchange between men, for the Duc de Bellegarde). Here, Lesbia has been renamed Philis, a stock name of contemporary pastoral love poetry, and the scene of amorous suffering has been brought entirely under male control. Sappho's powerful imagery has degenerated into a joke: how could this woman imagine that I am turning pale, etc., over her, when I am aware of nothing? When Malherbe penned this vision of Sappho as salon amusement in 1623, French Sapphic fictions were in the process of being revitalized through exposure to Ovid.

15. In "Louise Labé et la redécouverte de Sappho," Rigolot points out that Labé applied for the permission to publish her collection before any of the 1554 volumes that contain poems by Sappho had appeared. He suggests that she could have had access to these texts in manuscript. In addition, the Greek text of fr. I had been available since 1546. For information on both Labé's self-portrait as Sappho and her contemporary poets' reinforcement of this image, see the articles by Rigolot and Anne Freadman, as well as Rigolot's edition of Labé.

16. "[Phoebus] gave me the lyre that was accustomed to sing poetry of Lesbian Love."

17."Thus Love has so estranged you from yourself, / That one would say that you have been changed into another."

18. "Such a one I have seen who had in her youth / Condemned Love: afterwards in her old age / Burn with ardor."

19. "Thus Love takes his pleasure, in dictating / That the will of one will be contrary to the other's. / [A man] will not love, who will be loved by a Lady: / [A man] also will love, who will not be loved."

20. I would like to thank François Rigolot for having called this reference to my attention.

Chapter 1

1. "The literary tradition Ovid began, which existed well into the eighteenth century, in fact laps at the feet of the infant novel" (Moers, 147).

2. In the following pages, I will examine only the the novel's formulation in seventeenth-century France. However, I do not intend to imply that the pattern that I will trace was a unique occurrence. For example, a remarkably similar struggle for the right to speak with Sappho's voice was enacted some fifty years later in England. Nor do I wish to suggest a rigid parallelism between the foundation of the modern novelistic order and ancient practice, to imply, for example, that Ovid responded to Sappho because he was threatened by the women writers of his day. Ovid's appropriation of Sappho was so powerful in its complexity that he succeeded in positioning himself as an intermediary between subsequent writers and the paradigmatic female literary origin. That mediated response will be my subject here.

3. Recent studies by Marguerite Yourcenar, Edith Mora, and Marie-Jo Bonnet are all attempts to disengage Sappho's poetry from the legends surrounding her person. See also Mary Lefkowitz's analysis of the fictionalization of Sappho's biography.

4. In my discussions of the reception of Sappho's poetry, I will use adjectives such as "deviant" and "scandalous" to characterize the erotic triangle she proposes and the verb "normalize" to describe attempts to make this triangle conform to a heterosexual model. This vocabulary is intended to reflect the judgments and the standards promoted by the creators and critics of the French literary tradition.

5. I speak obviously from the point of view of today's reader. However, I hope to show from the response to Sappho across the centuries that the doubt in which she shrouds her founding erotic configurations is essential to the controversy she has provoked. Eva Stehle Stigers sets the erotic configuration of Sappho's poetry in opposition to that of the male poets who were her contemporaries. Her study is a convincing attempt at a reconstruction of the horizon of expectations against which Sappho positioned herself. See also John J. Winkler's readings of several Sappho poems as self-conscious meditations on the blindness of epic discourse.

6. For more on this issue, see the appendix.

7. As we we will see, this reading of the poem's principal emotion as envy of the man was particularly frequent in the period prior to and following the creation of the original psychoanalytic discourse on female homosexuality. For Freud's position, that the lesbian follows a male model of desire, see "The Psychogenesis of a Case of Homosexuality in a Woman" (18:145–72).

8. For a reading of fr. 31 as a model for female eroticism, see my "Female Voyeurism."

9. Jacobson, 281, n. 22. He quotes Denys Page and other authorities to support

this view. Yourcenar offers a reconstruction of the process by which Phaon could have been identified with Sappho (*La Couronne et la lyre*, 72.)

10. I will examine only the scenario of abandonment, Sappho rejected by male lover, that Ovid promoted and that, in his wake, seventeenth-century French writers defended and rejected. I will not, therefore, consider the scenario of abandonment which Sappho's poetry legitimated but to which Ovid nevertheless pays no attention, the woman writer abandoned by the beloved girl.

11. As the chronology of this chapter becomes more complicated, readers may wish to refer to the chronology in which the most important contributions to the creation of a French Sappho are listed.

12. The Robert dictionary traces the official appearance of "biographie" to the early seventeenth century. The *OED* cites Dryden as the first author to use its English counterpart (in 1683), and credits Addison, who presented Sappho to an English public, with the introduction of "biographer" (in 1715).

13. His name is often written "Tannegui Le Febvre." I have standardized the spelling of his name, and his daughter's, to "Le Fèvre."

14. Ovid's early translators at the beginning of the seventeenth century (Déimier, Lingendes) had already begun to Gallicize the poet's name as "Sapho." No explanation for this shift has ever been offered. Someone in the audience for a lecture in which I presented an early version of this chapter suggested that the removal of the second *p* was a form of castration. This theory would seem convincing were it not for the fact that, in general, Sappho's defenders initiate the excision of the *p* and, with the exception of Le Fèvre, none of them restores it.

15. Only David Robinson gives Du Four de La Crespelière's translation even a passing reference.

16. I will leave in French adjectives such as "galant" and "honnête," and for the eighteenth century "larmoyant," which were used to characterize literary styles of different periods but which have no true equivalent in English.

17. The *Poète goguenard*'s edition bears a title worthy of his pseudonym: *Les Odes amoureuses, charmantes, et bachiques des poètes grecs Anacréon, Sappho et autres galanteries de divers auteurs, en prose et en vers.* The title is the first indication of what will become the dominant eighteenth-century view of Sappho in which she is transformed into a typical court poet of the day, and promoted as a representative of the light amorous verse still in favor.

18. Although she does not cite it, the classical inspiration for Le Fèvre Dacier's stand was undoubtedly provided by the less discreet commentary in the ancient lexicon, the Suda: "[Sappho] had three companions or friends, Atthis, Telesippa, and Megara, to whom she was slanderously declared to be bound by an impure affection."

19. The fragment is number 47 in Mora's translation. Since Lobel and Page provide no translation from the Greek, I will always give a reference to at least one modern edition that does supply translations. My English translations of Sappho will be based on those of J. M. Edmonds, Marion Miller and David Robinson, or C. R. Haines.

20. Twentieth-century English editors generally no longer accept the attribution of the two epitaphs to Sappho, an attribution universally admitted until the nineteenth century. French editors, however, continue to include the poems (see Reinach, 204 and 205; Mora, 144 and 145).

21. Proof that Longepierre's nonsectarian presentation probably came too late

to widen the classical French "horizon of expectations" for Sappho is provided by the remaining translation of her poetry, a document that is surely the closest approximation of a late seventeenth-century "popular" view of the Greek poet available to us. Within months of the baron's edition, in the pages of the *Mercure galant,* the public paper of court society, appeared a version of Sappho by someone identified simply as "a provincial girl of good family, only eighteen years old" (July 1684, 104). The very existence of this translation testifies to the fact that, once the Le Fèvres introduced the French to Sappho, the spread of her influence was rapid and wide.

22. Let me cite a recent critic, Howard Jacobson, in support of this position: "I do consider the last six poems genuine, but have nonetheless ignored them here for a simple reason: the first fifteen *epistulae* and the last six are two distinct works. Not only were 16–21 written at a different time in the poet's life from 1–15, but they are quite different in their form, scope, and nature. These so-called 'double letters' are a work unto themselves and would demand separate and thorough treatment" (ix). The authenticity of some epistles is still disputed. For a recent discussion of this issue, in particular the evidence used to question the authenticity of the Sappho epistle, see R. J. Tarrant. Even though most critics currently accept *Heroides* 15 as genuine, it is unlikely that the debate surrounding this text will ever be permanently resolved, since it has remained open for centuries. Jacobson rehearses the arguments made by both sides in the authenticity debate (277). The epistle's authenticity is not important for my argument here, since in the seventeenth century the fifteenth epistle was always thought to be by Ovid, and his authority gave credence to the legend of Sappho it promoted. In my final chapter, I present the origin of this debate as an attempt to distinguish Sappho's authority from Ovid's and discuss the complex relation between this debate and the fictionalization of Sappho.

23. From this perspective, Jacobson's analyses are ultimately of limited use to proponents of Ovidian feminism: he stops short, for example, of contrasting the power and eloquence of these complaints with the less articulate discourse generally assigned classical literary heroines.

24. Jacobson's study is not to be confused with this critical tradition, despite his view that wit works against a sympathetic reaction to the heroines. Like Verducci, Jacobson seeks to defend Ovid's artistry and to grant the *Heroides* renewed artistic prominence.

25. (28.33–34). I quote Ovid from the Loeb Classical editions. The *Heroides* were translated by Grant Showerman. In general, I follow the English translations proposed in the Loeb editions, although I will on occasion modify these translations.

26. For example, in the article "Sapho" in his dictionary, Pierre Bayle concludes his list of the readings proposed for "mascula Sappho" with the explanation he presents as most authoritative: "It signifies the courage she had to make the leap from the White Rock of Leukas." The other interpretations suggested are "1) This word means that Sapho was a tribade; 2) it designates her attachment to intellectual pursuits, rather than the distaff and the spindle."

27. I follow Verducci's translation of *Heroides* 15 here and on occasion in the following pages.

28. The formula Ovid chooses to bestow an author's name on Sappho, "auctoris nomina Sapphus," renders a Greek genetive in Latin. It also masculinizes,

according to the Latin model, her author's name. (In her poetry, Sappho's name appears as "Psappha," a dialectal equivalent of "Psappho.") However, classicists assure me that Ovid's original readers would not have experienced this reaction to Ovid's formula, which they would have appreciated instead for its ring of high literariness.

29. The issue of whether Ovid did in fact invent the "epistola" or whether he had precursors in antiquity is debated in all studies of the *Heroides*. I am convinced by arguments for his originality.

30. Studies that discuss the influence of the *Heroides* include Laurent Versini, Charles Kany, and Bernard Bray, *L'Art de la lettre*.

31. See Alain Viala, 149. For additional seventeenth-century testimony, see Jean de La Forge, 8.

32. This tradition continued to develop until, by the end of the eighteenth century, the epistle was pronounced only a translation of Sappho and was included in editions of her poetry. Ovid's displacement is not an isolated phenomenon in the history of Sappho's fictionalization. For example, the authenticity of John Donne's Sappho epistle is currently being questioned.

33. They thereby anticipate a theory subscribed to by a number of Sappho's modern commentators who have suggested that Sappho's poems were "in reality love letters." I borrow the phrase from a twentieth-century proponent of this theory, Jean Hubaux (204). See also Jacobson (281, n. 40). See Longepierre (344) for a seventeenth-century formulation of this hypothesis.

34. On this quarrel and on the characteristics of the antithetical epistolary models, see Yoshio Fukui, especially 44–45.

35. A number of seventeenth-century novelists, notably Villedieu (Marie-Catherine Desjardins), one of the best-known women novelists, turned Ovid's technique against him and made him the hero of their amorous fictions. In her *Les Exilés de la cour d'Auguste* (1672), Villedieu initially assimilates him with the unfaithful lovers to whom the heroides are addressed. Her Ovid is "a professional changeling [*un inconstant de profession*]" (54).

36. I will write "Longinus" to refer to the figure long believed to have been the author of this treatise.

37. I quote "Longinus" in my translation of Boileau's translation.

38. I have modernized Boileau's French, a practice I follow whenever I cite early sources.

39. Thus Le Fèvre Dacier translates *phobeitai* as "tremble." In her commentary, she defines it as "the particular trembling that results when one is transported by furor . . . as if in a convulsive movement" (425). Boileau turns the convulsive tremor into a movement outside the self, a loss of self akin to madness.

40. Boileau's exclusion of some of Sappho's most forceful imagery cannot be attributed simply to neoclassical prejudice since Sappho's contemporary translators by and large did not share his squeamishness. For example, the young provincial gentlewoman, even though publishing in the semiofficial organ of court society, retains the physical image to which Boileau most strongly objects, and makes the poet say "I sweat."

41. Racine also eliminates those forms to which Boileau objected, the "cold sweat" for example.

42. For my reading of *Phèdre*, I stress Racine's distance from the fourth epistle. For a study of his proximity to Ovid's Phaedra, see Georges May (*D'Ovide à*

Racine, 139–45). Because I wish to promote Racine's Sapphic dialogue, I am also forced to ignore his debts to two central precursors, Euripides and Seneca. I do not deny that they are powerful models for Racine. However, in *Phèdre* Racine, no more than Ovid, does not create Sappho through a male poetic exchange: his identification with the original woman writer is as intensely personal, if not as sustained, as Ovid's. On Racine's debt to Seneca, see Charles Segal, *Language and Desire.*

43. Ariadne also figures in the *Heroides* (tenth epistle). For *Phèdre,* Racine follows the legend according to which she dies on Naxos: "Ariane, ma soeur, de quel amour blessée. / Vous mourûtes aux bords où vous fûtes laissée" (1.3.253–54).

44. Pierre Grimal notes that, for the description of Hippolytus's fall in his *Phaedra,* Seneca borrows the language Ovid used for his account of Phaethon's fall. Thus Racine goes back to Ovid via Seneca, as well as on his own (Segal, *Language and Desire,* 70, n. 19). See also Segal ("Solar Imagery," 151) for a discussion of the parallels between Hippolytus and Phaethon.

45. The first of the numerous contemporary French tragedies inspired by the story of Hippolytus to include an invented younger rival for Phèdre, by Mathieu Bidar in 1675, is part of the same movement to impose a new fiction of the desiring woman.

46. "That as yet no monsters tamed by me / Have won me the right to be as weak as he was."

47. "If any monster has succeeded in evading you, / Allow me to lay its honorable remains at your feet, / Or else the lasting memory of a beautiful death, / Making eternal days so nobly ended, / Will prove to all the universe that I was your son."

48. "Untamable bull, impetuous dragon / Its tail is curved up into twisted folds."

49. "Yes, Prince, I languish, I burn for Thésée, / I love him, but not . . . / The inconstant worshiper of a thousand different objects, . . . / But faithful . . ."

50. Hippolyte-Phaethon may also be linked to a third young male who falls to his death from the heights of his ambition, Icarus. The story of Icarus, son of Daedalus—the man who built the labyrinth and who gave Ariadne the thread that forged her relationship with the inconstant male—makes most explicit the youth's desire to follow in his father's path and to go higher than his father. In *Phèdre*'s opening scene, Théramène refers in passing to Icarus and his fall (1.1.14).

51. Both Seneca's *Phaedra* and Racine's explicitly evoke the classical example of the murderous mother, Medea. But the vision of Ovid's epistle being promoted in Racine's day implicates Sappho as well in this extreme scenario of the vengeance of the woman scorned for a younger woman.

52. The metamorphosis of the murderous mother into bird provides a clue linking Ovid's Sappho to Icarus. For his overly ambitious flight, Icarus dons artificial wings covered with feathers. Thus he plunges to his death in garb resembling that devised, according to Strabo, for the ritual *pharmakos* who was pushed from the White Rock of Leukas. Before the criminal was sacrificed to Apollo, the inhabitants of the region "tied all kinds of birds and winged creatures to him so that they might brake his fall by their fluttering." When Sappho is forced to take this leap, she replaces the young man whose ambitious rise she threatened to cut off. Paintings in a number of seventeenth-century French châteaux testify to the fact that the iconography of Icarus and that of Phaethon were intertwined at

that period. Judith Stein describes a 1797 drawing depicting Sappho in the traditional Leukadian execution garb (170).

53. Sappho's first eighteenth-century translator, François Gacon, completes this cycle by borrowing from Racine for his version of the Aphrodite ode. In the eighteenth century, the original woman writer was fictionalized into a more and more explicitly vengeful figure. By the end of the century, in Franz Grillparzer's *Sappho,* after Phaon abandons her for another woman Sappho, like Phèdre, begs the gods to avenge her by killing the pair with lightning bolts.

54. Segal provides a fascinating analysis of the function of the sword in Seneca's *Phaedra* as "the mark of the newer author replacing the older, the son replacing the father," as the textual locus where Seneca meets his literary fathers, Euripides and Ovid. However, in the case of the female literary precursor, Sappho, the capture of the sword signals not the smooth unfolding of the literary order but a violent rupture in it. Segal admits that at the end of the tragedy "the mother/wife, Phaedra, is no less powerful by her absence. . . . Her female desire serves as a symbol of what refuses ultimately to be confined and bounded as the unambiguously possessed object of the father and as the secure possession of a univocal language" (*Language and Desire,* 208–11, 220).

55. Critics who wish to stress Racine's (dangerous) proximity to the novelistic style of his day, especially to the female novelistic style, refer to him as the tragic poet of *préciosité.* See Emile Ripert for a discussion of Ovid's style as "*précieux*" (86).

56. For evidence that Huet also questioned Boileau's ability to speak for the ancients, see the Pléiade edition of Boileau (1072, n. 2).

57. The sentence's syntax presents Sappho's supporters as intellectually inferior. "[André Dacier] was the disciple of . . . Le Fèvre, father of . . ." (339). Anne Le Fèvre is syntactically doubly inferior, twice removed by prepositions from the primary authority, Dacier. On her remarkable erudition and scholarly accomplishments, see Farnham's study. Le Fèvre Dacier was to play an important role in the transmission of information about Sappho to England. Prominent early eighteenth-century English writers, as Farnham notes, studied her translation and, partly as a result, Sappho played in the development of the English novel a role parallel to that she had performed in France.

58. A volume preserved in the British Museum contains a response to the scholars whose envy, according to Anne Ferrand and to Anne Le Fèvre Dacier, leads them to obscure the contributions of women intellectuals. In his copy of Boileau's edition of "Longinus," André Dacier added in the margin next to Boileau's version of Sappho's ode his wife's translation of the same poem (see Farnham, 83). He thereby countermanded, if only for himself, the double suppression in Boileau's preface: of the original woman writer and of Anne Le Fèvre Dacier's efforts to restore her original status.

59. The *Lettres amoureuses* was published anonymously. However, in the copy of the *privilège* that concludes the volume, the right to publish is granted to Augustin Courbé and the work's author is identified as "le sieur de Scudéry." A reading of the volume makes it clear that Georges de Scudéry's name was used on a work of his sister's creation, a situation that was repeated for all the novels in Madeleine de Scudéry's vast production.

60. This image initially promoted by seventeenth-century authors—most prominently La Bruyère (*Des Ouvrages de l'espirit,* 37)—has today become a

commonplace for literary critics. Historians of the novel continue to affirm that in the seventeenth century women enjoyed a "privileged" position with regard to the love letter (see, for example, Bray's preface to his edition of *Romans d'amour par lettres,* 24–28). Critics also consistently fail to point out the content of the love letters whose female nature they promote.

61. The revised scenario Scudéry imagined for love letters has been allowed to slip through the pages of literary history. Each commentator proposes a different origin for the epistolary novel (Bray, 28; Versini, 35), and all their candidates follow the Ovidian model. Each of these proto-novels and actual novels, and most strikingly the genre's greatest commercial success, the *Lettres portugaises,* guarantees that the Phaethon figure will complete his rite of passage, and each displays with prurient fascination the suffering of the woman abandoned because she loved too passionately. Marie-Odile Sweetser discusses the proliferation of abandoned women in seventeenth-century French literature. The paternity of the *Lettres portugaises* is still questioned. However, I would not be surprised to discover that it was an attempt by a woman writer parallel to Scudéry's in the *Lettres amoureuses* to undo the Ovidian model by showing the abandoned woman's recovery of control when she learns to become a writer.

62. I will consider only the first volume of the *Femmes illustres.* The sequel seems to me mainly, if not entirely, a product of Georges de Scudéry's more overblown rhetoric. Scudéry was the first writer, a full thirty years before Le Févre Dacier and with only the precedent of I. Jacques de Bellefleur's 1621 translation of the *Heroides,* to Gallicize "Sappho" to "Sapho."

63. In her poetry, Sappho mentions a certain Eranna, who was traditionally identified, almost certainly erroneously, with the poet Erinna. Erinna, whose poetry is thought to have been influenced by Sappho's, probably lived in the fourth century B.C., but her dating is uncertain. On Erinna, see Mora, 122.

64. It is impossible to reconstruct Scudéry's sources for this vision of Sappho, but she could have had access to a fragment later included in Longepierre's edition, in which the poet chides a woman who has thought only of her beauty and so, unlike a writer, has no chance of winning immortality (LP 55; Reinach, 63).

65. One member of the younger generation of writers for whom Scudéry served as authorizing example, Catherine Descartes, revised fr. 31 to put herself in the narrator's position and cast Scudéry in the role of the beloved girl, concluding that the possibility of "often seeing and hearing [Scudéry] / Is a pleasure greater than the pleasure of the gods" (Rathery and Boutron, 403).

66. Staël, also motivated by a similar personal identification with the original woman writer, stresses almost identical physical attractions in the portraits of her Sappho figures.

67. Scudéry's precursor French Sappho, Louise Labé, presented a more sexually explicit view of the female desiring subject in her poetry, although it is doubtful that she intended to invite comparison between the geometry of desire she inscribed and that presented by the Sapphic narrator. On the complex question of Labé's relationship to Sappho, see François Rigolot's "Louise Labé et la redécouverte de Sappho."

68. This denegation of Scudéry's relation to sapphism is found in all early treatises on illustrious women. Scudéry's modern commentators continue this practice of announcing that Scudéry was known as the French Sappho and

immediately adding that her sobriquet was not intended as a commentary on her sexual preferences (see, for example, Aronson, 19).

69. Scudéry is always portrayed as as much a prude as Molière's "ridiculous" learned women. This image may even on occasion have (unconsciously?) inspired editors to alter Scudéry's works in order to make them comply with the image of the prudish literary woman. Thus, for example, the text of a letter in which Scudéry describes her novelistic credo has been altered to have her insist that novels must "conform" to the standards first of all of "decency" and then of "honnêteté," whereas the manuscript refers only to the demands of "honnêteté." Scudéry's 1670 letter is included in Rathery and Boutron's edition of her correspondence. (The passage in question is on p. 294.) This standard edition of Scudéry's correspondence was established on the basis of copies of the many letters in the Biblioteca Medicea collection made by Lechaudé d'Anisy. However, the manuscripts reveal many errors in these copies.

70. According to Le Fèvre Dacier, in the seventeenth century "Scamandronymus" was the most commonly accepted variant of the father's name (389). Perhaps because he backs away from the threat to paternal sexuality, Georges Mongrédien misreads Scudéry's fiction of the father's name: "nommé Scamandro*gène* dans le roman" (*Mademoiselle de Scudéry et son salon*, 24). I have consulted the first edition of *Artamène* as well as a number of other seventeenth-century editions; all of them contain the variant "Scamandro*gine*." I realize that printer's errors were frequent in seventeenth-century novels, but remain convinced that Scudéry's onomastic alteration, if unintentional, would not have remained uncorrected in a work so often reprinted in its author's lifetime.

71. Like everything in the portrait, these names are culled from a variety of sources. "Athys," Scudéry's spelling of "Atthis," figures in Sappho's poetry and is repeated in Ovid, also the source of "Cydnon" (this is the reading of Ovid's "Cydro" given in early French translations of the *Heroides*). "Erinne," as we have seen, refers to the poet whom Scudéry believed, on the Suda's authority, to have been Sappho's contemporary. She is introduced here, as in the *Femmes illustres,* to allow Sapho to encourage other women writers. I have not succeeded in tracing "Amithone" to any source, but I am convinced that it is not a gratuitous invention, since nothing else is.

72. For information on *préciosité* and on the literary activities of seventeenth-century salon women, see Dorothy Backer and Roger Lathuillère.

73. Ian Maclean discusses the active *précieuse* debate on the institution of marriage and some of the proposals for changing women's status within the institution (115–18).

74. Because of these fictions, Phaon, like Staël's hero Oswald after him, believes before he meets Sapho that it is impossible for a woman to be "learned without being ridiculous" (375).

75. Among early historians, see also Jean de La Porte, *Histoire*, 2:515. Among recent critics, see especially Arnaldo Pizzorusso, 115, also Larnac and Salmon, 85.

76. Perhaps in response to attacks by Valincour and others, a late seventeenth-century novelist, Anne de La Roche-Guilhen, revised the "happy end" Scudéry devised for her Sapho and made an unhappy love for Phaon the prelude to a successful marriage and motherhood. Her *Sapho ou l'heureuse inconstance* (1706) is an attempt to rehabilitate marriage for the female novel that culminates in a plot worthy of Marivaux. She is, to my knowledge, the only writer ever to imagine Sapho's marriage and motherhood as having taken place subsequent to her

involvement with Phaon. On the plots devised for their heroines by early women writers, see Nancy K. Miller's "Emphasis Added."

77. Boileau's dialogue is allegedly also directed against another writer of romance fiction, La Calprenède, but he actually refers very little to this novelist's work. The pretense of attacking a male novelist may also be part of a strategy to deflect attention from the gender-specificity of his critical project. Furthermore, in the dialogue Boileau breaks with standard seventeenth-century onomastic practice and speaks of "Scudéry" and not "Mlle de Scudéry," as though he were parodying the individual he terms " the author" rather than "the sister of the author with the same name."

78. On symbolic executions in seventeenth-century France, see the first chapter of Michel Foucault's *Surveiller et punir*.

79. In the preface to her edition of the *Heroides*, L'Héritier explains that she began to translate Ovid "to obey two women whose distinction is due to their merit as much as their birth" (viii–ix). Her dedication appears to be a response to Boileau's demeaning identifications of Le Fèvre Dacier and Scudéry. It would seem, therefore, that her version of Ovid's influential fiction was authorized by Sappho's most prominent female sponsors to reflect their views.

80. On the development of French literary history in the eighteenth century, see my "Classical Reeducation."

Chapter 2

1. In *Family Romances* (1908), Freud generally speaks of "the child." He makes it clear that it is a male child that he has in mind on the one occasion when he distinguishes between male and female children, only to dismiss the female on the grounds that "the imagination of girls is apt to show itself much weaker" (9:42).

2. On occasion, some of Sappho's French editors and translators claim to be aware of German scholarship but, as will become evident with the example of Billardon de Sauvigny, these claims are in general totally unfounded, simple gestures of scholarly chic. However, that the editor of an almost entirely spurious text feels free to cite the authority of the most enlightened Hellenists of the day does indicate how little the German tradition was known in France.

3. As late as the early twentieth century, no less an authority than Ulrich von Wilamowitz-Moellendorff still reveals his familiarity with some of the most outlandish Enlightenment fictions.

4. Bayle's article "Leucade" contains his version of Sappho's suicide.

5. Fabricius actually intended to speak of Phaon on a second occasion but instead of writing "Phaon" he speaks of Sappho's love for "Pampho," a Freudian critical slip that may reveal his eagerness to keep Aphrodite's boatman out of the picture he is painting. In any event his slip makes the editors of the 1791 update of the *Bibliotheca Graeca* so uneasy that they devote an extensive note to explaining that Fabricius could only have had Phaon in mind and that he could not have intended to write "Pampho."

6. For additional translations and more background on issues raised by fr. 1, see the appendix. Those who know Greek should be aware that the dominant pre–nineteenth-century reading of the verb in line 24 was "ethelois."

7. Barrin's translation is reprinted more than a dozen times between 1676 and 1740, making it the dominant vision of Ovid's text for the Enlightenment.

8. L'Héritier's rendition of Ovid's "non sine crimine" as "tendrement" is certainly a reference to Scudéry's "tendres amis," which carries, unlike Ovid's description, no implication of sexual intimacy.

9. Ovid's authority and, eventually, the authenticity of *Heroides* 15 always come under suspicion in conjunction with Sappho's sexuality. Together with her distrust of Ovid's authority, L'Héritier brings up, for the first time in modern Sappho scholarship, what will become known as the theory of the two Sapphos when in the nineteenth century it is the basis for the questioning of the authenticity of the Sappho epistles.

10. The second eighteenth-century translation of Sappho, by Antoine de La Fosse (1716), is simply a verse adaptation of Le Fèvre Dacier's prose renditions that remains faithful to its model.

11. The official version of Boileau's dialogue appeared a few months after Gacon's translation, but Gacon must have known the pirated editions and may, in addition, have had access to the manuscript prepared by Boileau in 1711.

12. Later in the century (1777), Billardon de Sauvigny even uses Racine to revise Ovid when he offers a version of *Heroides* 15 that resonates with echoes of *Phèdre*. (See, in particular, *Poésies*, 56, 65.)

13. All pre–nineteenth-century French translators replace "Aphrodite" with "Venus."

14. This reading of the troubling final verb form of line 24 dominated the French tradition for some hundred and fifty years, but it was particular to that tradition. For example, Raabe, one of the first to provide a translation in German (1794), offers a completely different, and even less satisfactory, solution: "he should kiss you to your heart's desire" (14).

15. Gacon's version is the first eighteenth-century precursor of Staël's Sapphic scenario, the older woman abandoned by her younger lover for a younger woman.

At the end of the century (1795), abbé Jean-Marie Coupé becomes the only other eighteenth-century French translator to offer a major revision of this ode. He makes the object of the erotic gaze the goddess Aphrodite: "He is equal to the Gods, he surpasses the Gods, the happy mortal who can gaze upon you, O Goddess of Cyprus" (146). The year before Gacon's translation appeared, Addison offers English readers Ambrose Philips's version of the ode, easily masculinized in English because of the absence of the agreement necessary for the Sapphic narrator's female signature. Lest any confusion remain, Addison prefaces the translation with "whatever might have been the occasion of this ode, the English reader will enter into the beauties of it, if he supposes it to have been written in the person of a lover sitting by his mistress" (*Spectator*, no. 229:539). Addison dismisses Boileau's translation, with its female signature, as "rather an imitation than a translation" (541). Like Gacon, Addison also opposes Sappho's "natural" style to "the conceits and turns of wit" of contemporary love poetry and proposes the masculinized translations of her odes he is publishing as literary models for "genuine and natural beauty" (no. 223:526, 528).

16. No scholar to date has drawn up a complete bibliography of Sappho translations and works that fictionalize Sappho. The reader desiring such a bibliography could combine the listings provided by Edith Mora, David Robinson, and Judith Stein to come up with a nearly complete bibliography.

17. The inevitability of this peculiar blend of sound scholarship and unfounded fabulation is unique to the eighteenth-century tradition.

18. Béatrice D'Andlau dates the song's composition at "about 1784" (103). Germaine Necker was seventeen or eighteen at the time. D'Andlau reprints it in a section "premiers essais," that is, works written before the first published short stories.

19. Canat notes Barthélemy's "uncontested authority" and calls *Anacharsis* "the Empire's favorite reading" (1:19, 1:20, n. 8).

20. This Sapphic assembly resembles a school rather than a salon. Here, Barthélemy is far ahead of his time. The Sappho-as-schoolmistress fantasy will only come into its own at the turn of the twentieth century, primarily in Germany and England.

21. I have not found this anecdote in any source from antiquity. The "modern" accounts of the White Rock of Leukas, such as Bayle's quite thorough listing of those believed to have perished in the leap, do not include Artemisia.

22. In 1801, J.-B. Chaussard published a continuation of both Barthélemy's and Lantier's voyage novels, *Fêtes et courtisanes de la Grèce: Supplément aux voyages d'Anacharsis et d'Anténor*. His portrayal of Sappho as a courtesan provides the clearest link between his precursors' fiction of her menacing heterosexuality and the theory of Sappho as prostitute widely promoted in the first half of the nineteenth century.

23. La Harpe begins his career by authoring new *Heroides* and ends it by composing a sixteen-volume course in literary study, *Lycée*, that exerted enormous influence in the early nineteenth century, when it was thought to represent the last canon of the ancien régime. In his *Lycée*, La Harpe declares that only two of Sappho's poems survive.

24. Louis Poinsinet de Sivry's 1758 edition, *Anacréon, Sapho, Moschus, Bion, Tyrthée, etc.*, as its title indicates, also participates in Sappho's reduction to textual promiscuity. He characterizes the tone he imposes on the poets he freely associates as "cheerful" (*riant*), thereby establishing himself as a follower of Du Four de La Crespelière and a precursor of Barthélemy in the tradition of Sapphic light verse.

25. Anacreon, Bion, and Moschus are all presented in the "pastoral poetry" section of the abbé Batteux's *Principes de la littérature* (1747), the *ars poetica* of Moutonnet de Clairfons's generation.

26. On the attribution of this poem to Sappho and the subsequent rejection of that attribution, see Miller and Robinson, 116–17.

27. Marie-Antoinette's *duchesse en gondole en trois parties* is shown in Penelope Hunter-Stiebel's *Menuiserie* (fig. 26).

28. It is ironic that his reading of the troublesome line 24, "I will bring him a slave, / At your feet in chains," should be the century's most accurate equivalent of Sappho's "against her will," "even if she is not willing," since Billardon de Sauvigny never considers that the poem could be addressed to anyone but Phaon.

29. The *Bibliothèque universelle des dames* is also known as the *Bibliothèque des Mlles Eulalie, Félicité, Sophie, Emilie de Marcilly*. The selection from Sappho is included in volume 8 of the some eighty volumes of *Mélanges*. In their one important departure from Billardon de Sauvigny's fiction of Sappho, the editors of the collection give a prowoman slant to the scenario of Sappho as victim of slander. They contend that Sappho was persecuted only by male poets jealous of her talent, whereas her fellow women writers never turned against her. "Are men really more wicked, or are women naturally inclined to make common cause, when the glory of their sex is at stake?" (8:99).

30. The vicomte de Parny was the only late eighteenth-century figure openly to admit Sappho's homosexuality. In "La Journée champêtre" (in his *Poésies érotiques*), he says he is "repulsed" by all erotic poetry with a homosexual object choice. He ends his discussion of "these tastes" with an exorcism of sapphism: "Priestesses of Lesbos . . . It's for us that [nature] made you beautiful" (113–14).

31. During the period of the creation of the "new" heroides, Blin de Sainmore also edited five volumes of the *Elite des poésies fugitives* (1764–70).

32. Sappho's new transience may have helped inspire a flood of ever freer adaptations of her poetry, especially fr. 31, at the end of the eighteenth century. Chénier rewrites it as an ode to Fanny; Lazare Carnot provides a curious, deist version ("He is equal to the Supreme Being. . ."). The fraudulent Sapho even generated other literary frauds. Vanderbourg includes an imitation of the ode in his 1802 literary fabrication, the *Poésies* of Marguerite de Surville, an alleged fifteenth-century poet. Those who were taken in by his trick would have extended Sappho's history in France back a century earlier.

33. At least one other poem, a fragment also uncovered in the most recent discoveries and apparently addressed to Sappho's daughter Cleis (LP 98; Mora, 55), is sometimes read as a political work (see Mora, 383). Denys Page, however, argues against this interpretation on the grounds that the line on which a political reading hangs is "incomprehensible, probably corrupt, in its present form" (*Sappho and Alcaeus*, 102).

34. Nowhere is Barthélemy's "reconstruction" more fully exploited than in Jean Larnac and Robert Salmon's 1934 "biography" of Sappho. Their mining of the political myth makes apparent the reason for the remarkable scholarly success of a mere novelization of Sappho's life: the fortuitous near-conjunction between the appearance of Barthélemy's fiction and the outbreak of the French Revolution.

35. Sappho's plot can also be considered the primal scene for Staël because it serves as the vehicle through which she works out her personal family romance. For an intricate reading of *la femme et l'oeuvre*, see Simone Balayé's *Madame de Staël: Lumières et liberté*. In *Madame de Staël, Novelist*, Madelyn Gutwirth suggests many ways in which the novelist's fictions can be read as reflections of her complex relation with her parents. Their elaborations of Staël's actual family romance reinforce in many ways the reading I will propose of Staël's fiction of the original family romance, the configuration at the origin of the patriarchal order. The fear of incest and the menace of the oedipal complex for the female child that Staël suggests in the Sappho legend only become explicit in Laurence Durrell's 1950 verse play *Sappho* in which the heroine unwittingly marries her own father.

36. Relevant passages concerning Delphine's *sensibilité*, passionateness, and superiority include: 1:6:42–44, 1:11:68, 1:23:110, 1:26:127, 3:11:407, 6:13:366. For citations from *Delphine*, I give part number, chapter number, and page number in Claudine Herrmann's edition. In her preface, Herrmann quotes (after Balayé) a contemporary critic of *Delphine:* "A passionate woman is not against nature, but she is against the nature of well-bred women" (11), demonstrating the social impropriety of Delphine and Barthélemy's Sapho, and justifying D'Auvigny's decision to make modesty and deference his Sapho's dominant traits.

37. Gutwirth cites Fauchery's critique—"the Revolution figures as only a distant frame for an essentially sentimental tale"—in order to modify it with a judgment with which I agree: *Delphine* is a revolutionary work because of its "momentum . . . toward personal freedom for women" ("La *Delphine* de Madame de Staël," 155, 161–62). Balayé shows how the novel's first critics for the most part attacked and on occasion applauded the presence of the Revolution in the novel. She also cites Staël's own defense of the necessity of the political context for the development of her love story (*Madame de Staël*, 123).

38. Staël's personal marital chronology paralleled fairly neatly the composition of *Delphine*. She began the novel in the last months before she obtained her separation from her husband, and in May 1802, near the time she finished it, the baron died while en route to her home in exile at Coppet, suggesting that liberation from a bad marriage could also provide an impetus to literary activity.

39. Théophile Gautier compares Staël to Sappho because both were political exiles, a punishment he feels both deserved for having interfered in the male preserve of politics (see Richer, 166).

40. For a discussion of Napoleon's increasingly conservative views at the time of *Delphine*'s publication, see Balayé, *Madame de Staël*, 90–92.

41. Sacy seems primarily to have been read outside of France. His novel was even translated into Russian (St. Petersburg, 1780).

42. The only other transvested Sappho I encountered appears in William Mason's 1797 *Sappho*. Before ending in tragedy, the play hovers on the border of farce in a plot closer to *A Midsummer Night's Dream* than to any legend of Sappho: when Sappho hears that Phaon loves a woman named Doris, she dresses as a man and becomes his amorous rival and, in an attempt to win Doris's hand, sings a free version of the ode to a beloved girl to Doris, who reclines on a bed of violets (the violet was Sappho's flower) (35–37).

43. Commentators on these fictions often remind us (pedantically) that this scene is completely anachronistic since in ancient Greece women were never allowed to watch naked men at sport.

44. Tresham did not number the plates. I consulted the edition in the Bibliothèque Nationale, Estampes Sb.26. For more on Tresham, see Stein, 159–61. I often rely on Stein's admirable research into the politics on which the late eighteenth-century iconography of Sappho is based.

45. Verri's influence, like Sacy's, is sometimes evident in unexpected places. For example, in Bréghot Du Lut's commentary on his 1835 translation of Sappho, the fine points of his version of the story of Phaon as Aphrodite's boatman (163) correspond exactly to Verri's vision of this scene, including certain details I encountered nowhere else.

46. Imperiale accidentally anticipates the next way the Sappho canon would be enlarged, with the early twentieth-century papyri discoveries. I cite the translation of the *Faoniade* by Grainville.

47. For citations from *Corinne*, I give book number, chapter number, and page number in Simone Balayé's edition.

48. Staël's extensive use of travelogue to, in Barthélemy's words, "set her story in action" may also have been inspired by his and Lantier's novels.

49. Mora was the first recent critic to discuss the resemblances between the plots of *Corinne* and Staël's *Sapho* (179–80).

50. I do not know how many of the Napoleonic Sapphic fictions Staël had actually read. An unpublished letter in a private collection proves that she knew Verri's novel.

51. The sentence is echoed much later in the novel when Oswald's young daughter Juliette asks her father: "What is Corinne, my father? [*Qu'est-ce que c'est que Corinne, mon père?*]" (20:4:575).

52. See Gutwirth, *Madame de Staël*, 173. "Improvisatrice" also enters English in reference to the great Italian performers of the late eighteenth century, especially Maria Morelli, who was so well known as "Corilla Olympica" that Staël added a

footnote to *Corinne* explaining that her heroine's name was to be seen as a reference to the Greek poet and not to the Italian improvisatrice (592, n. 29).

53. The Gérard painting was commissioned by Prince Augustus of Prussia at the suggestion of Staël's intimate friend, Juliette Récamier. He later gave the painting to Madame Récamier, who hung it in her salon, where *Corinne au cap Misène* presided over the first readings of the *Mémoires d'outre-tombe* in 1834. According to Chateaubriand's editor, Levaillant, the painting "caused to hover over them the figure of Madame de Staël, symbol of glory and its transience" (1:xxxi). The other famous portrait of Staël as Corinne, by Elisabeth Vigée-Lebrun (1808), alters dramatically the impact of this identification by portraying the literary woman in full possession of her powers. However, correspondence between the artist and her model reveals that Vigée-Lebrun had intended to use the background of Cape Miseno but had been dissuaded by "[Staël's] friends" (Stein, 92), who may have wished to avoid, during Staël's lifetime, the melancholy associations of the clifftop setting. Nevertheless, the setting she substituted, the temple of the Sibyl at Tivoli, is related in a less visible way to Corinne's suicide and is a reminder of the vengeance Staël added to the traditional Sapphic scenario.

54. Verri also gives his dark, passionate Saffo a blond, reserved sister. This sororal dichotomy between the dark courtesan and the fair virgin announces the nineteenth-century tradition of Sapphic doubles.

55. According to Napoleon's own testimony, Staël asked him, upon his return from Italy, which woman in modern times he most admired, to which he replied: "The one who has the most children." The emperor reports having said on another occasion: "The Empress Joséphine and Madame de Staël were at opposing ends of the scale from one another. One was woman, from the soles of her feet to the ends of her hair, the other was not even a woman in her . . . [genitals]" (cited in Gutwirth, *Madame de Staël*, 287).

56. Several Sapphic images produced by painters with Napoleonic connections, notably Tresham's and Gros's depictions of her suicide, feature her snakelike curls, suggesting that Sappho was a Medusa figure, a menacingly powerful fiction of the female.

57. One final canvas links Napoleon's artistic entourage to Sappho. David, commemorator of the emperor's most elevated moments, painted at the same period (1809) the strangely playful *Sapho, Phaon, et L'Amour*.

58. Chaussard explicitly linked the official Napoleonic Sapphic tradition to Boileau when he published an update of his *Art poétique* (1817).

59. The situation Tarczylo uncovers in eighteenth-century France should be contrasted, for example, with Lawrence Stone's findings about the same period in England. Stone notes the increasingly open presence of (male) homosexuality in eighteenth-century English life, as well as renewed attempts to punish practicing homosexuals (337). Louis Crompton confirms Stone's conclusions and notes the "unprecedented number of executions of homosexuals in England" in the late eighteenth and early nineteenth centuries (5).

60. The only Revolutionary aspect of the play's fictionalization of Sappho is the anticlerical shading Pipelet introduces. The high priest conspires with Sapho's treacherous friend Damophile in her plan to guarantee that Sapho will kill herself, first by arranging for a secret marriage between Phaon and Sapho's student Cléis. When this fails, the priest helps Damophile kidnap Phaon and Cléis and make it seem that they have run away together.

61. It is interesting that this rivalry, rooted in the daughter's desire to replace the

mother and the mother's fear that she will do so, is absent from Staël's Sapphic fictions, where readers familiar with the author's overtly oedipal fascination with her father and jealousy of her mother, well documented by Balayé and Gutwirth, might expect to find it developed. Conversely, the fiction Staël develops, the son controlled by paternal interdiction, might be more conventionally identified with a male novelist.

62. Pipelet portrays herself as the Revolution's official Sapphic bard, so her rejection of the political exile theory must signify an incapacity on the part of the ruling ideologues to accept the suggestion that a flight from the fatherland would be necessary in a fight for freedom. In the then prevailing view, only partisans of the old order, *émigrés,* left the paternal home.

63. Grillparzer could have had access to Staël's *Sapho* in a manuscript circulated by the Schlegels. See Tubach (170–173) for the opposed reading of Grillparzer's tragedy as a work suggesting, rather than repressing, Sappho's homosexuality.

Chapter 3

1. Switzerland's neutrality did not guarantee freedom of movement for either Staël (who was constantly under police surveillance) or her guests (who sometimes put themselves at risk to visit her).

2. In addition to the active tradition of scholarship and speculation, Sappho was frequently included as a footnote to the texts that, from the Revolution to the end of the nineteenth century, composed the ever more vast body of speculation on Woman. To cite only one early example, the second edition of Pierre Roussel's *Système physique et moral de la femme* (first published in 1798) contains an appendix, "Doutes historiques sur Sapho." In this curious addition to a curious compendium on female biology, Roussel develops the theory that Sappho could just as easily have drowned herself on Lesbos. If she traveled to Levka, it must have been in the hope of freeing herself from her unhappy passion (394–96).

3. In "Why is Diotima a Woman?," David Halperin proposes a parallel reading of the *Symposium.* This essay is part of a forthcoming study, *One Hundred Years of Homosexuality and Other Essays on Greek Love.*

4. Perhaps the most convincing testimony to the pivotal role philology intended for literature in the historico-politico-religious system it presented as the foundation of the modern nation-state, and to its presentation of the Germans as direct heirs of the Greeks, is found in Friedrich Schlegel's (1815) study of ancient and modern literature, an origin of the discipline today called comparative literature.

5. Welcker's heir, Ulrich von Wilamowitz-Moellendorff, still comments on Verri and Imperiale in his 1913 *Sappho und Simonides,* as though he were dealing with serious scholarly commentaries. In the years just prior to his study of Sappho, Welcker himself enlisted twice to fight Napoleon's army (in 1814 and 1815).

6. I will be concerned in this section less with the history of philology than with the pan-European dissemination of its theories and will try to recreate the clichéd image of Winckelmann rather than an overview of his contributions, for example. I therefore privilege certain texts like Müller's more central in other European traditions (in Müller's case, the Anglo-American tradition) than in Germany. I sometimes make an idiosyncratic choice of texts by scholars like Winckelmann, foregrounding those texts that were most widely disseminated.

7. *Sexual Life in Ancient Greece,* 183. The Hellenist Paul Brandt wrote his 1909

study of Sappho under his own name but used the pseudonym Hans Licht to sign his 1925–28 *Sexual Life in Ancient Greece*. I cite the expanded 1932 English edition of this work. Unless otherwise noted, translations from the German are mine.

8. In citing Winckelmann, I limit myself to his works available in translation to the contemporary French public.

9. See Richard Jenkyns, especially 132–34, on Winckelmann's belief that the Greek aesthetic sense originated with the omnipresence of male nakedness. Jenkyns suggests that the views of Winckelmann and some of the Victorians whose fascination with Greece he documents were influenced by their homosexuality. The same argument has been put forward about almost all of the German philologists I will discuss in this section. See, for example, Ernest Borneman's judgment that Hans Licht's views of Greek culture are all colored by his homosexuality (cited by Sally Tubach, 80). See also Judith Stein (197, n. 61, and 319, n. 125) on Welcker's homosexuality. Whereas knowledge of the sexual orientation of these scholars does not seem irrelevant to my reasoning here, I would prefer to keep such information marginal. In general, I agree with K. J. Dover's position that "the cogency of a philosophical argument, its power over the imagination, its moral and social value, and its influence over subsequent thought do not depend on the sexual orientation of its proponent" (153). In addition, for the period that concerns me here (1815–1920), the simple knowledge of an individual's own homosexual orientation does not seem sufficient to me: the degree of official persecution of homosexuality as well as the degree of personal repression of an individual's homosexuality seem to me both more relevant to the type of argument I will be considering here, and in general more difficult to evaluate.

10. For additional information on nineteenth-century German interpretations of Sappho, see the studies of Elisabeth Frenzel, Horst Rüdiger, and Tubach.

11. Welcker himself is still cited, for example by Page in *Sappho and Alcaeus*.

12. I will initially adopt the often controversial position, implicitly Welcker's, that *pederastia* can be defined as what is today known as homosexuality.

13. Neue's position is blind but not absurd, since any convincing reconstruction of the line must be metrically accurate.

14. The most influential German commentaries on *pederastia* were always translated. Probably because Meier openly asserts the sensuality of homosexuality, his study was only translated a century later. I quote from Pogey-Castries's expanded French edition (3).

15. The word is only granted admission in the supplement to the *OED*. For more information on the medical tradition, see Georges Lanteri-Laura. See George Chauncey and Faderman on the literature of sexual inversion, and Weeks on the homosexual as a product of modern capitalism.

16. In the introduction to the 1901 edition which I consulted, Symonds says that he wrote *A Problem in Greek Ethics* in 1873 and that the text was first published in 1883. I have found no trace of the 1883 edition in national library catalogs. Boswell states that the work was originally "privately printed" in 1873 (*Christianity*, 17, n. 25), but I have found no trace of an 1873 edition. The work must have been available before it is included, without the consent of Symonds's executor, in Ellis's 1897 study. Symonds also uses "homosexual" in *A Problem in Modern Ethics* (1891; see Boswell, *Christianity*, 42, n. 4). According to the

Dictionnaire de la langue du dix-neuvième et du vingtième siècle, the word was first used in German in 1869 by K. Kertbeny (Pseudonym of K. M. Benkert). Alain Corbin claims that the word first appeared in French in 1809 but gives no information about this otherwise undocumented occurrence (587).

17. I cite the English translation because the work was revised and expanded for this edition.

18. Elaine Marks discusses the prevalence of the pedagogical situation in fictions of female homosexual passion (357 ff.). However, in the Müller model Sappho is made a schoolmistress in order to deny her sexuality.

19. Directly related to this question of the gender of the aesthetic norm is the status of Sappho's person. Philologists often stressed the physical portrait, widely promoted in antiquity, of the tenth muse as small, dark, and ugly, the opposite, in other words, of the Aryan physical type. Léon Poliakov traces the beginning of the active promotion of the Aryan myth to the same period during which the promotion of philology and that of *pederastia* also are initiated. Indeed, no less important a figure in the creation of philology than Friedrich Schlegel is positioned by Poliakov at the origin of the Aryan myth (190). Nineteenth- and twentieth-century French commentators, especially those associated with the "Sapho 1900" movement, sometimes insist instead that Sappho was beautiful.

20. Wilamowitz thereby also manages to eliminate the threat posed by the exclusively female circle constituted around Sappho. In the introduction to *Communities of Women,* Nina Auerbach shows how female communities have always been the subject of wildly varying intepretations. Through the ages, the same kinds of questions have been asked about such groups that were formulated by Sappho commentators: (1) Were they schools? (2) If so, for what purpose? legitimate (to train women for socially acceptable, wifely duties)? or illegitimate (to lure them away from the world of men)? (3) If the schools trained girls to refuse men, did they advise them instead to embrace chastity, or did they corrupt their students by exposing them to sexual perversion?

21. Bachofen and his editors perform a similar dance around the term to be used here. He switches from German to Greek and says "arrenes erotes" and the German editors add in brackets "[die Männerlieben]." In the English edition, the term is initially given in Greek, a literal version of "male loves," and translated in parentheses (incorrectly) as "male homosexuality." This multilingual rite of onomastic avoidance may originate with Bachofen's implicit desire to position himself at a slight angle from commentary on *Knabenliebe.*

22. On interpretations of the Porta Maggiore fresco, see Stein, 21, 190. Mario Meunier reviews Pythagorean readings of the suicide (*Sappho,* 39–46). This leads him to compare Sappho and Saint Theresa (47), even to suggest that Sappho and Sévigné knew the same "burning maternity" (49).

23. The strange publication history of *A Problem in Greek Ethics* is described in n. 16.

24. The section's title, "Sexual inversion among Greek women," repeats the hesitation with regard to onomastic innovation evident at the study's outset. In his title, Symonds calls male homosexuality "sexual inversion," a term borrowed from the sexologists rarely found in his text. The linguistic dichotomy may signal either a simple reluctance to coin a noun based on an adjective only just created in Germany, or a decision to use the at least slightly more familiar term in the title and the (preferred) neologism in the text. In any event, Symonds simply shifts

immediately from "sexual inversion" to "homosexual" in his first page (as he does in the opening paragraph of his section on female homosexuality) without calling attention to his innovative use of neologisms.

25. When Swinburne proclaimed Sappho "the greatest poet who ever was at all," he echoed the exceptional status that Symonds, unlike German ideal love theorists, accorded her poetry (in *Studies of the Greek Poets*).

26. Though Welcker had previously waffled about the status of Phaon and the suicidal leap (in his commentary on Müller, Hillebrand even cites him as the origin of the inauthenticity theory [Müller, *Histoire*, 2:652]), he now resurrects Aphrodite's boatman to guarantee Sappho's heterosexuality. The shifting status of Phaon and of the Ovidian scenario with which, as we will see, he had become synonymous in the nineteenth century can serve to measure the power each philologist was prepared to claim for his personal authority: Phaon is such an outlandish figure that only scholars convinced of their credibility attempt to resurrect him.

27. What I term the pure doctrine of philology with respect to *Knabenliebe* continues to be preached today, virtually without alteration. See the two most recent studies, Harald Patzer's *Die Griechische Knabenliebe* (1982) and Bernard Sergent's *L'Homosexualité initiatique dans l'Europe ancienne* (1987). Sergent still repeats what is essentially Wilamowitz's view of Sappho's school preparing virgins for marriage.

28. Joubert was also the author of a defense of Napoleon I, thereby evoking the possible alliance between philology and Napoleonic fictions of Sappho. When Joubert's evaluation is compared with that of Émile Deschanel — also distorted by personal prejudice, to be sure, but far richer and better informed — one begins to wonder if French scholars' standing even in their own country may have been determined by loyalty to the positions of the reigning philologists. In other words, did Deschanel's independence from the philological party line contribute to the problems allegedly caused by his socialist politics? For another French rehearsal of the philological view of Sappho, see Alexis Pierron's 1850 *Histoire de la littérature grecque*.

29. See also Edmonds on Sappho's love of flowers (*Sappho in the Added Light*, 25–26). The enthusiastic persistence with which this argument is evoked by Anglo-American scholars made me wonder if scholarly traditions inevitably repeat clichés of national characteristics.

30. The often considerable delay in making German Sappho scholarship available in French is even more surprising when one considers that contemporary journals like the *Revue germanique* generally ensured the almost immediate transmission of German scholarly advances.

31. Boissonade offers only a variant on the dominant French version — "Or you [Sappho] will no longer desire it" — proof that he had found no textual evidence to back up his intuition. Alan Spitzer analyzes the intellectual ideals of Boissonade's day in their political context. His description of what he calls "the generation of 1820" provides the only indications I find convincing of the climate that could have made Boissonade's intellectual independence possible. It was also Boissonade who (in the *Journal de l'Empire*, 5 January 1810) proclaimed the authenticity of the *Lettres portugaises* and offered "proof" of the identity of their author, Mariane Alcaforado, demonstrating a consistent involvement with questions of the legitimacy of women's writing.

32. In the note K to his entry "Sapho," Pierre Bayle lays out the story of the two

Sapphos and categorically dismisses it, which may explain why it was never evoked in the eighteenth century when the association between Sappho and courtesans was first formed.

33. In *La Bible de l'Humanité* (1864), Jules Michelet promotes a chauvinistic vision of Sappho (the blend of Barthélemy and Visconti-Allier de Hauteroche characteristic of his national school). His biography does contain one innovation: writing shortly before the Franco-Prussian war brought on a renewed fear of depopulation, Michelet presented Sappho, for the only time in her history, as the mother of a son, a future defender of the fatherland. I am grateful to Frank Bowman for this reference.

34. Stein compares the Barrias canvas to the *odalisques* (274).

35. The earliest instance I have encountered of the linkage between the two Sapphos and Ovid's inauthenticity is in L'Héritier's commentary on her 1732 translation of the *Heroides* (349).

36. No editorial pairing has succeeded in replacing the original one, although at least two have been suggested: *Sappho und Simonides, Sappho and Alcaeus*.

37. Bréghot Du Lut uses one *p* on the title page, two inside. From the 1830s to the end of the century (when more exotic spellings are introduced), "Sappho" appears intermittently in France.

38. Bréghot Du Lut is the last translator to hint at the more complex sexual scenario that Boissonade had intuited—"her poems seem to betoken a passion that nature disavows" (161)—although he immediately backs down from this suggestion by declaring that all those who thus characterize Sapphism base their opinion on writers who lived long after the poet (162).

39. Veïssier Des Combes places a series of imitations after his translations, culminating in the vicomte de Vanderbourg's 1802 literary hoax, the version of fr. 31 allegedly composed by the fifteenth-century poet, Clotilde de Surville. For this fabrication, Vanderbourg normalized the poem's sexual orientation: it is addressed to a man and it's the other woman, the female poet's rival, who equals the gods. Both sections of the Veïssier Des Combes edition end, therefore, on a note of sexual respectability.

40. "Sticometrics," as Planchon defines it, is nothing more than the division of lines of poetry on the basis of meaning, providing a pause after each separate idea (7–9).

41. Victor Hugo was, of course, in exile at the time. Deschanel is the only commentator ever to have defined Sappho's politics as liberal: he pronounces her a "républicaine" (352).

42. I have passed over a number of translations that are remarkable neither for their quality nor for their lack of it. Marcellot and Grosset's 1847 *Odes d'Anacréon et de Sapho* repeats the standard biography and provides a relatively accurate, if bland, rendering of the two odes and four fragments. Joseph Boulmier's 1852 *Odes saphiques* is a volume in the spirit of eighteenth-century promiscuity: he blends Sappho in with poems of his own invention and imitations of the sixteenth-century Latin poet, Salmon Macrin. Dubois-Guchan's 1873 *La Pléiade Grecque* is perhaps the last edition true to the eighteenth-century vision: Sappho is grouped together with Anacreon, Alceus, Bion, Moschus, and so on. What the second "Officier de la Légion d'Honneur" to translate her passes off as her verse often owes more to Billardon de Sauvigny than to Sappho. Finally, Roche-Aymon's 1882 *Poésies d'Anacréon et de Sapho* uses the two odes and twenty-five fragments (bearing titles like "A sa mère," "A sa fille") to portray Sappho as a defender of marriage and the family.

43. Of all the eccentric commentaries on Sappho, Bascoul's may well be the most bizarre. He himself uses the adverb "feverishly" to characterize his obsessive compilation (2:Y4). He piles appendix on appendix, at the end no longer even printed but handwritten, as he finds everywhere confirmation of what he believes to be his unique comprehension of Sappho.

44. Bascoul contends, for example, that "Atthis" is "the proper name of Attica" and is inspired by "the custom in comedy of calling domestics by the name of their country" (2:53). The descriptions of the Sapphic comedies provided by Dover (174) offer a challenge to this theory.

45. Plate 3 is unusual in that Girodet does not supply a text to go with it. Coupin takes the liberty of deciding that it illustrates the poem "I slept, in my dream, in the arms of Cythérée" (5), which must be a reference to the ode "Le Songe" fabricated by Billardon de Sauvigny and long passed off as Sappho's (*Poésies*, 73–76). This invention was widely considered part of her corpus in the early nineteenth century (see, for example, L. Gorsse's 1805 epic).

46. See Miller and Robinson (108) on the controversy between "maiden" and "slender youth." Stein discusses Girodet's illustration in her section on homoerotic images of Sappho (295–96).

47. See Emeric David's review in the *Revue encyclopédique*.

48. Bergk's *Anthologia* is reedited several times during his lifetime, in addition to the posthumous reeditions I will discuss shortly. The year of the *Anthologia*'s original edition, 1854, is also the year of the discovery of the planet Sappho (the eightieth telescopic planet) by M. Pogspn. I know nothing about the astronomer's views of Sapphism.

49. Bergk's revolutionary decision may well be another proof of the influence of French Sapphic speculation on the German philological tradition: his reading may have been made conceivable in part because of mid–nineteenth-century French fantasies of the lesbian.

50. Only the commentator without ties to a national tradition, Bascoul, notes the strange lack of justification surrounding these major reversals. He accuses Bergk of having used "his authority" to "create" a new variant for the first ode. His infraction was so "monstrous" that Hiller and Crusius simply did not "dare maintain that woman [the female object of desire] in their reedition" (2:69). See William Calder (146–47) for an account of the heated dispute between Welcker and Bergk over line 24 and what Calder terms "the dread participle."

51. No dictionary is very precise about the sources on which entry dates are based. The Robert lists 1838 for "saphisme" 's appearance; the Grand Larousse gives 1842. As a noun, "lesbienne" appears in the 1862 *Complément* to the Academie Française dictionary. The adjective, as in the expression "amours lesbiennes," preceded the noun. The Robert situates "homosexuel" in 1906, the Grand Larousse in 1907. Only the *Dictionnaire de la langue du dix-neuvième et du vingtième siècle* uses an earlier date, 1891. Actual usage in all likelihood frequently antedated these examples. See, for instance, Baudelaire's use of *lesbienne* in 1845–48. In any event, it is clear that in French usage of "sapphisme" and "lesbienne" preceded and probably inspired English terminology, whereas the reverse implantation occurred with the vocabulary of "homosexual." English usage is discussed by many commentators; with reference to Sappho, see Judith Hallett (451) and Stein (257–58). Prior to the complex nineteenth-century situation, the dominant French terms were "tribade," "tribadisme."

52. Lebey was primarily a political writer, the author of two works on

socialism, a book on the 1848 revolution, and two studies of Louis-Napoléon Bonaparte.

53. Louÿs dedicates *La Femme et le pantin* "A André Lebey, son ami P.L."

54. The bisexuality of Wharton's edition is not limited to the "Ode to Aphrodite." See, for example, his parallel treatment of LP 102, the weaving fragment (116). In his "Life of Sappho," Wharton makes a convincing case for the implausibility of Barthélemy's political Sappho, a critique that did not convince the editors of the *Oxford Classical Dictionary* to honor their own scholarly tradition over the French (as Page does) and remove this late addition to Sappho's "biography."

55. The 1903 volume is not reproduced in its entirety in the two-volume 1923–24 edition, *Poésies de Renée Vivien*. In this chapter, I will try as far as possible to maintain an admittedly artificial division between Vivien's contribution as an editor of Sappho and the vision provided by her Sapphic fictions.

56. "Psappha," or "Psappho," is the correct dialectal spelling. This fact was first mentioned in France by Croiset; it was thus neither invented nor introduced by Vivien, as has been suggested.

57. As early as Neue's edition, doubt had been cast on the authenticity of "Cercola" (in French most often "Cercolas"), the name generally attributed to Sappho's husband: "Who could believe that there was someone in Greece with such an obscene name?" (2) (See Mora, 36, on the possible meaning of the alleged husband's name as slang for phallus.) Cercola's homeland, Andros, is the name of an actual island, but can also mean "Virilia" (Wharton's suggestion) or "Without Men" (Mora's). Wharton first proposed that these names were "invented in ribaldry by the Comic poets" (6).

58. In *Une Femme m'apparut,* the poet figure San Giovanni refers to "that hideous and bestial motherhood after the 'Ode to Aphrodite' and the ode 'A une femme aimée!' " (22).

59. Meunier goes further than any other chastity advocate in demanding equal rights for female homosexuality. He claims that these generous, chaste friendships functioned in an identical manner for men and for women (*Sappho*, 48–49; see also 30–31). It is hard to believe that Meunier's presentation of Sappho is not in some way a response to the German tradition. He spent several of the years between the two editions of his translation as a prisoner of war in Germany. See his account of life in German prison camps, *Un Camp de représailles* (1919), in which he describes how a German Hellenist (whom he refuses to name) wrote to ask that he be well treated. Meunier then becomes a celebrity for the Germans who, learning that he was only a sergeant, exclaim "France never knew either how to recognize men or to organize them" (15). He implies that, in the Germans' eyes, the lack of prestige awarded "the tradition" seemed to explain France's inferior nationalistic organization.

60. Page continues to express reservations with regard to the feminization of line 24. In America shortly before Reinach-Puech, Robinson provides both hetero-sexual and homosexual translations of the "Ode to Aphrodite," but gives the heterosexual version first (50). He also masculinizes fr. 31 into a poem to Phaon.

61. Reinach was the author, for example, of a history of the Dreyfus case, a study of anti-Semitism in antiquity, and a compilation of references to Judaism in Greek and Latin authors. It seems likely that Reinach's contribution to the edition was completed in the mid- to late twenties. Salomon Reinach, Théodore's father, was one of the first to question (in 1892) the foundations of the Aryan myth already

assuming great importance throughout Europe, and in Germany in particular (Poliakov, 267). It was also Salomon Reinach who collected Renée Vivien's papers and gave them to the Bibliothèque Nationale, sealing them until the year 2000. The Reinach family and the Sapho 1900 group shared a portraitist, the Dreyfus supporter, Lucien Lévy-Dhurmer.

62. Before Larnac and Salmon, only Coupé had developed a reading of Sappho's poetry as dealing solely with the exchange between the poet and her divinity: "Sappho is always speaking to Venus" (146).

63. Weigall, identified as "late Inspector-General of Antiquities, Egyptian Government," pays inordinate attention to local color and little to Sappho. Inexplicably, his biography was immediately translated into French where, largely due to Larnac and Salmon, it achieved a certain status—it is still cited by Richer in 1985. Milburn's work is a silly concoction, a fictionalization of the papyri discoveries of no scholarly (or literary) merit.

64. The theatrical chastity tradition is, for example, the clearest French influence on Grillparzer.

65. The Racinian image of Sappho as Venus's "prey" has a long life in France. The most extreme example of the poet's attempts to appease the angry goddess was imagined only in 1905, when Nonce Casanova depicts Sappho arranging to have all her students ceremoniously break their chastity vow by making love with a crew of brutal sailors (145)!

66. Indeed, the only long poem or play of the century without Racinian echoes is Emile Dario's 1862 *Sappho, élégie antique.*

67. Peyre declares that Rachel's presence at the Théâtre Français created "an unsuspected interest in Racine" (25).

68. Several of these playwrights are openly associated with the new monarchy. For example, Marc-Antoine Désaugiers *(Sapho à Leucade, intermède lyrique)* was a court poet who produced vaudevilles for virtually every event in the lives of the restored royal family (the marriage of the duc de Berry in 1816, the coronation of Charles X in 1825, etc.).

69. This theatrical tradition is thus the last literary model for the painterly iconography of Sappho's leap. Painters begin to represent this scene only when its literary popularity is already waning; by the time the suicide tradition is in full flower in painting, the scene has almost disappeared from Sapphic fictions and the event has been rejected by French Sappho scholars. (See, for example, Théodore Chassériau's 1849 canvas, and Gustave Moreau's 1867 and 1880 representations. See also Stein, chap. 6.)

70. See the article on Pradier's death in the *Revue de Paris,* July 1852. See also Claude Vignon's praise for the *Sapho* in his *Salon de 1852.* Confirmation that Pradier's figure still constituted the model for Sappho's iconography at the time of Daudet's novel is provided by Armand Silvestre, poet, critic, and early supporter of the impressionists. The stage direction for the opening scene of his 1881 play runs: "Sapho, alone, holding her lyre in the attitude of Pradier's statue" (7).

71. Daudet's only real nineteenth-century precursor for the creation of a Sappho prostitute with a heart of gold is Dumas (or his stable) who in the 1843 *Filles, Lorettes, et courtisanes* briefly portrays her as "the Greek Magdalene" (119).

72. Flaubert's *Salammbô* seems a likely inspiration for this spelling.

73. On the possible relation between fiction and reality in the history of female homosexuality in the nineteenth century, I agree completely with Alain Corbin's

conclusion: "It is at present impossible to write the history of female homosexuality. Outside of a worldly practice which exists from the 'anandrines' of the late eighteenth century to the rich Americans in Belle Epoque Paris, we know only the interminable pronouncements of doctors and magistrates on the proliferation of tribades in the bordellos and prisons. What we do know well, on the other hand, is the fascination that the lesbian exerts on the contemporary male imagination. . . . The masculine phantasms which lead to the medicalization of [the pederast], incite the poetization of [the lesbian]" (589).

74. The parodic characterization of Houssaye's play is actually a reasonably accurate description of what is, to my knowledge, the last Sapphic play. Francis Vielé-Griffin's 1912 *Sapho* (in which Sappho is blended with Mallarmé just as outrageously as nineteenth-century playwrights wove her voice together with Racine's) concludes with what seems to be a dialogue between Sappho and the White Rock. While numerous writers use Sappho as a vehicle to come to terms with Racine, this is the only case in which she plays a parallel role vis à vis Mallarmé.

75. This attribution is justified by Le Dantec (1:1592), of Baudelaire's editors the most attuned to matters Sapphic (he translated Sappho and wrote a study of Renée Vivien). The parody is not included in the more recent Pléiade edition. The recent biography of Baudelaire by Pichois and Zeigler attributes the parody to Baudelaire, Banville, Pierre Dupont, and Auguste Vitu (219). The two entries in the *Corsaire-Satan* are dated 24 November 1845 and 17 January 1846.

76. The poem was removed from the anthology's second edition (1858), after it became one of the condemned "pieces" of the *Fleurs du mal* in 1857.

77. Boyer's overnight success culminated in instant parody. Less than a month after his eulogy, Banville reviews, also in the pages of *Le Pouvoir*, *La Veuve Sopha*, *parodie de la Sapho de M. Philoxène Boyer* (16 December 1850).

78. In a prologue Banville composed for Boyer's play, he refers to Racine as "the master" before whose example the young playwright "trembles" (3–4).

79. Baudelaire was inspired for "L'Ecole païenne" by Daumier's caricatures of overused figures from antiquity, *Histoire ancienne*. The series of fifty plates appeared in *Le Charivari* between December 1841 and January 1843. "La Mort de Sapho," which depicts a vile hag being forced to the edge of a cliff by Cupid, is number 49 (January 1843). Before "L'Ecole païenne," Baudelaire had not mocked artists who depicted Sappho. See his review of Dugasseau's 1845 *Sapho* (ed. Le Dantec, 1:833).

80. In some of the most offensive Sappho commentary of the age, Gautier compares Sappho to Staël as female political exiles, only to conclude that their examples prove that women should stay out of politics and keep themselves busy with love, "without mixing the graceful pleats of their white tunics in with the somber cloaks of conspirators" (Richer, 166–67).

81. "For Lesbos chose me among all on the earth / To sing the secret of its budding virgins, / And I was in childhood admitted to the black mystery / Of frantic laughter mixed with somber tears; / For Lesbos chose me among all on the earth."

82. François Jean-Desthieux is convinced of the reference to Staël (74). A reference to an actual figure, Delphine Gay, has also been proposed (ed. Pichois, 1:1128, n. 1), but I find this possibility less convincing because it ignores the literariness in which Baudelaire so carefully anchors his lesbian. The connection

between "Delphine" and Staël for the decadent writer is confirmed by Barbey d'Aurevilly's *Le Bonheur dans le crime,* in which "Delphine" is the name of the first comtesse de Savigny and which also refers explicitly to Staël. Frank Bowman suggests that the primary reference is to Delphine de Sabran.

83. Only Vielé-Griffin outdoes Banville in his use of Sappho as patroness of art for art's sake. His 1912 play defines Sapphism as the search for perfect beauty and the total commitment to art (170–71), but with no suggestion of the erotic content associated with the use of similar arguments to justify *pederastia.* Sappho defines her "fertility" *(ma vie féconde)* as having trained her pupils to become poets (173).

84. Faderman discusses demographers' renewed fears of a declining birthrate in the late nineteenth century and suggests that literary vituperation against lesbianism might have been inspired by "fear of anything which might promote that decline" (281). In the case of Sapphic commentary, the fear that the Germans might get ahead was translated, paradoxically, into an allegiance with their philological tradition.

85. Verlaine was also the author of quite graphic clandestine lesbian poetry.

86. The most disquieting of these popular Sapphic texts is A. Hope's 1836 *Sapho.* His portrait of Sappho is sufficient to convey the tone of the work: "She is wretched, misshapen, with red hair, one near-sighted eye, the other missing, a hooked nose, the mouth of a negro, an elephant's teeth, gingerbread skin, a camel's figure, an ass's skin, that's Sapho" (8).

87. Baudelaire also inspired the contemporary pictorial convention of lesbianism. Courbet noted his debt to "Delphine et Hippolyte" for the 1864 *Femmes damnées* and the 1866 *Le Sommeil, ou Les Dormeuses* (Baudelaire, ed. Pichois, 1:1127).

88. Faderman notes the increase in antilesbian fiction, such as Adolphe Belot's 1870 *Mademoiselle Giraud, ma femme,* during the second half of the century (see her chapter "Lesbian Evils"). However, before the early twentieth century, such fictions are unrelated to fictions of Sappho.

89. "This name was in doubt and Bergk almost believed that she was called simply Mnaïs" (17). Due to breaks in the texts, there is still uncertainty about the spelling of this name and about which poems are written to this "Mnasidika"-"Dika."

90. Louÿs's little jibe could have prompted Wilamowitz to counterattack by republishing his review in *Sappho und Simonides.*

91. "Then the Unknown Woman, persuasive and formidable, terrible and gentle, says to me: — If you love me, you will forget your family and your husband and your country and your children and you will come to live with me.

"If you love me, you will leave everything you cherish and the places where you remember yourself . . . and your memories and your hopes will become nothing more than the desire for me. . . .

"And I answered her sobbing: I love you."

92. Gubar credits Vivien with having "tapped the energy of the decadents' alienated lesbian," with having first suggested that the " 'unnatural' longing of the decadents' Sappho turns the lesbian into a prototypical artist." "[Vivien] subversively implies that the lesbian is the epitome of the decadent and that decadence is fundamentally a lesbian literary tradition" (49). I have no disagreement with this reading of Vivien, but I still maintain that the essence of her portrait of the artist as lesbian is already in Barney's *Cinq petits dialogues grecs*—and that

Baudelaire, even though admittedly in a completely different ideological spirit, already creates the essence of the decadents' impossible self-portrait as Sappho, important elements of which are invented by Houssaye and Boyer. For an overly Baudelairean reading of Vivien that makes her work into a simple annex to *Les Fleurs du mal*, see Le Dantec's *Renée Vivien, Femme damnée, femme sauvée*.

93. In addition to the *Femmes damnées*, Jean-Desthieux's production is limited almost exclusively to the four volumes in which he preached that World War I had not concluded the hostilities, and announced that the continuing existence of "nationalistic gestures" would culminate in "the misfortune of the universe" (*Petite Entente*, 5). See *La Leçon de Pyrrhus* (1920), *La Petite Entente* (1922), *Les Dessous de la Petite Entente* (1921), and *La Paix est à refaire* (1933).

94. Psappha also commits suicide from unrequited love for a girl (unnamed) in Vivien's "La Mort de Psappha" (*Poèmes*, 1:88–93). In Vivien's "Dans un verger," Psappha's suicidal leap has a clearer cause: "Eros has broken my soul, as the wind / Twists the mountains and breaks the great oaks" (2:141). After her death, Eranna recites a paraphrase of fr. 31 and Damophyla declares that "Psappha . . . has suffered the anger / Of the Gods who, smiling, pursue their design" (2:143). Vivien thereby brings full circle the uncanny erotics of the Sappho-Phèdre identification, initiated by Racine, making Sappho at last victim of the gods, like Phèdre, but because of her love for a woman. The only fiction by a "Sapho 1900" writer that seems to have preserved the traditional scenario (suicide because of Phaon) is Lucie Delarue-Mardrus's two-act verse tragedy *Sapho désespérée*, whose title was changed to *Phaon victorieux*. I say "seems" on the basis of the titles. The play was never published and I have not succeeded in finding any information on the location of a possible manuscript. The tragedy was staged twice, by the Comédie Française in the Greek theater in Orange in 1906 and by the Théâtre Femina in 1913 with Lucie Delarue-Mardrus herself playing the role of Sapho. (Elaine Marks called my attention to this information, available in Emilie Sirieyx de Villers's biography of Delarue-Mardrus [29]).

95. "I will be, that night, the guest that you are afraid of seeing. / . . . / I will occupy my place, invisible, at table. / . . . / Like before, I will come to your bed, / It will be his kiss, but it will be my mouth. / You will desire me through his desire. / And once again you will give my name to your pleasure."

96. Frank Bowman warns me that this suggestion may be a fiction based on the public reputation of the Saint-Simonians.

97. Although Page generally supports English scholars (Mure and especially Symonds), he breaks with his native tradition on the schoolteacher issue (which he associates primarily with Wilamowitz) and reserves one of the first salvos of his essay "The Contents and Character of Sappho's Poetry" for it: "the theory finds no support whatever in anything worthy of the name of fact" (*Sappho and Alcaeus*, 111).

98. Faderman attributes the profusion of lesbian characters created by male French writers in fin-de-siècle literature to "a reaction to some dramatic signs of female independence" (254).

99. The first Sapphic fiction to place Sappho in an exotic setting is also at the origin of the decadent vision. Houssaye's drama opens in "Sappho's room" which is ornamented with "frescoes and mosaics."

100. The scenario of Sappho as her brother's rival for a courtesan (identified as either Dorique or Rhodope) was invented in antiquity by Athenaeus and Strabo. In modern times, it seems to have been developed exclusively by the French, who further embellish it by identifying the courtesan as the object of fr. 31 and the

brother Charaxe as Sappho's male rival in the poem. Saint-Marc, a Boileau commentator, seems to have resurrected the theory; Deschanel gives it its fullest modern development (344, n. 1). Maurice Donnay also uses this critical fiction in a literary work: a scene of his *Lysistrata* (1892) features an imitation of fr. 31 justified in this way (1:2). It is fitting that this scenario, in which the beloved woman rejects Sappho for her male double, enter the French tradition under the patronage of Boileau, who toned down the sapphic passion of fr. 31.

101. The only Sapphic novel of the period that makes no attempt to formulate a response to the medical tradition is Casanova's 1905 *Sapho: Roman de la Grèce antique*. The threat of Sapphic pedagogy is evident, but it is presented only as the loss of future citizens because her students pledge to remain chaste. Casanova simply repeats the most traditional Ovidian scenario in an overblown, long-winded style. He makes only one attempt to profit from his subject's sensationalism: a lurid frontispiece of a near-naked woman weighed down with exotic jewelry.

102. In a fascinating argument, Isabelle de Courtivron sees the virile *femme fatale* as betraying the desire of her male creators to be women, simultaneously to hand over a masculine role to a woman and accept for themselves a feminine one: she "was dreamed up as a warning against the eventual concretization of an appealing but destructive fantasy" (226).

103. On the contrary, in an interview granted Richard Hall for *The Advocate* shortly before her death, Yourcenar denies having known any of the Americans in Paris at the time of their initial impact on the French literary scene and claims that she knew Barney only "after 1954" (39). I would argue that the question still remains open because of Yourcenar's widely documented desire to, in Hall's words, "sidestep the issue of homosexuality" (38), especially, I would add, as it could refer to her own biography. Thus she remarked to a *New York Times* interviewer: "I live in Maine, so people call me a recluse. . . . Because I lived with a woman for forty years, people assume I'm a lesbian" (22 January 1981). It seems clear that, no more than Sappho's, Yourcenar's sexual biography will never be able to be written. I am grateful to Michael Cadden for a xerox of *The Advocate* interview.

104. Of Sappho, Yourcenar says only that "she was born on an island" (1126). We learn that Phaon "claims to be the son of a Greek of Smyrna and a sailor of the British fleet: Sappho's heart beats at hearing once more the delicious accent so often embraced on Atthys's lips" (1130). In Phaon, and possibly Atthys, Yourcenar repeats Sappho's geographic configuration: Greek surrounded by the more exotic Turkish.

105. My reading of "Sappho ou le suicide" coincides at times with Gubar's (see especially 60–62). However, I am less certain of Yourcenar's situation with regard to the international modernist lesbian community whose relation to Sappho Gubar so convincingly exposes.

106. Like his mentor Welcker, Wilamowitz fought against the French: he enlisted in 1870 (Calder, 136, n. 29).

107. Yourcenar, who debunks all the myths of Sappho's biography, nonetheless maintains the exile theory: "We know that the poetess was exiled from Lesbos following a political upheaval, and that she returned there when the defeated party returned to power" (*Couronne*, 69).

108. Yourcenar completed work on *Hadrien* on Mount Desert Island, Maine. She has toyed with the notion of her situation in the margins of the empire by pointing out that her island figures on maps of Louis XIV's Arcadie.

109. "Sappho's art has nothing bland, nothing soft or artificial" (*Couronne*, 72).

Epilogue

1. This entry is not an isolated case of English collaboration to preserve Wilamowitz's interpretive authority over Sappho. Let me give just one more example: the notes on Catullus 51 in C. J. Fordyce's standard commentary begin with a description of Catullus's model (fr. 31) which privileges the nuptial scenario Wilamowitz imagines for the poem (218).

2. Page thus defines the lifespan of scholarship's memory as a half-century. It would hardly be reasonable to insist that it should be longer, although it seems to me that some consciousness of the broad outline of a longer interpretive history could always held commentators to be mindful of interference from their own prejudices.

3. See Dover (179) on the culmination of Page's jealousy reading in the theory of Sappho's "penis envy" or "phallic awe." It hardly need be noted that Page is influenced not only by German philology's view of Sappho, but also by the Freudian interpretation of the eroticism of female homosexuality. (See Freud's "Psychogenesis of a Case of Homosexuality in a Woman." See also Irigaray's reading of Freud's position in *Speculum* and de Lauretis's elaboration of Irigaray's position.)

4. The beginning of line 24 is also related to what might be termed the line's mode, since it contains the adverb and the negative particle that modify the final participle. Such questions, related to verb placement (temporality, repetition, etc.) form the basis of Page's "control" interpretation. It is fitting, therefore, that English Hellenists deflect our attention there, away from the sexuality encoded in the line's ending.

5. Dover's equally measured reading of Sappho fr. 31 follows (177–79). Dover is virtually unique among Sappho commentators in that he is constantly on the alert for the blinding intrusion of personal prejudice: "The reader is warned that in any eventual decision between alternate treatments of this poem [fr. 31] there is a larger element of subjectivity than I would usually (if I perceive it in time) allow myself" (178, n. 19).

6. It seems likely that Woolf knew the work of English chastity theorists like Edmonds. I find it hard to believe that she did not also have Wilamowitz in mind, since her description of the state's policy on sapphism seems such a convincing parody of his arguments. She may also have known the work of Bascoul, the one medical doctor (whether a gynecologist, I do not know) to have concerned himself with Sappho's chastity.

Appendix

1. When referring to the Greek, I always cite the text given by Lobel and Page. I do not reproduce the poems in Greek on the assumption that specialist readers can easily consult this text.

2. Eva Stehle Stigers's reading suggests a way of combining these two strategies. She deflects attention from the traditional autobiographical reading by presenting the erotic orientation of Sappho's poetry as determined by *formal* concerns: "The formal problem facing Sappho was to find a way of presenting the female persona as an erotic subject: . . . Sappho's solution, to direct the erotic impulse toward other women, was perhaps a traditional one" (45).

3. For bibliography on these questions and discussion of the various points of view recently defended, see Anne Giacomelli.

4. This designation is generally accepted today. However, older editions assign

the poem different positions in Sappho's corpus. In Reinach-Puech, still the standard French edition, for example, it is fr. 2.

5. I came across in fact only one French translation that reproduced these lines accurately.

6. "The greatest obstacle to our understanding of the whole is indeed our ignorance of the relation of this man to the girl and to Sappho . . . : But we must not forget that the *man* was the principal subject of the whole of the first stanza, and we shall not be content with any explanation of this poem which gives no satisfactory account of his presence and his prominence in it" (*Sappho and Alcaeus,* 28).

7. In Girard's model, the desiring subject is always a man, or a woman, like Emma Bovary, created by a male author.

8. For background and an extensive bibliography on the jealousy theory and the issue of the man's centrality, see Emmet Robbins.

References*

Addison, Joseph. *The Spectator* 223 (15 November 1711); 229 (22 November 1711); 233 (27 November 1711).

Alletz, Pons-Augustin. *L'Esprit des femmes célèbres du siècle de Louis XIV et de celui de Louis XV.* 2 vols. Pissot, 1768.

Allier de Hauteroche, L. *Notice sur la courtisane Sapho, née à Erésos, dans l'île de Lesbos.* Dondey-Dupré, 1822. (This version is more complete than that in the *Journal Asiatique.*)

Aronson, Nicole. *Mademoiselle de Scudéry ou le voyage au pays de Tendre.* Fayard, 1986.

Auerbach, Nina. *Communities of Women.* Cambridge, Mass.: Harvard University Press, 1978.

Augier, Emile, and Charles Gounod. *Sapho, opéra en trois actes.* Michel Lévy, 1851.

Aulotte, Robert. "Sur quelques traductions d'une ode de Sappho au XVIe siècle." *Lettres d'Humanité* 17 (1958): 107–22.

Bachet, sieur de, trans. *Les Epîtres d'Ovide.* Bourg-en-Bresse: Tainturier, 1626.

Bachofen, J.J. *Myth, Religion, and Mother Right.* 1861. Translated by Ralph Manheim. Princeton, N.J.: Princeton University Press, 1967.

Backer, Dorothy. *Precious Women.* New York: Basic Books, 1974.

Badolle, M. *J.-J. Barthélemy.* Presses Universitaires de France, 1926.

Baïf, Antoine de. *Oeuvres en rime.* 4 vols. Le Breyer, 1573.

Balayé, Simone. *Madame de Staël: Lumières et liberté.* Klincksieck, 1979.

Balzac, Guez de. *Lettres.* Pierre Rocolet, 1636.

Banville, Théodore de. "La Semaine dramatique." *Le Pouvoir,* 18 November 1850.

Barney, Natalie Clifford [Tryphê, pseud.]. *Cinq petits dialogues grecs.* Editions de la Plume, 1902.

———. "Equivoque." *Actes et entr'actes.* Sansot, 1910.

———. *Souvenirs indiscrets.* Flammarion, 1960.

Barrin, Jean, trans. *Les Epîtres d'Ovide.* Audinet, 1676.

Barthélemy, Jean-Jacques. *Voyage du jeune Anacharsis en Grèce.* 1788. Reprint (7 vols.). De Buré, 1790.

Bascoul, J.-M.-F. *La Chaste Sappho de Lesbos et le mouvement féministe à Athènes au quatrième siècle avant J.-C.* Welter, 1911.

*Unless otherwise noted, all works were published in Paris.

————. *La Chaste Sappho de Lesbos et Stésichore.* Welter, 1913.

Batteux, abbé. *Cours de Belles-Lettres.* 1747. Reprint (4 vols.). Saillant, 1774.

Baudelaire, Charles. *Les Fleurs du mal.* Edited by Antoine Adam. Garnier, 1961.

————. *Oeuvres complètes.* Edited by Yves-Gérard Le Dantec and Claude Pichois. 2 vols. Gallimard, 1968.

————. *Oeuvres complètes.* Edited by Claude Pichois. 2 vols. Gallimard, 1975.

Bayle, Pierre. *Dictionnaire historique et critique.* 1697. Reprint. Desoer, 1820.

Beattie, A. J. "A Note on Sappho Fr. 1." *Classical Quarterly* 7.1–2 (January-April 1957): 180–83.

————. "Sappho Fr. 31." *Mnemosyne* 4th ser. 9–10 (1956–57): 103–11.

Belleau, Rémi, trans. *Les Odes d'Anacréon Teien traduites du grec.* André Wechel, 1556.

Benjamin, Walter. *Charles Baudelaire: A Lyric Poet in the Era of High Capitalism.* Translated by H. Zohn. London: New Left Books, 1973.

Bergk, Theodore. *Anthologia lyrica.* 1854. Reprint. Leipzig: Teubner, 1868.

————. *Anthologia lyrica.* Edited by Edouard Hiller. 1896. Reprint. Leipzig: Teubner, 1913.

Bibliothèque universelle des dames. Hôtel Serpente, 1787. (Sapho in vol. 8, pp. 95–131.)

Billardon de Sauvigny, Louis-Edmé. *Le Parnasse des dames.* 9 vols. Rualt, 1773. (Vol. 1 contains his translation of Sappho.)

[Billardon de Sauvigny, Louis-Edmé], trans. *Poésies de Sapho, suivies de différentes poésies dans le même genre.* Amsterdam, 1777.

Billy, André. *L'Epoque 1900.* Tallandier, 1951.

Blin de Sainmore, Adrien. *Héroïdes ou Lettres en vers.* S. Jorry, 1767.

————. *Lettre de Sapho à Phaon.* S. Jorry, 1766.

Boileau, Nicolas. *Oeuvres complètes.* Gallimard-Pléiade, 1966.

Boissonade, Jean-François. *Lyrici Graeci.* Lefèvre, 1825.

————. "Variétés." *Journal de l'Empire,* 3 December 1812.

Bonnet, Marie-Jo. *Un Choix sans équivoque: Recherches historiques sur les relations amoureuses entre les femmes, XVIe–XXe siècle.* Denoël-Gonthier, 1981.

Boswell, John. *Christianity, Social Tolerance, and Homosexuality.* Chicago: University of Chicago Press, 1980.

————. "Revolutions, Universals, and Sexual Categories." *Salmagundi* 58–59 (1982–83): 89–113.

Boyer, Philoxène. *Sapho, drame en un acte.* Typographie de Dondey-Dupré, 1850.

Brandt, Paul. *Sappho.* Leipzig: Friedrich Rothbarth, 1905. (See also Hans Licht.)

Brantôme, Pierre de Bourdeilles de. *Les Dames galantes.* Gallimard-Folio, 1981.

Bray, Bernard. *L'Art de la lettre amoureuse: Des manuels aux romans (1550–1700).* The Hague: Mouton, 1967.

————. ed. *Romans d'amour par lettres.* Garnier-Flammarion, 1983.

Bréghot Du Lut, Claude, trans. *Poésies de Sapho.* In *Odes d'Anacréon,* edited by J. B. Montfalcon. Crozet, 1835.

Calder, William M. III. "F. G. Welcker's *Sapphobild* and its Reception in Wilamowitz." *Hermes* 49 (1986): 131–56.

Canat, René. *L'Hellénisme des romantiques.* 3 vols. Didier, 1951.

Casanova, Nonce. *Sapho: Roman de la Grèce antique.* Société d'éditions littéraires et scientifiques, 1905.

Chateaubriand, François-René, vicomte de. *Mémoires d'outre tombe.* Edited by F. Levaillant. 2 vols. Garnier, 1949.

Chauncey, George. "Female Deviance." *Salmagundi* 58–59 (1982–1983): 114–46.

Chaussard, J.-B. *Fêtes et courtisanes de la Grèce: Supplément aux Voyages d'Anacharsis et d'Anténor.* 1801. Reprint (4 vols.). Chez les principaux libraires, 1821.

Chauvet, Joseph-Joachim-Victor. *Sapho, poème en trois chants.* Chez les Marchands de Nouveautés, 1815.

Cixous, Hélène. "Le Rire de la Méduse." 1975. Translated by Keith Cohen and Paula Cohen. In *New French Feminisms,* edited by Elaine Marks and Isabelle de Courtivron, 875–93. Amherst, Mass.: University of Massachusetts Press, 1980.

Corbin, Alain, et al. *Histoire de la vie privée.* Vol. 4, *De la Révolution à la Grande Guerre.* Editions du Seuil, 1987.

Coupé, abbé Jean-Marie. *Soirées littéraires.* 16 vols. Honnert, 1795.

Cournol, Hippolyte. *Sapho, tragédie lyrique en trois actes.* Didot, 1819.

Courtivron, Isabelle de. "Weak Men and Fatal Women: The Sand Image." In *Homosexualities and French Literature,* edited by George Stambolian and Elaine Marks, 210–27. Ithaca, N.Y.: Cornell University Press, 1978.

Croiset, Alfred. *Histoire de la littérature grecque.* Vol. 2, *Lyrisme.* Fontemoing, 1898.

Crompton, Louis. *Byron and Greek Love.* Berkeley and Los Angeles: University of California Press, 1985.

Dacier, Anne Le Fèvre, trans. *Les Poésies d'Anacréon et de Sapho.* D. Thierry, 1681.

D'Andlau, Béatrice. *La Jeunesse de Madame de Staël.* Geneva: Droz, 1970.

Dario, Emile. *Sappho, élégie antique.* Moissac: Larnaudes, 1862.

Daudet, Alphonse. *Sapho.* 1884. Reprint. Flammarion, 1887.

———. *Trente ans de Paris.* Marpon et Flammarion, 1888.

D'Auvigny, Jean Du Castre. *L'Histoire et les amours de Sapho de Mytilène.* 1724. Reprint. The Hague: Jean Neaulme, 1743.

David, Emeric. Review of *Recueil de Compositions,* by Anne-Louis Girodet. *Revue Encyclopédique* 38 (1828): 103–8.

Déimier, Pierre de. *Lettres amoureuses, ensemble la traduction de toutes les épîtres d'Ovide.* G. Sevestre, 1612.

DeJean, Joan. "Classical Reeducation: Decanonizing the Feminine." In *The Politics of Tradition,* edited by DeJean and Nancy K. Miller. *Yale French Studies* (Fall 1988): 26–39.

———. "Female Voyeurism: Sappho and Lafayette." *Rivista di Letterature Moderne e Comparate* 40 (1987): 201–15.

De Lauretis, Teresa. "Sexual Indifference and Lesbian Representation." *Theatre Journal* 40 (May 1988): 155–77.

Deschanel, Emile. "Sappho et les Lesbiennes." *Revue des Deux Mondes* 17 (1847): 330–57.

Desjardins, Marie-Catherine [Mme de Villedieu]. *Les Exilés de la cour d'Auguste.* Lyon: Amaulry, 1679.

Des Rues, François. *Les Fleurs du bien dire*. Lyon: Roche, 1595.

―――. *Les Marguerites françaises*. Rouen: Reinsart, 1612.

Dijkstra, Bram. *Idols of Perversity: Fantasies of Feminine Evil in Fin-de-Siècle Culture*. New York: Oxford University Press, 1986.

Donnay, Maurice. *Lysistrata*. Grand Théâtre, 1892.

Dover, K. J. *Greek Homosexuality*. Cambridge, Mass.: Harvard University Press, 1978.

Du Four de La Crespelière, Jacques [Le Poète Goguenard], trans. *Les Odes amoureuses, charmantes, et bachiques des poètes grecs Anacréon, Sappho et Théocrite*. J.-B. Loyson, 1670.

Dumas, Alexandre. *Filles, Lorettes, et courtisanes*. 1843. Reprint. Lévy, 1896.

Edmonds, J[ohn] M[axwell]. *Lyra Graeca*. 1922. Reprint (3 vols.). London and New York: Heinemann and Putnams, 1928.

―――. *Sappho in the Added Light of the New Fragments*. Cambridge: Deighton Bell, 1912.

Estienne, Henri. *Pindari Olympia Pythia, Nemea, Caeterorum octo lyricorum carmina*. 1560. Reprint (2 vols.). H. Fuggerus, 1566. (First edition does not include all Sappho texts.)

Fabricius, J.-A. *Bibliotheca Graeca*. 1704. Reprint (4 vols.). Hamburg: Liebezeit, 1725. (The entry "Sappho" is in vol. 1.)

―――. *Bibliotheca Graeca*. 4 vols. Hamburg, 1791. (The entry "Sappho" is in vol. 2.)

Faderman, Lillian. *Surpassing the Love of Men: Romantic Friendship and Love between Women from the Renaissance to the Present*. New York: William Morrow, 1981.

Farnham, Fern. *Madame Dacier: Scholar and Humanist*. Monterey, Calif.: Angel Press, 1976.

Fauchery, Pierre. *La Destinée féminine dans le roman européen du dix-huitième siècle*. Colin, 1972.

Faure, G.-A. *La Dernière Journée de Sapphô*. Mercure de France, 1901.

Ferrand, Anne Bellinzani. "Une Lettre de la présidente Ferrand sur Madame Dacier." *Revue d'Histoire littéraire de la France* 13 (1906): 326–31.

Fordyce, C. J. *Catullus*. Oxford: Clarendon Press, 1961.

Foucault, Michel. *Surveiller et punir: Naissance de la prison*. Gallimard, 1977.

―――. *L'Usage des plaisirs*. Gallimard, 1984.

―――. *La Volonté de savoir*. Gallimard, 1976.

Freadman, Anne. "Poeta (lst decl., n., fem.)." *Australian Journal of French Studies* (1979): 152–65.

Frenzel, Elisabeth. *Stoffe der Weltliteratur: Ein Lexikon Dichtungsgeschichtlicher Längsschnitte*. Stuttgart: Alfred Kröner, 1963.

Freud, Sigmund. *The Standard Edition of the Complete Psychological Works*. Edited and translated by James Strachey. 24 vols. London: The Hogarth Press, 1953–74.

Fukui, Yoshio. "Une théorie sur l'art épistolaire vers 1625." *Etudes de langue et littérature françaises* 1 (1965): 42–48.

Gacon, François [Le Poète sans fard], trans. *Les Odes d'Anacréon et de Sapho*. Rotterdam: Fritz et Böhm, 1712.

Gans, Eric. "Naissance du moi lyrique: Du féminin au masculin." *Poétique* 46 (1981): 129–39.

Giacomelli, Anne. "The Justice of Aphrodite in Sappho Fr. 1." *Transactions of the American Philological Association* 110 (1980): 135–42.

Gilbert, Sandra, and Susan Gubar. *The Madwoman in the Attic.* New Haven, Conn.: Yale University Press, 1979.

Girard, René. "Generative Violence and the Extinction of Social Order." *Salmagundi* 63–64 (Spring/Summer 1984): 22–49.

Giraud, Jean. "D'Après Sapho: Variations sur un thème éternel." *Revue d'Histoire littéraire de la France* 27 (1920): 194–203.

Girodet, Anne-Louis. *Recueil de Compositions dessinées par Girodet, et gravées par M. Chatillon, son élève; avec la traduction en vers par Girodet de quelques-uns des poésies de Sappho et une notice sur la vie et les oeuvres de Sappho par M. P. A. Coupin.* 1827. Reprint. Chaillou-Potrelle, 1829.

Gorsse, L. *Sapho, poëme en dix chants.* 2 vols. Giguet et Michaud, 1805.

Gourio, abbé Thomas. *Galerie littéraire.* Delloye, 1837.

Grainville, J.-B., trans. *Hymnes de Sapho, nouvellement découvertes et traduites pour la première fois en français.* Trainetelle et Lemarchand, l'an V [1796].

Grenaille, François de. *Nouveau recueil de lettres des dames tant anciennes que modernes.* 2 vols. Toussainct Quinet, 1642.

Grillparzer, Franz. *Sappho.* Translated by J. Bramsen. London: Alexander Black, 1820. (Original German edition 1818.)

Gubar, Susan. "Sapphistries." *Signs* (Autumn 1984): 43–62.

Gutwirth, Madelyn. "La *Delphine* de Madame de Staël: Femme, Révolution et mode épistolaire." *Cahiers Staëliens* 26–27 (1979): 151–65.

———. *Madame de Staël, Novelist: The Emergence of the Artist as Woman.* Urbana: University of Illinois Press, 1978.

———. "Madame de Staël's Debt to *Phèdre: Corinne.*" *Studies in Romanticism* 3 (Spring 1964): 161–76.

Haines, C. R. *Sappho: The Poems and Fragments.* London: Routledge, 1926.

Hall, Richard. Interview with Marguerite Yourcenar. *The Advocate,* 10 June 1982 and 16 February 1988.

Hallett, Judith. "Sappho and Her Social Context: Sense and Sensuality." *Signs* 4 (Spring 1979): 447–64.

Halperin, David M. "One Hundred Years of Homosexuality." *Diacritics* (Summer 1986): 34–45.

Heinsius, Nicolaus. *Notae in Heroidas P. Ovidii Nasonis.* Leipzig, 1658.

Hope, A. *Sapho.* Barba, 1836.

Horace. *Satires, Epistles, and Ars poetica.* Translated by H. Rushton Fairclough. Loeb Classical Library. 1926.

Houssaye, Arsène. *Les Confessions: Souvenirs d'un demi-siècle 1830–1880.* 4 vols. Dentu, 1885.

———. *Sapho, drame antique en trois actes. L'Artiste* (15 October 1850): 150–53; (1 November 1850): 167–72; (15 November 1850): 182–84.

Hubaux, Jean. "Ovide et Sappho." *Le Musée belge* 30 (1926): 197–218.

Hunter-Stiebel, Penelope. *Menuiserie: The Carved Wood Furniture of Eighteenth*

Century France. Exhibit catalog. Rosenberg and Stiebel, 18 April–14 June 1986.

Imperiale, Vincenzo. *La Faoniade: Inni ed odi di Saffo.* 1784. Reprint. Pisa: Dalla Nova Tipografia, 1803.

Irigaray, Luce. "Ce Sexe qui n'en est pas un." Translated by Claudia Reeder. In *New French Feminisms,* edited by Elaine Marks and Isabelle de Courtivron, 192–214. Amherst, Mass.: University of Massachusetts Press, 1980.

―――. *Speculum de l'autre femme.* Editions de Minuit, 1974.

―――. *This Sex Which Is Not One.* Translated by Catharine Porter. Ithaca, N.Y.: Cornell University Press, 1977.

Jacobson, Howard. *Ovid's "Heroides."* Princeton, N.J.: Princeton University Press, 1974.

Jean-Desthieux, François. *Les Femmes damnées.* Gap: Editions Orphys, 1937.

―――. *La Paix n'est pas faite: La Petite Entente.* Bossard, 1922.

Jenkyns, Richard. *The Victorians and Ancient Greece.* Cambridge, Mass.: Harvard University Press, 1980.

Joubert, Léo. "Alcée et Sapho." In *Essais de critique et d'histoire.* Firmin Didot, 1863.

―――. *Dictionnaire de biographie générale.* Firmin Didot, 1870.

Jouy, V. J. E. de. *La Galerie des Femmes.* 1799. Reprint. Tchou, 1968.

Juillerat, Paul. *La Reine de Lesbos, drame antique.* A La Librairie Théâtrale, 1854.

Jym, trans. *Sapho de Mytilène réhabilitée, traduction équirythmique.* Angers: Bruel, 1937.

Kany, Charles. *The Beginnings of the Epistolary Novel in France, Italy, and Spain. University of California Publications in Modern Philology* 21 (1937): 1–158.

Kauffman, Linda. *Discourses of Desire: Gender, Genre, and Epistolary Fictions.* Ithaca, N.Y.: Cornell University Press, 1986.

Knox, A.D. "On Editing Hipponax: A Palinode?" *Studi Italiani di Filologia Classica* (1939): 193–96.

Labé, Louise. *Oeuvres complètes.* Edited by François Rigolot. Flammarion, 1986.

La Bruyère, Jean de. *Les Caractères.* 1694. Reprint. Seuil, 1964.

La Forge, Jean de. *Le Cercle des femmes sçavantes.* Loyson, 1663.

La Fosse, Antoine de. *Les Poésies d'Anacréon et de Sapho avec la traduction en vers français de Mr de La Fosse.* Edited by Anne Le Fèvre Dacier. Amsterdam: Veuve P. Marret, 1716.

La Gessée, Jean de. *Premières oeuvres.* 2 vols. Anvers: C. Plantin, 1583.

La Harpe, Jean de. *Lycée.* An VI–XIII. Reprint. (16 vols.). Deterville, 1818.

La Jonchère, Vénard de. *Sapho, opéra en trois actes. Théâtre lyrique.* Barbou, 1772.

La Morvonnais, Hippolyte de. *Elégies et autres poésies, suivies de Sapho, drame lyrique en deux actes.* Ponthieu, 1824.

Lanteri-Laura, Georges. *Lecture des perversions: Histoire de leur appropriation médicale.* Masson, 1979.

Lantier, E. F. *Voyages d'Anténor en Grèce et en Asie.* 1797. Reprint (2 vols.) Buisson, 1801.

[La Porte, Jean de]. *L'Esprit de mademoiselle de Scudéry.* Amsterdam: Vincent 1766.

———. *Histoire littéraire des femmes françaises.* 5 vols. Lacombe, 1769.

Larnac, Jean, and Robert Salmon. *Sappho.* Editions Rieder, 1934.

[La Roche-Guilhen, Anne de.] *Sapho, ou l'heureuse inconstance.* La Haye, 1695.

Lathuillère, Roger. *La Préciosité: Etude historique et linguistique.* Geneva: Droz, 1966.

Lebey, André, trans. *Les Poésies de Sapho.* Mercure de France, 1895.

Le Dantec, Yves-Gérard. *Renée Vivien, femme damnée, femme sauvée.* Aix-en-Provence: Editions du Feu, 1930.

Le Fèvre, Tanneguy. *Abrégé des vies des poètes grecs.* Saumur: Lerpinière et Lesnier, 1664.

———. *Poésies d'Anacréon et de Sappho.* Saumur: R. Pean, 1680.

Lefkowitz, Mary. *The Lives of the Ancient Poets.* Baltimore: Johns Hopkins University Press, 1981.

L'Héritier, Marie-Jeanne. *Epîtres héroïques d'Ovide, traduites en français.* 1730. Brunet, 1732.

———. *Le Triomphe de Madame Deshoulières, reçue dixième muse au Parnasse.* n.p., 1694.

Licht, Hans. [Paul Brandt]. *Sexual Life in Ancient Greece.* Translated by J. H. Freese. London: Routledge and Kegan Paul, 1932. (Original German edition 1925–28.)

Lingendes, Jean de, trans. *Les Epîtres d'Ovide.* T. du Bray, 1618.

Lobel, Edgar, and Denys Page. *Poetarum Lesbiorum Fragmenta.* Oxford: Clarendon Press, 1955.

Longepierre, H.-B. de Requeleyne, baron de, trans. *Les Poésies d'Anacréon et de Sapho.* P. Emery, 1684.

Lorenz, Paul. *Sapho 1900: Renée Vivien.* Julliard, 1977.

Louÿs, Pierre. *Les Chansons de Bilitis.* 1895. Reprint. Charpentier, 1901.

Maclean, Ian. *Woman Triumphant: Feminism in French Literature 1610–1652.* Oxford: Clarendon Press, 1977.

Marks, Elaine. "Lesbian Intertextuality." In *Homosexualities and French Literature,* edited by George Stambolian and Elaine Marks, 353–78. Ithaca, N.Y.: Cornell University Press, 1978.

Marolles, Michel de, trans. *Les Epîtres héroïdes d'Ovide.* Veuve P. Lamy, 1660. (Preface by François Ogier.)

Mason, William. *Sappho.* 1797. Reprint. London: T. Becket, 1809.

May, Georges. *Le Dilemme du roman au XVIIIe siècle.* Paris and New Haven: Presses Universitaires de France and Yale University Press, 1963.

———. *D'Ovide à Racine.* Presses Universitaires de France, 1949.

Meier, M. H. E. *Histoire de l'amour grec.* Translated by L.-R. de Pogey-Castries. Stendal, 1930. (Original German edition 1837.)

Mercier, Louis Sébastien. *L'An 2440.* 1770. Reprint. Editions France Adel, 1977.

Meunier, Mario. *Un Camp de représailles.* Nancy: Berger-Levrault, 1919.

———. *Sappho, Anacréon et Anacréontiques.* Grasset, 1932.

Michelet, Jules. *La Bible de l'Humanité.* F. Chamerot, 1864.

Miller, Marion, and David Robinson. *The Songs of Sappho.* Lexington, Ky.: The Maxwelton Co., 1925.

Miller, Nancy K. "Emphasis Added: Plots and Plausibilities in Women's Fiction." *PMLA* (January 1981): 36–48.

———. *Subject to Change: Reading Feminist Writing*. New York: Columbia University Press, 1988.

Moers, Ellen. *Literary Women*. New York: Oxford University Press, 1985.

Mongrédien, Georges. "Bibliographie des oeuvres de Georges et Madeleine de Scudéry." *Revue d'Histoire littéraire de la France* 40 (1933): 225–36, 413–25, 538–65.

———. *Madeleine de Scudéry et son salon*. Tallendier, 1946.

Mora, Edith. *Sappho: Histoire d'un poète et traduction intégrale de l'oeuvre*. Flammarion, 1966.

Morel, Maurice. *Sapho de Lesbos*. Didier, 1903.

Morrison, Mary. "Henri Estienne and Sappho." *Bibliothèque d'Humanisme et Renaissance* 24.2 (1962): 388–91.

Moutonnet de Clairfons, J.-J., trans. *Anacréon, Sapho, Bion, et Moschus*. 1773. Reprint. Paphos [Paris]: J. Bastien, 1780.

Müller, Karl Otfried. *Histoire de la littérature grecque*. 2 vols. Durand, 1865. (Original German edition 1841.)

———. *The History and Antiquities of the Doric Race*. 2 vols. Oxford: Collingwood, 1830. (Original German edition 1820–24.)

Mure, William. *A Critical History of the Language and Literature of Ancient Greece*. 3 vols. London: Longman, Brown, 1850. ("Sappho" is in vol. 3.)

———. "Sappho and the Ideal Love of the Greeks." *Museum für philologie* 1.12 (1857): 564–93.

Nagy, Gregory. "Phaethon, Sappho's Phaon, and the White Rock of Leukas." *Harvard Studies in Classical Philology* 77 (1973): 137–77.

Necker, Jacques. *Oeuvres complètes*. 1821. Reprint. Darmstadt: Scientia Verlag, Aalen, 1971.

Neue, Johann Christian. *Sapphonis Mytilenae Fragmenta*. 1824. Reprint. Berlin: G. Nauck, 1827.

Orlando, Francesco. *Toward a Freudian Theory of Literature*. Translated by C. Lee. Baltimore: Johns Hopkins University Press, 1978.

Ovid. *The Art of Love and Other Poems*. Loeb Classical Library. 1929.

———. *Heroides and Amores*. Loeb Classical Library. 1914.

———. *Tristia, Ex Ponto*. Loeb Classical Library. 1924.

Page, Denys. *Sappho and Alcaeus*. Oxford: Clarendon Press, 1955.

Parny, Evariste Désiré de Forges, vicomte de. *Poésies érotiques*. 1778. Reprint. Brussels: Tarlier, 1828.

Pastre, Geneviève. *Athènes et le péril saphique: Homosexualité féminine en Grèce antique*. Librairie Les Mots à la Bouche, 1987.

Patzer, Harald. *Die Griechische Knabenliebe*. Weisbaden: Franz Steiner Verlag, 1982.

Perrault, Charles. *Réponse aux réflexions critiques de Mr [Despréaux] sur Longin*. N.p., n.d.

Peyre, Henri. *Bibliographie critique de l'héllénisme en France de 1843 à 1870*. New Haven, Conn.: Yale University Press, 1932.

Pichois, Claude, and Jean Zeigler. *Baudelaire.* Julliard, 1987.

Pierron, Alexis. *Histoire de la littérature grecque.* Hachette, 1850.

Pipelet, Constance [Princesse de Salm-Dyck]. *Sapho, tragédie mêlée de chants.* Privately printed, 1810.

Pizzorusso, Arnaldo. "La Concezione dell'arte narrativa nella seconde metà del seicento francese." *Studi mediolatini e volgari* 3 (1955): 114–25.

Planchon, Louis, trans. *Sappho retrouvée et Anacréon, traduction en vers sticométriques.* Desobry, 1846.

Poinsinet de Sivry, Louis, trans. *Anacréon, Sapho, Moschus, Bion, Tyrthée, etc.* Nancy: P. Antoine, 1758.

Poliakov, Léon. *The Aryan Myth: A History of Racist and Nationalist Ideas in Europe.* New York: Basic Books, 1974.

Proust, Marcel. "A Propos de Baudelaire." In *Baudelaire: A Collection of Critical Essays,* edited by Henri Peyre, 11–22. Englewood Cliffs, N.J.: Prentice Hall, 1962.

Raabe, A. G. *Interpretatio Odarii Sapphici In Venerem.* Leipzig: Ex Officina Sommeria, 1794.

Rable, Paul-Pierre, trans. *Anacréon français-grec, suivi de pièces anacréontiques de Bion, Théocrite, etc., des poésies de Sapho en vers imitatifs.* J. Claye, 1855.

Racine, Jean. *Phèdre.* 1677. Reprint. Seuil, 1962.

Rathery, Edmé Jacques Benoît, and Boutron, eds. *Mademoiselle de Scudéry: Sa vie et sa correspondance, avec un choix de ses poésies.* 1873. Geneva: Slatkine Reprints, 1971.

Redarez-Saint-Remy, Jules-Henry, trans. *Les Poésies de Sapho de Lesbos.* Hachette, 1852.

Reinach, Joseph. *La Grèce devant le Congrès: Conférences faites sous la présidence de M. Alfred Croiset.* Boivin, 1919.

Reinach, Théodore. "Nouveaux fragments de Sappho." *Revue des études grecques.* 15 (1902): 60–70.

———. "Pour mieux connaître Sappho." In *Publications diverses de l'année 1911.* Institut de France. Firmin-Didot, 1911: 51–70.

Reinach, Théodore, and Aimé Puech. *Alcée Sapho.* Les Belles Lettres, 1937.

Richepin, Jean. *Sapphô.* Marpon et Flammarion, 1884.

Richer, Jean. "Restitution à Gautier du texte 'Sapho'." *Bulletin de la Société Théophile Gautier* 7 (1985): 163–68.

Richter, Johann. *Sappho und Erinna.* Leipzig: Voss, 1833.

Rigolot, François. "Louise Labé et la redécouverte de Sapho." *Nouvelle revue du seizième siècle* 1 (1983): 19–31.

Rilke, Rainer Maria. *The Notebooks of Malte Laurids Brigge.* Translated by Stephen Mitchell. New York: Vintage Books, 1985.

Ripert, Emile. *Ovide.* Colin, 1921.

Robbins, Emmet. " 'Every Time I Look at You . . .': Sappho Thirty-One." *Transactions of the American Philological Association* 110 (1980): 255–61.

Robert, Marthe. *Roman des origines et origines du roman.* Grasset, 1972.

Robinson, David. *Sappho and Her Influence.* Boston: Marshall Jones, 1924.

Romilly, Edouard. *Sappho: La Passionnante—La Passionnée.* Editions Eugène Figuière, 1931.

Roussel, Pierre. "Doutes historiques sur Sapho." *Système physique et moral de la femme*. Caille and Ravier, 1809. (The original 1789 edition does not include text on Sappho.)

Rüdiger, Horst. *Sappho: Ihr Ruf und Ruhm bei der Nachwelt*. Leipzig: Dieterische Verlagsbuchhandlung, 1933.

Sacy, Claude de. *Les Amours de Sapho et de Phaon*. Amsterdam: Nihof, 1775.

Sainte-Beuve, Charles Augustin. *Portraits de femmes*. Garnier, 1845.

"Sapho à Phaon." *Mercure galant* (April 1713): 213–41.

Schlegel, Friedrich. *Histoire de la littérature ancienne et moderne*. 2 vols. Ballimore, 1829. (Original German edition 1812.)

[Scudéry, Madeleine de]. *Artamène ou le Grand Cyrus*. 1649–53. Geneva: Slatkine Reprints, 1972.

———. *Les Femmes illustres ou Les Harangues héroïques*. Courbé, 1642.

———. *Lettres amoureuses de divers auteurs de ce temps*. Courbé, 1641.

Segal, Charles. *Language and Desire in Seneca's 'Phaedra.'* Princeton, N.J.: Princeton University Press, 1986.

———. "Solar Imagery and Tragic Heroism in Euripides' *Hippolytus*." In *Arktouros: Hellenic Studies Presented to Bernard Knox*, edited by G. Bowerstock, 156–72. Berlin: Walter de Gruyter, 1979.

Sergent, Bernard. *L'Homosexualité dans la mythologie grecque*. Payot, 1984.

Showalter, English. *The Evolution of the French Novel 1641–1782*. Princeton, N.J.: Princeton University Press, 1972.

Silvestre, Armand. *Sapho*. Ollendorf, 1881.

Sirieyx de Villers, Emilie. *Lucie Delarue-Mardrus: Biographie critique*. Sansot, 1923.

Spitzer, Alan B. *The French Generation of 1820*. Princeton, N.J.: Princeton University Press, 1987.

Staël, Germaine Necker, baronne de. *Corinne, or Italy*. Translated by Emily Baldwin and Paulina Driver. London: George Bell, 1890.

———. *Corinne ou l'Italie*. Edited by Simone Balayé. Gallimard, 1985.

———. *Delphine*. Edited by Claudine Herrmann. 2 vols. Editions des femmes, 1981.

———. *Oeuvres complètes*. 17 vols. Strasbourg and London: Treuttel and Würtz, 1820–21.

Stein, Judith. "The Iconography of Sappho, 1775–1875." Ph.D. diss., University of Pennsylvania, 1981.

Stigers, Eva Stehle. "Sappho's Private World." In *Reflections of Women in Antiquity*, edited by H. Foley, 43–57. New York: Gordon and Breach, 1981.

Stockinger, Jacob. "Homosexuality and the French Enlightenment." In *Homosexualities and French Literature*, edited by George Stambolian and Elaine Marks, 161–85. Ithaca, N.Y.: Cornell University Press, 1978.

Stone, Lawrence. *The Family, Sex and Marriage in England 1500–1800*. New York: Harper and Row, 1979.

Sweetser, Marie-Odile. "Images de la femme abandonnée: Traditions, contaminations, créations." In *Onze nouvelles études sur l'image de la femme dans la littérature française du 17e siècle*, edited by W. Leiner, 63–76. J.-M. Place, 1984.

Symonds, John Addington. *A Problem in Greek Ethics being an Inquiry into the Phenomenon of Sexual Inversion*. Reprint. 1883. London, 1901.
———. *Studies of the Greek Poets*. London: Smith, Elder, 1873.
Tarczylo, Théodore. *Sexe et liberté au siècle des Lumières*. Presses de la Renaissance, 1983.
Tarrant, R.J. "The Authenticity of the Letter of Sappho to Phaon (*Heroides* XV)." *Harvard Studies in Classical Philology* 85 (1981): 133–54.
Thevet, André. *Les Vrais Portraits et Vies des hommes illustres*. 2 vols. Veuve Kervert, 1584.
Thomas, Antoine Léonard. *Essai sur le caractère, les moeurs, et l'esprit des femmes dans les différents siècles*. Moutard, 1772.
Touzet, M. *Sapho, poème élégiaque*. Veuve Duménil-Lesueur, 1812.
Tresham, Henry. *Le Avventure di Saffo*. Rome, 1784.
Tubach, Sally. *Female Homoeroticism in German Literature and Culture*. Ph.D. diss., University of California, Berkeley, 1980.
Valincour, Jean Baptiste Henri de Trousset de. *Lettres à Mme la Marquise *** sur le sujet de La princesse de Clèves*. Edited by J. Chupeau et al. Tours: Université François Rabelais, 1972.
Vallois, Marie-Claire. *Fictions féminines: Madame de Staël et les voix de la Sibylle*. Saratoga, Calif.: Anma Libri, 1987.
Veïsier Des Combes, Louis-Alphonse, trans. *Odes d'Anacréon et poésies de Sapho*. Duprat, 1839.
Verducci, Florence. *Ovid's Toyshop of the Heart: Epistulae Herodium*. Princeton, N.J.: Princeton University Press, 1985.
Verlaine, Paul. *Oeuvres poétiques*. Edited by G. Robichez. Garnier, 1969.
Verri, Alessandro. *Le Avventure di Saffo*. 1780. *I Romanzi*. Ravenna: Longo, 1975.
———. *Sappho*. Translated by John Nott. London: Cuthell and Martin, 1803. (Translation of *Le Avventure di Saffo*.)
Versini, Laurent. *Le Roman épistolaire*. Presses Universitaires de France, 1979.
Vial [Jean de Reuilly]. *La Raucourt et ses amies: Etude historique des moeurs saphiques au XVIIIe siècle*. Daragon, 1909.
Viala, Alain. *La Naissance de l'écrivain*. Editions de Minuit, 1985.
Vielé-Griffin, Francis. *Oeuvres*. 1912. Reprint (4 vols.). Mercure de France, 1930. (*Sapho* is in vol. 4.)
Visconti, E.Q. *Iconographie grecque*. 3 vols. Didot, 1808. (The entry "Sappho" is in vol. 1.)
Vivien, Renée. *La Dame à la Louve*. Alphonse Lemerre, 1904.
———. *Une Femme m'apparut*. Alphonse Lemerre, 1904.
———. *Poésies de R. Vivien*. 2 vols. Alphonse Lemerre, 1923–24.
———. *Sapho: Traduction nouvelle avec le texte grec*. Alphonse Lemerre, 1903.
Weber, Henri. *La Création poétique au seizième siècle en France de Maurice Scève à Agrippa d'Aubigné*. Nizet, 1956.
Weeks, Jeffrey. *Sexuality and Its Discontents: Meanings, Myths and Modern Sexualities*. London: Routledge and Kegan Paul, 1985.
Weigall, Arthur. *Sappho of Lesbos: Her Life and Times*. New York: Stokes, 1932.

Welcker, Friedrich Gottlieb. *Sappho von einem herrschenden Vorurtheil befreyt.* Göttingen: Vandenhoek und Ruprecht, 1816.

———. "Ueber die bieden Oden der Sappho." *Museum für philologie* (1856): 226–54.

Wharton, Henry Thornton. *Sappho: Memoir, Text, Selected Renderings.* London: Stott, 1885.

Wilamowitz-Moellendorff, Ulrich von. *Sappho und Simonides.* Berlin: Weidmannsche Buchhandlung, 1913.

Williams, Gordon. *Tradition and Originality in Roman Poetry.* Oxford: Clarendon Press, 1968.

Wills, Gary. "Sappho 31 and Catullus 51." *Greek, Roman and Byzantine Studies* 8 (Autumn 1967): 167–98.

Winckelmann, J. J. *Recueil des différentes pièces sur les arts.* Barrois, 1786. (Original German edition 1763.)

———. *Histoire de l'art chez les anciens.* Jansen, 1793. (Original German edition 1764–67.)

Winkler, John J. "Gardens of Nymphs: Public and Private in Sappho's Lyrics." *Women's Studies* 8 (1981): 65–91.

Wittig, Monique. "Paradigm." In *Homosexualities and French Literature,* edited by George Stambolian and Elaine Marks, 114–21. Ithaca, N.Y.: Cornell University Press, 1978.

Wolff, J. Christian. *Sapphus, Poetriae Lesbiae, Fragmenta et elogia quotquot in auctoribus antiquis graecis et latinis reperiuntur.* London: Vandenhoeck, 1733.

V. Wolff. "A Society." In *Monday or Tuesday.* Richmond: Leonard and Virginia Wolff, 1921.

Yourcenar, Marguerite. *La Couronne et la lyre.* Gallimard, 1979.

———. *Mémoires d'Hadrien.* Gallimard Folio, 1978.

———. *Oeuvres romanesques.* Gallimard, 1982.

Index

Abandoned woman, the, 46, 62; abandoned for a younger woman, 89–90, 191–92, 340n.18; and the epistolary novel, 76, 100; and male literary authority, 82–83; her physical degeneration, 87; promotion of the fiction of, 96, 337n.61; Sappho as, 28, 40, 51–52, 67, 192, 327–28n.4, 332n.10. *See also* Authority, male literary

Académie Française, 114, 298

Addison, Joseph, 5, 332n.12, 340n.15

Aelian, 16, 66, 233

Alceus, 159–60; as character in Sapphic fictions, 190–91, 258–59; his alleged relationship with Sappho, 214, 233, 236; his intersection with Sappho, 55; Müller's reading of his poems, 215

Allier de Hauteroche, L., 14, 232–34

Amazons, 107, 273

Anacreon, 95, 118; edited with Sappho, 34, 53; his alleged involvement with Sappho, 17

Andréas, Hélias, 31

Androgyne, the, 271, 294, 338n.70; Sappho as, 281–82, 295

Antinous, 225, 297

Anti-Semitism, 119, 347n.19, 351n.61

Anxiety of influence, the. *See* Rite of passage, authorial

Aphrodite, 52; in Sappho's poetry, 126–27, 319

Ariadne, 62, 64

Aristophanes, 118

Aristotle, 153

Armida, 178

Aronson, Nicole, 337–38n.68

Artemisia, 141, 341n.21

Aryan myth, the, 347n.19, 351–52n.61

Atthis, 59, 216, 236, 239, 250, 284

Auerbach, Nina, 347n.20

Augier, Emile, 259

Augustan age, the, 18, 73, 79

Aulotte, Robert, 34, 36, 329n.2

Authority, female literary: jealousy of, 94–96; usurpation of, by male writers, 77

Authority, male literary: and the usurpation of a female voice, 77, 83, 100. *See also* Transvestism

Authority, poetic: Sappho's authorization of, 6

Author's name. *(Nom d'auteur). See* Names, authorial

Bachet, sieur de, 80, 129–30

Bachofen, J. J., 203, 220–22, 224, 254, 270, 347n.21

Backer, Dorothy, 83, 338n.72

Badolle, M., 159

Baïf, Antoine de, 32, 34–36

Bakhtin, M. M., 63, 73

Balayé, Simone, 182, 342.37, 343n.40, 344–45n.61

Balzac, Guez de, 80, 82

Balzac, Honoré de, 259

Banville, Théodore de, 267, 273–74, 353n.78, 354n.83

Barney, Natalie Clifford, 249, 292, 294; as founder of "Sapho 1900," 279; *Cinq petits dialogues grecs*, 280–81, 354–55n.92; *Equivoque*, 284; relation to Pierre Louÿs, 279–80. *See also* "Sapho 1900"; Vivien, Renée

Barrias, F. J., 234, 349n.34

Barrin, Jean, 129–30, 138, 339n.7